The Invisible
WALL

W. Michael Blumenthal

The Invisible WALL

Germans and Jews

A Personal Exploration

COUNTERPOINT WASHINGTON, D.C.

A CORNELIA AND MICHAEL BESSIE BOOK

Library of Congress Cataloging-in-Publication Data
Blumenthal, W. Michael.
The invisible wall: Germans and Jews: a personal exploration /
W. Michael Blumenthal
"A Cornelia and Michael Bessie book."
Includes bibliographical references and index.
ISBN 1-887178-73-2
1. Blumenthal family.   2. Jews—Germany—Genealogy.
3. Germany—Genealogy.   4. Germany—Civilization—
Jewish influences.   5. Blumenthal, W. Michael, 1926–
6. Germany—Ethnic relations
I. Title
DS135.G5857   1998
943'.004924—dc21   97-47735

Printed in the United States of America on acid-free paper that meets the American National Standards Institute Z39-48 Standard.

A CORNELIA AND MICHAEL BESSIE BOOK

COUNTERPOINT
P.O. Box 65793
Washington, D.C. 20035-5793

Counterpoint is a member of the Perseus Books Group.

5   7   9   8   6   4

For the next generation—
ANN, JILL, JANE, AND MICHAEL EDWARD,
and especially for
BARBARA

The self-same song that found a path
  Through the sad heart of Ruth, when, sick for home,
  She stood in tears amid the alien corn
                    JOHN KEATS, "Ode to a Nightingale"

CONTENTS

Illustrations appear between pages 210 and 211.

PREFACE

First of all, there is the interesting question, "Who is a Jew?" Many answers are possible. I have chosen the one once given by Sartre: "A Jew is whoever the world sees as one, irrespective of religion." This definition works well for Germany, since there even those of Jewish descent who had been baptized continued to be considered de facto Jews long before the Nazis introduced their fanciful racial definition.

Second, while my book purports to deal with German Jews generally, the reader will note that much of the emphasis and many of the facts and stories relate to Prussia. That is an arbitrary decision on my part, but it is deliberate and not the product of either accident or ignorance. I realize that there were differences in the situation of German Jews between, say, Prussia and Bavaria—or more broadly between northern Germany on the one hand, and the southern and western areas on the other. Yet Prussia, and specifically Berlin, was the principal stage for the major events in the German-Jewish drama over time. Moreover, by far the greatest part of German Jewry was concentrated there. Giving in-depth attention and space to regional differences would have added some useful refinement and nuance, but it would not have substantially changed the reader's understanding of the major events. For those purists still dissatisfied, I offer my apologies.

Writing this book was an adventurous journey into uncharted territory, filled with the excitement of discovery. It began with only the germ of an idea, vast areas of ignorance, many questions, few answers, and no preconceived notion where it would lead me. For a nonhistorian, it was an experience with enormous intellectual challenge. In the end, I was much the richer for what I had learned about my people—and myself. My hope is that I managed to convey some of this through my stories, and that the reader will enjoy reading the book as much as I did writing it.

In a multiyear effort of this kind, there are many people who provide inspiration, encouragement, and help. I thank them all—including the many too numerous to single out for individual mention. To them I express my appreciation and my regrets. There are others, nevertheless, who played very special roles.

First and foremost, there was the enthusiastic support of my editors, Cornelia and Michael Bessie. They were a joy to work with. Mike's wisdom and advice on how to make this a better book were crucial along the way and kept me going. I owe much to Cornelia for her insightful comments and suggestions in reading earlier drafts. She did a great deal to improve the final product. I am grateful also to the people of Counterpoint—especially Frank Pearl and Jack Shoemaker—for their confidence and backing when this project was little more than a gleam in my eye. My thanks also to Counterpoint's managing editor, Carole McCurdy, and the rest of the competent staff who smoothed the rough edges and handled the myriad details preceding publication with professionalism and dedication. Tom Christensen's copy editing greatly improved the final product.

In Germany, I must above all acknowledge the important contribution of my research assistant, Dr. Ruth Federspiel. She was a valued colleague and collaborator for more than two years. She scoured German archives and libraries for me, discovered unknown sources, and served as willing guide during my frequent visits to Berlin. I thank her for her hard work and patience in the face of tight deadlines and too-frequent late-night calls and faxes.

There are many other friends in Germany who took a keen interest in my work. I want to acknowledge in particular Dr. Stefi Jersch-Wenzel, formerly at Berlin's *Historische Kommission,* and currently director of the Simon Dubnow Institute in Leipzig. She gave generously of her time. Her deep knowledge of German-Jewish history was of tremendous help to me in providing leads for sources and pointing me in the right direction. I am equally indebted to Professor Wolfgang Benz, director of the *Zentrum für Antisemitismus-forschung* at Berlin's *Technische Universität,* whose interesting insights, especially on the later years of German-Jewish history and the Nazi period, helped me a lot. Professor Wolfram Fischer, chairman of the *Historische Kommission* and Director of the Freie University's *Institut für Wirtschafts- und Sozialgeschichte* saw to it that the Institute's resources and library materials were opened to me.

In Oranienburg, the town historian, Hans Biereigel, was unfailingly helpful with background on the town and history of its now-vanished Jewish community. The staff at the *Brandenburgische Landeshauptarchiv,* Potsdam, was also of great help and deserves my thanks. At the *Otto Suhr Institut's* newspaper archives of the Freie Universität, Frau Kirschbaum-Reibe and Frau Kolossa equally merit special mention for going the extra kilometer in digging up relevant material.

The Leo Baeck Institute in New York was an invaluable resource. I thank Fred Grubel for welcoming me and Carol Kahn Strauss, executive director, for extending many courtesies. My special thanks go to the competent and cheerful Diane Spielmann, who dug up many vast treasures of relevant material.

At Princeton University, Professor Barbara Hahn stimulated my thinking about Rahel Varnhagen.

From Brazil, Irene Freudenheim sent me interesting material on Arthur Eloesser, her grandfather, and in Wengen, Switzerland, my ninety-five-year-old aunt, Edith Blumenthal Munter, the last survivor of the senior Blumenthals, reached deeply into her memory of pre–World War I family lore and Oranienburg life, thus adding much color to my understanding of the bare facts of our past.

I have left the most important people for last. These are, first of all, Karen Vasudeva and Marie Santos, my two faithful secretary-assistants. The former was quick, efficient, and competent in handling the preparation of the first part of the manuscript. To Ms. Santos fell the task of later doing the bulk of this work and assisting in the library research at Princeton. I could not have written this book without her.

My sister, Stefanie Blumenthal Dreyfuss, played a unique and invaluable role. She read and provided critiques of early drafts, stimulated my memory, offered ideas, and urged me forward with critical warmth and enthusiasm. Her unfailing literary taste won my admiration. It is she who, among many other good ideas, pointed me to the epigraph by Keats.

Finally, there are my young son, Michael Edward, and my wife, Barbara Bennett Blumenthal. It is their love—and patience—that kept me going. They know how much I owe them.

CHAPTER I

PROLOGUE

1

The SS *Marine Adder* was one of many assembly-line troop transports hastily built during World War II. An unsightly 12,000-ton vessel, painted battleship gray, she could carry as many as 3,800 men and equipment across the ocean in what is generously described as minimal comfort.

Except for a few small cabins for senior officers, the better accommodations consisted of a dozen or so large areas on lower decks, outfitted with double-decker bunks for forty-eight passengers each. That was the good space. The bulk of the passengers slept in large holds deep in the ship's bowels, where the bunks were stacked four high. The ventilation was poor and the air and odors vile—especially when the seas were rough and the seasick collapsed in the aisles before reaching the communal washrooms.

Actually, the *Marine Adder* did not see much World War II service. Commissioned in 1945, she was one of the last additions to the military's by then vast transport armada. As a late arrival, she played only a small part in bringing the troops home after the surrender of Japan. Thereafter, declared surplus by the Army, she was chartered by American President Lines in

1946 for basic transport and freight service between the West Coast and the Far East.

In the course of her unremarkable career, the *Marine Adder* was destined to spend much time in mothballs waiting for the next military emergency. Before being relegated to the scrap yards she finished her existence as a lowly car transporter. Given her level of passenger comfort, it was an appropriate fate.

Though the *Marine Adder* was anything but glamorous, she was nevertheless as beloved by the stateless Displaced Persons who traveled on her from Shanghai to San Francisco in September 1947 as the finest ocean liner ever built. For seventeen days she carried some one hundred of these former German and Austrian Jews across the Pacific from their enforced wartime exile in a Japanese-run ghetto to a new beginning in America. It was the last leg of an odyssey that had begun with their headlong flight from Nazi terror, in the wake of *Kristallnacht* with its smashed shops, burning synagogues, and concentration camps of almost a decade before. Finally the long, circuitous journey was coming to an end. The *Marine Adder* was the Ark delivering them to dry land, to a permanent home and to renewed hope.

September 24 was a beautiful day. The air was sweet and fresh, and the sky was a perfect cloudless blue. Twenty-one years old, with sixty-five dollars in my pocket, I was one of the refugee DPs coming to America on the *Marine Adder*. Most of us had been up since well before dawn, and now we stood pressed against the railings as the ship sailed through the Golden Gate into San Francisco Bay. Can there be a more glorious way to catch a first glimpse of the United States?

Stepping ashore at the Embarcadero, we were greeted by relatives and friends who had preceded us. Some had arrived quite recently; others—the "pioneers"—a decade or more earlier, soon after Hitler's rise to power. These we quickly dubbed the "Mayflower refugees" because to us—fresh out of our German-Jewish cocoon in Shanghai—they seemed so strange, so decidedly and even ostentatiously American in dress and demeanor and in the way they laced American slang and accents into their German.

Soon our small group of Shanghai survivors would be much like the others, eagerly taking our place in America. There had been some tough moments for us, stuck in wartime Shanghai as "guests" of the Japanese. We had never been really safe, and a few times, without being fully aware of it, we had come pretty close to disaster.

But that was all behind us, and now we were joining all those other survivors from Hitler's Germany—assimilated German Jews eager to assimilate into the New World. For the older ones the process would be slow and painful. But there was nothing to hold us youngsters back.

In the early years, the first arrivals had clustered together in places like the Upper West Side of Manhattan, which some called "The Fourth Reich," and in parts of Forest Hills in Queens. On the West Coast, similar enclaves had sprung up in San Francisco and Oakland. But our little group of latecomers quickly dispersed, each going his own way, grateful for the chance—at last—for personal fulfillment, security, and acceptance as future citizens with equal rights.

We came in exciting times to a country vibrant with the energy of millions of returning veterans, and many of us were privileged to live the American dream to the fullest. The younger generation flocked to the college campuses. Our parents had taught us that education was the key to a good life. "What you have learned, they can never take away from you," my mother often lectured me. Others pushed out into business and the professions and before long most had joined America's growing postwar middle class.

In Germany, the generation of our parents and grandparents had once played an important role and contributed to national life out of proportion to their numbers. In our newly adopted country, some of us would have the same good fortune. From among the 300,000 German-Jewish refugees who ultimately came to the United States, there would emerge Nobel Prize winners, leaders in the media and the arts, prominent educators, and distinguished professionals in law and medicine. One even rose to the lofty heights of Secretary of State.

I fell in love with this country from the first moment I set foot on American soil, when the taxi dropped me off at a tiny fleabag hotel on San Francisco's Ellis Street. I was young and full of resolve; this was the land of opportunity, and as far as I was concerned, the sky was the limit. Yet in my wildest dreams I could not have imagined the privileges that would one day come my way. Among them would be the honor to serve my adopted country as its Ambassador abroad, and as the 64th U.S. Secretary of the Treasury, only the third foreign-born citizen to hold that position.

2

I was born a German Jew and legally I remained one until that day in 1941 when the Nazis decreed that I was a German no more. At the time we were living—existing is more like it—in the tough environment of wartime Shanghai, the only place open to us after our headlong flight from Germany. As a youngster of fifteen, I do not recall feeling especially deprived when I first heard the news, though my parents were stunned.

For years I had little knowledge of the past, and even less interest or inclination to look back. Germany was where I was born, but what had happened there was mainly a bad memory, though fortunately a fading one. After arriving in San Francisco, nothing was further from my mind than to dwell on the past. The United States was my new home, and my imagination and energies were fully engaged by my American life, by the present and the future and by what I would make of it. The past was history— tragic, incomprehensible, and eminently forgettable.

For a long time, that is how it was. I became a citizen as quickly as the law allowed, and the federal judge in Trenton, New Jersey, the U.S. court nearest Princeton University where I was attending graduate school, scheduled the naturalization ceremony. And so for the greatest part of my life I have been a proud American citizen—nearly half a century now.

My adopted country has been good to me. I could educate myself, develop my talents, and raise a family, much as other immigrants and refugees have done before me and since. With an American wife and four American children, and with my share of material success, I have at various times been a teacher, businessman, banker, and government official. Small wonder, therefore, that my childhood as a German Jew soon lost much of its meaning and long ago became a blurred and unreal memory of the distant past.

Yet strange and unexpected changes occur as we grow older. For some, age may be primarily a matter of arteries. But for me that has not been the whole story. With the passage of time I discovered that the formidable

German philosopher Schopenhauer had a point when he observed that the first half of life gives us the text—and what follows supplies the commentary on it.

My ignorance about what had really happened in Germany began to bother me. If knowledge is the toupee that covers the baldness of our ignorance, then, with the passage of time, the cold draft over the top of my head became increasingly irksome. Slowly, step by step, my need to know about the past grew until it became too important to be ignored any longer. There were too many unanswered questions, not merely about my own family and their ancestors, but about that entire group of German Jews into which I was born. What had gone on between German Christians and Jews, and why? Why had there been such a promising beginning, so much hope and so much accomplishment—and so terrible an end?

3

When the modern history of the Jews of Germany came to an end in the mid-twentieth century, it was less than three hundred years old. The beginning was in 1671, after the end of the Thirty Years War, when the first of the Hohenzollerns, Frederick William of Brandenburg, known as the Great Elector, issued his Magna Carta for Jews and invited the first fifty families to come from Austria and settle in his realm.

It was not the first time, of course, that Jews had come to live there. The first Jew set foot on German soil many centuries earlier, probably around the time of Christ and possibly even before, and some have lived there ever since. After the Christianization of Europe, these Jews of Germany, the Ashkenazim, had more often than not been subjected to harsh discrimination and cruel treatment. There were good times for them and bad ones, periods of calm followed by long stretches of persecution or, worse yet, bloody massacres that decimated them and drove them out. In an unending cycle of periods when the desire to exploit and profit from their presence alternated with years when envy, and superstition, and Jew-hatred was uppermost, some towns would expel them even as others would again invite them in. Since the Middle Ages and the days of the Crusaders, life for Jews in Germany was so dangerous and difficult that their numbers had dwindled to insignificance by the fifteenth and sixteenth centuries. In Brandenburg, only a century before the Great Elector made the move that was to mark the beginning of modern German-Jewish history, they had once again been banished "for eternity." There had always been regional differences, of course, and in a strict sense Germany was never entirely without Jews for the past 2,000 years. Yet Prussia became the center for modern Jewish life in Germany and by far the greatest number of Jews settled there.

The Great Elector was not motivated by any affinity or love for Jews. Distaste for them—the word *anti-Semitism* had not yet been invented—was widespread throughout Europe, and Frederick William was no exception. But he was a practical man. He needed help to rebuild his country, devastated during the Thirty Years' War by marauding bands who pillaged and looted their way across the land and left behind an exhausted and decimated people. The Jews were only one of the several groups he brought in. Along with them came Huguenots from France, Protestants from the Palatinate and French Switzerland, Walloons, Salzburgers, and thousands of religious refugees from Bohemia.

Nevertheless, the Jews were different. From the very start, they occupied a special place in his realm—more segregated and regulated, taxed and exploited than any others. Yet, as the German states grew into the most powerful country in Europe, united by Bismarck into a single German Reich, the Jewish community grew and prospered as well. Eventually German Jews became something unique among the Jews of the world, and would occupy a special place in most areas of their country's national life.

The beginning was slow and inauspicious.

For the first one hundred years or so, except for a small minority of Court Jews who served the sovereigns as bankers and financial advisers, along with a handful of others in privileged positions, most Jews lived a restricted and marginal existence outside the regular stream of German life. They were, in effect, the sovereign's personal property, and their condition was governed by the Jew Laws, a set of special restrictive and exploitative rules that served as a steady source of profit for the many perennially impecunious German princes and rulers.

The restrictions and impediments placed on Jews—and the inventiveness in devising ways to tax and squeeze them—boggles the mind. No Jew could travel safely from one place to another without a *Schutzbrief,* a special letter of protection, sold at high prices. Even with the letter in hand, the levies a Jew had to bear were punitive. Jews—and only Jews—were taxed, and taxed again wherever they went and whatever they did.

Around 1700 it cost a Brandenburg Jew 150 taler,[1] plus a horse, to be allowed to travel to a fair, and more taxes were collected at the town gate of each place he passed. In Mainz, the customs duties levied on Jews defined them as merely another product, to wit: "Honey, Hops, Wood, Jews, chalk, cheese and charcoal."[2]

Jews needed special permission to marry; they paid taxes for births and deaths and were held collectively liable for the debts of their bankrupt and insolvent. Jews alone were subject to the hated *Leibzoll,* a body tax resented as a shameful and onerous burden.

But there was more. In the eighteenth century, Jews were forced to buy the output of the Prussian king's beloved porcelain factories—far above market prices, taking a loss on the resale. (For reasons lost in obscurity, exceedingly ugly likenesses of monkeys were in especially ample supply.) The porcelain racket, though, actually was an improvement over a cynical earlier practice—forcing the kosher-eating Jews to buy the wild boars the sovereign bagged during the royal hunt.

In addition to taxes, there were innumerable restrictions on what Jews could or could not do. Virtually nowhere were they permitted to own houses or land. They couldn't own stores facing the street and were forbidden to deal, trade, or work in a dizzying range of occupations or products. Craft guilds were totally closed to them. Jews couldn't deal in foodstuffs, wines, wools, or yarns; they couldn't be brewers and distillers; and they were officially barred from most manufacturing and many trades.

In practice, in fact, Jews were relegated to fulfill those functions—mostly money lending and petty trading—which had the lowest prestige and which few Christians wanted to do. Only a small number achieved the privileged status of "Protected" Jew, and were allowed to live in cities where they could pursue more hopeful careers alongside their Christian neighbors.

A small number of Protected Jews gradually reached middle-class status, but most others remained desperately poor. They lived in segregated communities, the ghettos and Jew streets, turned inward onto themselves, speaking their own language and wearing their own distinctive dress. Frozen in the past, they were governed by elders and rabbis bound to their religion and traditions, with little or no social contact to a Christian world that looked down on them as an alien and inferior people.

When change began, it came gradually at first. Eighteenth-century enlightenment brought new ideas as the old feudal order crumbled. Static societies gave way to the belief in man's right as a citizen rather than as mere subject, and neither German nor Jew remained immune to these changes. More and more Jews strained to break out of their narrow traditional confines, and more and more Christians tolerated receiving them in their midst. In Berlin and a few other German cities beginning around midcentury, small numbers of the more educated and cultivated on both sides began to meet together in universities, scholarly groups, and literary salons. As Jews moved into the cities in larger numbers, these contacts grew. Slowly the process of Jewish assimilation into the broader German environment got under way.

The powerful influence of the French Revolution with its new ideas of universal citizenship rights furthered this trend. It buttressed the views of those Germans who thought that the time had come to end the isolation of the Jews and to begin absorbing them into the wider society. They believed that Jewish assimilation should be encouraged, and that it would prove beneficial to both sides and eventually lead to the transformation of Jews from their reduced status as an inferior separate "nation" within Germany, into citizens with equal rights.

Finally, as the eighteenth century drew to a close, a series of legal reforms, first promulgated in France and Austria, were also applied in several German cities and states. A major milestone was reached in 1812, when Prussia abolished most of the more onerous and discriminatory provisions of the Jew Laws, granting the Jews citizenship rights—and duties, including the obligation of military service.

But it was in the nineteenth century when the truly dramatic changes occurred and when the assimilation of German Jewry into the mainstream of German life progressed so rapidly and far that one historian has appropriately called it possibly "one of the most spectacular social leaps in European history."[3]

Over the span of only a few generations, the Jews of Germany shed their medieval constraints, turned their backs on old rabbinic values, and entered the modern age. Brushing aside ancient ideas and religious bonds, they took full advantage of their newly won legal rights and eagerly seized opportunities in the world outside. Not only did they do so with a speed and to an extent unprecedented in Jewish experience, they also achieved extraordinary levels of success and prominence. In the process, their integration into non-Jewish life and their assimilation of German culture and habits of thought went further and faster than anywhere else in Europe.

The forces of modernity were altering the lives of Christians and Jews alike. Germany was in the midst of its belated industrial revolution. As economic conditions changed, the old social structure was crumbling with it. Railroads were being built at a rapid pace and new factories rose up everywhere. In trade and commerce, mercantilist patterns gave way to relationships reflecting the more unfettered interplay of market forces. Enormous new capital needs had to be met and these required new forms of financial organization and the creation of many new large and smaller banks.

It was a time of great ferment, at once full of opportunity and hope as well as of dislocation and fear. Under these circumstances the interaction of Germans and Jews was bound to be uneven and complex, yet the latter found the conditions quite congenial to their talents and ambitions: Jews were adventurous and eager to advance wherever doors were opening up—or could be pushed open—and in the process many swiftly absorbed the surrounding culture. They became important agents of change, often outdistancing their Christian competitors in pioneering new forms of entrepreneurship in finance, commerce, and industry. Before long, they came to dominate entire sectors of German economic life in banking, publishing, shipping, textiles, and many facets of the retail trade—activities where their historical experience gave them a particular edge.

By 1860, there were already twice as many Jewish as non-Jewish private banks in Berlin, and Jews helped organize the new banking giants that dominate the economy of Germany to the present day. Jewish capital and entrepreneurship developed the railroads and started some of Germany's largest industrial enterprises in the frontier electrical and chemical fields, in coal mining and in heavy industry.

There had always been a handful of very rich Jewish families, who amassed their wealth in preindustrial times as Court Jews and bankers to the nobility. But now a much greater number of Jews grew wealthy, and a few extraordinarily so. By 1908, nine of twenty-nine families in Prussia with the largest fortunes were Jews, as were as many as 20 percent of the lesser Prussian millionaires—surprising numbers, given the tiny percentage of Jews in the population as a whole.

Not all Jews, of course, prospered or became wealthy. Many never achieved more than very modest levels of income and some, especially the later arrivals settling in Berlin and other large cities, remained quite poor. Yet within one or two generations, a surprisingly large number reached at least middle-income status, and before long some of the better parts of Berlin had a disproportionate number of Jewish residents. Incredibly, though the city's population was only 5 percent Jewish in 1914, the Jews had become the source of a third of all the taxes collected.

The amalgamation of Jews into German society and the primary measure of their advancement was not, however, restricted to economic success. Their remarkable rise in business and finance was only one side of the coin. Their influence on a wide spectrum of other facets of German life, and the important role they soon came to play in the professions, science, journalism, and music and the arts was at least as important. Jews, in fact, became vital actors in virtually every aspect of Germany's intellectual life and above all in what the Germans cherished most: their culture.

Once outside the ghetto, Jewish involvement and contributions to German culture moved in parallel with their economic progress. In what became a two-way process, they rapidly absorbed German culture and habits of thought and, in turn, influenced German intellectual life in deep and far-reaching ways. It was this dynamic of mutual interaction that transformed the ghetto dwellers of yesterday into the secular modern German Jew.

Until well into the eighteenth century, the intellectual life of the Jews had been circumscribed by social isolation. They were insulated from the outside world, and their learning remained narrowly confined to what was taught in Jewish elementary schools and talmudic academies. Women received little or no formal education, and for men study and learning was largely focused on their religious heritage. Interest and knowledge about the environment outside this world was low. Few questioned the ancient strictures, traditions and prejudices—as defined by rabbinical leaders and ghetto culture.

Eighteenth-century enlightenment first weakened and then shattered these bonds. On the Jewish side, it was Moses Mendelssohn, the hunchback son of a poor Jewish Torah scribe, who became an early and influential apostle of what some later would call the German-Jewish symbiosis and who first and most powerfully symbolized the Jewish drive to move beyond the ghetto walls. At a time when most of his coreligionists still spoke only their own language, *Judendeutsch* (Yiddish), he became an erudite master of the German language, and the friend and equal of some of the best and brightest of Germany's intellectual elite. While holding firm to his Jewish heritage, he was the first philosopher of modern German Jews, the most prominent and influential of his people to build bridges to German culture and secular life, and a dedicated proponent of the view that it was just and beneficial to both sides that Jewry be liberated from discriminatory laws and medieval constraints. Jews, he argued, should and could be assimilated fully into German society in spite of religious distinctions.

Somewhat later, a few sons and daughters of the wealthy, mostly descendants of Court Jews, began to interact with Berlin's gentile intellectuals. A few extraordinary young Jewish hostesses established literary salons and intermingled with an eclectic group of educated Christians, including some from the uppermost Court circles and nobility. At about the same time, a new movement of Jewish enlightenment—the *Haskalah*—led to the establishment of a new type of reformed Jewish school, where the teaching of secular subjects alongside the traditional religious curriculum became the dominant theme.

These were merely early portents of much more dramatic and rapid changes in the position of German Jews. Several developments coincided. In most German states and in Prussia in 1812, reform legislation finally removed many of the restrictions on residence, choice of occupation, and access to education. Urbanization was now in full swing and new population, including many Jews, poured into the cities. The attraction of greater educational opportunity for them went hand in hand with their quest for enhanced status and economic advance. Strong emphasis on learning (albeit in a narrow Jewish context) had always been at the heart of ghetto life. Emancipation now transformed this tradition into an avid desire to branch out into the wider areas of Western culture and learning.

Belief in education, moreover, was one value that Jews and gentiles shared, and the nineteenth century was a time when fundamental educational reforms and a general flowering of academic pursuits was in full swing. Whereas in 1816 only 60 percent of Prussian children were in school, the advent of compulsory education brought more than 80 percent into the classroom thirty years later, and practically all by the mid-'60s. Advanced secondary education also made great strides, while fundamental reforms emphasizing the unity of teaching with research thrust the German university into the forefront of higher learning in Europe.

Jews moved into this environment with great energy and speed. They rapidly became much more urbanized than the Christians. By 1871 more than 20 percent of them were living in cities, compared to just 5 percent of the population as a whole—a pattern that intensified over the years. When Hitler came to power, two-thirds of all German Jews lived in urban areas— more than half were in the seven largest German cities, with the greatest Jewish concentration in the capital city, Berlin. Many new arrivals had been exposed to only a limited religion-oriented education before emancipation. Now they sent their sons and daughters to the better schools and universities in relatively far larger numbers than gentiles. In 1880, for every one thousand Prussian Protestants 5.2 were students at secondary schools; the equivalent number for Catholics was 2.3, but for Jews it was an incredible 33.6. Although barely 5 percent of Berlin's population was Jewish in 1893, almost a full quarter of all students in the city's *Gymnasia* were Jews, and in the best ones the number was higher yet. The same was true in the universities where, by the mid-nineteenth century, the proportion of Jewish students in relation to the total number of Germany's Jews was twice as high as the corresponding proportion of gentiles. By the end of the century it had become eight times as large.

The rush of Jewish students into education was eloquent testimony of the enthusiasm with which they adopted modernity. Intellectual accomplishment and economic success—*Bildung und Besitz*—became the values by which they measured their enhanced status in society. In both regards they succeeded so well that they came to occupy a highly visible place as an especially educated and economically dominant minority elite.

Once, the "Jewish question"—and anti-Jewish feeling—had evolved around religious differences. In the era of enlightenment the Jewish question was secularized from the church to economic, political, and social issues. But the animosities it generated were no less real, and by no means all barriers came down. Important limits remained, some formal and official and others informal, and less visible, but no less effective.

Just as heavy Jewish concentration in certain sectors of the economy had been a heritage of medieval restrictions on their occupational choice, so continuing patterns of discrimination gave rise to an analogous large over-representation of Jews in certain professional and intellectual fields—and in their virtual absence from others. For even after the disappearance of the Jew Laws, nineteenth-century German Jews were effectively excluded from two of the most important pillars of the society—the military and the bureaucracy. An unconverted Jew had virtually no chance of becoming an officer in the armed forces, regardless of how rich and influential his family or how much he might have distinguished himself on the field of battle. This policy of almost total exclusion persisted, with rare exceptions, until well into the years of the First World War.

The same discriminatory rules applied in practice to the civil service and the bureaucracy—from modest levels all the way to the top. In nineteenth-century Germany a Jew could be a doctor, lawyer, or scientist but not even a lowly clerk in the Kaiser's postal service or a conductor on his trains. Since German universities were state institutions, it also limited to rare instances and unusual cases the appointment of a Jew to tenured faculty status—the most treasured position in academia.

The predictable result was that educated Jews tended to move heavily to those occupations where discrimination had ceased to be a major issue—principally the professions, and science and the arts, and it is here that some achieved great distinction and a few acquired world renown. The numbers tell the story. The first Jews were admitted as solicitors only in the mid-1800s. Yet before Hitler came to power, in the first decades of the twentieth century, fully 16 percent of all German lawyers were Jews. In the Weimar Republic almost 10 percent of all doctors and 8 percent of dentists were Jewish.[4]

Many Jews became scientists and researchers, and they flooded to the theatre, into the arts, and to music, where they made their mark as some of Germany's best-known composers, conductors, and performing artists. There was also a strong concentration in journalism, as publishers and as writers and literary critics.

By the time of Weimar, there were few areas of German intellectual and professional life not profoundly touched by the Jewish presence. The majority, middle class and thoroughly assimilated from the ghetto culture of their grandfathers, retained their Jewish identity, even if they had substantially loosened the ties to their faith. They believed strongly in the German-Jewish symbiosis—the positive interaction of German Christian and Jew to the benefit of both. Though the road toward equality had been neither smooth nor direct, they were convinced that the gap was gradually being closed and that they would in time be fully accepted with a dual identity, at once German and Jew. It was a dream and a hope to which they were fully committed and in pursuit of which many donned blinders and shut out all contrary signals.

A minority of Orthodox Jews resisted the exuberant quest for assimilation and clung to traditional Jewish culture. After 1900, a small group of Zionists rejected assimilation altogether and turned their attention to Palestine instead. But these were exceptions. Most others felt profoundly German in language, culture, and outlook. It was as Germans that they saw their future and pursued their lives. And it was as Germans that they hoped that their contributions and commitment to the fatherland would eventually lead to the end of any remaining discrimination.

The hope was not without foundation. A lot of progress had been made over a short period of time, especially in the decades after 1870. Yet even during the best years of the Wilhelmine period and the Weimar years in the '20s, the true situation remained contradictory and mixed. Periods of progress were followed by regression. Deep-seated anti-Semitic sentiment, rarely dormant for long, waxed and waned depending on the times.

The old image of the Jew as Christ-killer and obstinate religious heretic had given way to many shadings of Judeophobia justified on political, social, and eventually pseudoscientific racial grounds. The idea of the Jew as religious outcast was replaced by the stereotype of the exploiter, speculator, and middleman, and then, under the Nazis, by that of the racially inferior subhuman who could never be a true German at all. The willingness of the population to accept these images varied in discouraging cycles and reached highest intensity in times of economic hardship, only to decline again during periods of prosperity and growth. Politicians rarely hesitated to avail themselves of Jewish help at one point and to play the anti-Semitic card at another.

Dislike of Jews was never far below the surface. At the beginning of the First World War, Jewish patriotic fervor was aroused no less than that of the gentiles. A hundred thousand Jews flocked to the colors; a third of them won medals and honors, and two thousand eventually received battlefield promotions into the officer ranks—a considerable breakthrough indeed. Twelve thousand Jews died in battle and many more were wounded. But far from legitimizing their claim to equality as contributing Germans, none of this stilled the Jew haters. When the war turned sour, it was the Jews who were blamed, and Jewish soldiers were accused of being shirkers who evaded military service at the front.

The climate grew much more tense during the Weimar Republic's short and troubled life. Paradoxically, this was the time when most of the remaining de facto barriers to full Jewish participation in German life were swept away. Jews rose in academia, in the world of the arts, and in the bureaucracy. The civil service was more open to them, and they participated actively in the political sphere across the spectrum from extreme left to far right. There were Jewish ministers and revolutionaries, and one had helped to draft the Weimar Constitution itself.

Yet, even amid all this apparent progress the signs of trouble accumulated. The country was in crisis. Jews were more in evidence, and they received more of the blame. Since a few Jews had participated in high positions in the international conferences on peace and reparations, it was now they who were increasingly blamed for the onerous conditions the Allies had imposed. And since some Jews had been among the revolutionaries and agitators on the far left, it was now "the Jew" who was the focus of the resentment and the hate. As the population reeled under the hyperinflation of the early '20s and ruinous unemployment at the end of the decade, it was Jewish bankers and speculators who were accused, in spite of the fact that Germany's Jews suffered no less from those disasters than anyone else.

The economic turmoil, political instability, and social upheavals that characterized the Weimar years were fertile ground for raising old resentments and prejudices to new heights. Some German Jews still thought that all this was once again only a temporary reverse, though they would soon find that they were sadly mistaken. In fact, it was the beginning of an irre-versible downward slide into disaster.

There were a few good years in the mid-1920s, but the trend toward an especially virulent and poisonous anti-Semitism did not abate. As Hitler appeared on the scene after the war, he availed himself of many of the old prejudices and racial theories that had long been prevalent on the German scene. The dislocations of a lost war and the lack of a truly democratic tradi-tion facilitated his task.

For Germany's Jews, the unimaginable happened when Hitler seized power in 1933. The wheel had turned full circle. In spite of the remarkable advances and contributions they had made, in spite of all their struggles and hopes, the modern history of the Jews of Germany now speeded to-ward a calamitous end for which no one had been prepared.

Germany's Jews had made an astonishing impact on Germany in many fields and far beyond the country's borders, but there had never been more than about 600,000 of them—a tiny minority of no more than 1 percent of the German people. During the first eight years after Hitler seized power, more than 300,000 managed to flee and some 70,000 died; since the Jew-ish population was over-aged, the rate of deaths greatly exceeded that of births. So, when the doors finally closed in 1941 and escape was no longer possible, there were only 163,000 Jews left. Most were deported to the East, and very few survived. Thousands took their own lives.

4

The road German Jews traveled in their rapid advance from medieval isola-tion to modernity over the course of a few generations, the place they were accorded in an ambivalent and fickle gentile world, the impact of gentiles and Jews on each other, and the range of diverse attitudes and reactions on both sides—all that is a unique story that raises many puzzling questions. The more I discovered about the history of my ancestors, the more these issues loomed in my mind and the greater became the urge to delve more deeply in a search for answers.

What was it like for Jews in Germany over the course of the past 300 years, before Hitler drove most of them out and murdered the rest?

What were the everyday lives of Jews like, the famous ones and the ordinary people? How did a Jew cope when he was little more than the king's chattel, and a source of tribute, and then later when he emerged from isolation and assimilated German culture?

How did Jews confront the legal barriers against them, as well as the subtler invisible ones once they became emancipated citizens? And how did they react when, though deeply patriotic and fully German, they were once more branded pariahs and outcasts? Why did so few recognize the dangers before it was too late?

What kind of people were they, and what were their dreams, hopes, and fears? Were they really accepted fully as Germans or was that only an illusion?

Why was it that so small a group with all of its own internal differences, diversities, and conflicts, facing an often inhospitable world, nevertheless was so productive and had so profound an impact on German and world culture, and even on Judaism itself?

And most importantly, why was it in Germany of all places—a country that prided itself on its advanced culture, where Jews had gone further than almost anywhere else—that Jew-hatred evolved into its disastrous and most deadly form and engulfed all of European Jewry? Anti-Semitism existed in all countries—was the German variety fundamentally different?

That is the most troubling question of all—why the holocaust was unleashed in Germany, and what explains the apparent toleration and active participation of a substantial number of Germans in it.

Historians have agonized over this question. No one has as yet come up with a fully satisfactory answer, though Harvard scholar Daniel Goldhagen, in his recent widely discussed book, claims to have found it.[5] In Goldhagen's view, German anti-Semitism was indeed special because German society was permeated with a unique and singularly hateful racist view of Jews that had evolved over a century or more. It held that "the Jew" was a subversive *Untermensch* out to destroy other races and that only his total elimination would solve the problem. It was, says Goldhagen, this uniquely German form of "eliminationist" anti-Semitism that most Germans had absorbed and that Hitler and his criminal regime utilized to recruit a hundred thousand or more "ordinary" Germans to become active holocaust perpetrators, and it is this that explains the silent acquiescence of the rest.

Not all historians agree with Goldhagen. Many, indeed, strongly disagree. Yet if he is right, the rapid advance of German Jewry prior to Hitler
is all the more astounding, and the Jews' failure to recognize the deadly
nature of the anti-Semitic forces arrayed against them, the more puzzling.

5

A number of excellent histories of the Jews of Germany have been written
over the years.[6] I am not a historian, and this book is not the kind of work
meant to break new ground, nor is it directly a study of the holocaust and
what brought it on. Rather, it is a book that tells the story of the life and
times of six Jews—five men and a woman, some famous, accomplished,
and rich, and others who lived ordinary middle-class lives.

I found them all in the Blumenthal family tree. What attracted me to
them was not really my (somewhat tenuous) relationship to these ancestors who lived in Germany over the span of ten to twelve generations.
The main reason I chose them lies in my fascination with their varied experiences as German Jews—their triumphs and their troubles—and because
their lives, each in a different time, reflect the German-Jewish relationship
from earliest beginnings to the end.

Their stories shed light on many questions raised by the Jewish experience in Germany. They also provide an interesting perspective on Goldhagen's thesis about the nature of German anti-Semitism and the sources of
the sickness that led to the holocaust—supporting some of his assertions
and raising questions about others.

As Germans and Jews encountered each other after 1671, their complex
relationship was troubled and rife with ambiguities. Christians saw Jews as
a distasteful, inferior, and alien group, depraved and damned for their sins
against Christ; Jews had erected their own walls and formed stereotypical
preconceptions during many years of isolation, and viewed Christians as a
largely ignorant, uneducated, uncultured, cruel, and unpredictable people.

When more and more Jews broke out of their isolation and bid for acceptance in the German world, they came up against deeply engrained Christian preconceptions and prejudices. Even as the formal barriers fell, these
attitudes prevailed and a less obvious yet no less formidable and painful

resistance to accepting Jews fully in the German midst remained in place. The burdens of history weighed heavily on both sides.

As Jews rapidly assimilated German culture, the bonds to their Jewishness were loosened, their horizons widened, and their aspirations changed. What they now craved above all was full civic equality and social acceptance in the outside world, and they tried to gain it in any number of ways: through hard work, intellectual achievement, patriotism, a craving for the outer trappings of material success, and sometimes—unconscious or not—a blatant aping of the least attractive and redeeming gentile attitudes and values. Their tactics and strategies changed with the times but the goal always proved elusive and was never fully achieved. Yet the Jews never stopped trying.

The lives and times of my six protagonists tell the story of what happened in the ups and downs of this process from 1671 to 1945.

Jost Liebmann (1640–1702) was one of the earliest ancestors. In the seventeenth century, life was hard and dangerous for Germany's Jews, who were still turned inward, and were hated and despised. Jost began as a poor, itinerant peddler of trinkets and cheap pearls and ended his days as Court Jeweler to the Brandenburg nobility and one of Berlin's richest men. At first he had no earthly possessions and not even the most elementary rights—only a fierce determination to achieve status and success in a hostile world. Always subservient to his master, deeply attuned to the constant risks a Jew faced, he was smart, ambitious, and restlessly striving. He knew how to use his charm but he could also be ruthless and full of guile.

He never questioned his self-image as an observant Jew—identity crises were not for him. He lusted for riches, and as Court Jeweler he rose to the highest levels of material success, but leadership of the small community of Berlin Jews was his equally coveted social goal.

Jost mirrors Jewish life in Germany during the early days. He began like most others, but later, occupying a special place, he helped lay the foundations on which future generations would build. He belongs to a small group of modern German Jewry's founding fathers.

Rahel Varnhagen von Ense (1771–1833), born as *Rahel Levin,* the child of a later age, was as prototypical for the awakening ambitions of Jews in her day as Jost was in his. She belonged to that generation of Jews who first tired of their restricted and isolated lives and dared to venture across the bridge from the Jew street into the secular world. Her hopes and her dreams, what she attempted and how she was received, foreshadow the experiences of those who would later follow in her footsteps.

At first, merely associating with important non-Jews was a thrill. For a long time she denied and sought to escape her Jewish past, but she discovered that it did her no good. She sought to marry into the gentile aristocracy but was rejected and found that her problems remained unresolved. Fervent patriotism, abandonment of her faith, refuge in Christian theology, support of liberal politics, and romantic notions of liberty—Rahel tried them all. Like a soldier, she climbed the gentile world's invisible walls only to be stopped short of her goal every time—and to marshal her energies once more and try surmounting them again. Her triumphs and disappointments, the self-delusions, and the need to cloak even from herself the true motives for the way she chose to live were all wrapped up in that remarkable woman's fascinating life.

Rahel occupies a key place in the history of German-Jewish relations. Though she published nothing, she achieved lasting fame in the literary world. Her Berlin salon was the meeting place for the cream of Prussia's intellectual elite at a time when the country was entering the modern world. As a Jew her importance transcends her role in Prussia's intellectual life. In her eagerness to win acceptance in the Christian world, and with her delicate sensibility to all the slights and nuances of barriers and rejections, she mirrors and anticipates the agonies of German Jews with similar ambitions in later generations.

Rahel is both an inspiring figure and a tragic one. She was highly intelligent, insightful, restless, and full of energy and ambition, and she played a remarkable role in Berlin at a crucial time. In her eagerness to be a true German, she was for many years impatient with her origins and lamented often that her birth as a Jew was her greatest curse. In the end—sadder but wiser—she found that the barriers against her were still in place, that she had remained an outsider even with her aristocratic name, and that it was her Jewishness which had been the true wellspring of the meaning of her life.

Giacomo Meyerbeer (1791–1864), a descendant of Jost Liebmann, was a towering figure of the nineteenth-century musical world and a celebrated composer of grand opera. His countrymen showered him with honors as a great German, even as they often denigrated him as an un-German "cosmopolitan" Jew.

A child prodigy and the son of a Berlin family of cultured community leaders with considerable influence and great wealth, he became the object of anti-Semitic envy while still a young boy. The experience deeply wounded him, leaving its scars on his psyche for the rest of his life. In Germany's love-hate relationship with its brilliant Jewish musical genius, and in its effect on his character, demeanor, vanities, and fears, Giacomo mirrors the ambitions and agonies of the deep yearning for recognition and acceptance of many German Jews.

Unlike Rahel, who chose to "cross over" and be baptized a Christian, Giacomo never wavered in his defiant pride as a Jew. His way to deal with the animosities he encountered was to engage in ceaseless striving for success, recognition, and fame in his chosen field.

Neurotic, always working, insecure, pessimistic, thin-skinned to criticism, and quick to see anti-Semitic motives behind every failure and rebuff, he remained a devout Jew but wanted above all to be recognized as a great German too.

Giacomo Meyerbeer's incessant drive to excel, his nervous energies, his melancholy sighs that *"Risches* [anti-Semitism] is forever," and his pained yet fatalistic acceptance of it as the unavoidable burden of all Jews, as well as his generosity mixed with both a hard-headed business sense and an insatiable desire to be loved, mirror the reactions of not a few other German Jews.

Neither his wealth nor approbation as a great composer gave him peace of mind. He won titles and honors throughout Europe, but it was never enough. His anxieties and insecurity continued, and he never ceased trying for yet another success. His love-hate relationship with Germany continued until the end. The Emperor of France, one of his greatest admirers, offered him the highest recognition he could bestow—a place in the Panthéon. Giacomo politely declined. It was his last wish that he be buried on German soil after he died.

Louis Blumenthal (1818–1901), my great-grandfather, was Meyerbeer's distant relative, a descendant of longtime Brandenburg Jews. His forebears

came to the province as peddlers generations earlier, but long ago they had
won the right to settle in its small towns as petty shopkeepers or traders in
dry goods and textiles.

Louis belonged to that generation of middle-class German Jews who
were the first to have fully absorbed German values and lifestyles. He lived
in the Bismarckian age and was proud and grateful for the civil rights
granted the Jews in 1871. A decent and honest man, respectful and approv-
ing of Prussian law and order, he was the Kaiser's loyal subject and a German patriot to the core.

Louis lived in the small town of Oranienburg—as did his son and grandson—and throughout his life he remained a small-town Jew. This little
Brandenburg town therefore will appear frequently in my book as an example for the evolution of Christian-Jewish relations outside Berlin. A respected local businessman and the founder of the town's little bank, he was
one of the first Jews elected to the town council and one of the first to play
an important role in Oranienburg's municipal affairs. For Louis, being a
good German came first, and though he was a leader of the local Jewish
community as well, he served it more as a duty, with a fond backward
glance to his Jewish past, than out of a deep commitment to Judaism or
because he was still a practicing Jew.

There were many middle-class Louis Blumenthals in the Kaiser's Reich,
solidly German in their outlook and convinced that Germany was Europe's
best country for a Jew. They sent their children to German schools and
educated them as true Germans. They were proud of German strength and
accomplishments and took secret pleasure in the advancement and growing prominence of Jews in German national life. Anti-Jewish discrimination hurt and pained them more than many were willing to admit. Even
in small-town Oranienburg, Louis remained anxiously watchful, though
there were others in his circle who preferred to ignore anti-Semitism or to
pretend that it was no longer a problem at all.

Arthur Eloesser (1870–1938) was a well-known critic of literature and the
stage, and a respected scholar in his own right. He was my maternal grandmother's brother, the "showpiece" in a family of merchants and traders,
the first to have had both the right and the resources to attend Berlin University and to eschew business affairs for more intellectual pursuits. Exqui-
sitely German in outlook and values, he lived and breathed German culture

and was an active contributor and participant in Berlin's literary and cultural affairs. For most of his life he knew rather little about Judaism. "The *mesusah*," he once wrote, "disappeared from the door when I was a child."

As a young man, he was a gifted student, a favorite of his teachers, with excellent prospects for a promising academic career. Yet he would quickly discover the reality of being a German Jew even after emancipation. The university was not a congenial place for someone like him, and a tenured professorship was not in the cards for an unbaptized Jew. Being forced instead to choose a career as journalist and critic was typical for educated modern Jews overrepresented in the "free" professions.

Arthur Eloesser reflects German Jewry's attitudes and experience in their best time—and in their worst. A German patriot, he volunteered for the war at the age of forty-five. A monarchist in the Kaiserreich, he embraced Weimar democracy and had high hopes that it would work. A humanist and social liberal—though we would today call him politically conservative—he shared the nostalgia of many Germans for the discipline and order of Germany's authoritarian past and viewed the troubled times of Weimar with concern and some fear.

He believed in Germany and in the Jews' place in it. He was the typical Jewish assimilationist for whom the German-Jewish "symbiosis" was a reality—the prototype of the thinking modern German Jew in his attitudes as a German and his distance from Jewish traditions; also, however, in his failure to confront the rising evidence of a spreading virulent anti-Semitism during Germany's troubled times of the 1920's and to question the underlying assumptions of his assimilationist views.

Like many German Jews, he did so only when it was tragically too late. When Hitler took power, the Nazis burned his books and he was forbidden to work as a journalist or to publish his works.

In the last years of his life, Arthur studied the Bible, rediscovered his Jewish roots, and became a committed Zionist. His children fled the country, and Arthur twice visited Palestine and rediscovered "the promised land." It was, this German humanist wrote, as if he had "come home." Yet each time he returned to Germany, and before he could emigrate, he died. His widow was murdered.

The last of the line is *Ewald Blumenthal* (1889–1990), my father. One of German Jewry's survivors, his life is a fitting mirror of how the story ended.

Jost Liebmann, his earliest known ancestor, had begun as a poor outcast, not accepted as a German citizen and branded as an inferior, alien Jew. With Ewald the circle would be closed. When he was born, German Jewry stood at its height. A half century later he fled the country much as Jost had lived in it three centuries earlier—an alien Jew without property or rights.

My father was a conventional, middle-class German Jew. His self-image was that of a German. He had served in the Kaiser's elite guards and fought for his country in the trenches of France. The Emperor had personally rewarded him with an Iron Cross, but before he escaped Germany to save his life, he was a prisoner in the Buchenwald concentration camp.

He never thought deeply about the anomalous position of German Jews, accepting it as the only thing he had ever known. His values were German, but in his emphasis on business success and respect for intellectuals, in a certain cautious timidity, and even in the attitudes and prejudices he unconsciously absorbed, he reflects the historical experience and outlook of many assimilated modern German Jews.

For five years he stayed in Germany and hoped that Hitler was only a bad dream. To leave the country was a nightmare—no country wanted him, and there was no place else where he really wanted to go. For years, he had said that he couldn't possibly live in Palestine "with nothing but Jews." In the end it was in just such a place—the Jewish wartime ghetto of Shanghai—where he would be forced to finish with his German past once and for all.

He died in San Francisco at the age of 101, a naturalized American for nearly forty years. He spoke with a strong German accent, retaining many good memories and a few of the worst ones. He only went back to Germany once—briefly. He didn't like to talk much about the past, and I think he felt that though he had once had a good life there, the rest had all been a disastrous delusion.

When I served in the State Department and the White House, he clipped every press item mentioning his American son and was immensely proud. And when I was appointed to the Carter cabinet as Secretary of the Treasury, he told me wryly, "As a Jew, that wouldn't have been possible for you in Germany, your country of birth."

CHAPTER II

ORIGINS

1

If someone had asked my parents where their families came from, the reply would have been Brandenburg or perhaps, reaching further back, East Prussia. My mother, a touch self-conscious, might have mentioned the province of Posen (now the Polish Poznan), making sure to add that her family had moved to Berlin long ago, when Posen was still a part of Prussia—and that Posen was not like Galicia. In the circle of my parents, the distinction between longtime residents and recent arrivals—the largely Galician *Ostjuden*—was important to the former for their sense of status and identity.

More distant roots? That question would have been met with blank stares. When I was young, many assimilated German Jews had grown quite hazy about their remote origins. The history they remembered was their history in Germany, beginning about where this book begins—the last part of the seventeenth century or the early part of the eighteenth.

But that, of course, is not the whole story. The distant past of Germany's Jews—indeed, of all Ashkenazim—can be traced back much further, all the way to classical times. There are some historians, in fact, who believe that the key to understanding Germany's Jews—their special character, who they were, and what they thought and did—lies precisely in that faraway past.[1] That, however, although it provides intriguing insights, is a subject for a book in itself and too far removed from the scope of this one. For our purposes, a few significant highlights and events suffice to put what came later into appropriate perspective.

In the beginning there were no Ashkenazim or Sephardim, only a Semitic people who came to be called Jews, named after the tribe of Judah, the Hebrew Yahudi. There is much that is unique about the Jews, above all, perhaps, that they have survived at all. They are, after all, the only biblical people to have endured intact to the present day. Given their fateful, often bloody history and their unending trials and troubles, that in itself is little short of a miracle. What is equally remarkable is that over much of their recorded history, they survived as a largely dispersed people. Ever since their Babylonian exile in the sixth century B.C.E., more Jews have lived outside their homeland than in it.

Most of the early details are uncertain and shrouded in the mists of the past. But we do know that well before the time of Christ there were large, flourishing Jewish communities throughout the Middle East and in the major Mediterranean cities. There were Jews in Babylon, Mesopotamia, and Phoenicia, in the Persian Empire, in Egypt, along the coast of North Africa, and later on in Greece. After the rise of the Roman Empire, large numbers of Jews lived in Rome and throughout much of the rest of Italy.

From the beginning, a great many were outside the homeland by force of circumstance rather than choice. A large part of the Jewish population had been exiled to Babylon six centuries before Christ. Later, when Titus destroyed the Temple in 70 C.E. and again, in the aftermath of the Bar-Kochba revolt sixty years later, as many as a half million Jews or more are said to have been carried off to Rome as slaves.

Yet not all who left their homeland did so involuntarily. Jews, along with Syrians and Greeks, were among the old world's most adventurous and enterprising travelers and traders. Some reached India and even China, where there is evidence that the so-called Kaifeng Jews may have first settled there not many centuries after the birth of Christ.

The succession of Roman procurators sent to govern Palestine imposed ruinous tax burdens on the people and drove many Jews off the land. As a result, substantial numbers left for essentially economic reasons in a steady flow of emigrants to Rome and other parts of the Empire. There is no precise information about total numbers, but we do know that it involved many—probably in the millions, more, indeed, than the number of Jews who remained behind, causing a contemporary of Caesar to observe that "it is hard to find a spot in the inhabited world where this race does not dwell or traffic."[2]

As to their arrival in Germany, no one knows for certain when a Jew first set foot on German soil, though there are stories claiming a presence well before the birth of Christ. Some historians cite reports of a Jewish presence in Roman towns and settlements near the Rhine and Danube rivers as early as 300 B.C.E. There are tales about Jews in the ancient city of Worms petitioning Herod to spare Jesus from crucifixion, and of beautiful Jewish maidens among Roman legionnaires encamped along the banks of the Rhine.[3]

Although these are merely legends, the hypothesis of a very early presence in Germany is not unreasonable. The Romans were the first people from an advanced civilization to arrive there, years before Christ, at a time when the indigenous tribes were still dressed in little more than pelts. They came, originally invited by the Gauls, to help repel the invasion of "barbarians" pressing in from the East. Crossing the Alps or traveling north from the Mediterranean through France, up the riverbeds of the Rhone, the Loire, and the Seine, they established their towns and encampments along the great rivers—the Rhine, Main, Mosel, and Danube. And in the wake of the Roman legionnaires came all the others: settlers and camp followers, wives, prostitutes, beggars, and gypsies, and of course the merchants and the traders. Given a substantial Jewish presence in Rome and the prevalence of Jewish traders throughout the classical world, the supposition that Jews were among the earliest arrivals is certainly plausible.

The first concrete evidence of a Jewish presence in Germany—locally made terra-cotta bottle stoppers and a menorah excavated from Roman ruins near Trier—dates back to the third century C.E. The elaborately carved stoppers depict manikins with clearly Semitic features and seem to make fun of such Jewish customs as circumcision, exclusiveness, and endogamy. They also give an idea of the occupations of these early Jewish settlers, to wit, wine-growing and the trading of slaves.[4] But the first really hard evidence attesting to the presence of Jews is generally thought to be two decrees by the Roman Emperor Constantine the Great in 324 and 331 C.E.

The first of these stipulates that the Jews of Cologne are eligible to be called to the Curia, or city administration—thereby bestowing on some of them the dubious honor of making them liable for Roman taxes. The later decree exempts the Chief Rabbi from this obligation.

In the pre-Christian era, leaving aside that a good many of their ancestors had been brought there against their will, the Jews in Rome and throughout the Empire seem to have led tolerable and normal lives. They were Roman citizens and enjoyed the same legal rights as all others, with no particular restrictions placed on their freedom of movement, their occupation, or the practice of their religion. They were merchants, shopkeepers and traders, artisans, farmers, and vintners,[5] and they had their scholars and rabbis who even then occupied a place of honor and respect among them.

Two exceptions, however, already distinguished them from others—and both would have fateful consequences when resurrected in a later day. For one thing, the Jews alone were liable for a special poll tax, the *Fiscus Judaicus,* justified as a substitute for the ancient tax once imposed for the support of the Temple in Jerusalem, and they were also—on religious grounds—exempt from military service.

Already the Jews seem to have voluntarily set themselves apart, focusing more on each other than on the outside world. Their pride in their faith and their sense of chosen mission made them seem somewhat haughty to others. They alone were the monotheists, passionately committed to what they believed was the only true faith, tenaciously determined to maintain the covenant with their God, and unalterably convinced that steadfast adherence to their laws and prescriptions would lead, in time, to the kingdom of God on earth.

This too would have lasting and bitter historical repercussions and would contribute to their reputation as stiff-necked resisters, to their "otherness" as a people with an alien culture and a sense of superiority toward those around them.

2

What role does chance play in the history of mankind?

What if a short Jewish tentmaker from Tarsus, a man named Saul, with crooked legs and bright blue eyes under heavy brows, had not had a vision telling him to go out and preach to pagans and Jews that the only way to salvation was to accept the crucified Jesus as the son of God? If this man, the true founder of Christianity, who is today called St. Paul, had not had his dream, would today's world be fundamentally different?

What if Mohammed, left as an orphan in the desert, had not been taken in by his uncle but had perished in the sandy wilderness of Arabia at an early age? What if George Washington had been captured in the battle of Trenton, or if the young Napoleon had died in the siege of Toulon? Indeed, what if a young girl named Klara Plözl had never come to be a maid in Alois Schicklgruber's household, eventually married him and borne him a son whom all the world knows as Adolf Hitler?

Are there fundamental forces that shape the fate of humanity regardless of personalities and individuals? Or is it that particular persons and events, by virtue of fortuitous circumstance, have a determining impact on the course of human history and experience, which in their absence might have taken a totally different turn?

These questions arise in any study of Jewish history, where the chance appearance of key figures and seemingly random milestone events have again and again played a fateful role in shaping the vicissitudes of Jewish existence.

The spread of Christianity is clearly one such example, perhaps the most dramatic one. But it is only the first in a long series of others.

When Constantius Chlorus, known as "The Pale," who was about to become Caesar of the Western Roman Empire, met and took as his *concubina,* or morganatic mate, a certain tavern maid named Helena, it became for the Jews another watershed. For out of their union emerged around 275 C.E. a son named Flavius Valerius Aurelius Constantinus, later called Constantine the Great, who would make a momentous decision affecting not only the course of Western culture but also the long-term fate of the Jews.

For Constantine (as for St. Paul), it began with a dream and a vision. When Constantine succeeded his father as Caesar of the West in Gaul and Britain, there were other Caesars who were his rivals. As he set out to do battle with one of his competitors, a certain Maxentius who held sway over Rome and Africa, it appears that somewhere near Colmar, before crossing the Alps, he and his soldiers reported seeing a shining cross. It was, he said, in a dream that night that he received the command of Jesus to take the cross as his standard. Thus Constantine became the first Christian Emperor of Rome, and when he died he was buried in the white robes of a Christian neophyte and not, as had been customary, in the purple of a Caesar.

Constantine's conversion marks the beginning of the Christianization of the Roman Empire with lasting—mostly baleful— consequences for the Jews. Broad religious tolerance had prevailed under the pagan Emperors. Now, as the pagans yielded to the new faith, it was the Jew who stood apart. He stubbornly resisted conversion, becoming a permanent thorn in the side of the state, a member of a sect that the Emperor at various times called shameful, contemptible, beastly, and perverse.

Discriminatory decrees soon followed. In 319 C.E. it was ordered that Jews be burned for stoning a convert. Later there were other edicts forbidding their ownership of Christian slaves or their circumcision, the conversion of any slave to Judaism, and on pain of death, Jewish-gentile intermarriage and the teaching of the Torah to gentiles.[6] Henceforth, the Jews in Rome and Italy were singled out as a nettlesome people and progressively deprived of their equal rights.

There were repercussions in Germany also, but for the next several centuries at least, the position of Jews remained less unfavorable there. It was a time when the Roman Empire of the West was in decline and the petty kingdoms of the Franks and other tribes ruled in Gaul and on the German side of the Rhine. These were rude, crude, and uncouth people, but since religion—a single true faith—was less of a factor for them than in Christianized Rome, the lot of the Jew was at first less onerous as well. Roman law, which had bestowed citizenship on him, still pertained, and as far as is known, the Jews of Germany seem to have lived under these tribes in relative peace and burdened with few discriminatory restrictions. But these are the Dark Ages, and detailed knowledge about conditions and events is scarce. However, over the next four hundred years two separate developments with future significance are noteworthy.

On the one hand, these are centuries when a flourishing commerce developed among the "barbarian" West, Christianized Byzantium, and the rising Muslim East. The nobility in Gaul and Germany greatly valued the East's jewels and ivory and their tapestry, silk, and spices. Exotic essences and perfumes were particularly welcome in an age not known for its cleanliness. Noble ladies and their men liked the "Jew smell"—the perfumes Jewish traders brought from the East, where there was strong demand for furs and for weapons and slaves. It is the Jews who, together with Greeks and Syrians, became the principal traders in this commerce. Jewish ships sailed the seas between East and West, and Jewish entrepreneurship and initiative benefited from these conditions in a world that was difficult and lawless but also full of opportunity and reward. The role of these Jewish seafarers and caravaneers was greatly valued, and it has been said that to an extent the tradition of an international Jewish network of traders and financiers, which endured to modern times, has its earliest origins in this period.

The second development of the period had equally far-reaching consequences, although its impact on Jewish life in Germany would prove less favorable. In the feudal order prevailing under the Franks and the other tribes—Burgundians, Frisians, and Swabians—land ownership passed to the warriors and vassals of the ruling elite. Allegiance to these princes, dukes, and lords—and their protection—was derived from status achieved in battle. Jews had neither military ties nor rural roots, leaving them in a kind of no-man's land, unprotected and with uncertain status. By the ninth century, therefore, when the Franks had gradually converted to Christianity and come under the influence of the Church, the Jews—without land or protection—found themselves isolated and vulnerable, easy targets for discrimination and abuse.

Yet for the next several centuries, the position of the Jews actually took a turn for the better. A new, more favorable ruler appeared on the scene: Charles the Great, or Charlemagne, as history remembers him. Crowned King of the Franks and Emperor of the West in 768 C.E., he established a new dynasty and led a renaissance in his Carolingian realm, the beginning of what in time became the Holy Roman Empire.

Charlemagne was strong-willed, intelligent, and pragmatic. He greatly expanded his kingdom, conquered the Saxons, fought and defeated the Lombards, and led expeditions against the Arabs in northeastern Spain. He vigorously promoted commerce, and for this he valued the enterprise and skill of the Jews, and so he protected them and gladly availed himself of their talents.

Charlemagne was the founder of German nationhood. As the Saxons and the Wends came under his sway, he continued to push outward toward the east. Along the Elbe, Saale, and Oder rivers his dynasty established scores of new cities at Magdeburg, Halle, Merseburg, ranging as far away as Prague, Bohemia, and Poland. Wherever he and the Carolingians went, traders followed, and it is along these flourishing routes of commerce that the Jews spread out and settled across Germany at key points and river crossings that later grew into towns.

Jewish life under Charlemagne and his Carolingian successors has some interesting parallels to the Jewish experience in the eighteenth and nineteenth centuries. Both were eras when critical turning points with lasting consequences took place. In the later period, the Jews emerged from the ghetto into modernity. Under the Carolingians they first became true Europeans, the culmination of an evolutionary process away from their oriental origins begun when their ancestors had left the homeland many centuries earlier. Henceforth, it would be the numerically superior Ashkenazim who would play the dominant role in world Jewry, distinct from those in and around the homeland, and the main carriers of a unique kind of Jewish-European culture developed in the diaspora.

On the one hand, the enmity of the Church toward Jews—"those who had murdered the Lord"—was already well established and reflected in a steady stream of Church edicts aimed at containing their presence among Christians. The conversion from paganism was recent and shallow, and many edicts were designed to isolate Jews from Christians lest the flock be contaminated by Jewish heresy. But there was also much jealousy of Jewish wealth and resentment of the lost tithes from Jewish nonbelievers. Though the discriminatory and often punitive decrees had an ostensible theological basis, many were at least as importantly the result of economic and financial motives.

On the other hand, the basic antagonism of the Church toward the Jews notwithstanding, much of what was decreed was kept more in the breach than in the observance. Charlemagne and his temporal successors largely ignored the edicts, treated the Jews as equals in most economic and political spheres, and allowed them to practice their religion without any significant restraints.

In a pattern that would be repeated many times in a later day, the Jews, though standing apart, had an important role to play in the system: they were needed, so they were tolerated and protected, sharing in the Carolingian renaissance and prospering under it. In addition to their roles as traders, merchants, and artisans, they were valued as physicians, scholars, and advisers. One of them, Isaac, is known to have been dispatched as Charlemagne's emissary to the distant court of the great Harun al-Rashid, returning four years later with the Caliph of Baghdad's splendid and astonishing gift of a live elephant, which Isaac had successfully transported in an arduous journey from the Middle East to Charlemagne's court at Aix-la-Chapelle.

Prosperity and royal protection led to a flowering of Jewish culture, and great academies of Jewish learning flourished in many of the larger German towns. But though life was good for them, the seeds of trouble were already germinating beneath the surface. Here lies the second parallel to modern German-Jewish history.

Gentile society was organized within a rigid class structure—nobles at the top, and clerics, soldiers, craftsmen, and serfs below them. Jews stood outside this structure and were relatively more prosperous and educated, but as a group, they were without secure social standing and recognized prestige. In contrast to the prevailing squalor of the towns—general filth, stinking streets, and poor houses—they lived among their own under conditions that were a good deal better. Within the voluntary separation of the *Judengasse,* the Jew street, they kept slaves, their houses were made of brick, their women rarely worked, and their dress was better, even splendiferous on holidays and special occasions. They had developed a language of their own, read books and were more literate, and walked with pride. Under the rabbis who were the scholars, arbiters, and judges regulating Jewish affairs, their life was more prosperous and more ordered.

These were the ingredients for future trouble. Jews were not only different, they were proud of it and made little secret of their disdain for many of the prevailing temporal rules and of their refusal to recognize any true king other than their Lord, or that the supreme law binding on them was the Jewish law and no other.

During the era of Carolingian rule up to the eleventh century, the Jews

of Germany grew in numbers and spread out across the land. They prospered in relative security and their culture deepened. But their separate
ways, partly forced on them and partly voluntary; their greater wealth; and
their position outside the established social structure proved a precarious
and dangerous mix in the face of the animosity of the Church and the ignorance and jealousies of the population around them. The time came when
it would lead to tragedy and disaster.

3

Clermont-Ferrand, in the Auvergne, is today a modern city of 150,000, the
industrial and tourist crossroads of the *massif central* in south-central
France.

Clermont is an ancient Roman town, founded in the third or fourth century C.E., long before it was joined with its twin city Montferrand. The
name means Hill of Light, but in the Jewish literature of the Middle Ages it
was often called *Har Ophel,* or Hill of Darkness. For it is here that an important visitor came at the end of the eleventh century C.E. to make a speech
that would have a lasting impact on history. For the Jews, the speech was—
like the Babylonian exile or the Christianization of the Romans—a major
turning point ending their better days under the Carolingians and ush-
ering in events that decimated their communities and forever worsened
the Jewish position in the gentile world and the attitudes of Jews and gentiles toward each other.

Pope Urban II, a Frenchman of noble birth, who had been Cardinal
bishop of Ostia, came to Clermont in 1095, seven years after his elevation
to the papal throne. Erudite, eloquent, and handsome, Urban was an important ecclesiastical reformer who held office during a period of severe
crisis and change in Christian affairs. His energies were focused on
strengthening the position of the Church and establishing clearer rules
and laws defining its position vis-à-vis Christian society and its temporal
rulers. His aim was to expand ecclesiastical influence and supremacy in
the affairs of the Christian world, and that was the purpose of his trip.
It was with this in mind that he arrived to speak at Clermont on November 27, 1095.

The Pope wanted to stir the enthusiasm and religious fervor of the believers and rally them closer to the bosom of the Church. To do so, like any astute politician, he chose a cause and a rallying cry that he knew would be well received among the faithful—nothing less than a call for a great crusade and holy war to liberate the Holy Land from the Muslims and free Jerusalem from the grip of the infidel, in the name of Christ.

The Christians of the East had for some time been asking for help against the encroachment of the Muslims, who had extended their sway throughout the Mediterranean and across North Africa as far west as Spain. More recently, Christian pilgrims to the Holy Places had reported intolerable indignities at the hands of the infidels. But gradually the Muslims had been losing ground, so the moment seemed opportune to call for the great Crusade and to urge the knights to strike a decisive blow in the long-standing Christian–Muslim struggle.

The battle cry was *deus volt*—God wills it. A Pope calling for war might seem strange to us today. But in Urban's day it was not. In a time of spiritual awakening, Popes did not disfavor war as a means of promoting their cause, blessing the battle flags of the knights and promising them spiritual rewards in this life and in the next.

It is unlikely that the Pope anticipated the enormous power of the forces he set in motion. For the Church and the rulers, the Crusade was a convenient diversion from many internal problems. For the impoverished knights, taking the vows of the Crusader meant adventure and the chance to escape their debts. And for the others—the unofficial bands of common people and rabble that followed them, there was the opportunity for food, loot, and excitement in an otherwise drab and dismal life.

A council of bishops began the planning on the very next day, and the Pope and others continued to carry the message throughout France and beyond. Within months, the first Crusaders, led by Peter the Hermit of Amiens, set out toward Constantinople and the Holy Land, arriving in Cologne in April, on what became a major route for the Crusaders—up the Rhine and down the Danube to Hungary and on to the East. But what was intended as an orderly movement of armed crusading knights soon turned into an undisciplined horde, as assorted bullies, adventurers, and local riffraff joined the throng, intent more on loot and pillage than on religious salvation. Two groups in the population became their particular targets: women and Jews.

In an age when women were relatively defenseless, the rabble that followed the knights had little compunction about their abuse and rape along
the way—and certainly not as regards the female Muslim prisoners taken
later on. Nor did their enemies hesitate to respond in kind, as described
somewhat salaciously by a Saracen writer of the period: "How many well-
guarded women were profaned . . . and pretty things put to the test, and
virgins deflowered and proud women dishonored and lovely women's red
lips kissed."[7]

But if women were a frequent target, the Jews became one even more so,
for they were not only equally defenseless but also a rich mark for loot.
Though some Crusaders like Peter had taken vows not to kill and could be
bribed to pass by the Jewish areas in peace, others were considerably less
squeamish and restrained.

Two factors, with their roots in the earlier past, contributed to the doom
of the Jews. For centuries the Church had agitated against them and accused them of every imaginable sacrilege, including the murder of the son
of God. Why, the people now asked, do battle with the infidel in the faraway East, without first avenging the death of Jesus on his murderers closer
to home? As the Abbot of Cluny put it: "What is the good of going to the
end of the world . . . when we permit among us other infidels who are a
thousand times more guilty toward Christ . . . ?"[8] Thus the seeds sown by
centuries of animosity and inflammatory rhetoric now became the religious justification for Jew killing.

The second factor making the Jews a ready target, however, lay outside
religious prejudice and the greed of the masses. The often self-imposed Jewish isolation now contributed greatly to their downfall. Living among their
own in the separate, more prosperous Jewish quarters, well before the time
when the authorities enforced their segregation, coupled with their ill-
concealed distaste of the habits and ways of the gentiles, made them stand
out as a readily identifiable and conveniently positioned minority ready
for slaughter.

The First Crusade began in 1095, and before the movement had run its
course over the next two centuries there were a total of seven others.[9] Again
and again, as the waves rolled over Jewish communities by the Rhine and
Danube rivers, there was mayhem and murder, though the first three Crusades were by far the worst. It was as if the first killing had set a precedent

and permanently opened the floodgates of anti-Jewish excesses among the people. From then on, for hundreds of years to come, the pogroms, the expulsions followed by recalls and renewed exiling, and the general degradation of the Jews never ceased for long.

It is during the two first centuries of disaster and decimation following 1096 that the attitudes of gentiles and Jews toward each other would be most deeply and permanently influenced and shaped. The life of the Jew among the Christians would never again be the same. His designation as an outcast has its origins in this period, affecting his character and his position as a hated alien, and marking him for centuries as the scapegoat for every calamity and disaster in the world around him.

4

The orgy of killing of the First Crusade set these calamitous events in motion. A holocaust, as this surely was, is rarely predicted in advance, and the victims are usually the last ones to see it coming. Perhaps that is because, by its very nature, a disaster of such epic proportions defies the imagination and lies beyond human grasp before the event.

In our own time, many German Jews did not see the signs of their impending doom; until virtually the last moment they simply could not envisage what was in store for them. As the Crusaders advanced on them nine centuries earlier, Germany's Jews faced a similar disaster of impending wholesale decimation and they were equally unable to recognize the storm signals ahead, though later Jewish chronicles have preserved a full account of the events.

Early warnings from their French cousins that the roving bands of Christian Soldiers of the Cross and their followers meant serious trouble were disregarded. What had happened in France didn't seem relevant to their own situation. They had lived relatively unharmed among the Christians for a long time. As would happen in the twentieth century, they trusted their neighbors and their government. Germany was different, they thought.

They were soon disabused of this idea. It was during Passover, on May 3, 1096, when the first horde of Crusaders under Emicho, Count of Leiningen, descended on the Jewish quarter of Speyer, looting and forcibly baptizing some, while murdering eleven others. At Worms and Mainz, over the next two weeks, it was infinitely worse, and before the rampage ended there, eight hundred Jews had died. "God wills it," the Crusaders cried, and the stunned Jews almost seemed to accept the battle cry as their own. Some sought refuge with the bishop, others tried to buy off their attackers, but rarely did they defend themselves, and when the mob approached, rather than risk forcible baptism, they preferred to die by their own hand, an act they called *Kidush ha Shem,* blessing the Name:

> They let themselves be killed and blessed the Name of the Lord; they offered their necks so that their head be cut off in the name of their Creator; some also laid hand on themselves. Thus they fulfilled the word of the prophet— "The mother is on her children and the father has fallen on his sons." Thus the one butchered his brother, the other his kin, his wife and his children; also the bridegroom his bride, gentlewomen their darling children. All accepted wholeheartedly the heavenly judgment, offering their souls to their Creator, crying "Hear, O Israel . . ." The enemy stripped them, and dragged them about and none was left except a few who were baptized by force.[10]

The atrocities at Worms lasted two weeks, but when Emicho and his mob moved on to Mainz at the end of May, the bloodletting was even worse, and before it was finished well over a thousand Jews had died there, many by their own hand. Virtually the entire community was wiped out in an orgy of killing and mass suicide over the next several days:

> The first to be encountered by the enemy . . . were the most devout, among them Reb Izchak ben R. Moshe, a great leader. They had refused to flee into (the bishop's) inner chambers merely to buy themselves another hour of life. Rather, they sat there, lovingly accepting the judgment of heaven, wrapped in their prayer garments and prepared to fulfill the will of their Creator. The enemy smothered them with stones and arrows and cut them down with their swords. And when those in the inner chambers saw how the enemy had overwhelmed them, they called out ". . . it is best to sacrifice our lives. . . ." And the women butchered their sons and daughters, and then themselves. And many men took heart and likewise slaughtered their wives, children and servants.[11]

Those prepared to submit to baptism might sometimes be spared, but only a few were willing to save themselves in this way. Incredibly, even those who had been forcibly baptized were so devastated that they preferred death, thus to expiate the dishonor of having to live among the un-circumcised Christians. In one such dramatic instance, described in the later chronicles of Jewish survivors, Mar Izchak and Mar Uri, two rabbis, set fire to the synagogue and chose self-immolation for themselves and their families rather than to bear the disgrace. First they killed their kin, and then: "He went to the House of Prayer . . . lit fires at every corner and door, and prayed amidst the fire to the Lord in a strong and beseeching voice." [12]

In town after town, and in every village where Jews lived, the mobs looted and killed. In Cologne, many Jews chose death by throwing them-selves into the Rhine. Whole communities were wiped out in the sur-rounding villages at Xanten, Mörs, Altenahr, and Kerpen. Farther south, at Regensburg, the Crusaders drove the entire Jewish community into the Danube and forcibly baptized them. Before it was over and the Crusaders had moved on, more than 12,000 German Jews had met their death. For the survivors, the only consolation was the news that Emicho and his co-horts had themselves been killed by the Hungarians, who apparently took a dim view of their marauding ways.

The First Crusade's period of slaughter finally ended in 1103 when Henry IV allowed the forcibly baptized Jews to return to their faith, decreeing his *Landfriede,* a peace bestowing immunity on "clerics, women, nuns, peas-ants, merchants, travelers, fishermen, hunters and Jews." [13]

Slowly, the survivors crept back to rebuild their homes, and for a gen-eration the peace held. But the bloodletting was not over; this was merely the beginning of a long period of suffering and death. In the twelfth cen-tury, the Second and Third Crusades began with similar massacres of Jews. Even though the king and occasionally clerics like Bernard of Clairvaux inveighed against the Jew killing, they were rarely successful, and the mur-der continued with never-ending outbursts of violence against Jewish communities at Boppard, Speyer, Halle, Erfurt, Frankfurt, and elsewhere throughout Germany.

For the Jews, the lasting significance of the Crusades lay not only in the terrible toll exacted on them. The disaster also left deep and permanent scars on both sides. Jews everywhere now were outcasts and fair game, sub-jects of denigration and derision forever exposed to official and popular discrimination and mistreatment. In the Jewish mind there remained etched deeply into the collective psyche a sense of helplessness, full of agony and self-blame. In time this resigned fatalism would serve as the basis for making a virtue out of their pariah status and enforced isolation.

Early in the thirteenth century, the Emperor proclaimed the Jews as his *servi camarae,* his personal property, protected by him but exploitable as an asset of the Crown and subject to his whim. The Church, though officially opposing outright slaughter, continued to add to the Jewish troubles. The Third Lateran Council in 1179 had inveighed against Christian money-lending, leaving the Jews, who had been excluded from most other occupations, as the principal source of credit—hated usurers in a dishonored profession, with negative implications for many years to come.

But it was at the Fourth Council, called by Pope Innocent III in 1215, that the greatest number of discriminatory rules and restrictions against the Jews were added in what has been called the high-water mark of medieval anti-Jewish legislation.[14] Innocent was an unyielding enemy of the Jews; he called them "Sons of the Crucifiers" and wrote that they were condemned to be the living witnesses to their sins: "It is pleasing to God that they should be suppressed by the servitude they earned when they raised sacrilegious hands against Him."[15]

Henceforth Jews were to be officially separated from Christians—thus foreshadowing the fateful practice of segregating them in ghettos. They could no longer hold public office, have sexual intercourse with Christians, or employ Christian servants. Living apart, they were ordered to wear the distinctive Jew badge, dress with a peaked hat, and pay heavy taxes on their property. Once converted, they were strictly forbidden to return to their faith. Moreover, the Council's propagation of the Doctrine of Transubstantiation—the Host as the living body of Christ—added Host desecration as yet another pretext for Jewish persecution to all the other false accusations of Jewish thirst for Christian blood, ritual murder, and child killing at Passover.

Bloody outrages against Jews continued throughout the thirteenth and fourteenth centuries, with rarely a time when somewhere in Germany Jews were not being set upon, massacred, or expelled. In 1243, the first recorded charge of Host desecration led to the devastation of many Jewish communities. A worse slaughter, with the same justification, occurred in Frankfurt a few years later. In 1286, many Jews died in Munich after being accused of drinking the blood of Christian children during their Passover rites, and in 1298 a poor knight with the curious name of Rindfleisch (beef meat), alleging a ritual murder in the town of Röttingen, instigated the massacre of thousands of Jews throughout Germany. During the Armleder riots, which continued for two years beginning in 1336, bands of roving rabble armed with pitchforks who called themselves Jew batterers (*Judenschläger*), roamed through Franconia, Swabia, and Alsace, wreaking havoc on dozens of Jewish communities including that of Mulhouse, which was almost totally wiped out.

The height of Jewish suffering, however, was reached during the terrible years of the Black Death from 1347 to 1352, when all of Europe was in the grip of fear and anguish over the ravages of a dread disease that killed as many as twenty-five million, a quarter to a third of the entire population.

It was an event that one historian has described as "the most terrible physical calamity in historic times."[16] The medieval world was no stranger to the scourge of diseases like leprosy, scurvy, and influenza, for which no one knew a cure. But this pestilence that descended on Europe was different. It killed vast numbers indiscriminately and rapidly—usually in three or four days. No one was safe—neither rich nor poor, soldier nor servant, priest nor layman, peasant nor city dweller. Places where crowding and the concentration of people were greatest, such as monasteries, were particularly hard hit. Before it was over, of 375 bishops alive in 1348, 207 had died, also 25 of 64 archbishops and 9 of 28 cardinals.[17]

We now know that the cause was *Pasteurella pestis,* bubonic, septicemic, and pneumonic bacilli probably imported by oriental rats on ships docking at Marseilles and other Mediterranean ports. From there the disease spread through France, England, and Germany and across the rest of Europe, reaching Russia in 1351. No one understood what was happening or knew what to do, and the resulting helplessness and mass hysteria in the face of imminent death for all is hard to describe.

The rich blamed the poor, and the poor the rich. Soothsayers, quacks, and charlatans had a field day. Astrologers looked to the stars and concluded that it was all because of an unhappy conjunction of Saturn, Jupiter, and Mars. The Church explained it as divine punishment for a sinful world.

Yet all this was to no avail, and none of the traditional cures—purging, bloodletting, potions, or vinegar treatments—was effective. New remedies such as fasting, dieting, purifying the air by fire, and fumigation with incense worked no better, nor did more outlandish ideas, such as those of the Medical Faculty of Paris, which opined that baths and sexual intercourse were particularly dangerous and likely to have fatal results.

It was in this climate of fear and terror that the people were gripped by a form of mass neurosis and madness that led to wild excesses in behavior. Some turned to mindless superstitious religiosity. Throngs of half-naked flagellants wandered through the streets beating themselves in the hope of divine forgiveness. Others resorted to orgies and licentiousness, and the breakdown in normal restraints led to a pervasive lawlessness exceeding all previous bounds. And so it was not long, amid the turmoil and the derangement, before the masses turned on society's outcasts—first the lepers and then, with a bloody vengeance, on the Jews.

The retribution wreaked on Germany's Jews was terrible. It began when the rumor gained currency that the deaths were not divine retribution at all but a *pestis manufacta,* a pestilence deliberately caused by the Jews to punish Christians for their past outrages against them. Put to the torture, some Jews had been made to say that they indeed had been at fault: "because you Christians have destroyed so many Jews," a tortured victim had shouted at Breisgau; and at the castle of Chillon, near Lake Geneva, a similar confession had been extracted.

Soon the news spread of elaborate Jewish plots to poison wells with infernal potions and magic brews. Even though the king and the Church tried to protect them, and the Pope himself issued a bull absolving Jews of responsibility and blaming the devil, nothing could stop the crazed rabble. Throughout Germany, sixty large and 150 smaller communities were wiped out. Six thousand Jews are believed to have died in Mainz alone. At Strassburg, on St. Bartholomew's Night, August 23–24, the entire community was burned at the stake, and the same occurred at Frankfurt and Cologne, where more than 2,000 died in the flames of a mass pyre.[18] At Nordhausen, the Jews asked for time to prepare themselves, and died by their own hand in mass self-immolation.

The plague killed Jews and Christians alike, but for the former it became the occasion for yet another in the seemingly endless series of massacres and disasters that had stretched over more than two centuries. Of the many thriving communities that had existed in Germany prior to the Crusades, not many were left when the fourteenth century drew to a close.

5

As the next century dawned, much had changed for the Jews of Germany, and none of it was for the better. The Age of Death had lasted for several hundred years. Tens of thousands had perished; others had escaped eastward through Bohemia and Moravia to Poland and the Slavic areas. For the rest, life had become difficult and precarious and these remnants of what had once been flourishing communities now lived scattered across the land, subject to severe restrictions.

Throughout Germany, as elsewhere, the rules of the compulsory ghetto, first promulgated during the Third Lateran Council, were coming into force with increasing severity. In Frankfurt, as of 1462, 110 Jewish survivors lived segregated in the *Judengasse,* behind portals guarded by a Christian gatekeeper and tightly shut at ten o'clock each night. Punitive taxes were the order of the day, the threat of pogroms was ever present and expulsions were frequent—at Cologne in 1424, Speyer in 1435, Augsburg in 1439, and later in Mainz and Ulm as well. One place would banish them, while another would decide it needed them and readmit them, usually at a high price. Sometimes, after a few years, the very town that had expelled its Jews "for eternity" would again call them back to fill the void in money lending and trading.

In Swabia all Jews were imprisoned, their property confiscated, to be released only upon the cancellation of all debts owed to them.[19] In Brandenburg the back and forth of bloody punishment, expulsion, and return was particularly frequent. No sooner had some Jews been allowed back, when a short generation later yet another disaster descended on them. In 1510, for example, a potter named Paul Fromm was apprehended in the theft of a gilded Host from a village church, which he had allegedly sold to the Jews for their sacrilegious purposes.

What followed is typical of the day. Thirty-five Jews were arrested and tortured repeatedly until they finally "confessed" their guilt. On the day of their punishment, a great spectacle was organized for the amusement of the masses. On Friday, a feast day, the town nobles, wise men, scholars, and theologians gathered in the market place, seated high up on a three-tiered wooden stage. Below them sat judges, scribes, and other officials, all avidly watched by the spectators.

Slowly and solemnly, the condemned were led to the market square, Fromm at the head of the procession, followed by the Jews in their long caftans and white peaked hats. Fromm was tied to a rack, an iron chain around his neck, and exhibited to the people. Finally, he was singed ten times with hot irons and eventually burned to death. The Jews, three at a time, were similarly killed, but not until a rabbi had said a prayer while the condemned sang praise to their creator. Two Jews who had converted to Christianity were favored with the privilege of a mere beheading, rather than the more painful death on the pyre.[20]

Yet even during this somber period Germany was never totally without Jews, although the numbers now were small—no more than a few thousand at most. If not for the great trek eastward of those escaping the reign of terror, perhaps the Jews of Ashkenaz might not have survived at all.

A few Jews had gone to the eastern areas in earlier times, but now it was Poland and Lithuania to which they flocked in large numbers. Poland lay in ruins from the devastation of Tartar invaders and a series of friendly rulers was eager to have the immigrants' help in the rebuilding. In 1264, Boleslav the Pious was the first to issue a Charter of Protection for them. In the next century, Casimir the Great was particularly hospitable, encouraged, it is said, by his beautiful Jewish mistress.

Under their liberal policies Jews were granted broad rights, allowed to live where they wanted and to travel freely. They settled widely in towns and villages throughout Poland, became an important force in revitalizing trade and commerce, and worked as artisans and financial agents, estate managers, and "tax farmers," interposed between the people and the nobility. Allowed a large measure of self-government and autonomy, they developed a rich communal life, religion and scholarship flourished, and their numbers increased greatly. At the beginning of the fourteenth century only a few thousand Jews lived in Poland. By 1500, their number had risen to 50,000, increasing again tenfold to half a million within another century and a half. The birth rate was exceptionally high, so that in time—even when conditions had become much less favorable for them—Poland and Lithuania were home to well over a million Jews.

This eastward migration and the extraordinarily rapid growth of a large Jewish population in Poland, Lithuania, and parts of western Russia, is of great importance. It is in large part due to this that Western Jews survived, and it is this pool of people that became a major source for the rebirth of German Jewry through a re-emigration westward after the seventeenth century.

From the early days of their arrival, Polish Jews had tended to cluster in their own areas and to reconstitute their inward-looking religious and cultural life. Their language remained the Yiddish mixture of middle high German with Hebrew and Latin words. Enforced ghetto segregation or widespread restrictions on where they could live were not a significant issue, except later in Krakow and in a few larger cities. Real ghetto culture, therefore, has its true origins not here but in the West, Germany included. Its impact on Jewish traditions and habits, and on Jewish psychology, is critical for understanding future developments and deserves brief mention.[21]

Strictly enforced segregation of Jews behind ghetto walls was first implemented in Spain and Portugal, and in Venice after 1516—hence the Italian name *geto,* or iron foundry, its site in that city. In time, the practice, with some local variation, spread elsewhere, and nowhere was it accompanied by harsher and more comprehensive rules than in Germany.

Typically, the ghetto or *Judenstadt* was confined to one or more narrow streets, twelve feet wide, in the worst part of town. With no chance of enlargement as populations grew, houses tended to be high, often meeting at the roofs, since only vertical expansion was possible. Overcrowding, squalor, and unsanitary conditions were endemic and sunlight was sparse. Moreover, since the Jews could not own real estate, they were perennially exposed to the gouging of Christian landlords. Access was through a single gate, locked inside and out. No Christian was allowed in at night or on major holidays like Easter, when the inhabitants were strictly forbidden outside the ghetto walls.

The rules regulating what the Jews could and could not do were endless. The tax burden was oppressive. They could not ride in a carriage or employ

Christians. Distinctive dress, with the Jew badge, was required at all times. Shops outside the ghetto were forbidden. Jews were barred from handicrafts and the liberal professions. In some instances, to control their numbers, only the firstborn was allowed to marry, and occasionally all inhabitants had to submit to forced Church services—and to strict controls meant to prevent them from blocking their ears.

What remained for the Jews was trading in secondhand goods, primarily old clothes. Without shops, they became peddlers, and their traditional role as money lenders triggered pawnbroking and dealing in gold, jewelry, and precious stones. Overall, life was degrading, stultifying, and unhealthy and led to a general impoverishment of the population.

And yet, paradoxically, it was these very restrictions and the Jews' isolation that also created a varied, often rich social life and became the key to future Jewish culture. To survive within the ghetto walls, the Jews established their own microcosm of the outside world and their own rules of behavior, social morality, and traditions, some of which would prevail into modernity.

The Chief Rabbi and his council administered temporal as well as religious affairs. Adversity and closeness spawned self-help organizations for charity and hospitality to travelers, for learning, and for education. Jews developed their own mail system and rules to discourage outbidding on the rents paid to Christian landlords. Community organization was tight, with a common bake house, dance hall, and public bath—and the synagogue at the center. Jews were thrown on themselves; their tradition of domesticity and the importance of Jewish family life have roots in ghetto culture.

To be sure, life was harsh, and in time no less than one in ten Jews was reduced to beggary. But even under the limiting conditions of the ghetto, the Jews created an environment of relative peace, serenity, and even of some joy, retaining their pride and making a virtue of their isolation.

6

It was fundamental changes in the world around them which first gave rise to changed circumstances and new opportunities for those Jews who had survived in Germany.

Until the sixteenth century, the feudal state was under the sway of one ruler and a single Church. Government and business were based on moral concepts that required submission to Church teachings, and these rigidly excluded the Jews. But now a new order of individual states evolved, each pursuing its quest of political and economic advantage through mercantilist concepts of self-sufficiency in manufacture and trade. In this type of early capitalism, making money became a prime goal, and poverty was no longer regarded as a virtue. In this era of court absolutism, the local prince, duke, or petty ruler replaced the Church as the all-powerful arbiter of human affairs. The primary purpose of the state was to serve his needs and political ambitions—and that required an expanding economy and the financial resources to sustain it. For this, more population was needed, capital had to be marshalled, industries organized, and new patterns of trade and commerce developed.

In this context the Jewish problem took on a different and more secular dimension. Religious strictures were now less important. Jews became useful for what they could contribute to the goals of the state. As it happened, their particular talents and historical experience proved highly relevant to what was required.

The recent schism in the Church also had a considerable and, on balance, positive impact on the position of the Jews. Not that the Protestant religion was any more favorably disposed toward them than Catholics, or that Protestant leaders like Calvin or Luther were any friendlier than the Popes of Rome. True, Martin Luther had at first come to their defense, partly because it was politically expedient in his fight with Rome, and partly in the hope of converting them through kindness. But as political circumstances changed, and attracting Jews to Christianity proved no easier for him than for Catholics, he turned violently against them. In time his hatred for Jews and the harshness of his prescriptions for dealing with them if anything exceeded that of the Church in Rome. In fact, eventually his shrill and intemperate anti-Jewish rhetoric became so violent that it served, some four hundred years later, as a favorite source for quotation by the Nazis in justifying their anti-Semitic measures.

What mattered is that in the fight between Protestants and Catholics, the Jew was essentially a bystander and the Jewish problem a decidedly secondary issue. In Germany, moreover, there was yet another factor with far-reaching consequences for the Jewish minority. The Thirty Years' War, pitting Catholic areas against Protestant areas, raged across its territory, devastating and depopulating the land and leading eventually to the creation of well over two hundred de facto separate political entities, territories and city states tied together only in theory but in fact independent to make their own treaties and to pursue their separate political goals.

Jews had stood apart from the war's controversies. Expelled from the major urban centers, except for the few city ghettos, and scattered across the countryside under the protection of local nobles, they had eked out a meager living as money lenders, pawnbrokers, and peddlers. They had suffered along with the rest of the population, paid the heavy taxes, and endured the hardships. But in the ghettos and behind the shield of their local masters, they had nevertheless been somewhat more secure than others. In fact, the conflict had created opportunities for them to supply the protagonists while the war raged—and to serve the rulers when it finally came to an end.

One important development of the period, which profoundly shaped the evolution of modern Jewish life in Germany, is that the war and its aftermath gave rise to a new institution and a new occupation for a selected few—that of the Court Jew.

As banker, financial agent, mint master, and purveyor of war supplies and luxuries for the local ruler, the Court Jew became as much a fixture at court as the Court Physician or Court Jester. Emulating the splendor of the palace of Louis XIV at Versailles, each prince and ruler wanted to rebuild his territories, but each had at the same time an insatiable need for the luxuries that added luster to the pomp and grandeur of his court.[22] It was the Court Jew's job to serve these purposes. In the process, he often rose high in his master's service and achieved influence not infrequently extending beyond the economic into matters of politics and diplomacy. Freed from the restrictions that encumbered Jews elsewhere, he could travel and live as he wished. Personal wealth and influence were among his rewards, and all Court Jews took full advantage of this, although not always with sufficient prudence and restraint. It was, therefore, also a dangerous profession, subject to court jealousies and intrigues, exposed to the envy of others and always at risk as a lightning rod for popular resentment against the ruler.

Court Jews are important in the history of Germany's Jews. Though they adopted many of the styles and habits of the world of the court and became considerably more worldly and emancipated than their isolated brethren, they nevertheless retained their attachment to their people and used their position of influence to benefit them. They were the first German-Jewish aristocrats, the first emancipated Jews to move into the gentile world, and in some cases, the ancestors of the top levels of German Jewry in later generations. Many became patrons of Jewish culture and learning and were appointed leaders and spokesmen for the community.

Unfortunately, there was a less positive side to this coin. The Court Jew could be helpful in good times, but when he fell from grace—an ever-present risk—the impact on all Jews could be severe. That, precisely, was the fateful case of one famous, early Court Jew—a certain Lippold, who in 1556 had succeeded another, "the faithful Michel," as Court Purveyor to Joachim II, Elector of Brandenburg. From all accounts Lippold was clever and indefatigable, but also greedy and unscrupulous, and when he fell, all of Brandenburg's Jews were made to suffer.

Lippold ingratiated himself with the Elector by catering tirelessly to his taste for wine, women, and song. He quickly grasped his master's weakness for trinkets and jewels for his mistresses, cloth and favors for his courtiers, and luxuries for himself. When a favorite, the young Magdalena, had a wish, Lippold was ready to meet it—at a price, of course: A little box for her dolls, a golden necklace, a bit of sugar candy for eight taler, a tumbler for nine and a half, velvet for a dress, and much more. Lippold's books are full of these entries recording his business with the Elector.[23]

In gratitude, the Elector appointed him Chief of all of Brandenburg's Jews, collector for Jewish and other taxes, Master of the Mint, and administrator of the coin of the realm. Lippold became indispensable to the ruler; he grew extraordinarily wealthy, partly by running all manner of entrepreneurial activities on the side, money lending and pawnbroking included.

Tax collectors and pawnbrokers are never popular, particularly if they are unscrupulous corner cutters, and Lippold was no exception. When the Elector died, retribution came swiftly. His successor had Lippold arrested the next day, and the anger of the people against the debauchery of the old Elector and his mint master preordained his doom; two years later Lippold was put to death, drawn and quartered on the rack. But "a Jew is a Jew," and so the entire community had to bear the brunt of his downfall. In 1573, all

Jews were driven from Brandenburg, not to return until Frederick William, the Great Elector, called them back a hundred years later.

Not all Court Jews were as rapacious as Lippold, nor as unfortunate. There were dozens who served at the courts of Germany's rulers and many served faithfully and well. Most became wealthy founders of dynasties of Jewish bankers and merchants, the early leaders of the broader emancipation of Germany's Jews. We shall frequently encounter their descendants over succeeding generations.

7

Will Durant has called the ability of the Jews to recover from misfortune "one of the impressive wonders of history, part of that heroic resilience which man in general has shown after the catastrophes of life."[24] His observation is meant to apply to all of the Jewish people. But nowhere is it more to the point than in the case of Ashkenazi Jews—and in particular to the survival and eventual renaissance of Germany's Jews.

At the end of the Thirty Years' War, Jews had lived somewhere on German soil for at least a millennium and a half, and probably longer. They had come as free citizens with equal rights—vintners, merchants, traders, and colonizers among the indigenous tribes. Some had occupied respected positions as scholars, physicians, and advisors. At first they had lived in relative peace and prosperity and then, for many centuries, they had endured unimaginable hardship and suffered through unending cycles of disaster and death.

They had come to Germany with a deep attachment to their ancient religion and never surrendered it though it became the principal source of their distress. Abandoning their faith as the world around them was Christianized would have saved them untold suffering. Yet they stubbornly clung to their religion even when they had to die for it or were made pariahs without honor or rights.

Few people in history have faced so many indignities, and so much misfortune for so long a time. Survival and regeneration under these circumstances is little short of a miracle.

One thousand five hundred years of separation from their Oriental origins had transformed the Ashkenazim into Europeans, albeit a special and unique minority. Their isolation had reinforced ancient tendencies to look inward and to focus on themselves. Looked down on and tormented by others, they had, as if in self-defense, begun to look down in turn on their tormentors. Having been made outcasts, they learned to glory in their fate and to make it a badge of virtue.

Long periods of persecution and suffering taught them stoicism, acceptance of adversity, and above all the techniques of survival. The frequent expulsions, flights, and forced dispersions through many lands far beyond Germany's borders cemented their sense of a common destiny. Their fraternal ties with Jews everywhere created bonds and networks that became the foundation for commercial and financial advantage at a later stage. Stereotyped as fit only for a few occupations, they learned to excel in them and to live by their wits.

Finally, in the isolation of their faith, without a homeland and with only their religion to sustain them, they made it the focus of their spiritual and intellectual lives, and this in turn led to a love of learning, of literacy, of abstract thinking, and of intellectual pursuits in general. Their separation from the surrounding civilization brought about the development of their own language, literature, and culture. And as outsiders, cut off from society's institutions, mutual need led to the growth of their own communal structures and their own folkways, rules, and social traditions. All of these factors not only explain their survival but also are at the root of their traditions and their character.

Their story is one of miraculous survival, but it is also a history full of paradox: Isolation over centuries was painful, but it was also the key to their survival as a people. Segregation was a bitter pill, but it also ensured their preservation. Stubborn resistance to conversion caused untold suffering, but it was also the foundation for a rich culture and their love of learning. The death of many and the flight east of most others was a disaster, but it was also the source of regeneration—the basis for the subsequent expansion of Jewish communities in Germany. Exclusion and grinding poverty were a curse, but they also taught the Jews how to recognize and seize opportunity, to adapt rapidly to changes in economic conditions and to turn them to their advantage. Discrimination and restrictions led to

deep frustration, but in time they also became the wellspring of their pent-
up energies, their restlessness, and their drive for acceptance and personal
success.

When, late in the seventeenth century, the Jews gradually reentered Germany's Christian world, it was very much as products of these special factors, which had produced unique skills, qualities, and character traits. Of
course, like people everywhere, Jews were a diverse group, with the same
weaknesses and human foibles as others. Their stultifying ghetto isolation,
while extreme, did reflect the outside world: the negative alongside the positive, areas of ignorance and superstition alongside wisdom, and narrow-
mindedness mixed with instances of spiritual grandeur. Seventeenth-
century Jews, no less than Christians, had their fools as well as their sages,
thieves as well as scholars, rogues as well as the righteous, bigots as well as
liberals.

CHAPTER III

ANCESTORS

Jost

The town of Beeskow would like to have a wealthy Jew.

Tax Commissary Leyser to King Frederick William I

June 26, 1720

Jews are the country's locusts . . . you must chase them away.

King Frederick William I to his son

Jan. 22–Feb. 17, 1722

1

The gown had a train carried by six countesses. It was made of silver bro-
cade studded with diamonds, and its owner, only eight days old and a
crown placed on his infant head, wore it over his diapers. The royal orchestra was augmented for the occasion by twenty-four trumpeters and two
drummers, and the city's church bells tolled for a solid hour. The entire
court and all its nobles and grandees stood in attendance as the boy's
grandfather proudly carried him to a specially made solid-gold basin for
the ceremony of baptism. Beside it lay the infant's umbilical cord in yet
another golden container, inscribed *Friedrich, Prince de Prusse et d'Orange,
né le 24. Janvier à 11½ heures du matin.*

Thus, in the first days of February 1712, the newest prince of the Hohenzollerns made his first public appearance amid the full array of pomp and court ceremony that Frederick I, his luxury-loving grandfather, could muster. One day, as Frederick II, this newborn would reorder the map of Europe and make Prussia's military might the fear and envy of her neighbors. But that was in the future. For now, on this day of baptism and celebration in 1712, the kingdom's citizenry reveled in their good fortune—the arrival, finally, of a male heir to the Hohenzollern throne, and for good luck a *Sonntagskind,* a little prince born on a Sunday.

By universal agreement, this happy outcome of the fourth try for a son by Crown Prince Frederick William of Prussia and the Princess Sophie Dorothea was a good omen. Only one of their first three children, the chubby-cheeked jolly little Wilhelmine, had survived her birth. Each of her two brothers had lived only a few days, succumbing for reasons variously described as having to do "with their teeth," or with too strenuous a baptismal rite. In truth, medical knowledge was still limited, infant deaths were common, and where understanding was lacking, legend and superstition were apt to flourish. With hindsight, neither the king nor his people need have been concerned. The sturdy Sophie Dorothea would best the odds by a fair margin and carry fourteen pregnancies to term, with nine of her children surviving infancy.

The grandeur of the celebration was no surprise. Ostentatious ceremony and baroque pleasures were the order of the day at the court of the newborn's grandfather, whose ambition it was to emulate Louis XIV and his most splendid of all splendiferous courts at Versailles. Years later, his grandson would say of his grandfather—a soft man who adored feasts, ceremony, and court etiquette—that he confused shining splendor with true greatness, that he "loved the flower and neglected the fruit." He was a ruler who had a taste for the elaborate and a willingness to spare no expense in indulging it. Whatever the occasion, Frederick I wanted to live in a sumptuous manner. In his first act in 1688 after the death of his father, the Great Elector of Brandenburg, he had arranged for ceremonies that stretched for a full three months from death to burial. When the mortal remains were finally laid to rest, he had ordered that his father be dressed in a red velvet coat trimmed with pearls and diamonds, and with his bejeweled sword and scepter placed at his side.

His greatest ambition, harbored since youth, was to elevate the Hohen-zollern dynasty of Margraves and Electors to royal status, and from the moment he succeeded his father he worked tirelessly to bring it about. No cost in money—or in men—was too high, and it had taken thirteen years of scheming, shifting alliances, and hard bargaining to realize his great dreams.

By siding with the Habsburgs against the Bourbons in the War of the Spanish Succession, the deal had been struck: eight thousand Prussian soldiers for the Austrians in return for the Vienna Emperor's acquiescence to a Prussian throne. In triumph, at Königsberg in 1701, Frederick III, Elector of Brandenburg, had placed the crown on his own head. After long and convoluted negotiation to accommodate the legal position of Leopold, Emperor of Austria and the Holy Roman Empire, it had been agreed that he would henceforth be known as Frederick I, by God's Grace, King in (but not *of*!) Prussia. It was a fine distinction, but to the Austrian Emperor it had deep meaning nonetheless.

The celebrations surrounding this milestone event had been elaborate—and very expensive. For his triumphant return to Berlin, no less than seven large and elaborate ceremonial gates had been erected, and as he entered the city in his gilded coach through the first of these triumphal arches, twenty maidens in white dresses stood to greet him. The feasting lasted day and night for an entire month.

For the self-crowned Frederick I, this was the style in which to rule as a king. The cost mattered little and the perennially depleted state of his coffers, though a nuisance, was never a deterrence. If the Crown Princess worried over the lack of funds for even her most basic household needs, that was regrettable. Still, the royal yacht, *Liburnia,* twenty-five meters long, with twenty-two cannons, would be built at great cost in Belgium and laboriously transported overland to Berlin. Not, to be sure, to make Brandenburg into a great sea power, but merely to sail the Spree River strictly for his amusement. And if the expense of his own large household with its multitude of councillors and chamber servants, its six court physicians, its numerous pages and lackeys, and its thirty-six court musicians (including the castrated Court Alto, Antonio Cambiola) brought his finances to the brink of bankruptcy, then new means and strategies for handling these ex-

penditures would have to be found. A king, after all, had advisers to work
out these matters, to invent new taxes and new ways to raise money, and
to find suppliers willing to sell on credit and bankers willing to lend.

Jost Liebmann, his late Court Jeweler and his father's favorite Court Jew
as well as his own, had understood the situation well—the opportunities
and also the risks. In 1712, at the time of the grandson's baptism, Jost was
no longer alive. He had died ten years earlier, but lived just long enough to
witness his patron's coronation—and to supply the jewels for the event.
Merely the gems for the new queen's crown were said to have been worth
at least 300,000 reichstaler—a truly staggering sum, the equivalent of millions in today's dollars. The cost was so stupendous, in fact, that the Legate
of Hanover, Herr Hensch, had snidely reported to his master that most of
them were rumored to have only been loaned for the occasion. (Given the
delicacy of the information, he had, however, prudently reported this juicy
item of gossip to Hanover in code.)

For Jost, it had been good business all the same—another occasion for
handsome profit in satisfying the never-ending appetite for jewelry of his
lord and the court nobility. Three years before, in 1698, seven large diamonds worth 45,000 taler had been supplied, and in the eight years since
Frederick had succeeded his father, he had sent bills to the court for six
times that amount.

The problem was that deliveries were one thing, but timely payment another. The king routinely paid his debts very late and rarely in cash. The
revenues he derived from his Jews for their letters of protection and the
many other taxes and special contributions imposed on them had once
been a good source of revenue for collecting his bills. But the king's ambitious plans and expensive tastes had long since exceeded his income from
the Jews. Jost, being no fool, had thus come to realize that it was as important to be imaginative about negotiating for alternative means of payment
as it was to have the right merchandise to accommodate the royal taste.
One solution was to persuade the king to pay "in kind," to be granted a
profitable concession, such as the monopoly over a local mint, to be allowed to lease one for a while, or else to supply the silver for minting purposes at the appropriate profit. As a case in point, that was how he had
been paid for the king's outstanding debts in 1697, when it was he who had
been given the profitable rights to the mints of Magdeburg and Minden.

That is also how Jost had become influential and rich, worth, it was rumored, upward of 100,000 taler at the time of his death, in our terms a millionaire many times over, and reputedly the richest Jew in Berlin. That is also how he had been able to live out his days in undreamed luxury for a Jew, how on a voyage to Holland, armed with Frederick's special letter of protection, he, the Jew Jost Liebmann, had traveled north across the land unimpeded by borders and town gates, accompanied by a train of servants in the comfort of a carriage drawn by a team of twelve horses.

But it had not always been so. The king's father had started out a great deal more modestly only a few decades earlier—and so had Jost.

2

On December 1, 1640, when the father, young Frederick William, only twenty years old, became Elector of Brandenburg-Prussia, the prospects for his country could hardly have been worse. He had inherited a patchwork of separate and disparate territories without rhyme or reason, ranging from the Dukedom of Kleve in the West to totally disconnected East Prussia in the East, and the Mark Brandenburg, Ravensberg, Cammin, and parts of Pomerania in between. Some years later, three more areas—Magdeburg, Minden, and Halberstadt—were added to this crazy-quilt pattern of possessions, the result primarily of past inheritances, historical accident, and leftovers from deals made in war. About the only things the parts of the whole had in common were resistance to central authority, separatist tendencies, and a mutual dislike for each other.

The Thirty Years' War, now at an end, had devastated the country and left it in a terrible state. Swedish mercenary armies had occupied the territory, and land and people were depleted and worn out. Population had declined by between a third and a half; fields lay idle, food was scarce, and famines were common. Starvation, low resistance to disease, and waves of pestilence and intestinal illnesses had exacted a heavy toll. Worse yet, the effect of man-made disasters had been exacerbated by many years of bad climatic conditions—an unusually extended period of low temperatures and increased precipitation beginning in the mid-sixteenth century, the "little Ice Age," which decreased growing seasons and further compounded the starvation and misery. Little wonder that, in its dismal state, no one in

Europe took the country or its new ruler seriously. The future was very much in doubt.

Historical hindsight is wondrously illuminating. Although the prospects looked grim and somber in 1640, we know today that Frederick William's reign was actually a major turning point—the beginning of the rise of Brandenburg-Prussia, and eventually of Germany, as the strongest nation in continental Europe. The man who became known as the Great Elector was in fact the first in a succession of Hohenzollern rulers who transformed the motley territories under their control into a powerful and aggressive nation.

Their formula for success was never based on any notion of enlightenment or attention to the people's will. Indeed, when such eighteenth-century ideas swept across Europe, they would take hold in Germany much later than elsewhere. The early Hohenzollerns succeeded because, on the whole, they were single-minded absolutist rulers and superior organizers who created a society and a system of government more structured, driven, and regimented than any other. They enforced the strictest discipline among their soldiers and officials—obedience to the death, or *Kadaver-gehorsam,* it came to be called—and it was their pliant bureaucracy and the good fortune of being blessed with competent advisers and a docile citizenry that were the keys to their achievements.

The first Hohenzollern rulers were at times cautious, at other times aggressive, adventurous, and even reckless. At critical moments they were just plain lucky enough to benefit from the stupidities and shortcomings of their foes. The strongest and most successful among them were also prejudiced, ruthless, and highly despotic. Yet they and their advisers could be practical and pragmatic when it counted, willing to use whomever and whatever was needed to achieve their aims.

3

History remembers Frederick William as the Great Elector because it was he who overcame the greatest initial odds and was the first to lay the foundations for the rise of Prussia as a major European force.

On March 4, 1643, more than two years after he came to power, he entered Berlin to receive the homage of its people. It was his first visit to the largest town in the heartland of his possessions, and it must have been a profoundly discouraging experience. Berlin was a miserable place. Pestilence and disease had reduced the population to probably no more than six or seven thousand. Though spared actual fighting within its walls, Berlin had avoided plunder and destruction only by paying exorbitant ransom to the Swedish occupiers. Now coffers were empty and the buildings stood in disrepair. Almost a third of all houses were totally abandoned. Very few of the streets were paved, and wells were clogged and unusable. The bridges across the Spree River were in such poor shape that heavy carts could hardly make it across. Garbage and night soil lay in the streets and pigs foraged among the refuse. Food was so scarce that there was nothing to feed the Elector and his entourage, "not even a mouthful of wine," as one of his advance scouts had been constrained to report.

The Elector's private purse was in no better shape; occasionally he had been forced to borrow a paltry fifteen taler, merely for his family's food and drink. He had, however, soon taken drastic steps. Fifty kilometers to the north, pleasantly situated along the banks of the river Havel, lay the village of Bötzow, an appealing, once-prosperous agricultural spot, which, like the rest of his lands, had suffered its share of woes from war and disease. Some years hence it would win the heart of his young wife, Luise Henriette, who found that it reminded her of her Dutch ancestral home. To please her, he later built a castle there and in her honor renamed the place *Oranienburg* for the Dutch House of Orange, the ruling family of the country where he had been educated and married. In 1643 he had taken a different course and pawned the village and its surroundings to a local noblewoman, a certain Frau Ursula von Knesebeck. The liquid funds thus secured he began to apply to the rehabilitation of his capital city.

Yet Berlin was not his central preoccupation. Frederick William was still a young man, but he was determined and pragmatic, a clear thinker and politically astute. As a youth, in Holland, he liked the openness there to new ideas, and had seen that a country's wealth and strength could be enhanced by the vigorous promotion of domestic commerce and trade. His impatience has risen steadily as he observed his weak father's ineffective advisers fail in their political maneuverings during the Thirty Years' War.

Now his main goal was to knit his disparate possessions into a single state, strong enough to become a factor in the power politics of Europe and to protect its borders.

The policies of his predecessors, who relied on shifting alliances and political maneuvers, had been an obvious failure and had led the country to ruin. From this, the Elector drew a conclusion that has stood the test of time to the present day: diplomacy works best when backed by military strength. What was needed, he decided, was a credible standing army as the backbone of his state, and it is this that became the primary focus of his thinking, from which his interconnected policy initiatives derived.

A sound military establishment, he realized, must rest on a healthy economic base, and like most of his contemporaries he had a mercantilist view of the world. He believed that the key to prosperity and strength lay in the accumulation of wealth in the form of all manner of specie, such as gold, silver, and coin. Such wealth, it was thought, came from favorable balances of trade, best achieved by vigorously promoting exports while protecting the home market. In turn, favorable trade and a stronger economy would generate the tax revenues needed to pay for the support of the troops. Finally, to accomplish all this, new people had to be found—in part to repopulate his depleted lands, and in part to inject new initiative and dynamism into Prussia's trade and her productive strength.

There was, however, one important barrier to his progress, and it required a good many years and all his considerable political skills to overcome it. The issue was the traditional power of the estates and the limits it placed on his power to act as he wished. The problems of local politics and military power were closely intertwined. To achieve the latter, he had to resolve the former. How he did it would have far-reaching consequences in Prussia for many years to come.

It was a time when the concept of a strong nation state along lines the Elector had in mind was still a novel and not altogether welcome idea. His predecessors had been the largest landowners, but true rulers more in name than in fact. Real power to tax and to govern in the various localities had remained with the estates—the large landowners, city patricians, prelates, and knights. Even the power to raise armies and make treaties required the approval of these notables. But now, during the confusion of the Thirty Years' War, the estates' impotence to act independently had also become clear. Deflation, economic decline, and financial crises had weakened their position, and the Elector made skillful use of this state of affairs to advance his aim of achieving political change.

With realism, ruthlessness, and guile, Frederick William advanced step by step to bring the estates under his control. In 1653 he made his first deal with the Brandenburg nobles, or *Junker*. For a half million taler, he freed them from taxes, ceded them outright ownership of their lands, and gave them full control over their peasants and local affairs. The money he used to build up his military strength, growing his army from a ragged band of six thousand into a centralized, reorganized, and more disciplined standing force of twenty to thirty thousand soldiers. As his strength grew he brought around the rest of the estates in the West and East Prussia as well.

But as he succeeded in amassing the critical powers for himself, he rewarded the *Junker* not only by ceding them their lands and the freedom to exercise local controls. He also persuaded their sons to serve as officers in his army, and initiated the practice—much extended by his successors—of appointing them to the top jobs in the administration of the state. It was a fateful decision, for in this way the *Junker* class became the backbone of Prussian aristocracy, an elite accorded a special place in the nation's affairs with wide social and political consequences for generations to come.

With a larger and better army at his back, the Great Elector achieved greater authority not only with the estates at home, but also in his dealings abroad. He could now play a more active and effective role in the wars and political maneuverings between Europe's principal nations, where Catholics fought Protestants, and the Swedes, French, Austrians, Poles, Saxons, and Dutch struggled for advantage in an endless ballet of shifting alliances and pacts. Brandenburg-Prussia had ceased to be a helpless pawn in this game.

As Frederick William had suspected, political power did indeed flow through the barrel of a gun. In 1660, at the Peace of Oliva, having allied himself with the Swedes in their battles against the Poles, he was rewarded with important booty to prove the point—the elimination of the last vestiges of Polish rights in his East Prussian lands. It was an important prize, the beginning of further victories abroad, and a good basis for moving forward with the many changes and new policies at home.

4

The circumstances of an unknown, impecunious seventeenth-century Jew hardly bear much comparison with those of the hereditary ruler of Brandenburg-Prussia. Yet there are analogies that come to mind. Like the Great Elector, Jost, though far removed in his utterly distant and different world, reached manhood full of ambition, great energy, and an iron determination to succeed. Jost, too, faced seemingly insurmountable obstacles—and overcame them to an astounding degree. And Jost also became a trail blazer for later generations of his people, much as the Elector built the foundations on which his successors would later stand.

Jost was a generation younger than the Elector, and he first came to Hamburg at a time in the early 1660s when the latter, recently triumphant at Oliva, was beginning to stir the pot at home. He came from Halberstadt and Hildesheim, where he had been born and raised, a young man barely past twenty, full of eager impatience to make his mark in one of the few activities open to a Jew—money lending, perhaps, or trading in old clothes, cloth, cattle or horses, skins, wines, or—best of all—precious metals and gems. His problem was that he was also quite poor. The few cheap amber stones in his pocket, his total worldly riches worth some twenty or thirty taler, were far from enough capital for even a modest beginning.

Straitened circumstance and hand-to-mouth existence were the common fate of virtually all Jews at the time. Setting out on the road, Jost was just another poor Jewish traveler joining the many other wanderers and vendors moving from place to place, trading and dealing, exposed and vulnerable and accustomed to live by their wits. Most were away from home for many months, en route to or from the fairs at Frankfurt, Leipzig, or Brunswick, buying here and selling there, living precariously and dependent for rest, shelter, and a place to pray on a thin network of relatives and coreligionists along the way.

But, Jost was special. He was unusually hard-working, smart, driving, and ambitious, but also a young man with a pleasing personality who understood human nature and knew how to impress. He was, as his aunt Glückel would record in her diary one day, "a pretty student of the Torah, he knew how to talk business, and he seemed altogether a clever lad."[1] He was also, from the beginning, blessed with good luck—the right person at the right moment in the right place. At the time he was still known as Judah Berlin, the name he had been given at birth. Later he would change his first name to Jost, which sounded more German and grand, though why he chose Liebmann over Berlin is not known.

As Jost was making his way north, Brandenburg's banishment of Jews, enacted in the previous century, was still in effect, though elsewhere in Germany Jews lived in small numbers spread out across villages and towns. These were the remnants of Germany's earlier flourishing communities of Jews. For centuries these survivors had lived a marginal existence outside regular society, excluded from the crafts and most occupations, cowed, fearful, and always under pressure against the threat of expulsion or worse. These were Jost's people, and though their situation differed from place to place, it was nowhere very good. Yet, economic conditions were finally looking up, and the Jews, too, were beginning to hope for some benefit from the change. Hildesheim and Halberstadt, the places of Jost's origin, had long harbored small Jewish communities, Halberstadt's being older, larger, and somewhat more settled. As to his destination—the free and in-dependent *Reichstadt* of Hamburg—the city fathers there had regularly veered between tolerating their Jews and throwing them out. More than once, Hamburg's Jews had been forced to scamper for refuge into neigh-boring Danish Altona, only to drift back again when the authorities re-lented or found it useful once more to invite them to return.

To Glückel of Hameln, a remarkable woman whose husband Chayim was Jost's uncle and whose niece he would one day wed, we owe a record of how Jost launched his career in Hamburg after arriving to stay at their house. It is one of the many stories recorded in her now famous diaries, a unique chronicle of the trials and triumphs of Jewish life in her time.

How long it took Jost to make his way to Hamburg from Hildesheim is not known, but it cannot have been an easy trip. Regular postal coaches were not yet in service, carriages were expensive to rent, and even a horse was clearly beyond his means. Like other poor Jews, Jost therefore traveled mostly on foot, for safety in daylight only, a bag on his back, keeping to the main routes and alert to the ever-present dangers and exigencies of the road.

Today Germany's fast trains cover the distance of a hundred miles in an hour, but for Jost it was a trek of many days or weeks. In the villages, local

urchins were apt to point and laugh at him, perhaps to shout "Yid" and to
throw dirt or hurl stones. Jost knew that it was the better part of wisdom
to ignore them if he could, to stay out of trouble, smile pleasantly and to
move along. Taunts and insults were some of the lesser problems he had to
face; the headache of finding a place to eat, sleep, and pray was more difficult to resolve. Most country inns would not accept a Jew, and to locate a
friendly roof was rarely a simple task.

There was no escaping all this. Distinctive dress or the yellow badge were
no longer, as they had once been, a matter decreed by law. Yet it was still
quite simple to recognize a Jew. Beards, not then common among Christians, were one distinguishing mark, though some Jews like Jost would
soon discard them along with their earlocks, so as to blend more unobtru-
sively into the rest of the human scene. Still, Jewish dress remained characteristic—the simple black long coat or cloak, the flat cap called the *barret,*
and the distinctive kerchief tied around the neck. The cardinal rule was to
dress simply and not to arouse suspicion or envy. Every Jewish community,
in fact, had its sumptuary laws to ensure that these rules were observed,
such as no velvet, damask, or silk for the women; no jewelry and no fancy
blond wigs for the men.[2]

For someone as poor as Jost all this was irrelevant, since there was not
much chance of any sign of wealth. A Jew in transit was safest when he
looked threadbare, which was certainly the common condition of most of
the travelers moving from place to place. The road was a dangerous place,
and highwaymen were common. With his wares on his back, suspected of
carrying money and valuables hidden in his cloak, the Jew was an inviting
target wherever he went. It was by far the greatest hazard he faced—to be
assaulted or robbed or, worst of all, perhaps to pay for an unfortunate encounter with his life.

It is just such a disaster that gave Jost his start. His relative Chayim Hameln was a trader in cheap pearls who had started at the bottom some years
before, making small loans to peasants, dealing in secondhand cutlery, ribbons, and trinkets and buying up old gold door-to-door for resale at the
fairs. With Glückel and their several children—eventually there would be
fourteen—he lived with other Jews in the neighborhood they called *Di
Gas,* the Jew quarter of Hamburg by the *Dreckwall,* the city's refuse dump
and the least desirable part of town. Di Gas was an area of crooked and

narrow streets where Jews rented their rooms; owning houses was not yet allowed.

Inside the houses, the furnishings were quite simple, and yet it is here that Jost found a haven from the hazards of the road. Crowded with beds, trunks for bedding, mirrors, a plain table, and chairs, these buildings contained the familiar signs of the Jewish life: Sabbath candlesticks and candelabra, goblets, ceremonial dishes, and Hebrew books and scrolls. Here, with Chayim, he could attend the synagogue and take part in the Sabbath. And here with his relatives he would eat the special Jewish dishes he liked— perhaps *tsimes,* a dish of raw turnips, carrots, cabbage, and greens, or gefilte fish made from pike, kasha, and the special *barkhes* bread baked for the Sabbath, apple kreplach, and especially the yellow *rüben,* a carrot the color of money, which was said to bring good luck.[3] Around the table, he would join in the songs, gossip, jokes, and perhaps, when the Sabbath was over, do a little business as well.

By dint of hard work and long absences from home, Chayim's business had gradually prospered. He had acquired some capital, employed an assistant named Mordecai, and extended the range and scope of his trading beyond the distance he could walk or cadge a ride. The unfortunate Mordecai, however, had recently been robbed and killed by a highwayman on the open road who, Glückel wrote, had shouted "stinking Jew" and shot him dead through the head. Fortuitously, it seems, Jost arrived just in time to take poor Mordecai's place.

Years later, Glückel, who was given to mixing deep religious faith and good business sense into occasional philosophical asides to her children, commented in some awe on Jost's beginning: "Observe, my dear children, how, God willing, He can make much of little, how Judah Berlin with a capital as good as nothing achieved great wealth and became a great man."[4]

A quick deal was struck. Within a week, armed with Chayim's letters of credit, Jost was sent off to Danzig to buy pearls from the East, and now that he had the capital he set about to make it work. Two years later his share of the profits was eight hundred to nine hundred taler, a decent sum and enough of a stake for the kind of trading on his own account he had always had in mind. The time had also come to get married—yet another opportunity to expand his capital base, now that his bargaining power for a reasonable dowry had been greatly enhanced.

In Hanover, as was the custom among the Jews, a local *shadkhen*—the marriage broker and go-between for the time-honored negotiation preceding a marriage deal, was put to work. The families were deeply involved, and amid much community gossip and rumors there were lengthy discussions, maneuvers, and bargaining for advantage before the contract was set. The bride, rarely much older than fourteen, had little or nothing to say. For Jost, the choice fell on Malka, a daughter of Reb Samuel of Hameln, a brother of Chayim, and the dowry was five hundred taler, a modest sum but acceptable to both sides.

His capital thus further augmented, Jost was ready to continue his climb up the ladder of success.

When, years later, Jost had become the richest and most powerful Jew in Berlin, it would be said that his insatiable acquisitiveness, his ruthlessness, and his unrelenting drive for advantage had been as much responsible for his success as good fortune, a pleasing smile, cleverness, hard work, and wit. The observation is probably not far off the mark, for these are the qualities most Court Jews shared in lifting themselves from the confines of Di Gas. Perhaps it was the only way, though it is true that it did not greatly endear them to their fellow Jews.

That Jost, for one, could be tough and unyielding in driving a very hard bargain seems not to be much in doubt. He was also what we would call today quite "litigious," forever embroiled in one or another financial feud, and prone to all manner of lengthy legal fights and maneuvers in pursuit of advantage and monetary gain. Jews settled disputes of this kind among themselves, before their rabbis and *parnassim,* the community elders, who were the arbiters called to rule in accordance with talmudic concepts and traditional norms.

In one such dispute, Chayim's partnership with Jost eventually came to an end. The amounts at issue were now more substantial—several thousand taler were involved—showing, if nothing else, that the fortunes of both parties had by then substantially improved.

Jost outmaneuvered his uncle and erstwhile sponsor with ease. Most good lawyers know that it is as important to try a case in a favorable venue as it is to appear before a sympathetic judge, a lesson that Jost apparently understood clearly. Being forced to argue his case against Jost before the rabbis of Hanover, where his nephew had friends and relatives but Chayim was relatively unknown, cost the uncle an adverse judgment and one-third of his wealth. Glückel laments the misfortune but records its acceptance with the fatalism characteristic of her world. For Jost, the victory was merely the springboard for bigger and better things to come.

5

It was on the last day of February 1670 that the sound of trumpets and rolling drums heralded to the people of Vienna the decision of their Emperor to expel every one of the city's four thousand Jews. The banishment "for eternity," as was often the case, turned out to last only a few years, and the Emperor soon felt obliged to resort to convoluted theological reasoning to justify their return. But at the moment, the news—long rumored and hoped for—was greeted with general satisfaction by the city fathers, guilds, merchants, and public at large. So great, in fact, was the delight at the university that the rector saw fit to commemorate the event in the official register, as *Anno quo ab imperatore Leopoldo Vienna a Austria relegato sunt Hebrae* (The year when Emperor Leopold expelled the Jews from Vienna and Austria).[5]

A substantial Jewish community had existed in Vienna on and off for hundreds of years. Time and again the Jews had bought the privilege of residence with heavy taxes and large contributions and loans; only a few years earlier their rights had once more been confirmed—upon payment of a substantial amount. Now it had all come to naught, Jewish pleas had fallen on deaf ears, and even the warnings of his own officials that arbitrary cancellation of rights bought and paid for might shake Christian confidence in his word had failed to dissuade the Emperor. The Pope himself had weighed in against the move, but the ultra-Catholic Leopold I, Holy Roman Emperor and King of Bohemia and Hungary, and his equally fanatic Empress, the Spanish Margaret Theresa, had in this instance proved literally "more papal than the Pope."

The Empress had suffered a miscarriage, there had been a fire in the palace, and Bishop Kollonitsch, her bigoted confessor, had repeatedly assured her that it was all because of the hated Jews. Leopold was greatly under the influence of his wife, and among the public there was enough superstition mixed with envy and the hope of commercial gain to favor the idea. So the Emperor had ended his hesitation and issued the order to expel the Jews.

In Brandenburg, the Great Elector followed these events with care and was quick to recognize an opportunity. His Resident in Vienna had kept him advised of developments, and once the Emperor had made the expulsion order official the Elector let it be known that he was disposed to allow some forty or fifty Austrian families to settle in his realm, though naturally only those with sufficient means. The benefit, it was hoped, would be the Jews' diligence and energy, along with their international connections as merchants and traders. The arrangement, in short, fit neatly into his overall program of repopulation and economic development.

Negotiations between his privy councilors and representatives of the Viennese Jews advanced smoothly toward a satisfactory conclusion, and so it was that on May 21, 1671, Frederick William issued his historic edict officially allowing the first fifty Jewish families to return to Brandenburg and settle there for an initial twenty years. The time limitation was a unique feature of the Elector's edict. No other Prussian immigrants were ever similarly restricted.

The edict was a major turning point for the Jews of Germany, effectively ending a hundred years of exclusion from Brandenburg dating back to the Lippold disaster. Later they would call it their Magna Carta. Though discriminatory in many ways, the order was nevertheless simple, straightforward, and relatively benign. It authorized the Jews to settle in Brandenburg and specified their right to travel, own homes, open shops and stalls, sell their goods from carts, freely journey to fairs, and trade in new and old clothes and in cloth of all kinds. As a special concession, they were permitted to bring their own slaughterers and teachers. Their payments were fixed modestly at an annual eight taler for a family, with only a small extra tax for each wedding, plus the obligation to pay the *Aksize* and other local taxes assessed on the general population.

Nothing in the decree shows any awareness of the administrative headaches to come, yet it is nevertheless revealing of how the Jews were viewed. They should come quietly, they were instructed, and take care to remain inconspicuous and not to offend the sensitivities of the non-Jewish world. There could be no public synagogue, but private services in their homes were allowed, during which derogatory or blasphemous talk against the

Christian religion was strictly forbidden. Any houses they built or owned might have to be sold back to Christians, they were warned. Finally, there was explicit caution against a litany of evils Jews were generally reputed to favor: to wit, no usury, no trading in stolen goods, no cheating of Christians, and no importing of "bad" coin.

On September 10, 1671, the first two families of Benedikt Veit and Abraham Riess received their letters of protection for Berlin, and other families soon joined them and settled in other Brandenburg villages and towns. It is this date that future generations would celebrate as the founding of the Jewish community of Berlin.

There were objections to bringing in the Jews almost from the start—and they came from two entirely different camps. On the one hand, the guilds and estates looked upon the influx with ill-concealed displeasure and concern. They considered the Jews unwelcome strangers and intruders into the established order. Jews had a reputation as aggressive merchants and tireless competitors likely to upset prevailing arrangements and hitherto protected positions. That is precisely what Frederick William had in mind, but the guilds and estates were anything but pleased.

The handwriting, however, had been on the wall for some time. Long ago, the Elector had taken a first step by allowing Polish Jews to trade in Brandenburg and to pass freely from place to place. When he subsequently issued numerous letters of protection to his Jews in the duchies of Halberstadt and Minden, the early fears of unwelcome changes had been confirmed, and when the guilds and estates saw this policy repeated in Kleve and elsewhere, their alarm had risen further. Most recently, the Elector's unusually strong reaction to a mob's ransacking of a private Halberstadt synagogue—an official one was forbidden—was additional evidence that he was determined to enlist Jews in support of his policies and to protect them vigorously if necessary. If for the Jews, then, the edict of '71 was a welcome sign of hope, it was for the gentile classes merely the final confirmation of what they had feared. Their resistance was immediate, and a steady stream of complaints and petitions rained down on the Elector almost from the start, beginning with the tailors of Frankfurt who bitterly protested the new competition.

Some time later, a particularly nasty broadside was delivered by the combined country estates, accusing the Jews of every conceivable foul act, such as that "they run through villages and towns, peddling and pushing their mostly old and slipshod wares at ruinous prices . . . entice buyers and cheat them . . . do business on the hallowed Sunday . . . are clandestine usurers and deal in stolen goods."[6] During the Swedish invasion Jews again came under fire, and there were more petitions accusing them of cowardice, disloyalty, and running away, and years later still the Memel guilds in East Prussia presented their bill of particulars against Jewish competitors.

In general, these complaints had little effect, though they always caused tension and nervousness among the Jews and deepened their insecurities and concerns. The Elector, determined to push forward with his plans, had firmly decided that the Jews would be allowed to play their part. Later, his son was even more urgently in need of funds, and the revenues generated by Jews had by then become too important to be passed up.

Resistance also came from another and surprisingly different quarter, and initially with more tangible results. The dissenter in that case was none other than Israel Aaron, the Great Elector's Court Jew in Berlin. If the gentiles feared the threat of competition, Aaron was no more pleased, and for him the probability of damage was palpable. For years, as the capital city's only Court Jew, he had enjoyed the prominence and prosperity of his monopoly as supplier to the army and the court. Solidarity with his coreligionists was one thing; potential threats to his unique role were quite another. Like most Court Jews of his day, he was acquisitive and aggressive, determined in the protection of his interests, and not excessively burdened with scruples when it came to advancing his cause. The influx of the Austrians into Berlin would place his position at grave risk. He was not about to surrender without a fight.

Israel Aaron had come to Berlin at the Elector's behest after the end of the Swedish War. His presence in the city thus antedates the arrival of the Austrians by about a decade. With Benedikt Veit and Abraham Riess, he can lay valid claim to being one of the three *Stammväter,* or founders of the Jewish community in Berlin. The son of a family of Jews from Lower Silesia, he had begun his service to the Elector by supplying his armies during the war, furnishing silver for the Königsberg mint and keeping the court well stocked with "wine, victuals and assorted other goods." Along the way, he had prudently exchanged his father's colorful, possibly descriptive name of Geizvogel (a less than flattering surname that loosely translates as "skin-flint" or "miser") for the more benign one of Aaron, which, however, had not altered his, or his wife Esther's, reputation for corner cutting, mean-ness, and sharp deals. While Frederick William was often appallingly late in paying his bills, Israel and Esther appear to have treated their own credi-tors even worse.

Two years before his death in 1673, when the Austrians were about to arrive, Israel succeeded in convincing the Elector to protect his position and to shore up his unique role. How generous to allow the refugees to come, he slyly complimented Frederick William in his plea. Yet the greater the number of Jews allowed in Berlin, he warned, the more likely that un-authorized ones might slip in. Ensuring that the new arrivals brought ample capital should be an absolute prerequisite; this, he assumed, would require further limitation on the number of immigrants allowed. And while this matter was being considered, he added, would the Elector per-haps reconfirm the letters of protection for his family and for him?[7]

In the end, his lobbying had a substantial effect. Instead of the ten Aus-trian families originally approved for Berlin, Israel succeeded in having the number reduced to just two, and to have his own letters of protection duly reaffirmed. When he died two years later, Esther succeeded in taking his place as supplier to the court. Israel's passing, it must be said, was not greatly mourned anywhere in Berlin.

6

Jost was a widower when he came to Berlin to wed Esther Aaron, née Schul-hoff, herself widowed since Israel's death.

He had buried Malka in Hildesheim not long before, but then Jost had never been one to let much grass grow under his feet. Since breaking with Chayim he had come far, furnishing metal at a good profit for several of the Elector's mints and winning the favor of Dorothea, the Elector's ambitious second wife. At Magdeburg, where he had leased the mint master's job, there had been lengthy and perilous litigation—again; this time quite pub-lic and beyond the protective umbrella of rabbinical control. The issue was suspicion that he had been clipping the coin, a not infrequent complaint and probably true. Nonetheless, his persistence, nimble footwork, and good relations with the court shielded him and smoothed the way. On January 27, 1677, Esther petitioned the Elector for a letter of protection for her groom, and only three days later her request was granted and Jost could take Israel's place.

The Berlin that he now could call home was much changed from the rundown and pitiful backwater of thirty years ago. As elsewhere across the Elector's lands, the pace had quickened and the impact of his reforms was making itself felt. Now that he had broken the power of the estates, the country was in the midst of a period of strong development and growth. From this point forward, over the forty years spanning the remainder of his rule and that of his son, the foundations of a strong, centrally governed Prussian state were put in place, and the face of the country—and of Berlin—was greatly transformed. The town bustled with activity and opportunity. Jost had chosen the time of his arrival well.

The big difference was that the Elector now had ample money, and was willing to spend it liberally in pursuit of his aims. The time when he had been forced to borrow a few taler merely to pay for his food had long since become a dim and distant memory. By far the greatest source of revenue now was the *Aksize,* an indirect consumption tax levied countrywide. During the first two years of the war against the Swedes, he had been able to collect some seven hundred thousand taler from this tax alone. By 1688, the year of his death, the one million subjects of his realm were paying over three million taler into the privy purse, a truly enormous sum.[8] The influx of the Jews had also helped. They were his *Regal*—a personal asset to tax as he pleased—and as their numbers grew so did the taxes and contributions they paid. All the more so because while the Elector had at first been rather moderate in his demands, his son and successor, the extravagant Frederick I, later showed considerably less compunction in squeezing the Jew for all he was worth.

The country's low birth rate and population sparsity had been deemed so serious in the early years that Herr Samuel Pufendorf, Court Historiographer, had seriously mused about the necessity of forcing the better classes to marry and reproduce. This radical solution the Elector had seen fit to ignore, having found ways to solve the problem by more practical means. For one thing, birth rates quickly accelerated once the economic upturn gathered some steam. Thereafter, the persecution of Protestant minorities throughout Europe provided opportunities that the Elector and his advisers were quick to grasp. He opened the doors wide to these religious refugees, treated them as favored new citizens and offered them varied inducements to come, in stark contrast to the restrictions he had placed on the Jews. As a result, by 1700, Prussia had attracted some twenty thousand French Huguenot *refugiés* alone, and these were soon joined by Waldensians from Piemonte, Walloons, Swiss Protestants, and eventually a good many Bohemians as well.

The resulting improvements in wealth and population were important enough in themselves, but for the Great Elector they were merely the means to achieve his principal goal—the creation of a large standing army and an effective Prussian military force. For the war with the north he had more than tripled the number of his soldiers to a total of 22,000 men, and after Oliva he could afford to keep more than half of them under arms. In the battle of Fehrbellin, fifteen years later, he won his great victory over the Swedes with an army doubled to 42,000 men, and he again kept many of them in uniform once victory was won.

Thus the Elector made Prussia's army a force to be reckoned with and the way this was done changed the country and people in lasting ways. The privy council was transformed into a *Generalkriegskommissariat,* a central core of senior ministers responsible for collecting the taxes and revenues to finance his expanding force. Its officials, the military and tax commissioners, became the all-powerful backbone of the state, while the sons of the impoverished nobility were encouraged to serve in the army and bureaucracy and singled out as the country's exclusive new elite. Before long, it was this privileged class of Prussians who ruled the roost and whose power, through their control over the purse, extended to all aspects of economic life.

This tightly administered system became the hallmark of Prussia for generations to come. The goal was to create a strong centralized state with the army at its core, but historians later observed that it had turned out the other way around, that Prussia had emerged as an army with merely the appendage of a civilian state. In the next century, when Prussian militarism and state regimentation had evolved even further under subsequent

Hohenzollern kings, Mirabeau quipped that Prussia was a state hatched from a cannonball, not a monarchy with an army, but an army that had treated itself to a state.[9]

Within Prussia's unique culture of militarism, regimentation, and bureaucracy, Germany's Jews now had their peculiar, uncomfortable place. They contributed their special talents to the country's development and growth and took advantage of its dynamism, drive, and opportunities for advancement, while never quite succeeding in shaking themselves free of the arbitrary and discriminatory rules imposed on them alone. Yet it was thus that Germany's destiny, and theirs, became inextricably intertwined, and that the special and singular mix of regimented German and discriminated Jew would give rise to unique and fateful results for both.

7

Israel Aaron's early success to limit the influx of Jews into Berlin proved short-lived. In spite of the best-laid plans, a lot more Jews than the Veit and Riess families soon arrived in the capital city and settled in the length and breadth of the Elector's lands. Managing their influx and their affairs became increasingly complex and soon greatly taxed the administrative skills—and the patience—of the Elector, and later of his son and their advisers. For most Jews, even with letters of protection, life would be no bed of roses for a long time.

When Frederick William died in 1688, he had come far in implementing his plans. The wheels had been set in motion, but much remained to be done, and it was left to his son to carry on with what he had begun. Though softer, less of a leader, and more interested in representational glitter than administrative detail, the new king did not deviate much from his father's line, allowing his ministers a free hand to continue the initiatives and programs started in previous years.

The problem was not that the Jews failed to contribute to the hoped-for revenue into the privy purse. In fact, quite the contrary was the case. It was more that their numbers were hard to control, the complaints of gentile merchants and guilds never seemed to end, and the Jews themselves were a difficult and fractious lot, given to much internal dissension and petty spats. Furthermore, their increasing numbers soon raised all sorts of new questions that no one had foreseen. A veritable blizzard of paper with rules, ordinances, orders, complaints, answers, arguments, and counterarguments was being unleashed, and the law of unintended consequences was making itself felt with a vengeance.

Controlling the numbers turned out to be the most difficult task. Once the doors had opened even a crack and word spread that Prussia's Jew policies had become more benign, there seemed no stopping the inward flow. The number of the *Vergleitete,* those granted official letters of protection and residence, had been gradually increased, and along with them had come their rabbis, teachers, scribes, slaughterers, servants, and community retainers—mostly *Unvergleitete,* or residents on sufferance without permanent rights. As the numbers grew, so did the complexity of their affairs, and that was another problem. But the greatest concern was the illegals, who had no right to be in the towns and villages at all, not to mention the itinerant peddlers and beggars. To the chagrin of the authorities and the legal Jews whom they held responsible, many more of these unwanted coreligionists now showed up at town gates and villages, and neither punishment nor fines proved effective to stem the flow.

To East Prussia, Jews came from the pogroms of Poland and Lithuania. Others fled from Cossack rampages in the Ukraine. Elsewhere they filtered back from Austria, Bohemia, the Palatinate, and from along the Rhine, expelled, drawn by economic opportunity, or just by the hope of tolerant treatment from a more lenient king. By the end of the century at least six thousand Jews had spread across Prussia's villages and towns. In Frankfurt an der Oder the official count doubled over the span of a dozen years; at Halberstadt, Kleve, and Minden around a hundred families were allowed to settle in each place; in the area of the Neumark, to the east of Berlin, local authorities reported 596 "official" Jews. In some towns such as Halle, smaller communities arose where there had previously been none at all.[10]

Even the little village of Bötzow—the place the Elector once had pawned—now had its Jews, though that was only one of the changes there. Now called Oranienburg, in honor of the Elector's first wife, it was no longer the depleted village that Ursula von Knesebeck had leased. Its prosperity over the years had been greatly enhanced, the population had risen, and it now had a model dairy farm, nine hundred sheep, a new bakery, and a brewery with monopoly rights for supplying the surrounding area with its brew. There was especially great pride in a spanking new little baroque *Schloss* (castle) named *Luisenhof,* which the Elector had ordered to be built for his wife at the edge of the town.

Jacob Isaak and Abraham Solomon had been coming to Oranienburg to sell their merchandise for years, and though the locals were wary of these nonbelievers, they liked their prices and the credit the Jews were accustomed to extend. A few of the merchants had grumbled about giving them permanent rights, but the two Jews and their families were nevertheless lucky enough to get letters of protection right after the edict of 1671 and settled down peacefully, dealing with wool, cloth, cattle, and skins. In 1688 the local magistrate reported that Oranienburg was home to a total of twenty-one Jews—six men, four women, eight children, and three servants.[11]

There is nothing like public money, liberally dispensed, to spark a boom—as the Oranienburgers had learned to their delight. Lady Luck had first smiled on them on that day in 1650 when Luise Henriette of Orange, the Elector's wife, had quite by chance discovered the town while hunting with her husband in the forests and fields nearby. Twenty-six years old at the time, she was both beautiful and intelligent, which may account for her success in persuading her husband to redeem Ursula's lien, and to give her the entire community and all within it as his spousal gift.

When Luise died prematurely at the age of 39, her *Luisenhof Schloss* had already been built. The stones—and the masons—had come from Holland just as she had wished, as had artisans and farmers to tend her nine hundred sheep, her dairy, and her other enterprises financed via the privy purse. She was, it was said, an astute businesswoman, good not only at attracting government funds but sharp to maximize the profits and taxes she extracted from her Oranienburg properties. Town chroniclers praise her for bringing wealth and employment to the town, though they note that her ingenious system of fines elicited much less enthusiasm among the local folk. Using bad language in the town hall cost a citizen a stiff five taler, and merely entering the town's Council Room during a session without proper license was punishable with yet another substantial sum.[12]

The Jews Jacob and Abraham would certainly have been the last ones to complain. They were the founders of Oranienburg's small enclave of Jews, much as small numbers of their brethren were establishing themselves in the towns and villages nearby. These were Prussia's newly arrived country Jews, and they were understandably grateful for a home and eager not to make waves.

Yet Berlin remained the greatest magnet of all. When the Veit and Riess families had first arrived, Brandenburg's principal city was still a small, run-down provincial place. A generation later, it had become a royal city aspiring to compete with the splendor of other kings, a mushrooming little metropolis whose population, by the turn of the century, had tripled to over fifty thousand.

Many of the ramshackle old houses had been torn down or spruced up and the "new cities" of Friedrichstadt and Dorotheenstadt had risen nearby. More canals and bridges had been built and there were many new palaces and stately homes. Completion of the Oder-Spree Canal greatly enhanced the importance of the port by diverting traffic from the mouth of the Oder River and routing it through Berlin. The development by Huguenots and other immigrants of important new industries, especially textiles, dyeing and wool, and the presence of a sizable permanent garrison of several thousand soldiers and dependents had further stimulated economic life.

Above all, Berlin was now the center of the new Prussian monarchy and the residence of a free-spending king. The evidence was visible everywhere and favorably commented upon by travelers from afar. John Toland, an English philosopher who visited there in 1706, applauded the broad new streets lined with linden trees "as in Holland," the pretty canals, clean drawbridges, and the new homes of senior ministers "which give the left-over old houses the appearance of ugly little dwarfs." The port filled with heavily laden river barges greatly impressed him, as did the vibrant city life, especially the new amphitheater by the town wall "wherein bears, lions, bulls, oxen and other wild beasts do battle, a good many of which are permanently kept in caves and holes below."[13]

At the center of all this stood Frederick I, who spared no expense to indulge his taste for splendor. Andreas Schlüter, his favorite sculptor and architect, built him a magnificent new palace, and no sooner had it been completed when the king ordered the number of rooms doubled, and royal stables put in place to accommodate at least 450 horses. At the edge of town, the queen had yet another palace built for her, complete with cere-

monial gardens and an opera house where the Crown Prince was cast in
the role of Cupid and made to dance solo—an unlikely assignment—
for which the austere later "soldier-king," Frederick William I, was poorly
suited indeed. The king sponsored the creation of an Academy of Arts, and
charged his favorite, the mathematician-philosopher Gottfried Wilhelm
Leibniz, to organize an Academy of Sciences to promote agriculture and
industry and to supervise a new Prussian system of education.

Historians have called this king a master of feasts and virtuoso of taste.
They were, in fact, very expensive tastes, which perennially taxed and depleted the royal purse. Expenditures for food and wine doubled in the first
decade of his reign, and the sums he spent on jewelry and clothes were
estimated at more than one million taler. The cost of new liveries alone
rose threefold.[14] For all this, even the sizable income from the *Aksize* no
longer sufficed, and it was left to the ingenuity of his officials to invent new
ways to squeeze the people for more cash. Yet whatever the king got was
not enough, and so an assiduous effort was soon underway to tap an especially convenient and fertile source for new funds—his Jews. It was they
who were made to bear the heaviest burden of all, and for whom no end
of special Jew assessments were devised.

By the turn of the century, Israel Aaron's success to limit the Jewish presence in the capital to a handful of wealthy Austrians had long since become
a distant memory. Well over a hundred families now lived in the streets
leading to Jew Square, the *Judenmarkt,* the center of the Jewish presence in
Berlin. They were a sizable group of more than seven hundred persons in
all, with their own class structure, social stratification, and all the traditional features of Jewish community life. The first Austrian families, the
Court Jews, and a few leading rabbis and physicians were at the top of the
heap, each with their followers. They were split along factional lines, competing for a dominant voice in community affairs. Below them, as a kind of
middle class, were the bulk of the others, including the fortunate officially
sanctioned, *Vergleitete,* the smaller money dealers, pawnbrokers, merchants, and petty traders, plus a few butchers, barbers, engravers, teachers,
and scribes whose skills were in demand. Many were still poor and lived
from hand to mouth, always hard at work to make their way, never quite
certain what new problem would arise or what new tax, special assessment,
or other new difficulty the next day would bring. At the bottom were the

workers, the *Unvergleitete* servants, retainers, transients, illegals, and all the rest. Their situation was by far the most precarious of all.

For Berlin's Jews, life was as full of opportunity and hope as it was difficult and complex. On the one hand, there was promising scope for business and financial gain. For Isaac Veith, who dealt in horses, the king's vast stables and the demands of the nobility and the army were an excellent market. For *Petschierstecher* (engraver) Levin Joseph, there was plenty of work in and around the court. Henoch Salomon, Anschel Meyer, and Levin Samuel, the three ritual slaughterers, had no difficulty selling their excess meat in town, and even Carpel Levi Wulf, the musician, found the community large and prosperous enough to support himself with performances on special occasions and feasts. The money lenders had plenty of business from the nobility and high-living Berliners perennially in debt. Others, perhaps Fischel Moyses, Levin Levi, and a Jew simply known as Ephraim, or a woman described as "Leiser David's widow," did good business from their stalls and sheds around the city's new arcades.[15]

Yet even with good business, the mood around the *Judenmarkt* was not always the best. To the Jews' innate fearful wariness, deeply ingrained from the past, there was the added uncertainty of a king whose frequent demands for more money were a constant worry and a heavy load. Berlin Jews, indeed most Jews in Prussia, still lived isolated lives amid a population who feared and disliked them and a king who was always asking for more. They remained a helpless minority whose fate was hostage to forces over which they had no control.

Would this greedy king ever say "enough"? As soon as the new Elector had succeeded his father, the Jews had paid to have their privileges confirmed. Then, in September 1689, they had been asked for a special 20,000-taler contribution "in view of the many liberties they enjoyed." Over the years, this was followed by a steady drumbeat of new demands—money for raising new regiments, lump sum payments for defense, for the king's crowning, or merely, as in 1710, to prevent some new chicanery like the threat of having the wearing of a special "Jew mark" restored. There were taxes for each servant, for births, and for weddings where one-fourth of the dowry was owed to the king, and never-ending "fines" for all manner of real or imagined infractions for which the Jews collectively were held to account. If the king's seal was stolen, it was assumed that the culprit must be a Jew and that a collective fine was due. If it was decided that too many *Unvergleitete* lived in Berlin, a doubling of their head tax was suddenly decreed. When the *Aksize* tax was raised, it was Jewish goods—textiles, cattle, wine, spirits, or even Jewish books—that were most heavily taxed.

The sum total of all these demands often far exceeded the Jews' ability to pay. Sometimes royal "precepts" were simply ignored or observed only in the breach, and tax-avoidance schemes were elevated to a fine art. The Jews protested and pleaded their case unendingly, and each year there would be new commissions and audits to investigate compliance and to check on Jewish income and wealth. Always there was much bargaining with officials until the issues were resolved, with no less controversy among the Jews themselves on how the load would be shared.

8

When Jost had wed Reb Samuel's daughter Malka in the '60s, he was an unknown young man taking a traditional wife. Fifteen years later, when the widower Jost and Esther Schulhoff-Aaron joined forces, a great deal more was at stake. Malka's moderate dowry had augmented the young trader's starting capital on the way up; the marriage to Esther was the final link in a chain of events putting him into the big time in Berlin. At the court, where there was business to be had on a grand scale, Malka and her five hundred taler would have been of little account; the connections of the Court Jewess, however, were an asset that no dowry could have bought.

"*Die schöne Esther*" is said to have been as attractive as her famous namesake in Jewish history, who delivered her people from a tyrant's hand. Unlike that other Esther, however, Jost's second wife was of a harder cut, as clever, grasping, and ambitious—and as little loved—as both men she wed. After Jost's death in 1702, even the king's own advisers were careful not to cross her in overt ways, and throughout the sovereign's lifetime she remained a dominant and feared figure at the court and among Berlin's Jews. There was a persistent rumor that she alone had leave to appear unannounced in the king's chamber. Though probably untrue, it is evidence nevertheless of the respect and fear with which her power was viewed.

Jost was a gambler who knew how to take risks. For a long time he had dreamed of the wealth and power of the favored few, those who had risen to become Court Jews and were advising and supplying Germany's princes and kings: there was Jakob de Jonge, the Great Elector's Court Jew in East Prussia, for one; Elias Gomperz in Kleve was another; and, above all, there had been Israel Aaron in Berlin. Theirs was the pinnacle of success to which Jost aspired, yet he knew that they were forever hostages to the vagaries of capricious fate. The sad ending of Lippold, the arrogant mint master who had forgotten that his position was entirely dependent on his ruler and suffered the consequences in an iron cage, and the ups and downs of the famous Samuel Oppenheimer in Vienna confronting his implacable enemy, Bishop Kollonitsch, served as poignant warnings. Jost was aware of these risks and long ago had concluded that it was prudent to move with caution and always to hedge his bets. Knowing the power of women, he was especially attentive to the Elector's wife, but remembering also the husband's mortality he started early to pay assiduous attention to the insatiable needs of their son, the future king.

Jost's progress is clearly reflected in the listings of Berlin's Jews.[16] At first he is identified merely as "Jew," and husband of the deceased Israel Aaron's widow; five years later, in 1682, he stands out in the official records as "Court Jew" and "Jeweler to the Court." Prudently specializing in the gems, gold, and silver treasures he knew best, he started small but steadily expanded the scope of his affairs. His first bill to the court was for a modest 175 taler, easily settled from the profits of the Halberstadt and Minden mints. By the early 1680s, Jost's business with the Elector had grown substantially. Year by year the court's debts to him mounted for a lengthening list of expensive goods—a large diamond ring for his master, a bejeweled bracelet, the Elector's gift for Mecklenburg's prince, and diamonds and rubies for the delegates of Denmark and Cologne. In the last years before the Elector's death, tens of thousands of taler were paid Jost and Esther out of Jew taxes and profits from the various mints. By then, Jost had achieved substantial wealth, but his greatest power and profits would come when the son had finally taken the throne. The years of careful attention to the successor and his wife now paid off in a major way.

Like most Court Jews, however, Jost never forgot where he belonged. He had special privileges and dealt almost exclusively in the Christian world, but the emotional bonds to his people remained unbroken and strong. He shared their culture, attitudes, and religion, and his character bore the imprint of a common heritage and past. Far from standing apart from Berlin's restless and contentious community of Jews, he felt intimately connected to their affairs. His riches and influence at the court satisfied his lust for power and success and had given him special standing among Christians and Jews alike. But for Jost that was not enough. To be recognized a Jewish leader and a patron of Jewish culture and learning was as important to him as the attainment of great personal wealth. He wanted to be the *primus inter pares* among Jewish aristocrats, the most important of Berlin's Jews and the dominant voice in their affairs. Toward that goal, he and Esther were willing to compete, maneuver, and intrigue with as much energy and persistence as they did in the pursuit of their commercial affairs on the outside.

As soon as he could, Jost made his presence felt. Within a few years he succeeded in replacing Israel Aaron as one of the Berlin chief elders, charged "in the name of the king" to take part in all community meetings, and to ensure that all Jewish regulations were kept and the interests of the state preserved. Using this position to maximum advantage, he did not hesitate to employ it aggressively to advance his family's cause and to extend his influence in internal Jewish affairs. He secured special letters of protection for his sons, succeeded in having his brother Isaak appointed Chief Brandenburg Rabbi, and saw to it that the next generation of Liebmann-Schulhoffs were well placed in key community posts in and outside of Berlin.

He scored a great victory when he successfully maneuvered to have the Elector grant him the coveted right to a private synagogue, winning out over the competing ambitions of Abraham Riess, whose family synagogue was ordered closed. The aroused Riess family and their followers replied with petitions and pleas and, for years to come, the "fight of the synagogues" thus unleashed was fought with equal parts of ferocity and intrigue, splitting Berlin's community into warring factions grouped around the Liebmann and "Austrian" cliques and their friends. Long after Jost's death, the two sides continued to scheme over the question of whose synagogue would survive, to the annoyance of the king and his advisers, who grew weary of the constant quarrels, protests, and petitions over synagogues, rabbis, and the election of elders. The struggle over the synagogues continued for more than a decade until finally, in 1714, both private houses of prayer were closed and the first official synagogue allowed to rise.

As the state expanded its central powers and steadily encroached on the independent rights of guilds and estates, Jewish self-rule came equally under attack. Increasingly, the king's officials injected themselves into the management of Jewish affairs and their religious and cultural life, which the medieval practice of self-rule had previously left undisturbed. Ironically, it was the disunity of the Jews that often provided the opening for the state to make its weight felt—thereby further adding to the tensions and pressures complicating their lives.

The unpredictable demands and contradictory attitude of the king added to Jewish nervousness and fear. The Elector's edict of 1671 had been a simple ten-point document, straightforward and relatively benign. At first, his son had left these rules undisturbed, though he had demanded handsome payment for reissuing the privileges his father had granted the Jews.

But on January 24, 1700, the shopkeepers guild once again complained, and he used the occasion to tighten the screw with a harsh revised decree. The tone was markedly less friendly, and ten additional provisions reflected both his greed as well as his ambivalence toward Jews. It was clear that for this ruler the Jews were little more than a cash cow to be milked dry. While threatening them with expulsion because of their alleged cheating, internal dissension, and the presence of illegals in their midst, he offered to show them mercy by assessing them a whole range of new fees. He doubled their protection costs, imposed new fines, and reimposed the hated Jew *Leibzoll,* the body tax from which the Great Elector had ordered them freed. In total contrast to the negative rhetoric of the decree, however, he actually suggested that a few more rich families come to Berlin, provided they paid him a significant additional amount.

But his proposed new rules also reflected his basic antagonism toward Jews. The ten points he added imposed controls over their freedom to elect elders, appoint rabbis, and otherwise manage their own affairs. Some years later, in a particularly unwelcome move, he authorized the official reprinting of an especially virulent anti-Jewish polemic by one Johann Eisenmenger, a Christian theologian whose ostensibly scientific yet badly distorted two-volume study, *Entdecktes Judentum* (Jewry Uncovered) was a frontal assault against the Jews. Eisenmenger's thousand-page opus attempted to prove that the Jews were guilty of every conceivable sin, often misquoting and distorting Jewish religious texts, and would for years be the basis for German anti-Semitic incitement. It was the first in a series of many such efforts.

All in all, life for the Jews remained difficult and harsh. Perhaps it is not surprising that in the streets near the *Judenmarkt,* quarrels and jealousies were more in evidence than joint efforts and a common purpose that might have improved their ability to withstand the hostile pressure of the outside world. Harmony and cooperation are generally easier to marshall when matters go well. Times of fear and uncertainty over individual survival and the basics of life rarely bring out the best and noblest instincts in man.

9

Never wish for a new king. After centuries of trouble and uncertainty, Germany's Jews craved stability and were deeply skeptical of change. The present might not be very good, but at least it was known and understood; change brought uncertainty with results that might well be worse. It was a pessimism justified by the past.

When, on February 25, 1713, the king died, the lesson would once again be learned. Hardly a year had passed since he had carried his grandson to the golden basin in a gown adorned by Liebmann jewels. Jost had been dead for a decade, but Esther, feared and disliked by both Christians and Jews because of her propinquity to the throne and her ruthless and grasping ways, continued to bask in the patronage of the court. Liebmann-Schulhoff sons, stepsons, and in-laws had been placed in leading positions in the capital and elsewhere, and daughter Hindchen was married off into the Hertz Bär family of prominent Frankfurt Jews. (One of her descendants, a composer of grand opera who called himself Giacomo Meyerbeer would, a few generations later, reach heights of acclaim in Germany unimaginable in Esther's day.)

Now the king was dead, worn out at fifty-seven by years of high living and feasts, and his son had taken the royal throne. Court Architect Schlüter designed the sort of elaborate coffin its occupant would have liked, and with due pomp and ceremony Frederick I was laid to rest in his Berlin

Dome. It was the last concession his son would make to his father's taste
for the ornate.

Only a week later, on March 6, the newspapers announced that "His
Majesty is determined that the magnificence must stop. . . ," and that "Herr
Schlüter is to go into service to the Muscovites."[17] The architect was not the
only one to be dismissed forthwith. The royal pages were sent off to be
cadets, and most servants in the palace kitchens were put to work elsewhere, the king having decreed that no more than twelve persons could
eat at his table at one time. Palaces were closed; horses, jewels, and works
of art sold; and salaries drastically slashed. The royal budget was reduced
by four-fifths.[18]

The new king was a miser, and he quickly brought Esther's time of glory
and power to an unceremonious end. He hated her as a symbol of the waste
that had bankrupted the royal purse, quickly confiscated her riches, and
placed both Esther and her son under house arrest. Their days as Court Jews
now were over, and Esther died a year later at Frankfurt an der Oder, away
from Berlin.

Frederick William I was the third of the four Hohenzollerns who made
their country great. He ruled in a transitional age when the rigid social order of the past was giving way to the enlightened despotism of a strong
central state. It was a time when manufacture and trade were replacing
long-held beliefs in the evils of money, credit, and interest; when rationalism began to displace medieval theories about a God-given station for each
layer of society; when education opened people's horizons, and new technologies in industry and manufacturing were changing old ways.

The new king reflected the contradictions of his age, but he was like no
other ruler who ever sat on a European throne—as totally unlike his father
as his famous son would one day prove to be unlike him. It is that son
whose conquests would earn him the epithet "Great," yet his quirky, irascible, and eccentric father was fully as remarkable a ruler as he. Much of
what Frederick the Great was later able to do would have been impossible
without the foundations his father laid.

They called him the "soldier-king." He was a short, barrel-shaped, red-
faced man, whom the Lord had blessed neither with grace nor good looks.
He was simple, crude, and direct, and yet his character was contradictory
and extraordinarily complex. He scrimped and saved to make his army

great, but he loved it so much that he rarely risked it in war. His temper was legendary, yet in his foreign policies he was cautious in the extreme. He spent endless hours enlarging and controlling the state purse, yet wasted untold taler and many hours drilling his cherished *"Lange Kerle,"* a group of giant soldiers so tall and gangly as to be utterly useless in a real fight. He had little interest in music, the arts, and most newfangled ideas, yet he was the first European monarch to introduce compulsory education, and in a twenty-year period he built over seventeen hundred Prussian schools.

He clung to a traditional, childlike religiosity, disliked Catholics, and had contempt for Jews. Time and again he would order them punished or expelled, only to relent and forbid his subjects to abuse them outside the law. He was also a violent man, who believed in meting out instant justice with his cane. The story is told of a Polish Jew in Potsdam who tried to avoid crossing the king's path. "Why do you run away, Jew?" the king asked, whereupon the man confessed that, frankly, he was afraid. "Imbecile," the king shouted in a rage, "you are supposed to love me, not fear me"—all the while raining down blows on the hapless man's head.

He was, above all, an organizational genius. An arbitrary autocrat who believed in the virtues of duty, hard work, and the fear of God, he took as his motto—in the polyglot French-German of the day—*ordre parieren, nicht raisonieren* (order and obedience, no arguments). Whether as a state official or a soldier, the idea was that in Prussia one received orders and was expected to execute them without question.

His true love was the army, and to make it great he totally restructured the administration of the state and its finances, thus putting his stamp on German society for generations to come—some would say even to the present day. In the brief quarter century of his rule over a still primitive and poor country, he established a modern standing army eighty thousand strong—and yet left a treasure of eight million taler stored in casks in the cellars of his *Schloss.* To achieve this, he greatly boosted revenues by merging the collection of taxes and administration of the royal domains into a single all-powerful general war commissariat in Berlin. Its very name— *General-Ober-Finanz-Kriegs-und-Domänen Directorium*—must have instilled awe and fear in his citizens. He divided Prussia into "cantons" of five thousand inhabitants each, stationed his regiments amongst them, and held each canton accountable to a royal tax commissioner who had to collect the revenue and recruit replacements for his troops. It was these officials who gradually came to dominate every aspect of Prussian civilian and military affairs.

With vastly increased revenues, he promoted the building of canals, bridges, and roads to support the expansion of industry and commerce. Above all, he succeeded in convincing the landed gentry that it was an honor to serve the state. He preached thrift, honesty, and blind obedience, drilled his troops incessantly, and expected his officers to do the same. In time, it was these aristocrats who became the country's powerful, often arrogant ruling elite while their sons served as the backbone of the military's corps of cadets. Elsewhere in Europe, the nobility hung around the court with little to do but to feast and fawn. By contrast, it was the soldier-king's major accomplishment to establish the Prussian tradition of honor derived from service in the army and the state. Even the lower ranks, forcibly recruited and drilled to blind obedience, would later take the spirit of military order and control with them when employed as petty officials and city servants.

Thomas Carlyle called Frederick William "Drill Sergeant of the Prussian Nation."[19] He did militarize his country—he was the first European monarch to wear a uniform at all times—yet through his administrative genius and his example of honesty, thrift, and hard work, he did much to lay the foundations for the powerful Prussia of future years. Life for his people was never easy under his stern rule; for the Jews it was the beginning of a particularly trying time.

10

At first there was no obvious sign that the new king's accession to the throne was the beginning of what one Jewish commentator later called "*Die Eiserne Zeit*"[20] (the iron time), a very hard and painful period indeed. The early signals were somewhat mixed.

On the Sabbath before the new year in 1714, Queen Sophie Dorothea had come with the king's ministers in a retinue of twenty carriages to witness the inauguration of Berlin's long debated new synagogue, and so much benign royal attention was considered a good sign. Chief Elder Hirschel Fränkel bowed deeply as he ushered the royal party into what many considered one of the finest temples in Europe. Court Embroiderer Aaron Isaak, whose daughter was to be wed during the same ceremonies, was overcome with joy and pleasure.

The king's prompt confirmation of existing rights was taken as another positive omen. Though he had used rough tactics to extract a three thousand taler payment for the synagogue, and though the confirmation decree had been expensive and involved thirty-two paragraphs of dos and don'ts couched in unpleasant rhetoric, none of it seemed a cause for immediate concern. It was only in the course of the next several years, as a new and painful policy of harassment and restriction unfolded, that this king's deep antipathy toward the Jews became painfully clear.

Year by year he tightened the vise under the pretext of either a complaint from a Christian or some real or imagined Jewish transgression. Step by step, the scope of Jewish business was reined in, punishments escalated, and every element of their lives controlled. The opening of new stores in Berlin was limited and the goods that could be sold severely reduced. Dealing in spices, dry goods, spirits, skins, and the buying of wool was totally forbidden. A new ceiling on the interest chargeable on Jew loans was also decreed and violators punished with confiscation of their entire capital. Meat could no longer be sold to Christians, nor houses bought without special permission. Most children of *Vergleitete* were either ordered expelled or allowed to stay only against payment of heavy new fees.

Edict XLVI, a particularly nasty one issued on Christmas Eve 1725, illustrates the general mood of the king: "If a Jew knowingly buys stolen goods," it said, he will be "whipped, brandmarked and expelled." A few months later, he decreed that Jews caught cheating on money be "beaten with sticks and chased away."

Thus it went, seemingly without end. In Berlin the Jews groaned under Frederick William's lash; so much so that there was, it is said, greatly renewed interest in when—at last—the Messiah might appear. The culmination of their troubles came in 1730, when the king issued a new, even lengthier *General-Privilegium,* which codified the piecemeal rules he had promulgated in previous years—a compilation so complex and painful that it took a full decade of argument, pleading, and debate—and the expulsion of several hundred Jews from the capital—before some of the provisions were softened and the decree put into effect.

In part, the king's edicts merely reflected his irascible, impetuous nature. Whenever his temper flared, he was apt to issue a new blast. The story of Levin Veit, who had supplied the mint with silver and died leaving insufficient funds to settle his debts, was a case in point. It so enraged the monarch that he declared all Berlin Jews coconspirators, locked them in their synagogue, surrounded them with soldiers, and eventually assessed them eight thousand taler for the mismanagement of their affairs. Interestingly enough, the edict made its appearance at the very time the king was in a permanent rage over the escape attempt of Crown Prince Frederick, his son, who could no longer bear his father's oppression and capricious moods. The delegate of Brunswick reported home that His Majesty had fallen into such a *"maladie,"* that Herr Stahl, the Court Physician, had been called into urgent attendance and that all manner of medicine had to be ordered from the apothecary.[21]

The sheer number of rules also demonstrated the king's penchant for detail and his irresistible urge to organize and control every element of the ever more complex Jewish affairs. When the first Jews arrived, the rules were relatively simple; seventy-five years later, their numbers having greatly risen, the sheer quantity of unanticipated questions being put to the king by his officials was getting out of hand, and the thicket of rules and prescripts had become confusing in the extreme. Could a widow stay after her husband had died? What if she remarried? What of her first as against her tenth child? How long could rabbis and their students and teachers stay? What if they married *Vergleitete*? What about inheritances, houses, travel, disputes, and so forth? For each of these nettlesome questions a new regulation would be issued. For each, yet another new question would arise or unexpected loophole open—thus putting Prussian *Gründlichkeit* (the urge for thoroughness) and Jewish ingenuity permanently to the test.

The basic reason for the king's harshness, however, was his fundamental dislike of all Jews, his presumption of their basic dishonesty, and his hope that they might one day just die out or disappear, either through baptism or expulsion. "Why do they hang on to their religion," he once asked, "given that they have for so long waited in vain for their Messiah to come?" The answer he liked best was that the stubborn Jews clung to their hopeless faith for one reason only—"for profit." His actions were calculated to contain Jews as a necessary evil, always to be watched and controlled, while exploiting them financially for the maximum benefit of the state.

It was a policy that necessarily led to no end of contradictions and inconsistencies, since the king was also a pragmatist, and his officials often reminded him of the usefulness of the Jews and the financial benefits to be derived from keeping them around. When his rage would get out of hand, it would be these officials who would argue with him, try to circumvent his orders, or otherwise weaken their intent.

11

During the early hours of May 31, 1740, the soldier-king rapped the floor by his bed with his cane. Using his pet name for Queen Sophie, he ordered her to rise. "Get up, Fiekchen," he barked, ". . . now I shall die."

Weakened by strokes, ill with the gout, and tortured with pain, he knew that the end was near, yet he remained irascible to the last. When he saw a stable boy saddling horses below his window with yellow saddles over blankets that were blue, he insisted that one of his retainers go to make sure that the culprit be whipped forthwith. His son, Frederick, who had suffered untold indignities during his father's life—and whose best friend the king had ordered beheaded in front of his eyes—knelt at his bedside, and when the old monarch was dead, it is said that he wept.[22] Whether the king's Jews did the same is not known, though the likelihood seems exceedingly remote.

It had been seventy-five years since the first Jews had been allowed back. Three generations had now called Prussia their home, and during this short period a great deal had changed. The country was no longer weak, vulnerable, and poor. Population was now over 2.5 million, placing it thirteenth among European states and tenth in territorial size. Prussia's efficiently organized and well-equipped army was smaller only than that of Russia, Austria, and France, and its quality was already second to none.

Consistent economic policies, a culture of frugality in expenditures, and obedient discipline in civil and military organization had helped Prussia to make greater strides than most European states. Manufacturing, agriculture, and trade had substantially grown and the treasury was full.

Among its many new inhabitants there were now some ten or twelve thousand Jews, though they were most certainly not "citizens" like others. For all intents and purposes, they remained the Prussian state's slaves, an oppressed, tightly regulated minority living on sufferance in a hostile world. Their numbers had risen vastly beyond what the kings had planned, and neither Prussian discipline nor intimidation, ordinances, and restrictive rules had been effective in stopping the inexorable inflow. For Jews, no less than others, Prussia's opportunities were an attraction impossible to resist and, paradoxically, its "law and order" environment, however harsh for them, was an added factor drawing them in. The threat of the mob had always been the Jews' greatest fear, but under the stern discipline of the Hohenzollerns they knew that in Prussia at least their physical safety was assured.

They had settled widely across Prussia's villages and towns. Sizable communities were established in Halberstadt, Frankfurt, Magdeburg, and above all in Berlin. In the countryside, the largest number of Jews were scattered across Mecklenburg, Pomerania, East Prussia, and Brandenburg. Most of them, especially outside the towns, remained poor and severely restricted in what they could do.

The lucky ones had been granted letters of protection under which their residence in Prussia—but not necessarily that of their children—was legally assured. Most others had only temporary permits, and everywhere there were Jewish floaters, wanderers, and occasional thieves precariously in search of a place to stay, dependent on the charity of their brethren and forced to live by their wits.

Jewish lives were still quite limited, and horizons remained narrow and confined, a circumstance not much different from that of the gentile world at large. In the first part of the eighteenth century travel was still difficult and expensive, and the average citizen rarely ventured much beyond the radius of the twenty kilometers from his home he could cover on foot. Even Emmanuel Kant, Prussia's greatest philosopher, never left his native Königsberg.

Most Jews were not yet Germans in any real sense of the word, and their religion and traditional teachings remained at the center of their intellectual lives. They still spoke their own language of Yiddish, and few had either interest or understanding of more secular knowledge and of non-

Jewish affairs. Firmly bound to a distinct community that their rabbis and elders dominated and tightly controlled, they were, in their own way, more educated than the gentiles among whom they lived. Yet theirs too was a culture full of superstitions and walls, and their literacy was largely restricted to the Talmud and the study of ancient laws.

But neither for German nor Jew had time entirely stood still, and neither group would for long remain untouched by the changes the Hohenzollerns had labored so long and hard to achieve. At midcentury, in the eighth decade since their return, the first signs appeared that the position of the Jew in Prussia was undergoing evolution and change, much as the rest of the population was changing under the impact of Prussian development and growth. Change brought a ferment of new ideas and ambitions among both gentiles and Jews—and nowhere were the seeds of change germinating more clearly than in the capital city of Berlin.

In spite of all the efforts to keep them down, close to fifteen hundred Jews now lived in the streets surrounding Berlin's Jew Square. Around them the capital was experiencing explosive growth, its population nearing the hundred thousand mark. One in five citizens was either a soldier or a dependent attached to the sizable garrison quartered in the town. Expanding manufacture and commerce had greatly improved economic life and raised the promise of yet more opportunities and greater prosperity ahead.

The king had thundered and threatened for years in his drive for a more orderly life, and the fruits of his labors were everywhere to be seen. There were firm rules about when and how to sweep the streets—precisely to the midpoint of the pavement, every second day. The hours of lighting oil lamps were strictly controlled, as were the igniting of fires and the locking of windows and doors. With Prussian thoroughness, an inspector of lanterns and thirty night watchmen had their precise instructions on how to check on locks, with fines for everything from dirty chimneys to unswept yards. Discipline was harsh and punishment severe—for thefts above fifty taler death by hanging had been decreed. The gallows—two for Christians and a separate one for Jews—were, it is said, rather busy.[23]

Yet, all in all, Berlin pulsed with energy and drive. The port was busy and commerce thrived, more broad avenues had been paved, and more streets were lit. The passageways were thronged with merchants and visitors from out of town, drawn by the variety of offerings in popular entertainment and in culture and the arts.

For decades the soldier-king had worked hard to develop Prussian manufacture and commerce and to create the financial structure to support the country's expanding economic base. He had exploited the Jews and kept them down, yet he had also used them to build Prussia up. He had threatened and thundered about them as "locusts" in the people's midst and yet, when it suited him, he had freely bestowed individual privileges on those he expected to help his cause. It is doubtful that the implications of his contradictory policies were clear to him at the time. The unintended consequence, however, was to elevate some Jews to vital roles as employers in manufacturing and wholesaling and as traders underpinning Prussia's growing economic strength.

Along with the early Court Jews and their heirs, this group now became the new Jewish economic elite and the increasingly indispensable agents of economic progress and change. The Gumperts, his Court Jews and the suppliers to his mints, had moved into banking and the manufacture of tobacco. In Dessau, it was Jews who made velvet, ribbons, and silk, and in Stargard, Marcus Elias and Solomon Arendt were the crucial middlemen whose financial and distribution skills made possible the growth of some of the king's favorites, the manufacture of wool products, piece goods, and wigs. Near Mecklenburg, at Wittstock, Jews with capital financed the local weaving of cloth, and Jewish manufacturers of gold, silver, and leather goods gave increasing employment to the people of Berlin.[24]

The number of these entrepreneurs was still quite small and most still stood apart from other facets of German life, yet it is through them that the position of the Jew began to be newly defined—and it is principally their children who would carry the torch in the years to come. No Jewish middle class or intelligentsia in a more secular sense had as yet emerged; that would come later, though the foundations were now in place. Gradually, but still only dimly perceived, a new pattern for the unique role of the Jews in German economic life began to emerge.

For the Germans, the Jew had become at once an important contributor, valued, needed, and even respected for what he did better than anyone—but also a necessary evil, always a second-class citizen, inferior in status and the target of fear, jealousy, and scorn. For their part, the Jews reacted with unparalleled energy, striving, and an incessant drive to achieve. A few became quite indispensable and grew wealthy and proud, even too proud— and a handful were now extremely rich.

Was it possible that in time a healthier positive relationship could emerge from this mixture of prejudice and need, distance and pride, and love and hate? Would a future era of enlightenment and new concepts of the rights of the individual overcome these biases and the gulf that had inhibited normal contacts on both sides for so long? Could the Jews be integrated into German life, or would it forever remain a union between unequals, locked in an uneasy mutual embrace of need tinged with dislike?

It was impossible to know. Few Jews dared to venture much beyond their own world; few gentiles could yet see far beyond the stereotyped image of the alien Jew in their midst. It is the children and grandchildren of the generations of Jost and his sons who would be the pioneers, the ones to break new ground and to seek a more normal relationship with the only country they had ever known. And that same generation of gentile Germans would rethink their attitudes and put forward their own ideas.

Change, however, was in the air. We know today that as the new king wept at his dead father's bed there were already those among Christians and Jews who would soon reach out for something different and new. In Dessau, Moses Mendelssohn, the son of a poor Torah scribe, set out for the bright lights of Berlin and in 1743 talked his way past Berlin's city gate for Jews. Some years later he would emerge as the foremost champion and advocate for a new way. In Frankfurt an der Oder, Benjamin Lemos was being admitted to the study of medicine, one of the first Jews allowed into the university's hallowed halls. Elsewhere Hindchen Liebmann, Jost's daughter, became the matriarch of a family dynasty; one of her descendants would be celebrated as one of Germany's great musical geniuses, and another as a respected poet. Around the same time, a young Jew named Markus Levin emerged from an early life in Brandenburg's woods where it is said he lived as a member of a band of Jewish vagabonds and thieves. In those days such people were harshly dealt with by the officers of the king. Markus, legend has it, had been branded as punishment for his crimes, and bore his mark of shame permanently embossed on his derrière. In later years, we will encounter him as a well-established, wealthy jewelry merchant in Berlin, a patron of the theatre and the father of a daughter who bore a noble name and became the talk of Berlin.

The first generation had been the ancestors; the next were the pioneers in the struggle for a more normal place for Jews on the German scene. In Oranienburg, Wittstock, Halle, Frankfurt, and above all in Berlin, it is their generation and the gentiles of their time who would write the next chapter of the history of Germany's Jews.

CHAPTER IV

PIONEERS

Rahel

To be a Jew! And now my entire life is a bleeding to death.

How revolting, degrading, insulting, senseless, low my environment, which I cannot escape; a single contact alone soils me, sullies my nobility. It is an eternal struggle! All of life's beautiful things pass by me, as a visitor passes a stranger, and I must live unrecognized, with the unworthy.

Rahel in letters to David Veit

1795

The thing that all my life seemed to me the greatest shame, that was the misery and misfortune of my life—having been born a Jew—this I should on no account wish to have missed.

Rahel on her deathbed

1833

1

When the soldier-king died in Potsdam shortly after three o'clock in the afternoon of May 31, 1740, the son did not linger long at his father's side. His tears dried, Frederick quickly left for Berlin, sent a curt note to his wife to join him there, and the next day stepped out on the balcony of his palace to take the oath of office, after which he stood and looked pensively at the cheering crowd below.

Crown Princess Elizabeth and most of Frederick's entourage and friends had remained at his personal residence at Rheinsberg to await developments. After years of chafing under his father's harsh control, the son had finally been allowed a measure of independence, and it is at Rheinsberg, in a small *Schloss* designed for him by his friend the sculptor and architect Georg Wenzeslaus von Knobelsdorff—who would later build him the much grander Sans Souci palace at Potsdam—that he had spent the last four years, probably among the happiest of his life.

The mood at the Rheinsberg court-in-waiting had been one of anxious expectation, and when the news finally came that the old curmudgeon was truly dead, joyful anticipation of good times ahead was much more in evidence than mourning or grief. When one of Frederick's courtiers, Baron Bielfeld, was awakened with the news of the monarch's death and expressed his doubts, Knobelsdorff assured him happily that the old king was indeed "dead, dead as a doornail," and that, as they would "dissect and embalm the corpse, he will never return." Thereupon Bielfeld jumped out of bed and knocked over a small table from which some coins fell to the floor, as Knobelsdorff reproached him good-naturedly: "You are collecting pennies when it is going to rain ducats on us." The new queen appeared looking lovely in a black and white negligee to receive the homage of the court, followed by a splendid, almost festive breakfast before everyone rushed off for the journey south.[1]

If, however, Elizabeth shared visions of a glittering future at her husband's side, she was soon to be greatly disappointed. Frederick, who had been forced by his father to marry her against his will, had maintained friendly relations with her at Rheinsberg. He claimed that he had paid his "tribute to Hymen" there, though some said they had lived more like brother and sister. In fact, the king and his advisers had on numerous occasions found it necessary to urge Frederick to be more assiduous in attending to his husbandly duties and to provide for dynastic succession. He appears, however, to have been quite lax in that regard and, in any case, there was never to be a tangible result.

The reasons for Frederick's attitude remain unclear. Throughout his life, he had little or no romantic interest in women and much preferred the company of men, with several of whom his relationship was loving and intense. Perhaps he was a homosexual, but if so, probably more a platonic than an active one. He certainly never had similar close relationships with women—and definitely not with his wife. Much later, when someone compared him to Solomon, he sighed: "Solomon had a seraglio of a thousand women, and by no means considered he had enough of them; I have only one and that is too much for me."

Frederick, in fact, now separated from his wife. Thenceforth, from the first day of his accession to the throne, they would rarely again spend even a single night under the same roof. In the years ahead she lived in the Berlin Palace, while the king stayed at Sans Souci, from which she was strictly banished. He insisted that she receive all honors due her as queen, and his own attitude toward her remained one of correct politeness, though at times he found it difficult to mask his underlying indifference. He did not lay eyes on her for the entire period of the Seven-Year War, and when they finally met again, the best he could do was to greet her with the words, "Madam, you have grown fat."

For Elizabeth, then, her arrival in Berlin was not the beginning of good times but the start of fifty-five years of isolation and loneliness. The boredom eventually transformed her into a crank and a shrew, but her husband cared little about all that. At the moment he had other things on his mind. He immediately left Berlin for his grandmother's palace at nearby Charlottenburg, and a few days later set out for Königsberg in East Prussia to attend the traditional ceremonies of homage there. His grandfather had made a great show of the same journey, at the head of a retinue of eighteen hundred carriages and thirty thousand horses. Frederick avoided such pomp and went virtually alone in a small traveling carriage, accompanied only by two of his closest friends.

Almost immediately after the ceremonies at Königsberg, Frederick was back in Berlin, seized by a frenetic zeal to take up his new responsibilities as Prussia's ruler. He recalled some of his friends whom his father had exiled abroad and, in a whirlwind of activity, issued a flood of orders and decrees, most of them unimaginable in his predecessor's time.

First, he reopened the Berlin Academy, which had been closed, and asked the French philosopher Pierre Louis Moreau de Maupertuis to head it. Next, he abolished torture for civilians (but not the flogging of soldiers, which was considered indispensable for military discipline). He decreed that henceforth all religions were to be tolerated, and he ended censorship of the press and of books. Because it had been a cold winter, followed by a poor harvest, he opened the public granaries and ordered that food be sold cheaply to the people.

All this and more he managed to do in a single week. It seemed that he had long ago planned exactly what to do when the time came and was intoxicated with the pleasure of getting it done. Once, while in this mood of giddy excitement, he roamed through the streets of Berlin, distributing cash among the city's poor.

In July, in the company of a young Venetian named Algarotti, who was a friend from his Rheinsberg days (some said they were lovers), he went to visit his sister Wilhelmine at Bayreuth, where she had been married off some years earlier to the local heir apparent. After a side trip to Strasbourg, which he and Algarotti tried but failed to do "incognito," he stopped in Kleve for his first meeting with Voltaire. The two had long corresponded but never met face-to-face, and the French philosopher was so thrilled with the pace and thrust of the Prussian king's reforms that he took to addressing him as "Your Humanity." They had a pleasant meeting, and talked of liberty and the immortality of the soul—while warily assessing each other behind a screen of extravagant mutual compliments. It was the beginning of a complex relationship destined to have its share of ups and downs.

Soon thereafter, Frederick was back at home, ready to conquer new worlds. Prussia—and Europe—would not have to wait for long.

2

Frederick II was twenty-eight years old when he took the throne, a young crown prince seemingly full of idealism and enlightened goodwill. A year earlier he had written a book he called *Antimachiavel,* which, as it happened, was published almost exactly at the time he became king.

It was, by general consensus, a juvenile and repetitive work, stocked with truisms and lugubrious sermons. Intended as a refutation of Machiavelli, it inveighed against a prince's arbitrary rule and condemned avarice, treachery, and foul play. The principal purpose of a ruler should be justice, the young Crown Prince wrote. He should be kind, gentle, soft-hearted, and humane, and his most precious quality should be his private and public morality. Above all, he should avoid unjust wars. A prince bent on conquest, said Frederick, was little better than a highwayman—except that one was destined to wear a crown and the other a noose.

In view of these enlightened and peace-loving sentiments, no one anywhere was prepared for what would soon follow. For, within a few short months, contrary to every sentiment expressed in *Antimachiavel,* Frederick crudely precipitated a war.

In October, Charles VI of Austria had died suddenly and his daughter, the young Empress Maria Theresa, had succeeded him to the throne. Against the advice of his ministers, Frederick quickly determined to take advantage of the momentary confusion in Vienna to seize Silesia, Austria's richest province. When Otto von Podewils, his first minister, had pointed out the illegality of such a step, he breezily replied that "a formal claim is a question for ministers. It is your affair."

Using subterfuge and pretense, he plotted the sudden and unprovoked attack in secret. One night in December he appeared at a masked ball in Berlin, dressed as a domino. The next morning he rode off at the head of his troops to press the attack. Europe watched stunned and shocked as in the two ensuing Silesian wars Frederick showed daring to the point of recklessness on the battlefield, risked and sacrificed thousands of his troops, outmaneuvered his enemies, took advantage of good fortune, and in the end, emerged victorious. On the political front he was equally unscrupulous and uninhibited—and no less successful. He switched allies more than once, time and again betrayed them, and engaged in one duplicity after another until finally, in 1745, all was won, and the humiliated Maria Theresa was forced to sign a treaty ceding Silesia to her Prussian enemy.

So much for the "Antimachiavel" and his high moral standards. The peace-loving king had gone to war and done everything he had once condemned. His anomalous character and the full measure of his inconsistent attitudes, his unpredictability, and his moral hypocrisy now were apparent and would, throughout his remarkable time as Prussia's ruler, repeatedly confound all those whose lives he touched.

He had extolled the virtues of peace and forbearance, but quickly started an unprovoked war. In 1742, when he had prevailed against the Austrians at the battle of Mollwitz, he had written his brother, "may God protect us from a second battle, equally bloody and murderous." Yet he had continued the war for another three years, at the cost of many thousands more Austrian and Prussian casualties, the depletion of his finances, and much suffering among his people. When it was finally over, he reverted to his favorite role as philosopher-king at Sans Souci, devoted to his collection of paintings and antiques, to music, poetry, and fine conversation, musing with Voltaire and his friends about the goodness and evil in man. He said he wanted everyone to "seek salvation in his own way" and thought of himself as enlightened, but he ruled as an absolutist with little respect for the views of others. Ten years later, in 1756, he once again reversed course, and with an army even bigger than before once more went off to war, inflicted enormous hardship on his people, almost lost his kingdom, and did not return for seven years.

Frederick II was the last of the four absolutist rulers of Prussia who together laid the foundations for their country's greatness. In history, he became Frederick the Great, the most analyzed and studied of the Hohenzollern kings, and the greatest of them all. To say that he was also the most complex, inconsistent, contradictory, and unpredictable is to state the obvious.

He had an enlightened attitude toward religious and political freedom and issued edicts accordingly, yet he rarely took advice, ruled as if he were the country's sole owner, demanded mechanical obedience from subordinates, and frequently showed a cynical contempt for people and their views. His writings reflect a remarkable open-mindedness for his time, yet his actions often bore witness to a stubborn bigotry. He was at times careful, self-critical, and modest—and rash, reckless, and egotistic at others. When it suited his purpose, he did not hesitate to double-talk and to prevaricate shamelessly, yet he could also be scrupulously honest and frank. In some situations he was coldly calculating and in others he acted with an impulsive ferocity beyond all reason.

Innumerable books have been written about him, including endless character studies. What has fascinated and puzzled historians above all is his fondness for saying one thing while doing another, and his extraordinary mixture of essentially antithetical character traits. Were they innate, or primarily the result of years of honing the skill of pretense while under his father's heel?

The father wanted a son in his own image, another "soldier-king" to think and to rule just like him. But young Frederick hated barracks life and the endless drills that were his father's specialty. His interests in flute playing, poetry, Latin, and Greek were precisely those his father detested most. Their personalities could not have been more different, and the clash between them was as inevitable as it was constant. But it was an unequal struggle, and the son soon learned that open opposition or rebellion was painful and futile. In the end, it became a kind of game of pretense, with the son seemingly submitting and doing as he was asked, while secretly pursuing a life of his own.

Was it then that Frederick had learned the art of a double life or was that always part of his basic personality? In a self-characterization, he once said that he was "a philosopher by inclination; a politician by necessity." Voltaire, a keen student of human nature, may have been closer to the truth when he observed that he was some of both, that Frederick was seized by a sort of "double enthusiasm" to think and to act; that he tended to pursue both to excess—and that sometimes one got in the way of the other.[2]

Whatever the reason, those who dealt with the Prussia of *Fredericus Rex* had to learn the hard way that what he said was not necessarily what he did, and that the outcome of this contradictory mixture of word and deed was hard to predict.

His ministers and his own people had to learn the same lesson—and his Jews had to learn it most of all. It is yet another paradox of their history that Prussia's Jews were, at first, more painfully affected by his inconsistencies than any other group of his subjects, and that in the end, he may, by virtue of his inconsistencies, unwittingly have done more to accelerate their assimilation, and their legal emancipation, than he ever intended or could have imagined.

3

When Frederick took the throne, few if any among Prussia's Jews read German books, let alone understood the French that the king and his friends favored. "No one speaks anything but French; German is for soldiers and horses," Voltaire had reported after his arrival in Potsdam.[3] Yet, if not many Jews had actually read the king's *Antimachiavel,* they no doubt knew of it and can be forgiven if the book's lofty sentiments and his decree on religious freedom had raised their hopes that better times were at hand. Berlin's Jews, in particular, had suffered under the father's harsh 1730 rules and never ceased to plead for some amelioration of their heavy burdens. With the liberal young king on the throne, would there not be some easing of the restrictions?

If this was their hope, they were to be greatly disappointed. Like everyone else, Berlin's Jews soon discovered that theory and practice were not one and the same thing in Frederick's Prussia—and especially not as applied to them. Religious liberty as a general concept was one thing; the specifics of easing up on the Jews were quite another matter. The king actually wanted the regimentation and strictures imposed on them tightened even further. Contrary to their hopes, the Jews soon found that rather than things getting better, they actually got decidedly worse.

The reality was that Frederick found the Jews fully as distasteful as his predecessors. Like his father, he viewed them as usurers given to swindling and deceit, a dangerous element requiring close supervision and restriction. In the introduction to the new *Generalreglement* for Jews, eventually promulgated in 1750, he noted that he considered it his duty to protect Christians from their underhanded practices by strictly limiting their number in proportion to the general population.

It had taken a full decade for the new law to come into effect, and seven years of study, argument, pleading, and debate from March 27, 1743, the day when the king's senior official, Herr Generalfiskal Uhden, had first submitted his proposed new *principia regulativa.* In the early years, busy with his Silesian wars, the king had left it to his officials to assess existing circumstances and make proposals for new rules. Yet in the guidelines he sent them, he had posed a set of detailed questions that ominously signaled what he had in mind: limit the number of Jews severely, restrict the size of their families, retain only the wealthiest, get the maximum in contributions from them—and chase away the rest.

Given the Prussian penchant for bureaucratic thoroughness, there had ensued a seemingly unending effort of counting Jews, surveying where they lived, how they earned their living, what they paid in taxes and contributions, and the like. In Berlin and elsewhere, Jewish scribes were kept busy responding to official questionnaires and supplying innumerable lists with the most detailed data. Thus, early in 1744, Berlin's elders were obliged to submit a particularly ludicrous roster describing and justifying every one of the community's servants, explaining, inter alia, the need for one rabbi and four assistants, two cantors and two chanters, three beadles for the synagogue, seven absolutely essential gravediggers, six equally necessary attendants for the sick, three butchers, two bakers, several scribes and printers, bath attendants, and of course, the indispensable guardians at the Jew gate to keep out the poor and the itinerant.[4]

Every so often, while this process was under way, the king would send his officials yet another curt instruction or marginal note, voicing displeasure over some alleged Jewish practice and ordering, in frequently rude and inflammatory language, some further restriction on them.

In October 1742, the officials were informed that the king demanded enforcement of the existing *Verbot* (prohibition) against Jewish peddling and wanted the strictest measures to prevent the surreptitious infiltration of alien Jews. Soon thereafter, they were told that the king opposed additional permanent residence permits. "Unless there is a convincing need," it was said, "His Majesty considers it damaging and detrimental."

Sometimes the king himself took pen to hand. In the town of Strausberg, the Protected Jew Caspar Jochem faced bankruptcy and requested a six-year moratorium to pay his creditors. The very idea enraged Frederick, and he so informed his minister in no uncertain terms. Where would it lead, he asked, if such frauds were accorded periods of grace? "In my lands," he said, "if any Protected Jew is so much as suspected of bankruptcy, he and all of his family should lose their privileges forthwith—nor should their place be taken by another family of Jews."[5]

As his officials—often more realistic and reasonable than their sovereign—struggled with these instructions, Christian merchants stoked the fires with a steady drumbeat of complaints. In 1743, the guild of French and German merchants once again protested against their Jewish competitors. Let them learn an honest craft as in Poland and Bohemia, they suggested, disingenuously ignoring that no Prussian craft guild would admit a Jew. Some time later, the leather merchants also protested Jewish competitors, and the general guild of Berlin merchants was not far behind. Meanwhile, the Jews themselves would make proposals, plead their inability to raise the mounting contributions, or assert the hardships placed on their children, such as limits on their marriages, conduct of a separate business, prohibition against living apart from their parents, and the like.

If the years under the old soldier-king had been their *"Eiserne Zeit,"* what now confronted the Jews under the philosopher-king was no better, and possibly worse. In 1760, the Russians had briefly occupied Berlin and extracted a large "loan" from the inhabitants. Berlin's Jews had to contribute a disproportionate share, and the occupiers indulged in a cruel joke by specifying in the loan document that repayment would occur "when the Messiah comes."[6] Getting their money back from the occupiers was perhaps the least of the reasons why indeed, after two decades of restrictions and wars under *Fredericus Rex,* his Jews had reasons to pray ever more fervently for their deliverer's arrival.

4

In October 1743, during the Silesian wars, Mendel Heymann and his wife Bela sent their youngest son to Berlin to continue his studies there. Mendel was a Torah scribe and synagogue custodian in the Jewish community of Dessau, southwest of the capital. Bela, it so happens, was a cousin of Elija Wulff, whose father, the Court Jew Moses Benjamin Wulff, had years earlier been a victim of Jost's and Esther's intrigues for the favor of the Great Elector and who, in turn, was distantly related to the family of Glückel of Hameln. Displaced from Berlin, he had moved to Dessau and become one of the leaders of its small, pious community.

Mendel and his Bela were loving parents and devout Jews, but their son was ready for more advanced talmudic studies, and traveling to another place to be with the right teacher was an accepted practice. A shy, slight, somewhat hunchbacked boy, only fourteen years old, Moses arrived a few days later at one of the Berlin city gates through which Jews were allowed to pass.[7] There he was critically questioned by a municipal official and by Löbel Spier, the Jewish gatekeeper whose duty it was to keep out illegals and undesirables, and who eventually issued him his official pass.[8] The new arrival signed his name as Moses mi-Dessau (Moses of Dessau) but soon began to call himself Moses Mendelssohn. He would never again live in any other place, dying in Berlin in 1786, the same year as the king.

When Moses first passed through the Jew gate of Berlin, it was inconceivable that any Jew, and certainly not this insignificant young student of the Talmud who hardly spoke German and was admitted on sufferance, would in his lifetime achieve great renown and universal respect, not only as the driving force for the legal emancipation of Prussia's Jews but also as a celebrated secular philosopher and master of the German language. Neither Christian nor Jew could in the 1740s envisage a Jew in this way, and least of all could Moses Mendelssohn have foreseen the role he was destined to play.

According to one of the many lists prepared at the time he came to the capital city, there were then 335 Jewish families living there, comprising precisely 1,945 persons—a lot more, to the king's great frustration, than the 120 families stipulated a few years earlier. It was the largest Jewish community in Prussia, highly stratified and organized according to wealth and status in line with the elaborate regimentation and classification system that the authorities had imposed. In the subsequent 1750 *Generalreglement,* the formal codification actually recognized six distinct Jewish classes: On top, a handful of "generally privileged" Jews, with rights somewhat akin to Christians; next, a group of ordinary *Schutzjuden* (Protected Jews), allowed permanent residence but with limited mobility and heavily circumscribed rights to pass the coveted status on to their children; and a third "extraordinary" group who had rights of residence only in their own lifetime, and only for themselves. Below these were the three least privileged classes, into which Mendelssohn was automatically placed. They were the merely "tolerated" ones—teachers, community retainers, and servants, who could neither marry nor engage in outside business and who were entitled to stay only as long as needed and employed.

"Worthy of a cannibal," Mirabeau had called Frederick's law, which was so onerous and restrictive that the Jews had requested that it not be made public, lest it undermine their ability to trade and to maintain their international credit. The rules remained the legal basis for Jewish life in Prussia for more than sixty years.

The Jews never ceased to beg for relief; eventually a coalition of Christians and Jews would argue for the law's total abolition, and no one would influence their thinking more than the young Moses from Dessau. But that only came a generation later, when a political and social revolution had swept Europe. When Moses arrived in Berlin, real change and true legal emancipation were unimaginable and the focus was, at best, on easing the most onerous aspects of the restrictions.

For the moment, it looked as if the rigidly oppressive conditions under which the Jews had been allowed to live in Prussia for a hundred years would persist forever. Circumstances, if anything, seemed to be getting worse. The future looked decidedly unpromising and any significant change for the better appeared out of the question. Yet, in fact, the tough days of the 1740s and '50s were the proverbial darkness before the dawn, the low point from which in a single generation a rapid process of fundamental change would totally transform the Jewish situation.

No one at the time saw the signs. Practically everywhere in Europe, Jews were still prisoners of their medieval bondage. True, Parliament in London had just voted that in the American colonies (but not in England itself) Jews were to be granted citizenship rights after seven years, and in Denmark and the Netherlands they were also relatively free. But these were the exceptions, and Berlin's Jews consoled themselves that even with all their troubles, they were not as badly off as most coreligionists elsewhere. In White Russia and the Ukraine, Jews were being killed and driven out by the thousands. In Poland, gangs of rioting Cossacks and peasants, the *Haidamacks,* were on a perpetual rampage, and ritual trials were still common. Jews were without any civil rights in France or in Austria, and in Italy they were confined to the old ghetto of Venice and to the one in Rome, which was worse yet. In Spain no Jews were allowed at all, and as late as 1739 in Portugal, they were still burned at the stake as apostates.

Berlin's Jews knew all that, and although their troubles were many, they preferred to count their limited blessings. While heavily restricted and taxed to the hilt, at least they were safe from pogroms and mobs in Frederick's stern and orderly Prussia and could live in the old way, piously turned inward and submitting to their fate. In the year before Moses arrived, they had inaugurated a *Beth Hamidrash*—an advanced talmudic school—which was attracting students from near and far, and it was there that Moses continued his education.

As was the custom, his education in Dessau had begun at the age of five—in Berlin, in fact, boys started even earlier, at age three. Soon after Passover, a father would accompany his young offspring to school, the teacher would place him on his lap, and the first lesson would begin—reciting the Hebrew alphabet, first in regular fashion and then backward. Next, the child would be taught the first two verses of Leviticus, and when it had been mastered, he would be offered some honey smeared on the letters of the page, to be licked as a sweet reward. In subsequent years, there were daily classes from morning till evening, and more rewards for good and diligent study. Parents took the responsibility for their sons' education seriously, at least until age fourteen. Illiteracy was a shame, and quite rare.

The old practices and spirit of piety, narrowly focused and strictly limited to religious subjects, still prevailed. Secular knowledge was off limits. The rabbis, fearing the outside world, did not allow it. "No man is entitled to sit at two tables, the one Jewish and the other secular," one of them had written, warning that "the wisdom of the Torah and that of [secular] philosophy are different" and insisting that Jews "stay away from the study of philosophy; any of its ancient or later interpretations are forbidden."[9] Even the owning and reading of "foreign" books was disallowed. Punishment of violators could be severe, including, in some cases, banishment from the community.[10]

It was in this traditional, narrow, and unpromising environment that Moses settled upon his arrival. The Jews were worried by Frederick's antagonisms and unpredictability, and there was no evidence that these would soon be eased. They continued to live clustered together in Sankt Nikolai parish, in the heart of old Berlin. It was not a ghetto in the medieval sense, and there were Christians and Christian churches in their midst, but most Jews lived in close proximity, in the Spandauer and the Klosterstrasse and in the various alleyways coming together at the nearby Molkenmarkt.

Nearby, in the Heyderreuthergasse, was the synagogue where the Jews prayed. The temple was the center of community life, an imposing structure that some considered the finest anywhere. Inside its main door the Jews had proudly affixed a plaque to commemorate the royal visit at the time of inauguration in 1718.

Tightly tied to the old ways and traditions, the young Moses could hardly have detected any signs of economic or social changes to come. A handful of young Jews were beginning to resent the intellectual restrictions and to look with interest at the world around them. One or two had been admitted to universities to study medicine, though the rabbis had warned against it. Moses Mendelssohn was himself a most unusual young man, a devout and committed Jew but nevertheless determined to move beyond purely Jewish knowledge, and he began to do so soon after he arrived. In the 1740s he taught himself German, French, English, and Latin; somewhat later, he learned Greek as well. This led him to discover great philosophers and theologians, such as Hume and Locke, also Spinoza, and the Germans Leibniz, Reinbeck, and Christian von Wolf.

Thereafter, there was no holding him back. Within a decade, encouraged by a few well-placed Jewish patrons who saw his brilliance, among them Isaac Bernhard, a silk merchant who employed him as his children's private tutor, he began to write—in German—thus to come to the attention of the outside world and to establish friendships with prominent non-Jewish Germans, especially Gotthold Lessing, the dramatist, and Friedrich Nikolai, a publisher and bookseller.

Only a little more than a decade after his arrival, young Moses Mendelssohn began to emerge as an eloquent spokesman for change and for a new relationship between Germans and Jews. Eventually, he became a great German philosopher, poet, and thinker in his own right. When he died, Goethe would say of him that "we have lost one of our [*sic*] worthiest men."

Moses Mendelssohn and his Christian friends provided the intellectual fuel for fresh thinking by a new generation of Christians and Jews about the place of the disenfranchised Jewish minority in German society. The confluence of their ideas with historical changes in Europe and elsewhere would be the true key to the important changes to come.

Paradoxically, Frederick's wars would also play a vital role. In 1756, Maria Theresa, still bent on revenge, moved to reverse the course of events that had cost her Silesia. To forestall her, Frederick invaded her ally Saxony and again marched off to a war lasting seven long and painful years. Now he needed the Jews—at least a few of them—in ways he had not anticipated. Once more principle gave way to expediency, and the Jews would soon have new opportunities and be transformed in ways that no one had foreseen.

5

In his youth his name was Mordecai Loeb Cohen. Later he changed it to
Markus Levin, though when and why remains as uncertain as much else in
his early life, including his first two marriages and the children he is said
to have fathered from them. With his new, more German name, however,
Rahel's father Markus reflects the changing character of Germany's Jews
during Moses Mendelssohn's time.

The few accounts we have of him are of a colorful figure, shadowy and
slightly mysterious, the kind of man who generates anecdotes but few hard
facts. Perhaps the rumors about his early years, roaming the land outside
the law—and of having been branded for it—are mere legend. What is
fairly certain, however, is that he began life poor and without permanent
rights in Prussia. Un-German and unassimilated, he was then one of the
many Jewish traders on the move from place to place in search of their
lucky break. His language was Yiddish, which he continued to speak at
home throughout his life. Beyond the usual smattering of Hebrew and talmudic studies, he had grown up devoid of any formal education.

One is reminded of Jost Liebmann. Like him, Markus Levin was a man
of high intelligence and great personal strength, tough and unrelenting, a
sharp businessman—sometimes excessively so—and one who, with hard
work and good luck, had established the foundation of his later wealth as
a supplier of gems to the court of Charles of Lorraine in Brussels. Around
1740, when Frederick claimed first the Prussian throne and then Silesia and
young Moses of Dessau presented himself at Berlin's town gate, Markus was
reported augmenting his capital with, among other things, trading in
money and jewels at the Leipzig Fair.

A quarter century later, much had changed for the erstwhile tormentor
of Maria Theresa, as well as for the young student of the Talmud and the
roving Jew with the reputed mark of shame branded on his buttock. The
king had become a devoted champion of peace, Europe's hardest working
monarch and an occasional poet of dubious talent; young Moses had won
fame as an erudite philosopher; and Markus cut a wide swath in postwar
Berlin as a vain and unconventional Jew of means, one of the new breed of
"arrived" businessmen who had prospered during the war and now mixed
with the rising bourgeoisie in Frederick's vastly changed postwar Prussia.

The transformation was greater for the branded Jew than for the greatest of all Prussians. Frederick was back at Sans Souci, tending his dogs, entertaining his friends, and issuing floods of orders, now building up and developing his country rather than making war. But for Markus Levin, entirely new vistas had opened up. Having greatly augmented his wealth during the war and become a Protected Jew, he was no longer content to live apart from the wider world around him. He preferred theatregoing and the company of actors to the traditional confining Jewish ambiance of rabbis and talmudic scholars. He had shaved his beard and in appearance he was hard to distinguish from a Christian. Dressed in his fancy clothes, walking stick in hand and head held high, his erect stride and self-confident air exuded satisfaction with himself and his status—and a determination that the world know it.

Chaie, a girl from a traditional family of country Jews in the little Brandenburg town of Zehdenick, was his third wife. For a while it seemed that there might be no progeny from their union, but after several miscarriages, the first child was born on May 19, 1771, the Monday of Pentecost. Markus and Chaie named her Rahel.

They lived at No. 26 Spandauerstrasse, at the corner of Königstrasse. The spell having been broken, several more children followed—a year after Rahel, Mordechai, who (like his father) changed his name to Markus; next Liepmann, who later called himself Ludwig; Rose, another daughter; and just five years before their father's death, the youngest boy, Meyer, who eventually chose the more German-sounding name of Moritz.

Rahel would later lament that her childhood had not been a happy one. Chaie was a weak woman given to bouts of melancholy and incapable of providing much support for the children, let alone her precocious eldest daughter. Her father remained old-fashioned in family matters; he ruled with an iron hand and was a hard man to love. Long after his death, Rahel would describe him as a despot pure and simple, "a rough, strict, violent, moody, brilliant father, virtually mad." He had, she said, practically broken her heart and deprived her of any independent will to act[11]—a considerable exaggeration, as we shall see.

The house at Spandauerstrasse stood in the middle of the Sankt Nikolai district of old Berlin where most Jews had always lived. The Berlin of Rahel's childhood and youth was, however, much changed from the town to which Moses Mendelssohn had sought admission a scant generation ago. Back then, Frederick had hectored his officials to keep the Jews in tight check, granted few of them the coveted privileges, and embarked on years of conquest and war.

Meanwhile, Berlin had twice been occupied by foreign troops and more than once Prussia's fate had hung by a thread. Miraculously, the king had finally prevailed, but postwar Prussia was evolving in a world on the eve of revolution and in the grip of fundamental change. In an environment where nothing was standing still, the situation of the Jews had also been greatly altered. During the years of war, for one thing, the king had found it convenient to become a bit more lenient in granting letters of protection, and many Jews were now better off, and a few had become fabulously rich.

Frederick's expensive wars had nearly bankrupted the country; the Seven Years' War alone cost a staggering 130 million taler. Even with his father's cash hoards, heavy taxes, and substantial subsidies from his English allies, there had still been a large shortfall in the financing of his incessant needs. To close it he had taken the easy way out and chosen the time-honored method of governments that spend more than they can borrow or tax. In the modern world, it involves running the printing presses; in Frederick's pre-paper-money day it entailed minting more coin and reducing the precious metal contained in each. The effect in both cases is the same: ruinous inflation, rapidly rising prices for basic foodstuffs, and hardship and grumbling among a citizenry burdened by oppressive taxes. Prussia's fate was no different.

Once he decided to finance the war on the backs of the people, Frederick was understandably anxious to deflect public discontent and let others take the blame. The best way, he shrewdly concluded, was to turn over his six mints to private leaseholders and shift to them the responsibility—and the onus—for the cheapened coin.

His officials had advised against it, but His Royal Majesty had insisted. For the lessee, who had to find the metal and mint it at a fixed price, it would be a highly risky and dangerous business, never far from bankruptcy and disaster. But there was also potential for great profit if one was blessed with luck and knew how to maneuver with daring and skill. The more coins the leaseholder was asked to churn out and the cleverer he was in buying the metal and doing the job, the richer he might become. The greater also the people's envy and blame for the rising prices. For the king it was quite an acceptable arrangement.

One problem remained. Christian bankers had neither the capital nor the international connections to find the metal, let alone the stomach to take on the personal and financial risks involved. What better candidates, then—and what more convenient lightning rods—than his rich Jews? The obvious solution was to enlist their help in exchange for granting some of them new privileges—while ensuring, of course, that his officials continue to limit and keep out the rest.

Veitel Heine Ephraim, an old favorite whom Frederick had chosen as his Court Jeweler when still the Crown Prince, and whom he would later install as Chief Elder of Berlin's Jews, was appointed one of the leaseholders. Other wealthy Jewish bankers were also chosen. Daniel Itzig, Hertz Moses Gompertz, and Moses Isaak were Frederick's "Mint Jews." They ran the mints during the long years of the war, often advanced him needed funds, and skillfully fed his incessant financial appetite even when disaster seemed imminent and defeat near at hand. In the process, they all became very wealthy without, however, enriching their reputations. Quite to the contrary, one of the king's most hated coins the people had taken to calling the "Ephraimit," and all manner of unflattering stories and nasty rumors about the leaseholders' chicanery and illicit enrichment had circulated widely among the people.

There were others, of course—Christians included—who had profited from the wartime economy, and for other Jews some of the new talers had trickled down as well. Subagents had been installed in some of the mints, which is how Markus Levin had been able to accumulate considerable wealth. Smaller bankers, money merchants, and war suppliers had done good business, and a network of Jewish "retailers" had roamed far beyond Prussia's borders, busily buying up old coin for melting and reissue at the mints. In the process, some of the lucky ones were granted letters of protection, and Markus had been able to claim his in 1762.

Thus the war became a turning point for Prussia's Jews, and Frederick's policies in the ensuing years of peace provided yet further opportunities for them. A new class of businessmen had arisen during the war and was expanding in peace, and with them came a changed outlook and attitude toward the attractions of secular life.

In 1763, the king returned to Berlin, gaunt, aged, and tortured with gout, a wiser and greatly sobered king. A hundred and thirty thousand Prussian soldiers had been lost in the war, and almost as many Austrians. Inflation, misery, and outright starvation were widespread in the country. The price of grain had more than trebled, and in Berlin the traditional loaf of bread, the *Groschenbrot,* had shrunk to a third of its prewar size. As winter approached, almost a third of Berlin's population of one hundred thousand was certified as destitute, and free bread had to be distributed to them to prevent imminent hunger riots.[12] The country was virtually bankrupt, and the people were as tired and exhausted as their sovereign.

Once again, Frederick made another of his complete turnabouts. Henceforth, he would no longer be the terror of Europe and the instigator of wars but the staunch champion of peace; no longer bent on battlefield glory but tirelessly in pursuit of Prussia's rehabilitation and of what he called *rétablissement*—the development of his greatly enlarged realm; expansion of its manufacturing, trading, and financial strength; and reform of education, the law, and the functioning of the society in general. Soon his subjects found themselves thrust into an environment of restless activity, goaded and commanded by their self-styled "First Servant of the State," who trusted no one, demanded to know everything, and insisted on making all decisions himself. Rising before 5 A.M. each morning and laboring till late at night, he remained *toujours en vedette* (always at the center of the action), as he once put it to his friend the Marquis d'Argens.

He held all strings in his hands. After his death, even a small part of the flood of his cabinet orders would fill forty-four volumes, plus twelve more volumes of the *Acta Borussia,* a compilation of official documents. A cynic who did not trust people, he had few close relationships, considered his whippet hounds his best friends, and asked that he be buried with them at Sans Souci when he died.[13]

Frederick discouraged individual initiative, demanded total obedience of his ministers and bureaucrats, and insisted on stern discipline. The Prussia he created became ever more a military and police state, but one where in an odd way sternness and laxity were allowed to exist side by side. Orders had to be obeyed blindly, corruption was punished severely, and military discipline remained harsh. Disobedient soldiers and deserters were still subject to the barbaric custom of "running the gauntlet," where they were beaten half to death. Ever the eccentric, he often personally attended these bloody spectacles, but he could cry bitter tears at the deaths of his mother and sister. Nor did he—as was happening elsewhere—eliminate serfdom or infringe on the privileges of the nobility. Yet he forbade censorship, allowed dozens of new newspapers to flourish, loosened the hold of religion on his people, promoted science and music and arts, and even tolerated carousing and widespread whoring in his capital city.

Prussia remained an agricultural country, the largest in what was still a loose federation of German states with a multiplicity of princes and courts. By the 1770s, however, Frederick had succeeded in making it the fourth biggest manufacturing nation in the world, and for this he found it once again to his advantage to enlist his Jews.

In the context of a world in flux, *Fredericus Rex,* enlightened despot and reformer, was a transitional figure standing between the old and the new, between eighteenth-century absolutism and nineteenth-century democracy. He presided over fundamental changes in the economic, political, cultural, and social lives of his people, and by the end of his reign, he had created new environments in every sphere of public life—in religion, art, music, industry, and in all manner of new ideas. Though he may not have intended it, the last two decades of his reign saw the emergence of a rising bourgeoisie and of a somewhat more open, if not yet democratic, society. Unwittingly, this autocratic king had been the pathbreaker for the rise of more bourgeois power.

6

Frederick's later years were the years of Rahel's childhood. Growing up was difficult for her, and looking back on the early years she once sighed that "no one could have experienced a more tortured (*gepeinigte*) youth." From the beginning, her health had been precarious. As an infant, she spent her first weeks in a carton, swaddled in blankets, so tiny that her survival was in doubt. All her life, in fact, she remained sickly, easy prey to infections, with periodic attacks of "weakness" and, in later years, plagued by all manner of real and imagined afflictions.

Young Rahel was slight and unprepossessing. She was a small girl with tiny hands and feet, a largish head on a small body and an oddly shaped face with a disproportionate chin, but dark, penetrating, and curious eyes. "A superior head on an inferior body," her close friend David Veit said. Under the thumb of her arbitrary father and a mother who provided little comfort, the hypersensitive Rahel was often unhappy, much given to suffering and self-pity, dissatisfied with her appearance, and resentful of the limitations of her life as a Jewish girl growing up in late eighteenth-century Berlin. It was evident from her earliest years that she was highly intelligent and unusually precocious. Years later, her husband would relate the story of how, at the tender age of twelve, she had become so preoccupied with serious philosophical thoughts about God and the immortality of the human soul that she once fainted dead away at the dinner table when suddenly overcome by doubts.

She had no formal education at all. Much to the discomfort of the rabbis and traditionalists, the first Jewish *Freischule,* where secular subjects other than Hebrew and the Talmud were taught, had opened its doors in 1778. It was, however, a school for boys only. In the Prussia of the 1770s and early '80s, female education was hardly the vogue.

The first girls' school, for Christians only, came into being in 1786; for Jewish girls there were none until twenty years later. Educating daughters in any formal sense had not been customary for Jews, although here and there a few of the most advanced and free-thinking were now pioneering a more progressive approach. The rich Daniel Itzig, who had both the requisite wealth and number of in-house students at his disposal—Madame Itzig having presented him with sixteen offspring in twenty years—had taken the unusual step of establishing a modern educational facility right in his own home, where private tutors instructed not only his sons but also his numerous daughters in German, French, history, music, and other nontraditional fields. Recha, Güttchen, and Lea, the three youngest of the many Itzig daughters, were Rahel's contemporaries. She must have envied them for their exposure to the wider world of knowledge.

Markus, however, was not as progressive, and he considered a formal education for his daughter quite unnecessary. At a time when the walls of the closed Jewish world were gradually crumbling and exposure to secular thought and contacts with Christians were becoming more common in her father's circle of friends, Rahel and her young Jewish contemporaries grew up as if "members of a savage tribe," as one of her later biographers described it.[14] Uninterested and ignorant of Jewish learning, she was equally unschooled; but she was irrepressibly curious about the secular world and impatient at the limits her circumstances placed on her personal and intellectual freedom to be a part of that world.

This lack of formal schooling always rankled Rahel and remained one of her frustrations. It is why she was later apt to deprecate herself as an "ignoramus" and to lament that "I was taught nothing." In fact, her sharp mind and thirst to know and to understand, along with a lifetime of voracious reading and listening, resulted in a remarkable self-education, even if some gaps remained. Jew-German, written in Hebrew letters, was her first language. That is surely why the many volumes of her diaries and the thousands of letters to her friends are composed in the sometimes faulty, poorly spelled peculiar German-French mixture she had taught herself. Perhaps it is also why she chose not to publish her writings but instead sought to make her mark as a literary hostess and social catalyst.[15]

There was much to see and learn in the Berlin of Rahel's childhood, and it thrilled her when her father, decked out in all his finery and looking more like a Christian than a Jew, would allow her and the younger Markus to accompany him on his walks past the city's sights and landmarks.[16]

Around the corner from their house, along the river and near the *école militaire* at Burgstrasse 25, they would pass Daniel Itzig's imposing mansion. A generation earlier, Itzig père had started out selling horses and cattle to the army, and when in 1748 his son, Daniel, had married the fruitful Miriam (as it happens she was the daughter of the same Benjamin Elias Wulff whose cousin had wed Moses Mendelssohn) he was still of modest means, his great fortune having been made during the war years as one of the king's mint leaseholders.

In 1761 Daniel Itzig had been given Christian rights, and now he lived like one, only better. To build the Palais Itzig, he had bought the main structure from a Prussian nobleman, added four adjacent houses to it, and engaged a distinguished architect who labored several years to combine them and to create an impressive facade. The mansion, set in a decorative garden with fountain, boasted the luxurious rarity of a bath, many fine paintings, and even a small synagogue for private use.

After the war, Itzig had acceded to the king's wishes and invested some of his wealth in a range of manufacturing enterprises—a tin factory, one for leather products, a plant to produce vegetable oils, and an iron works in the Harz Mountains. The companies owed their existence more to royal pressure than business opportunity, and none were destined for great success or lasting fame. But this was not the case when it came to Itzig's substantial real estate holdings—particularly one outside the city gates, a small estate and dairy that bore the name of the Prussian minister von Bartholdy, from whose family the property had been bought. Years after his death, Daniel's granddaughter, Lea, would marry one of Moses Mendelssohn's sons, and Felix, their offspring, a baptized Christian with Bartholdy added to his name, would make it famous as a composer of some of the nineteenth century's finest church music. One wonders what Daniel Itzig, a leader of the Prussian Jewish aristocracy whom many called the Prince of the Jews, would have thought of it.

Itzig's was not the only imposing residence the Levins might pass. Across the Molkenmarkt past the city hall, they would have come upon another of Berlin's most elegant homes, famous for its unusual interior staircase, cleverly lit with a lantern hidden above it. Moses Isaak, Itzig's partner, had bought it from a royal minister, and now his heirs lived there. Like his erstwhile partner, Moses had acquired great wartime wealth, and when he died, his estate was valued at a solid three-quarters of a million taler. He had begun as a lowly moneylender, but after the war he called himself "banquier" and sought to enhance his reputation with generosity and good deeds to Jews and Christians alike.

The most sumptuous of all the mansions of the newly rich Jews, however, was the one they called the Ephraim Palais. Old Veitel Ephraim, now deceased, had commissioned the building just after the king had granted him Christian rights in 1761, and there was nothing remotely like it anywhere else in Berlin. The place was occupied by Veitel's sons and had become a major tourist attraction. Visitors and locals came to stare at the elegant Corinthian columns supporting a balcony adorned with an intricate wrought-iron railing. Inside, Veitel had built himself a unique "Chinese" room, decorated his other chambers with exotic hand-painted paneling, and constructed a winding staircase made of precious wood.

Veitel's grandfather had been among the first fifty Viennese families allowed to settle in Brandenburg, but as recently as the 1730s, the Ephraims had still been so strapped financially that their annual payments to the community had amounted to less than one taler—17 groschen and six pfennig, to be precise.[17] Veitel's wife, Elke, brought a substantial dowry with her, but the real basis for his business success and wealth had been the good luck that Frederick had quite early taken a liking to him and made him his Court Jeweler while still at *Schloss* Rheinsberg. During the king's wars, no one had been more daring or more fiercely competitive in the minting business than Veitel Ephraim—and none of the Jewish leaseholders, it must be said, had earned themselves more envy and animosity from the people. On the other hand, after Veitel died, Voltaire, perhaps impressed by the aura of wealth and Veitel's power and success, effusively likened his virtues to those of Moses and Solomon combined ("Il était plus sage que Moïse et avait plus d'esprit que Salomon").[18]

In their meanderings, Markus Levin and his children would probably have turned toward Berlin's most beautiful thoroughfares. One of these was a broad avenue for riders and pedestrians, where four rows of linden trees lined a central path that Berliners called Unter den Linden; the other was the equally handsome Leipzigerstrasse. Strolling there in the leisure hours to take in the sights and sounds of Frederick's reconstructed Berlin, they would have encountered growing numbers of Jews who, decked out in their finery, mingled with aristocrats, visitors, and the city's bourgeoisie *en promenade*. Among them might well have been a rising young entrepreneur with his daughter Malka and her three sisters.

Malka's father, Liebmann Meyer Wulff, had been too young for the minting business during the war, but he liked the "big deal," had a sharp eye for it, and was rapidly enhancing his wealth. Some day he would be the richest man in the capital and Berliners would call him their Croesus. Malka, by then, would be the respected Madame Amalie Beer, married to a great-great-grandson of Jost's daughter Hindchen,[19] and mother of famous sons—one a promising poet and the other Prussia's most acclaimed composer of grand opera, the first Jew to bear the title of *Hofkapellmeister* (Court Conductor).

Unter den Linden was now Berlin's most impressive avenue and the king had spared nothing to embellish it. Early in the 1770s, he had peremptorily ordered forty-four unsightly old houses razed to the ground and replaced with more stately ones. Visitors frequently remarked on the sumptuous architecture of the new buildings. The Lustgarten and Royal Opera Square at one end of the avenue and the vast forestlike park known as the Tiergarten at the other were the favorite destinations of promenading Berliners, among which large numbers of well-dressed Jews could be observed.

Markus and his friends liked the opera and were enthusiastic participants in Berlin's theatre life, and he must have enjoyed showing his children the impressive Opera House. Frederick had ordered it built in the 1740s, with the Royal Library next to it, his brother Henry's palace across the square, and the *Zeughaus,* Prussia's largest armory, nearby. During his father's time, in an atmosphere dominated by pietist theologians, the theatre, playwrights, and actors and actresses had been regarded with suspicion and deemed frivolous and morally suspect. Now that had greatly changed.

Plays had previously been performed in French only, presented at the Comédie Française on the Monbijouplatz. Theatre spoken in German hardly existed at all, and what there was had been mostly harlequinades, buffoonery, and burlesques. With enlightenment, however, came a flowering of the German language, and now Berlin had a new theatre dedicated to German plays, the Teutsche Kommödie. To great acclaim, Döbbelin, the director, had shown Lessing's *Minna von Barnhelm* there, delighting audiences by poking fun at Prussianisms; his *Emilia Galotti,* condemning aristocratic privilege and praising new bourgeois values, had been equally popular. Goethe's *Götz von Berlichingen,* repeatedly roused audiences to "stormy" applause—though the king, who liked nothing much unless it was French, had seen fit to denigrate it as "bad imitation of Shakespearean platitudes." Frederick, it appeared, cared for the German Goethe no more than he did for the English Shakespeare. Later, in 1783–84, Schiller's *Die Räuber, Fiesca,* and *Kabbale der Liebe,* with the great actor Fleck in the lead, had also been well received.[20]

Markus and his circle liked to give dinners attended by prominent theatre people whose relationships with the Jews not only reflected affinities but also served a mutual self-interest. Jews and theatre folk, for one, both remained society's outsiders and the *soirées* were, for both sides, occasions to mix with the higher gentile circles. The Jewish men were dazzled by the actresses and liked to flirt or pursue more intimate connections with them. The perennially impecunious actors and actresses, for their part, enjoyed the style, culture, and wit of the Jews, but also their wealth and willingness to spend liberally or to make personal loans to them on favorable terms.

Rahel, exposed from a young age to her father's hospitality and theatre connections, was fascinated by this window to the outside world. Markus, in turn—however he otherwise tormented her—grew to appreciate her "wit," insight, and gift for the clever remark and saw that his young daughter's presence at his soirées was an asset welcomed by the invitees. For Rahel, it was a first experience with the possibilities of a literary and social salon.

7

Berlin's vast parklike forest, the Tiergarten, was the other destination of choice for excursion-minded Berliners. On weekends, the city gatekeeper would be on permanent alert for well-dressed families wishing to pass into its greenery beyond the end of Unter den Linden. Lifting the barrier, and his cap, he would pocket the customary tip, and the strollers and picnickers would continue on their way into their favorite forest.

For the better-class Christians, *déjeuners* and coffee parties at Tarone's establishment in the Tiergarten were quite the thing. For Jews, that was not an option, since few were as yet ready to breach the deeply ingrained taboos of their dietary laws. Yet the children wanted their cakes, and Markus, like all Berliners who could afford it, was equally intent on his *Kaffee*.

Coffee had only recently been introduced in Prussia, the king having had much less difficulty in that instance than he had encountered in persuading farmers to grow that strange, novel "apple of the earth," the potato, and in getting the public to accept it as a staple alongside their beloved bread. His father had been so exasperated with the resistance to potatoes that he had threatened to cut off the ears and nose of any farmer failing to comply. Acceptance of the new tropical brew had been quite another story. It quickly became a fashionable luxury beverage and the king derived substantial revenue by tightly controlling the rights to roast the beans. *Le tout* Berlin was thrilled to pay the price and to drink up.

Markus's special treat was a five-groschen trip home by horse-drawn carriage—the tariff for these taxis, like virtually everything else in bureaucratic Prussia, being clearly fixed for every destination—with a final stop for refreshments at Philip Falk's restaurant and *Kaffeehaus* in the old city, the only kosher eatery in Berlin.[21] Thereafter, returning from a more carefree day than Markus might, in his youth, have dreamed possible for a Jew, they would pass one more place worthy of note.

The house, with its small garden, at Spandauerstrasse 68, was far from splendid, but it was one of the most respected, and passersby stared at it fully as much as they did at the palaces of Ephraim and Itzig. In 1748, Lessing had lived there, and in the 1750s Nikolai, the famous bookseller and protagonist of German enlightenment, had made it his home. Now Moses Mendelssohn was the resident. He was Prussia's best known and most respected Jew, and the man whom even in France they called, with great deference, *"le juif de Berlin."* In the forty years since he had been admitted to Berlin on sufferance, he had advanced to be one of the most erudite German-language philosophers of the enlightenment and a cultured spokesman for German Jewry, blending the heritage of his people with the philosophy of the age.

Mendelssohn began as a private tutor in the home of Isaak Bernhard; later he had entered Bernhard's business and eventually had risen to manage the entire enterprise. In 1754, over a game of chess, he had met the German dramatist Lessing, and the two developed a close lifetime friendship. Soon after they first met, the German had been so impressed by the humanity, wisdom, and intellect of his hunchbacked Jewish chess partner that he had, without the latter's knowledge, arranged for the publication of one of his early philosophical essays, *On Chance Happenings.* In a way, Lessing had anticipated Moses Mendelssohn by writing, even before the two had met, *Die Juden,* a play in which he had done the hitherto unheardof and portrayed the principal Jewish character in a highly favorable light. In a later play, *Nathan der Weise* (Nathan the Wise), he modeled the equally admirable main protagonist after Moses Mendelssohn himself.

Just how revolutionary Lessing's picture of a Jew had struck many is illustrated in the critique of the earlier work by the Christian theologian David Michaelis, who protested that it was, in effect, simply unbelievable and not true to life: No Jew could be that virtuous! Commenting on this review, Moses had minced few words in a public rejoinder. Is it not a "humiliation and . . . impudence" he had asked, "to deny a whole nation the probability of being able to show a single honest man? A nation from which all prophets and the kings arose . . . ?"

In time, Mendelssohn had become famous as a secular philosopher; one of his major works, *Phaedon,* so impressed contemporaries that some had begun to call him a German Socrates. At the same time, he had also emerged as the principal spokesman for the view that Jews and Germans could coexist in harmony and with equal rights, and that it was time for them to do so. But he never wavered in his commitment to his religious faith. To build bridges, he had translated the Pentateuch into literate German, and his last great work, *Jerusalem,* was an eloquent defense and explanation of Judaism in its relation to the state. When the well-meaning Swiss theologian Johann Lavater challenged his beliefs and sought to convert him, Moses publicly rejected him with an emotional defense of his religion.

The seminal event during Mendelssohn's time, however, was the publication, in 1781, of Prussian State Councillor von Dohm's epochal treatise, *On the Civil Betterment of the Jews,* the starting point for the first serious debate about the position of Jews in Germany and a key event on the road to their eventual legal emancipation. No one was to have a greater impact on the substance of Dohm's ideas than Moses Mendelssohn, and no one would influence more profoundly the gradual evolution of Christian thinking about improving the status of German Jews.

As Rahel was growing up, these events were just beginning to unfold. Instead of a tiny handful of Court Jews, a growing number of upper- and middle-class merchants had taken their place, establishing the economic base for further advances and loosening their social isolation from the outside world. They were sober, hard-working professionals, proud of their accomplishments, more assimilated, more German in their culture and outlook and more in touch with Christians than any of their ancestors.

They still faced many injustices, but they were nevertheless proud to be in Prussia, proud to be "Frederick's Jews." Many were enthusiastic supporters of the enlightenment and hopeful that its values and evolving bourgeois society would facilitate their further progress. Most of them also looked favorably on the *Haskalah,* the particular form of Jewish enlightenment urged by Moses Mendelssohn to loosen stifling and exclusionary rab-

binical rules and talmudic restrictions and to open up Jewish minds to
greater involvement with secular ideas. Their children, Rahel among them,
were especially receptive and impatient to explore these new frontiers.

Yet it was still a bittersweet period, full of stress, ambiguities, and frustrations. In spite of changing outlooks and improved circumstances for some,
Jews remained Prussia's least-favored minority, still subject to the onerous
1750 rules, still heavily taxed, still restricted in number, and still unequal
in every respect. Internally, painful new rifts had opened up. There had
always been squabbles and petty jealousies, and the Berlin community had
never been particularly harmonious, but now the disquiet was greater
than ever.

In the transition from a ghetto existence to secular culture, bitter arguments had erupted between the rabbis, supported by traditionalists, and
the more assimilated community members no longer willing to follow their
lead. The rabbis were losing their grip and tensions ran high. For as long as
anyone could remember, they had enforced their old rules and sanctions
largely without outside interference. Now, as Prussia's legal system evolved
and matured, the king's officials interfered more often, imposing their own
ideas based on the legal reforms of their sovereign, who had never much
cared for the Jewish rules he liked to call "the Law of Hottentots."

Meanwhile Frederick, though more tolerant of rich Jews than before,
never wavered in his fundamentally negative attitude nor did he allow
his officials much leeway. Unmoved by Dohm's treatise, he dismissed it
blandly with the comment that "more could not have been expected." He
summoned Mendelssohn to Sans Souci, but chose to absent himself and to
let one of his aristocrats see him, and when the Royal Academy voted to
make the Jewish philosopher a member, he vetoed the decision.

The king's basic policy—squeeze the wealthy and keep out the rest—
remained in effect. Jews still had to pay assessments on every conceivable
occasion: for births, weddings and funerals, fees for recruits and for fire-
fighters, a body tax when crossing borders, calendar taxes, and the annual
payments for their protection in general. Virtually no one was exempt.
Mendelssohn too was forced to pay the body tax when he traveled to Dresden; allegedly the payment was recorded, alongside the rest of the day's
collections, for the transit of assorted merchandise—including "one Jew
and one ox." As late as 1769, Frederick actually introduced a particularly

nettlesome and disliked additional contribution, announcing that he had "graciously resolved" that Jews receiving protection or wishing to buy a home would henceforth be obligated to purchase specific quantities of porcelain from the struggling royal factory, one of his pet projects. Domestic resale of the overpriced product, even at a loss, was strictly forbidden, and exporting it proved well-nigh impossible.

And even as Markus Levin and his friends were at the theatre or taking their children on pleasant city walks, less fortunate Jews were still being turned away at the gate. In his diary, Solomon Maimon, an impoverished young Talmud scholar from Poland who later achieved fame as a profound commentator and critic of Kantian philosophy, recorded the bitter experience of being expelled from Berlin in 1779 by the Jewish gatekeepers and of falling, weeping, on the ground before them.[22]

Rahel grew up among these contradictions, this mix of the old and the new. Frederick's Prussia was exciting and full of intellectual ferment, and she wanted desperately to be a part of it. There was progress and there was hope, but most of the traditional barriers remained, and she felt them keenly. She would, in fact, continue to feel and suffer from them throughout her entire life.

8

Rahel considered having been born Jewish a *Falsche Geburt,* her misbegotten birth. It weighed on her as the heaviest burden of her life, and on her deathbed she still remembered it as "the thing that all my life seemed to me the greatest shame." In an early letter to David Veit, she lashed out against the "revolting, degrading, insulting, low environment that I cannot escape," and insisted that she would never accept "having been born a *schlemiel* [fool] . . . and a Jew!" Sometimes the shame of Jewishness stayed with her even when asleep. Once, she wrote Veit, she had dreamed that at her birth some extraterrestrial being had thrust a dagger into her heart, with the words, "Be a Jew!" Now, she wrote him, "my entire life is a slow bleeding to death." On other occasions, in a more philosophical mood, she would merely lament the inevitability of her fate, observing with resignation that she greatly disliked society's classes and could not accept their limitations, but that, alas, "one belongs to one anyway!"

Her father had built a solid financial foundation, introduced his children to gentile clients and friends, broadened their education beyond strictly Jewish learning, and given them a taste of the secular world. Predictably, it had disconnected Rahel and her contemporaries from their Jewishness, and now their entire lives became one long struggle to be accepted and to take root in that other world they had come to crave.

When Markus died in 1791, Rahel, freed of his petty tyrannies and fascinated by outside society, was determined to "invent" her own life and thrust herself into the effort with much youthful enthusiasm, optimism, and hope. Under the impact of what was happening throughout the world, there was *Aufbruchstimmung* in Berlin—a mood among the avant-garde of upheaval and change. Court life, under Frederick's successors, was decidedly dull. The young intelligentsia, fascinated with liberal ideas, thought it fashionable to cross social lines to meet like-minded souls in unusual settings. What united the young literati, scholars, aristocrats, actors and actresses, dilettantes, officers, and rising bureaucrats was their restlessness and impatience with the sterile past and a desire to experiment with the unconventional, and sometimes the outrageous. Daring ideas stimulated them, they liked or tolerated nonconformity and eccentricities in dress and demeanor, and they were eager for new forms of sociability and lifestyles outside established class-conscious society.

In former times, few aristocratic Christians would have been likely to know many Jews, let alone to be willing to meet them socially. But now they were intrigued by cultivated Jewish families whose salons beckoned with a stimulating environment, whose wealth and taste impressed them, who patronized the arts, who had a love for literature and learning, and who shared their interests in unconventional ideas, intellectual gossip, and the latest books.

Suddenly, the mixed salon where Jews and gentiles mingled was "in," and Rahel was quick to recognize its possibilities as a bridge to the outside. At a time when self-development was the ideal, she too wanted to discover herself, taste what life had to offer, and escape the traditional limits and dependencies of family and status. The salon was the place where contacts with interesting people, including Christians, were made, where her inferior social standing would make no difference—where everyone was equal. Once she had written to David Veit, "Why don't they take me for what I am? I am always Rahel."[23] In the free atmosphere of the salon, perhaps this problem would disappear.

Her first experience with this kind of social life was her father's eclectic group of non-Jewish friends. She had also attended alluring affairs at the home of the respected physician and Kantian philosopher Markus Herz, presided over by Henriette, his much younger wife. Henriette, known for her beauty and grace, had first learned the art of the salon at her husband's affairs where scholars met for serious scientific and philosophical debates. But that was a bit above her head, and so she had eventually branched off on her own. Now she hosted a parallel salon, next to her husband's, where a younger crowd of Christians and Jews came together, attracted by the husband's distinction and his young wife's charm. Among others, they included the two Humboldt brothers, Alexander and Wilhelm; Count von Dohma, a senior Prussian official; Karl Gustav von Brinckmann, a Swedish diplomat; a charismatic preacher named Friedrich von Schleiermacher; and the brilliant young Friedrich von Schlegel, who enthused about Greek poetry and held the guests in thrall with his ideas about the mysteries of human development. It was an ever-changing, always interesting, and enchanting crowd, and even Mirabeau, visiting Berlin before his death in 1791, had put in an appearance.

It had not escaped Rahel's notice that other young Jewish women of her circle, with backgrounds and ambitions similar to hers, were attending these functions with considerable personal success. Moses Mendelssohn's eldest daughter, Brendel, who now called herself Dorothea, often could be encountered at the Herz affairs. She had been married off by her father at age fourteen. Now in her thirties, she was as determined as Rahel to break into the German cultural scene. Not many years later, she would leave her husband and her religion to marry the young Schlegel, ten years her junior. The granddaughters of Veitel Ephraim, Marianne Meyer and her sister Sara, did their own entertaining and were frequent guests at Henriette's. They had the good fortune to be both attractive and rich, a happy combination of assets that eventually led to marrying into the nobility and the exchange of their Jewish names for aristocratic ones.

What Rahel and these women had in common was their overwhelming desire for validation in the non-Jewish world. Moses Mendelssohn had said that a Jew deserved to be accepted as a valid human being. Though he maintained his own religion, he had held it as moral and proper to be accepted as an equal alongside Christians. These women, however, wanted to go further. They aspired not merely to acceptance next to Christians, not only to recognition of their individual worth, but to true assimilation into German culture and society. They had studied German and French, read the classics, Wieland and Schiller, Lessing and Fichte, and above all Goethe, whose words they had made their mantra and whose "Community of *Gleichgesinnte*"—the classless society of the like-minded—was their ideal. More than the Jewish men of their generation, perhaps because they did not have their businesses to absorb and fulfill them, it was the women who had the keenest sense of exclusion and who had grown unhappily impatient with their origins and the narrowness of Jewish life.

Yet Rahel's situation was different from the others in a number of ways. Henriette was beautiful, with an erudite husband who had opened doors for her; the Meyer women were attractive and rich; Dorothea's father was famous. The unmarried Rahel had no such assets. Small and unprepossessing, she was neither rich, nor beautiful nor backed by a powerful husband or father. As to money, with her eldest brother now head of the family and without resources of her own, she was entirely dependent on him for financial support.

What most distinguished Rahel from the others, however, was her remarkable personality—the "wit" she had inherited from her father, her own special warmth, empathy, and intellectual agility, her way with the piquant remark at the right time and her passionate, yet appealing *Schwärmerei,* a rapturous and impassioned enthusiasm about literature and the arts, and about her guests and their lives. This was her great asset and the key to her magnetic personality, which attracted leading lights to surround her and made her Jägerstrasse "garret" into Berlin's most important salon.

Karl Gustav von Brinckmann, the Swedish Secretary of Legation whom Rahel had met at Henriette's, was one of the first to climb the stairs at Jägerstrasse to take tea with her. The stairs were steep and the rooms small and narrow, but the Swede was entranced with his hostess. He was smooth, cultured, talkative, intelligent, and a bit of a dandy, but well connected in the Prussian aristocracy, and Rahel's rare personality greatly intrigued him. Though she often lamented her lack of formal schooling, she had, in fact, more than made up for it, having learned German, French, and some English. She was widely read, played the piano and the violin, and was up to date on the latest in literature and the theatre. Brinckmann especially admired her empathy, her listening abilities and conversational skills, and her readiness to delve into matters of personal psychology and innermost feelings. In time, others in his circle of friends began to accompany him up the same stairs, and Lise, Rahel's maid, began pouring tea for an ever-expanding circle, among which the earlier additions were von Burgsdorff, a Prussian *Junker,* and the flamboyant Countess Pachta.

By the mid-1790s, Rahel had progressed further in inventing a new existence for herself than she might have hoped. More and more aristocrats and intellectuals now regularly came to visit, drawn by the thrill of the unconventional setting, the intellectual piquancy of the gossipy conversation, and the serious talk amid the inevitable flirtations and affairs of the heart. Wilhelm von Humboldt and his wife Karoline were frequent guests, as was his brother Alexander, the scientist and explorer; they mingled with actors and actresses, adventurous young Jews, and Christian preachers and philosophers. Even Rahel's brothers were present on occasion, getting their taste of the social possibilities. Not many years later, her younger brother Liepmann would opt for baptism as the most direct step to assimilation—emerging in the process as Herr Ludwig Robert instead of Liepmann Levin.

Rahel loved and admired her guests, but most of all she reveled in her new freedom. In the summer, she accompanied the actress Friedericke von Unzelmann to the Bohemian spas where *le tout* Berlin took the waters. Back in the capital, she wrote to Veit, she had daringly gone for a carriage ride on the Sabbath "in broad daylight." An underlying ambivalence must still have been there, since she confessed to him in the same breath that she would have denied it, if anyone had seen her. Later she would refer to the '90s as "her best years." Yet they ended badly.

In the winter of 1795, she had met Count Karl von Finckenstein at the theatre and fallen in love with this "blond soul," while he, like others in her salon, had been smitten by her personality and charm. It was the beginning of a long, tortuous four-year "engagement." Rahel had struggled in an emotional back-and-forth to advance the relationship from engagement to marriage, and dreamed of becoming the Countess von Finckenstein. Her fiancé wavered and dallied, sent her sentimental letters, agonized, struggled—and never could quite marshal the courage to take the final step. He belonged to one of Brandenburg's oldest aristocratic families. In the salon, the Jew and the *Junker* had both been individuals, and it had all seemed so easy. Outside, once he was back at his family's estate, he remained a scion of Prussian *Junkers,* while she was still the Jew. Finckenstein lacked the strength to break through these barriers. Later it turned out that even those of his friends who were visitors to Rahel's salon had advised him against marrying her, some in the strongest terms. Individual relationships were one thing; bringing a Jew into their society was quite another matter—the crossing of an invisible line.

Deeply hurt, Rahel had abandoned the quest, and left for the cover of the anonymity of a foreigner in postrevolutionary Paris, where no one cared greatly whether this Prussian woman was Christian or Jew. She had suffered her first great setback, and she had left Berlin discouraged and defeated, full of world-weary disappointment, which, she wrote, had "turned her to stone." The illusion had been shattered that her feelings of exclusion and inferiority could permanently be resolved in her salon among aristocratic guests, and that she could win true acceptance in their world. It was the first time that she had been taught a lesson that would be repeated more than once in her life—that there were limits to the acceptance of Jews, and ever-present subtle barriers to their full integration into society, with unseen but no less real lines of demarcation.

9

The industrial revolution sweeping Europe was having profound effects on life in the countryside, and also in the cities and their squalid urban slums. With changing patterns of production, new barons of industry and commerce had appeared, and landed aristocrats were in trouble. Emerging bourgeois society was asserting new rights and questioning old privileges. Aristocratic preeminence, the power of the Church, and kings and their courts were under pressure and the political landscape, domestic and international, was in upheaval.

In France, the king and queen had walked to the guillotine in 1793. Their executioners were at each other's throats, but their revolution remained the fear of Europe's kings and the hope of its young. While the Austrians and French were battling in Europe, Napoleon had made himself master of Egypt and was advancing in Syria. Soon he would return to the Tuileries and proclaim himself First Consul. Poland had been divided up—for the third time. The British, meanwhile, were busy in India, the Marquis of Wellesley having presided over the dismemberment of the rich Kingdom of Mysore. In America, the revolutionary hero George Washington had died and the formidable Thomas Jefferson, much admired in Europe, had been elected the republic's third president.

With politics and economics undergoing a vast transformation, intellectual life in the Western world was in ferment. In his *Wealth of Nations,* Adam Smith—who with David Hume was one of the two great figures of the Scottish enlightenment—had propounded the virtues of laissez-faire and roundly ridiculed the conventional wisdom of mercantilism and state intervention in trade and commerce.

Scientific knowledge had greatly expanded. Discoveries in physics and chemistry, advances in mathematics, progress in medicine, and exploration of previously unknown parts of the globe were opening up new vistas and stimulating the imagination. Joseph Priestley, at age sixty-seven, had published his stellar work on electricity and done pioneering studies of oxygen. James Watt's invention of the condenser made the steam engine possible—the first two having just appeared in Berlin for the first time. Eli Whitney's cotton gin was revolutionizing the textile industry, and just before 1800, Aloys Senefelder, a young German, had invented the art of lithography. In France in 1790, Antoine-Laurent de Lavoisier, the father of modern chemistry and an early proponent of scientific agriculture, had gained fame with his breakthrough table of thirty-one chemical elements—but lost his head in the revolutionary maelstrom of Paris. At the Berlin Academy, the mathematician-scientist Leonhard Euler had perfected calculus and made breakthrough contributions over wide fields ranging from mechanics, optics, and acoustics to astronomy, chemistry, and medicine. The world was being shorn of its unknowns. James Cook had explored the Pacific and discovered Hawaii. Vitus Behrendt had traveled up the northeast coast of Siberia. Alexander von Humboldt, the adventurous German aristocrat, was about to set out for an exploration of South America.

Creativity in the natural and social sciences coincided with an era of unusual artistic inventiveness, and a vast flowering of music and literature. Mozart had recently died. Beethoven, barely thirty years old, had just completed his Symphony no. 1 in C Major. Haydn, his teacher, had finished the twelve London symphonies. Paganini, at age seventeen, was already being acclaimed as the greatest violin virtuoso ever.

In Germany, Kant, Hegel, Herder, and Schlegel were leading a remarkable generation of philosophers, dramatists, and poets. Above all, it was the time of Goethe and Schiller and of Weimar as the center of German culture and literary achievement. Goethe's *Sorrows of Young Werther,* which had appeared a quarter century earlier, especially stirred the imagination of the young.

The literary style of the period became known as Sturm und Drang, the "storm and stress" of a new generation yearning for change, questioning class hierarchy, defying convention, and revolting against social limits. Here and there young rebels appeared in public unwigged, bare-headed, and with open shirts. Morals were loosening; "feeling" was everything. "Werther fever" had Rahel and many of her female contemporaries in its thrall. Goethe was their idol for, more than any other, he had expressed the generation's sentiments by dramatizing, in Werther, the conflict between prevailing morals and personal desire.

Yet Prussia remained one of the more stable places in Europe. The king's senior bureaucrats continued to run a police state, and the military were still in evidence everywhere. The class system remained frozen, and the citizenry was loyal to their king, respectful of authority, and obedient to the traditional zeal for regimentation and rules. Still, the intelligentsia and some of the upper-level young were restless.

The kingdom now was a major player in Europe with a population increased to ten million, partly by natural growth and immigration but in large measure by virtue of conquest and annexation. To Brandenburg, East Prussia, Westphalia, and the Rhine provinces, Frederick's exploits had added Silesia and Saxony, while the Polish divisions had greatly enlarged Prussian territory in West and South Prussia and netted at least two and a half million new subjects—including, paradoxically, one hundred and seventy thousand additional Jews. In all of Prussia there had previously been only fifty thousand; now, with four times as many, keeping them down was no longer a simple matter. In the province of Posen there were areas where one in four city dwellers was a Jew, and as many as half of all the merchants and professionals. In many places, the Jews were too important to be kicked out; applying the 1750 law in those places was impractical, but giving them free rein was equally unacceptable. Administering Jewish affairs was increasingly complex, and the pressure for new ideas was mounting.

Berlin had continued to grow and, with 170,000 inhabitants, it was now one of Europe's major cities. Fifty years of restriction, however, had actually led to a slight decrease in the number of its Jews. Fifteen years before, there had been almost four thousand; around 1800 there were several hundred less, though their importance to the city's and kingdom's economic life remained as great as ever.

Frederick the Great had died in 1786, shrunken and physically weak but with his iron will intact till the end. His nephew and successor, who held the throne for eleven years, was cut from a very different cloth. A young man in his prime, taller and more imposing than his ascetic, vinegary, and monastic uncle, Frederick William II loved life and women—and never ceased to devote substantial energies to the enjoyment of both. He was also softer, not overly smart, much dependent on questionable advisers, and in direct contrast to his uncle's religious skepticism, a devout and bigoted Christian who communed with ghosts and was given to mythic raptures. When it came to the capital city he had, however, followed Frederick's policies and continued to invest in more fine buildings and imposing monuments.

Berliners, who thought their city with its thirty churches, impressive houses, and broad avenues one of Europe's most beautiful, were particularly proud of the Brandenburg Gate with its bombastic victory chariot perched atop it. The new king had ordered the architect Carl Langhans to build him this *porta triumphalis* and followed up with a splendid new theatre, the Schauspielhaus, and an elaborate rebuilding of the *Schloss*.

Yet Berlin was a city of unusual contrasts. The representative splendor of the new areas was set off starkly against grim poverty and squalor, and the sumptuousness of the wide avenues diverged sharply from the filth and stink of the lesser streets and alleyways where garbage was thrown into the open, and chamber pots emptied into gutters. "Have Berliners no sense of smell?" the visiting Russian historian Karamzin asked plaintively, adding that he had been forced to permanently "hold his nose" when walking the streets.[24] A company of sixty ex-soldiers saw to it with military efficiency that the pretty lanterns in the better streets were kept fueled and lit. But elsewhere there was no illumination at all, and people stumbled through the dark, at the mercy of robbers, thieves, and heaps of rubbish blocking their way.

Anomalies such as these added to the excitement and spice of city life. While the rich rode by in their carriages and the upper classes flocked to the theater, haughty *Junker* officers and their families mingled with the public, Jews, visitors, pickpockets, and, soon after dark, squadrons of ladies of easy virtue. Permissiveness was common, licentiousness widespread, and morals generally loose in what had become a wide open city: by official count there were 358 streetwalkers, and no fewer than eighty bordellos ready to serve all pocketbooks and tastes.[25]

The king himself set anything but a good example. "Officially" married twice, he had in typical rococo fashion morganatically "wed" several others on the side and produced a dozen mostly illegitimate children. In sharp contrast to his uncle, he found the fairer sex utterly irresistible and was prone to fall desperately in love—and to bed one object of his infatuations after the other. Sometimes it would be a countess or a court attendant, at other times an actress or even a laundress. His favorite for years was the daughter of an oboist, a commoner upon whom he had bestowed the title of Countess von der Mark. His uncle had found the sexual and romantic proclivities of the nephew quite disgusting and, with resignation, observed long ago that "cet animal est incorrigible."[26]

Among so much moral laxity in some matters, the ubiquitous bureaucratic regimentation and the pervasive presence of the military—one in six Berliners was a soldier—never failed to impress first-time visitors from abroad. No sooner had he reached his room, Karamzin related, than his landlord handed him a police *Fragebogen* (questionnaire) with "the same questions . . . just answered at the city gate, but with one new one— namely, through which gate I had entered!"

Goethe, on his first visit to Berlin had, in some wonderment, reported to his friend Charlotte von Stein, that the streets "teem with horses, carriages, guns and armaments," and that at Prince Henry's table, he had encountered "generals by the half-dozen."[27] Dino Alfieri, an Italian poet who had visited Berlin somewhat earlier, found the spectacle highly foreign and distasteful, and wrote home that he had left "this giant Prussian barracks . . . with the appropriate disgust."[28]

As to the prostitutes and houses of pleasure, they too were at all times carefully counted, registered, and of course taxed. Physicians were regularly sent to examine the staff, pregnancies were carefully noted, and those with child confined for the duration before being allowed to reenter the tax-generating ranks. In Prussia, permissiveness and sin still required order and organization.

10

Rahel had fled Berlin deeply disappointed and shamed. Yet the image she invoked in her letters of a despondent woman in the grip of numb inactivity was as inaccurate as it was melodramatic. Rahel was a fighter, and whatever she may have believed, passive acceptance of her fate was not in tune with her restless personality—neither in Paris nor in Berlin, where she flung herself back into the old salon life within less than a year.

She had gone to Paris in the company of the Countess von Schlabrendorf, a friend who had her own reasons for wanting to leave town. The Countess was an unorthodox aristocrat who favored a bohemian lifestyle that had put her in the family way. As the two women prepared to leave, Rahel enthused about the impending adventure in a highly revealing letter to her. The illegitimate child was her personal "good fortune," Rahel wrote. With the infant, theirs would be a "family" of three; the idea thrilled her and she promised her love and limitless support in the prospective Paris togetherness. But in almost the same breath she let slip yet another thought, revealing her ever-present fears and insecurities. She said she had sensed that the Countess's mother harbored hidden feelings of resentment against her for reasons, obliquely implied, probably having to do with her Jewishness. Was it possible that the mother might now see her in a new light?[29]

Rahel craved social contacts and intense interaction with people she liked and admired, as a means, she said, of personal discovery but really also of gaining legitimacy and acceptance. Always, however, there remained the underlying insecurity of the Jew and restless activity to deal with it. It's hard to fathom all her turbulent feelings at that moment, but it may well have crossed her mind that if marriage to Finckenstein was not to be, perhaps the new relationship with the Countess and her newborn would let her get past the hurt over the rejection and, at the same time, legitimize herself at least to Frau von Kalkreudt, the Countess's mother. No one knows how much time Rahel actually spent as a loving family member with the Countess and her newborn in Paris, though it cannot have been all-absorbing and it certainly was temporary. Once back at home, there is no longer much mention in her letters about the Countess and her child.

Upon her return to Berlin, Rahel quickly took up where she had left off, and soon her circle was wider than ever. In the morning she wrote letters; in the afternoon and till late at night she entertained or was seen at the theatre or the opera. All of the old guests were back, joined by new and even more illustrious ones—romantic poets like Friedrich von Schlegel and Ludwig Tieck, actors and actresses who came after the theatre, both Humboldts, and Friedrich von Gentz, a young intellectual later turned politician and adviser to Prince Metternich at the Congress of Vienna. Gentz, who like Rahel had started out full of idealism and in search of self-discovery, had already greatly sobered and turned realist, if not reactionary, and was on the way to becoming a strong nationalist and defender of traditions. Though the two maintained warm personal relations in her salon, he was in fact—not unlike others who came to her—behind her back also an unabashed anti-Semite. Once he wrote to Brinckmann that "never has a Jewish woman—without a single exception—known true love." Rahel probably knew this, yet she chose to ignore it and continued to welcome him. The most distinguished of all her new guests, however, was none other than Prince Louis Ferdinand, a nephew of Frederick the Great, who met Pauline Wiesel, his latest paramour, at Rahel's salon, with the hostess acting as the understanding confidante of both.

Once again Rahel was living through others, to buttress her self-confidence and sense of belonging. Yet for the moment she was personally at loose ends and caught up in "aimless sociability," as Wilhelm Humboldt described it. For a while, questions of religion and God—neither Christian nor Jewish, but an amorphous otherworldly providence—preoccupied her. Then, once again, Rahel became engaged to be married. After Finckenstein, she had said that it could never happen again. Yet 1802 found her desperately in love, with Don Rafaél d'Urquijo, a Spanish diplomat. If it had been her first fiancé's "blond soul" that she had then found irresistible, it was now the Spanish aristocrat's Latin good looks. For a while their affair was full of passion, but her friends considered the second engagement as hopeless as the first. The two were basically incompatible, the Spaniard was insanely jealous, and the affair gradually cooled amid quarrels and scenes until, in 1804, it ended as had the first. In later years, Rahel would refer to Urquijo as her "Spanish Purgatory," observing that this episode "showed to what depth a person can sink."[30]

She was now a woman in her mid-thirties. After two failed engagements, she was still single, still alone, still in search of status and acceptance, and still unhappy and unfulfilled. But in 1806 there was worse to come. Prussia was drawn into a catastrophic war against Napoleon, and her troops, ill-prepared and poorly led, were disastrously defeated at the twin battles of Auerstedt and Jena. The king, his court, and the aristocracy fled Berlin, and most of Rahel's friends went with them. Prince Louis Ferdinand, her good friend, killed in battle and stripped of his clothes by French hussars, lay buried in the village of Saalfeld.[31] Prussia, humiliated and in shreds, lost much of her territory, and on October 27 at four o'clock in the afternoon, under the thunder of cannons, Napoleon triumphantly rode through the Brandenburg Gate to occupy the city.

With Prussia's defeat, Rahel's salon came to an end. It was the beginning of a period she later called her years of desolation.

The salon period had, as it turned out, been merely a short interlude when a vanguard among Berlin's Jews, wealthy and more educated than the rest, seemed to be gaining a measure of acceptance in German social life. But it had been a false spring, and their progress had been more apparent than real. True integration into German society had never been in the cards. Now the humbling of Prussia ushered in a renewed period of reaction and chauvinistic nationalism among German intellectuals and the upper bourgeoisie. There was suddenly a distaste for progressive ideas and a nostalgia for tradition, and even those few Jews who previously had found some open doors were again excluded. Anti-Semitic prejudice, never far below the surface, was again in the open.

Rahel and the young men and women from privileged families, ready to have done with their Jewishness as the price for admission into German society, felt isolated and rejected. Some had already been baptized, and some of the women had married aristocrats, yet few were truly accepted. Even with their newly acquired titles and their wealth, the women remained *mauvaise societé,* the baptized Baron Arnstein became *le premier baron du vieux testament,* and the snickering behind their backs rarely stopped.

For the vast majority of Prussia's Jews there had only been limited progress anyway. The doors had never opened for them, there was little social contact with Christians, and life went on pretty much as before.

The illusions of Rahel and her friends to the contrary, Prussia's Jews were still a disliked minority, still aliens without rights, still specially taxed and restricted, and still with a public image not greatly different from the past. The famous Freiherr Knigge, a sort of "Emily Post" of his day whose treatise on *Umgang mit Menschen* (On Dealing with People) was required reading in all literate households around 1800, had expressed the prevailing sentiment clearly: "Jews are born merchants . . . with a character full of negative peculiarities," he explained to his readers. Those who achieve higher cultural levels tend to exchange "the simplemindedness and orthodoxy of their customs for all the evils and foolishness of the Christians." Though some Jews were capable of great wisdom, learning, and generosity, he wrote, as a group they were a secretive, suspicious lot, ever on the chase for riches and reluctant to part with money. Above all, if doing business with a Jew, Knigge warned, "keep your eyes but not your purse open. . . . A Christian cannot rely on their . . . promises."[32]

11

In the countryside of old Prussia outside Berlin, even less had changed. The number of Jews allowed to settle in the small towns and villages had grown very slowly; in all of Brandenburg there were still not much more than eight thousand of them and the rules against accepting more from the eastern areas remained tight. In the little town of Oranienburg, there were at most a dozen families. They lived quietly among the Christians, selling their cloth and textiles from small shops or trading with local farmers in

grain, cattle, and horses, a few prospering slowly. Occasionally, a poor beggar Jew or unauthorized hawker would appear at their door and in accordance with the 1750 law, Herr Persch, the town clerk, would dutifully note
this irregularity and request instructions from higher-ups. There was, for
example, the vexing case of one Meyer Jakob, recently arrived in Oranienburg, who was the subject of Persch's report on January 14, 1792. His entire
possessions consisted of "one shoe, one boot, and a torn overcoat." A native
of Silesia, Jakob was a "vagabond and drifter" who had worked in Copenha-
gen as a tanner, traveled between Stettin, Glogau, and Töplitz, been hospi-
talized and expelled from Berlin, and now was sick again and under the
care of Oranienburg's Jews. What was he to do with him, Herr Persch had
inquired? That case, however, was less complicated than the one concerning the beggar Jews Hirsch Heyman, his wife Lea, and their four children.
According to Persch's investigation, they had roamed the province of Brandenburg begging for alms from local Jews. How was he to handle this large
family, in view of the several children?[33]

Following orderly Prussian procedure, Oranienburg's Chief Councillor
Borman, Persch's superior, continued to sign the required quarterly Jew
reports—even no news had to be duly noted. Delays were not tolerated;
the law was still the law. "Where is your report?" Berlin had inquired ominously on September 2, 1795. To which Borman had replied hastily and
full of contrition a few days later that "it is most dutifully and obediently
[*schuldigst und gehorsamst*] reported to Your Excellency, that in the months
of May, June, and July, no alien or otherwise itinerant unauthorized Jew
has appeared here."[34] Until well past the turn of the century, Herr Borman
would take care never again to miss his required quarterly Jew reports.

Oranienburg Jews maintained contact, socialized—and intermarried—
with relatives and friends throughout the area, as was the case when the
Simons and the Isaaks linked their offspring in marriage. No marriage broker had really been necessary when Levin Simon had become engaged to
Henriette Isaak, whose family had the coveted residence permit for the
town of Brandenburg, on the river Havel. Though an intermediary had
been employed to put the final touches to the marriage contract, this had
been primarily for reasons of appearance and tradition. The fathers of bride
and groom were both dealers in cloth who did business together. For years,

in good and bad times, they had backed each other and stayed in each other's homes when traveling. They had known Levin and Henriette practically from birth. The children had been born a year apart, the boy in 1791 and his future wife a year later, and their eventual marriage had often been alluded to—jokingly at first and then more seriously when they reached their teens. Both families remained observant Jews, and both took pride in their relatively secure status as the king's established country Jews.

Modest people of modest means, the Simons and Isaaks rarely traveled to Berlin—the trip was costly and took time, and the capital city was too fast and sophisticated for their taste. Yet, like many country Jews, they did have relatives there. Some of these had become important, and that was a great source of pride, and duly noted in their carefully kept genealogical tables. The Simons always pointed to their connection to the famous Rahel Levin who was the talk of Berlin. And when years later, Levin and Henriette married off their daughter to young Louis Blumenthal, a recent arrival in Oranienburg from nearby Wittstock, he had contributed additional ancestral luster with his connections to Jakob Hertz Beer, whose wife, the daughter of the fabulously rich Liebmann Meyer Wulff, traced her ancestry all the way back to Jost Liebmann. Her young son, Meyer, was said to be a musical genius.

Their connection to these prominent and successful Berlin Jews was a comforting reminder that they were part of a clan long resident in Prussia, real Germans even if still not citizens, people who were important and had made good. Contemplating their Brandenburg roots and basking in the reflected glory of the Berlin relatives served to set the Isaaks and Simons apart and gave them that precious gift, the sense of security, stability, and belonging every Jew craved.

Not much had recently been heard of Rahel, though rumor had it that in prior years she had entertained poets, countesses, and royals; that her brother had been baptized and now called himself Ludwig Robert; and that Rahel had herself begun to use that name when traveling.

Liebmann Meyer Wulff, however, remained much in the news. The ambitious merchant with an eye for the big deal whose daughter, Malka, Rahel had known since her youth, had in the ensuing years become fabulously rich and now lived in a fine house rivaling the Itzig and Ephraim palaces. He had amassed a small fortune selling grain to the Prussian army, but he

had scored his major coup with concessions for the lucrative Berlin–
Potsdam postal route and the Prussian State Lottery.

In recent years, Wulff had become so wealthy that he had actually advanced money to Berlin and single-handedly underwritten some of Prussia's loans. No wonder they called him Berlin's Croesus.

Malka, his daughter (after 1812 she would call herself Amalie) had become a prominent and respected personality in her own right. Married to
the rich sugar merchant Beer, she was by all accounts an extraordinary
woman. At the turn of the century, Amalie had started a salon of her own,
albeit a very different one from Rahel and Henriette. Many of Berlin's leading citizens came there, and it was her magnificent house, her exquisite
hospitality, the good food served on the finest china, and the extraordinary
musical offerings of Madame's evenings that attracted them.

Amalie had been raised to be a lady, and early on music had become the
focus of her life and the center of the Beer household—along with their
religion. She felt the burdens of her Jewishness no less than the *salonières*
and their circle. Jewishness, however, was for her a given, a part of her very
being; abandoning her faith was unthinkable. Indeed, though Rahel and
Henriette would occasionally attend her musical soirées, Amalie had nothing but contempt for "those frantic demoiselles," willing to do anything in
their quest for assimilation.

Her eldest son, Meyer, was born in 1791, the same year as distant cousin
Levin Simon, but in greatly more dramatic circumstances. Ever respectful
of Jewish tradition, Amalie had set out from Berlin for the Beer ancestral
home in Frankfurt an der Oder, there to await her first-born's arrival. The
baby, who would many times later demonstrate the same talent for drama
that he displayed in this debut, had decided otherwise. So it was that on
September 5, Jakob Liebmann Meyer Beer made his appearance not in the
Beer house in Frankfurt, but instead in a horse-drawn carriage near the tiny
postal station of Tasdorf.

His family called the boy Meyer, a common Jewish name, but one he
never liked and would eventually find ways to discard. His grandfather,
who had sired four daughters and hoped in vain for a son, was so thrilled
by the arrival of the family's first male heir that he had at once settled a
large sum on him that made him financially independent for life.

If Meyer was destined to have a gilded youth, it was most certainly not an idle one. Surrounded from birth by his mother's music, he quickly gave evidence of an extraordinary talent of his own and of a tireless industry and devotion to develop it. At age four he astonished his family with his capacity to recall long and complicated musical passages, mastered complex harmonic combinations, and showed an interest in inventing some of his own. To his doting and devoted mother, such talent merited nothing less than the very best in training and teachers. Accordingly, since her determination and energies were as limitless as her contacts and finances, it was Munich's distinguished Franz Seraphinus Lauska, erstwhile House Musician to the Duke of Serbelloni in Rome, and her occasional house guest, Muzio Clementi, whom she had recruited to instruct and assess him. The verdict, rendered before the boy was seven, was unanimous and unequivocal: the child was indeed a musical wunderkind, possibly even a second Mozart.

In 1801, at age ten, tenaciously promoted by his mother, Meyer had made his public debut, playing among other pieces a Mozart piano composition that drew rave reviews from the critics. All of musical Berlin came to hear him, and the *Allgemeine Musikalische Zeitung* waxed enthusiastically about the remarkable talent of "Liebmann Bär, the new little Jewish virtuoso."

His doting mother, never doubting her son's talents, engaged the very best teachers to instruct him, spoiled him endlessly, and dressed him in the finest clothes. After his first public appearances she had commissioned a fashionable Berlin portrait painter to capture her prodigy's elegant appearance on canvas and used her influence for its display at the Prussian Academy of Arts. In the painting he was clad in yellow silk trousers, a black bolero jacket topped by a velvet collar, and white stockings and patent leather shoes. His image hanging in the prestigious academy, Berlin's newest musical wunderkind had quickly become a sensation—for more reasons than one.[35]

True enough, the young man was a great and much talked about talent, Berlin was proud of him, and the portrait was remarkable. Yet to exhibit a young Jew's likeness at the royal academy was altogether too much. In the prevailing climate of conservative reaction, Berlin was not ready for that, and the issue quickly became a cause célèbre and rallying cry for active anti-Semites, led by Prussian Councillor Karl Friedrich Wilhelm Grattenauer. No Jew, argued Grattenauer, should be permitted to so defile the academy's hallowed halls. Others agreed and amid the hue and cry, Madame Beer was forced to beat a hasty retreat after a mere two weeks, removing the painting forthwith to the Beer villa.

It was the first time that young Meyer learned that merely being a Jew was enough to be considered second-class. The incident had a deep impact on him, and he would never forget it. It instilled in him a deep and lifelong sense of insecurity and a hypersensitivity to real or imagined slights and criticisms—but also a fierce determination to prove himself through his accomplishments in music.

Grattenauer's campaign was seen by Berlin's Jews as a painful reminder that the prejudices against them had not abated and were, if anything, again on the rise. He had been bold enough to lead his campaign against Jewish influence in the open. Years earlier, he had considered it prudent to do so anonymously with a pamphlet entitled *Wider die Juden* (Against the Jews). In it, he had accused Jews of being a corrosive element in society "since the time of Tacitus." In Grattenauer's view, there were no distinctions on religious or individual grounds. All Jews were alike; indeed, the baptized and more assimilated ones aroused his particular ire. These were, he said, an underground army pretending to be different from the others, who were actually especially busy undermining German life.

At the time it first appeared, his hate sheet met with only limited support, but now his arguments fell on more receptive ears. Rahel's friend Gentz, for one, was much impressed, and many of her erstwhile salon guests were also listening. In the new mood of patriotic reaction and romantic hankering for a return to old traditions, even Prussia's foremost thinkers, among them Kant, Fichte, and Herder, were not entirely unsympathetic. Soon a number of young intellectuals would band together in a salon of their own, the *Teutsche Tischgesellschaft,* whose stated goal it was to promote "German spiritual chivalry and truth." Its members included many who had once been Rahel's guests. Their by-laws specifically excluded "women, Frenchmen, philistines, and Jews."

Rahel suffered greatly as she contemplated these anti-Semitic setbacks in her "years of desolation." Young Meyer Beer had learned the same lesson even as Berlin celebrated his first successes. Most Jews had never doubted it. The question was whether their legal emancipation would eventually cause gentile sentiments to change.

12

Perhaps she was too self-absorbed to realize it, but the very events that had once again disappointed and isolated Rahel also were the impetus for a chain of events that finally brought legal equality to Prussia's Jews. Military defeat had produced a wave of nationalistic and reactionary responses by those who found comfort in idealizing a simpler and purer Germanic past. That was one side of the coin. The other was that it energized those who had long argued that Prussia's administrative institutions had to be modernized if the kingdom was to regain its former strength. The result was a confrontation between two groups of aristocrats: on one side, reactionaries and romantics who feared the loss of their privileges and spoke of recapturing old "Germanic values"; on the other, progressive bureaucrats determined to strengthen society through reform from above. In the end, it was the latter who carried the day.

Not that the reformers were any great friends of the Jews. Many were just as prejudiced against them as their opponents, and the first of them, Karl Freiherr (Baron) von und zum Stein, the king's principal minister from 1806 to 1808, was an outright anti-Semite who made no secret of his view that Jews like Liebmann Meyer Wulff had enriched themselves through trickery by taking advantage of Prussia's internal confusion—which his reforms were now designed to correct. Stein had no interest at all in enfranchising the Jews through his reforms, and if given a choice, he would gladly have chased most of them away. Among his successors, Count von Dohma, though he was said once to have proposed marriage to Henriette Herz, and Freiherr von Altenstein, Dohma's colleague, shared some of the same deeply ingrained antipathies of the aristocracy against the Jewish minority. They too were motivated not by goodwill, but purely by perceived necessity and practical considerations. Only Wilhelm von Humboldt, Rahel's old friend, and Karl August von Hardenberg, the last in the string of reformist ministers under whose aegis final emancipation was finally achieved, were deliberate progressives in dealing with the Jewish issue.

It is ironic, therefore, that Stein's municipal reforms, promulgated just as he left office in 1808, were the first real breakthrough on the road to Jewish enfranchisement. Stein fought for these changes as an indispensable prerequisite for eliminating the influence of royal advisers in the management of state and local affairs. Under his new law, citizens, qualified by residence and income, would elect their own representatives to city councils, assess taxes, and manage their own affairs. He resigned just as the law took effect, and it became clear that as the law was written, one of its by-products was that a significant number of city Jews were suddenly qualified to vote. Prussia being Prussia, his successors insisted that there could be no allowance for exceptions: Qualified Jews, too, were now citizens at the municipal level, though not yet citizens of the state. And—lo and behold—in the very first elections, a few of them were actually elected to the city councils.

It was a historic development for the Jews, and it broke the dike of their legal exclusion for good. If they voted in the cities, bureaucrats asked, why could they not bid on the royal domains being sold off under the rural reform program? There was always the practical consideration that excluding Jewish capital might threaten the program's success. Furthermore, the kingdom of Westphalia, under Napoleon's influence in the west, had already granted the Jews full civil rights, and in the east the same had happened in Poland and Austria. If Prussia were to hold out, might not its Jews migrate elsewhere to the detriment of the Prussian economy?

Though many fiercely opposed the Jews, the logic of these arguments carried the day—Prussia alone could no longer exclude the Jews. One senior official summarized the choice succinctly: "If Jews are detrimental, chase them away; if they are needed for the benefit of the state, give them their rights." Half measures no longer sufficed.

In spite of the opponents' polemics against this infamous new "*Judenstaat,*" the king had given his final accord, insisting only on adding vague language providing that details on admitting Jews to the bureaucracy and military were to be worked out later—a fateful loophole, soon amply exploited by those who hated the changes.

On March 11, 1812, Hardenberg affixed his signature to the final Edict of Emancipation. For Prussia's Jews, it was their Magna Carta and—as a Christian official put it—"the realization of a dream as ardently wished for as the coming of the Messiah." Their gratitude knew no limits, and the elders immediately took pen to hand to inform their sovereign that they were "deeply moved . . . and dare to place [our] profoundest thanks at the feet of the throne," promising him "boundless acts of loyalty" to prove their citizenship had been well deserved.

For a hundred and fifty years, Jews had been tolerated but not accepted. They had suffered from their psychological isolation and longed to end it. The indignities and rejection had deeply hurt them and spawned a wide range of stratagems in response—from fatalistic acceptance by some, to "crossing over" through baptism, to an incessant striving to prove their worth, by others. Now many hoped that an entirely new era would begin. Perhaps legal emancipation would finally lead to opening the doors for full Jewish integration into all of German life.

Did Rahel, just then preparing to leave Berlin, or young Meyer, the musical prodigy readying the Munich premiere of his first opera, share such hopes? Perhaps—but certainly not without skepticism and doubt. Both had already had experiences that shaped their outlook, which neither could forget. Meyer would always remember Grattenauer's attacks on him and retain a lifelong pessimism about changing gentile attitudes and a hypersensitivity about perceived slights and unfavorable reviews, which he ascribed to anti-Semitic spite. "*Risches* [Jew-hatred] is forever," he would frequently sigh.

Rahel, twenty years his senior and chastened by personal setbacks, had permanently lost some of her youthful enthusiasm. In middle age, she had not given up the fight but she, too, had greatly sobered about the prospects.

The time after 1806 had been her worst years, when the world seemingly had collapsed and the future looked bleak. No longer had she been in the center of an exciting life, mixing with people she admired. Once more she felt abandoned, rejected, a prisoner of her hateful birth. She had quarreled with her family, and now she lived alone, strapped for funds, with only her old servant to look after her. For a while she seemed resigned to her misery, and her letters to remaining friends were sad and serious, even pathetic. She was nothing, she wrote, and was "hurt, tortured, and annihilated." When her mother died, she wrote, "now I am no one's daughter, sister, lover, wife or even citizen!"

Yet, as always, her black mood did not last long. By 1808, writing to her old friend Brinckmann, her tone once more had changed. "I sit here alone," she wrote him, "all my old friends are gone . . . but . . . I remain unchanged. The reverses have given me a new hardness and renewed my innate spirits and strengths." The first signs of defiance, of her determination not to give up, were once more beginning to show.

Recently, two young men had come into her life, both many years her junior. One, Alexander von der Marwitz, she considered her intellectual superior. They talked endlessly, and it was he, she later said, who made her see things as they were—that the cards were stacked against her, that society would never open up to her, that the social barriers against her "wrong" birth were too high. Face reality, Marwitz had counseled her. Take what you can, and cease to fight for the unattainable. The other young visitor, liberal, naive, still unformed but deeply captivated by Rahel, who was fourteen years his senior, was Karl August Varnhagen. Seven years after they first met in 1807, Rahel would become his wife.

Varnhagen was from a good family, yet poor and without clear prospects, a desultory student of medicine and somewhat of a dilettante who much preferred literature and poetry to his studies. Though Rahel soon became his mistress, it was from the beginning an unequal relationship and it matured only slowly. Rahel at first resisted it and never felt great passion for him, while he was from the start much under her spell. She saw herself as his mentor and teacher—in her letters she frequently called him "my child" or "dear son"—and only gradually found herself attracted to the one quality she had missed in all her previous lovers: his genuine love for her, and his willingness to accept her as she was, for herself and without reserve.[36]

There remained much uncertainty and many ups and downs in their peculiar and uneven relationship. Rahel, still at sea, wondered about her future. Varnhagen, unsure, unformed and impecunious, cast around for his own place in life. In the Napoleonic War, he had served as an aide to a Prussian officer, and when some years later Napoleon passed through Prussia en route to Moscow, and Prussia had again declared war on France, he had managed to win a captaincy and gone off once more as a general's adjutant in the field.

It was the watershed year of 1812, and it would prove a personal turning point for Rahel and Karl Varnhagen. When the Russians occupied Berlin, she fled the city and made her way, via Breslau, to Prague, where many of her old friends had taken refuge. Once more she had a new mission. A true Prussian citizen now, it was the moment to be patriotic, and for a while she threw herself into collecting money and caring for the wounded. Varnhagen, meanwhile, had parlayed his military contacts into a peacetime appointment as a Prussian diplomat. He had also uncovered an obscure and somewhat questionable hereditary right to a title, and added the aristocratic "von" to his name.

When he again proposed marriage, Rahel hesitated no longer. On September 27, 1814, she married him. Four days earlier she had been baptized and taken Christian names. Rahel Robert, née Rahel Levin, was now Frau Friederike Antonie Varnhagen von Ense.

Varnhagen, she thought, was her last chance, and so she had taken it. In her search for identity she wanted status and to be near people of rank with socially acceptable names. With one of her own, she hoped that she had now crossed the great divide.

But had she? "I hear . . . that Varnhagen has now married the little Levy woman. So now she has become an Excellency and an Ambassador's wife. There is nothing the Jews cannot achieve," her friend Wilhelm von Humboldt had commented acidly when hearing the news.

13

The year 1812 was a fateful one for Prussia, and for the Jews. In March, a reluctant Frederick William III yielded to his reformist ministers and signed the royal decree bestowing full rights of citizenship on his Jews. Then, in the spring, Napoleon marched through Prussia at the head of a powerful army of half a million men, and in June he crossed the river Niemen and invaded Russia.

Six months later, the ice and snow of Russia's vastness had defeated him. Moscow had been put to the torch before he could reach it. Napoleon barely managed to escape capture, and when he reached Paris at year-end, only twenty thousand ragged and exhausted stragglers remained of his once vaunted troops.

The time to settle accounts had arrived. For seven years, Napoleon had occupied the kingdom, reduced it to half its former size and imposed his arbitrary will. Now that the tide had turned against him, Prussia made common cause with his Russian adversaries and rose up in a war of liberation. Before long, much of the rest of Europe had joined Czar Alexander and the Prussians in a grand alliance, the Belle Alliance, to rid itself of the once invincible French Emperor.

In February 1813, the Prussian king called for volunteers to form regiments of chasseurs and territorials, ordered general mobilization and universal conscription, and issued a stirring proclamation, *To My People,* calling on his subjects to join in the uprising. For unusual acts of bravery there were to be peacetime rewards and a glorious new decoration—the Iron Cross, patterned after a historic emblem of the old Teutonic Order and reminiscent of the feats of valiant German knights in bygone days.

Patriotic enthusiasm was at a fever pitch. Within a few weeks more than fifty thousand volunteers had signed up, including a large number of students and young intellectuals. By year-end, some three hundred thousand Prussian soldiers—6 percent of the entire population—were under arms. Among them, for the first time, were substantial numbers of young Jews, eager to be in the vanguard of the volunteers, to validate their recent enfranchisement on the battlefield and show that they were as ready as Christians to do their duty for Prussia.

By October it was all over. Napoleon had defended himself like a tiger but lost the decisive encounter with the forces of the Belle Alliance at the battle of Leipzig. He was all for fighting on, but his generals refused him, and in March of the following year they sued for peace and surrendered Paris. Banished into retirement as Prince of Elba, he would make one last try to return, but at Waterloo Napoleon's dream once more to snatch victory from defeat ended for good, and the Allies gathered at Vienna for a congress to organize the peace and reorder the map of Europe.

For as long as anyone could remember, the notion of Jews serving in the military had been unthinkable. The prevailing view of the Jew was that of a coward, given to haggling and dealing, incapable of valor and unsuitable for service in the king's army. Opponents to Jewish emancipation had seized on this dishonorable picture as an argument against giving them their rights. Others had maintained that, all other considerations aside, no Jew could serve as a soldier because his religion prohibited fighting on the

Sabbath. The response that no such restriction existed, that Jews had fought with valor as far back as Roman times and been commended for it by Ptolemy and Caesar, and that elsewhere in Europe they were even then serving with honor fell on deaf ears. A Christian, it was said, simply could not rely on a Jew.

When emancipation at last became a reality, the diehards had continued to oppose Jewish military service on principle. Special, more stringent rules were suggested for their soldiers. For a time, the proposition was seriously debated of assigning Jewish communities collective responsibility for deserters—on the assumption that Jews were more likely than Christians to run away from battle. In the end, none of this succeeded and the reformers prevailed. Under the new law, a Jew would have the same rights and obligations as anyone else.

The war of liberation, coming on the heels of their emancipation, was the first opportunity to prove their opponents wrong, and Prussia's Jews seized it eagerly. The word *fatherland* had taken on special meaning, and Jewish communities outdid themselves with acts of patriotism. More than a thousand young Jews—students, artisans, merchants, teachers, and doctors—rushed to volunteer. By war's end, the number serving in the military was, in proportion to their total number in the population, not much inferior to that of Christians.

Jewish families supported the war effort with extravagant gestures. "Jews give whatever they own. . . . In the list of war donors the Jews are at the top," Rahel reported to her brother in 1813. Berlin's Jewish merchants donated more than seven hundred reichstaler for the war effort—the first installment of a much larger sum they would contribute in coming months. The small community in Breslau turned over five thousand reichstaler, and Prussia's principal newspaper, the *Vossische Zeitung,* reported that Jews were collecting silver forks, knives, and spoons in their synagogues, that children were bringing their piggy banks, and that one Jewish butcher had thrown in his golden wedding ring as a sign of gratitude for his newly won citizenship.

Inspiring tales of Jewish heroism in battle circulated among them. Dozens of Jewish doctors volunteered to care for the wounded, a fair number dying from typhus and assorted battlefield infections. When a young Breslau Jew named Hilsbach, heavily wounded, had thrown himself against the enemy in the very presence of the king and subsequently died of his wounds, the story was retold many times. At the battle of Leipzig several dozen Jewish soldiers had paid the ultimate price, a total of seventy-two Jews had won the coveted Iron Cross, and a few had even been decorated with the Russian Czar's Order of St. George.

Though the Jews eagerly played their part, instances of discrimination and anti-Jewish slights nevertheless persisted. Yet, for a time even the cynics and pessimists were silenced, and most Jews began to belittle such incidents as relics of the past. A Jewish volunteer named Schwarzbraun, somewhat short and with Semitic features, answered his comrades' barbs by cheerfully volunteering for extra duty, doing favors, and showing special devotion with acts of quiet bravery. Another volunteer told of two coreligionists who had met Christian insults by challenging their comrades to join them in leading the charge into battle—and paid for it with heavy wounds. Meno Burg, a Jew who had been among the first to volunteer, refused to be discouraged when he was summarily ousted from an elite regiment upon discovery that he was a Jew. After a lesser unit accepted him, he reacted not with anger but gratitude and optimistically cited this as proof that prejudice could be met with persistent diligence and patriotic deeds.[37]

Those who did not serve were apt to have feelings of inadequacy and guilt. Ludwig Robert, Rahel's brother, was one of these: "What is to become of me?" he asked his sister, adding, "I cannot become a soldier; I don't ride and on foot I would be in the sick bay within the first week.[38] Even young Giacomo had pangs of conscience. His brother Wilhelm joined up in October 1813 and won battlefield honors in Silesia and Saxony with the First Regiment of Hussars, winning a rare promotion to lieutenant. Giacomo was full of admiration but could not bring himself to do likewise. While his brother put himself in harm's way and the battles were raging, he continued his studies in Vienna, immersed in the social life of balls, concerts, and musical soirées. Yet in 1814, writing to his old teacher Aron Wolfsohn, he confessed that "I cannot hide the fact that I have been disloyal . . . and this decision will poison my honor.[39]

It was a time when the Jews of Germany were elated and full of hope. Having proved their loyalty, most thought that in the postwar world their recent enfranchisement would surely bring them the acceptance they craved and a more respected and secure place alongside their Christian countrymen. It was happening elsewhere in Europe and soon, they hoped, it would be the same in Prussia as well. But the reality, when peace came, would once again disillusion them.

14

Not only was there no further postwar progress, but it was the beginning of another painful period of reverses and renewed anti-Jewish discrimination. Prussia was not yet ready to integrate Jewish citizens into its national life.

Frederick William III had issued his appeal for volunteers with the pledge that "certain reward will accrue to those who distinguish themselves."[40] Two years later, returning Jewish veterans discovered that it was a promise from which they were not to benefit. Though, in theory, they were equal citizens, Frederick's ministers now were unanimous that neither the bureaucracy nor the military should be more open to Jews than in earlier times.

The Minister of Justice felt strongly that "the presumption of an inferior morality is not invalidated by transitory bravery." His colleague, the Minister of Finance agreed, though he used somewhat loftier terms: "The moral condition of Jews," he counseled, "their religious concepts, customs, and education require palpable improvement before, in addition to general citizenship, the right to government employment can be accorded them." The idea of Jews in the police, for instance, would greatly offend the sentiments of the lower classes, the king was told. As to making an exception for those decorated with the Iron Cross, the Minister of the Interior bluntly brushed that aside with the observation that "the valor which this decoration denotes is not the only virtue needed for public service."[41]

These were not isolated rebuffs. Even as the rabbis in their synagogues loyally celebrated each anniversary of the great victory at Leipzig, a public debate raged as to whether it might not have been a mistake to extend the franchise to the Jews in the first place.

In the end, the law was allowed to stand but ruled to apply only within Prussia's borders of 1812. For the areas returned after the war, it remained unimplemented, and in its place were left twenty-one separate sets of rules of varying severity, some not much less restrictive than in medieval times. Even in old Prussia, the enfranchisement of Jews was systematically re-

stricted and undermined. The promise of opening up academic jobs to unbaptized Jews went unfulfilled. Officer ranks in the military once again
were closed and no Jew was to be promoted above sergeant. Officers' pen-
sions earned at Waterloo were to be forfeited and no elite guard regiment
was henceforth to accept a Jew. Eligibility for elective offices—mayor, for
instance—was also proscribed. No unbaptized Jewish doctor was allowed
in a public health post, nor could a Jew be a pharmacist or a surveyor.

The rollback in Prussia was, in fact, part of a general reversal of Jewish
fortunes throughout Germany. In some areas the rights won under Napoleonic occupation were canceled outright and in the Free Cities of Lübeck
and Bremen a movement actually got under way simply to expel all Jewish
residents. Everywhere—from Austria, Bavaria, and Württemberg in the
south to the kingdoms of Westphalia and Hanover in the north—basic
rights were either abrogated or reduced, and new limits were placed on
where Jews could live and what they could do.

The principal reason for these changes was that in Prussia and most of
Germany the old reactionary forces, rather than the liberal reformers, had
once more taken charge when peace came. Their postwar goals were to restore aristocratic privilege and absolutist rule, to counter the rise of the
bourgeoisie, and to sweep away whatever vestiges of Napoleonic reforms
and popular rights they could. Prussia's intelligentsia and university students were strongly opposed to this kind of restoration of the old privileges
of the aristocracy. They wanted instead an all-German Constitution and
German unity. In reaction to the years of weakness and foreign domination, their demands became linked to a glorification of all things "Germanic." The extreme nationalism of Prussia's foremost philosopher, Johann Gottlieb Fichte, was greatly admired.

Though Germans were deeply divided on most issues, there was, however, one thing on which all sides agreed—that it was best to put the Jews
back in their place. Anti-Semitism was once more in fashion. At the newly
founded University of Berlin a respected professor named Rühs led the
charge. He seized on the prevailing Teutomania, linking Germanic virtues
with old notions of an exclusive Christian state in which the Jew was an
outsider and could not be a true citizen. Their rights should be reversed, he
argued. They should once more pay special taxes and no Christian should
ever again be asked to fight next to them. In Heidelberg another academic

named Fries went further. Because Jews endanger the welfare and character of true Germans they should all be expelled, he argued. To the consternation of the Jews, such views from respected academics, far from being rejected out of hand, gave rise to renewed debate among the intelligentsia. A veritable flood of pamphlets ensued, and as many scholars took one side as lined up on the other.

The rising tide of anti-Semitic polemics quickly took on more popular forms. In 1812, an unemployed physician had written a play, *The Jew School,* which was so scurrilous—and so bad—that it had been banned. Now the piece was resurrected with a new title, the king was prevailed upon to authorize its presentation, and with a well-known actor appropriately named Wurm (Worm) in the lead, it played to overflow crowds who applauded his broad caricaturizing of every negative Jewish stereotype. Elsewhere, hate sheets for the broad masses again made their appearance and were passed by the censors. One of these, the *Judenspiegel,* explained that solving the Jewish problem by killing them was not morally wrong, just against the law. A better solution was to sell Jewish children to the English for employment as slaves in the Indies. The men should be castrated, while Jewish women were candidates for service in houses of ill repute.[42]

There was even worse to come. In 1819, the wave of renewed anti-Jewish agitation turned ugly and attacks on Jewish citizens accompanied by mob looting spread from one German city to another. The first spark was ignited in the Bavarian town of Würzburg, where the students were in a revolutionary mood, full of Teutomania, and resentful of resurgent aristocratic privilege. Looking for trouble, they readily found it by turning on the Jews. Shouting the medieval anti-Jewish slogan *Hep-Hep*—a Latin acronym for *Hierosolyma est perdita* (Jerusalem is lost)—they marched on Jewish houses and shops, joined by a plundering mob that smashed and burned Jewish property and beat Jews wherever they crossed their paths.

The incident gave impetus to an epidemic of anti-Jewish riots throughout Germany, and before it ended, shouts of "Hep-Hep," "Juda Perish," and "Death and Ruination to the Jews" had been heard from Bamberg, to Karlsruhe, Heidelberg, Frankfurt, and Hamburg, and eventually in Berlin as well. By then, the authorities were thoroughly alarmed, fearing that what had seemed a harmless safety valve for dissatisfaction, with the Jews as convenient scapegoats, was threatening to lead to more general revolt. As they moved to suppress the riots, the students themselves pledged to desist—

not, as the *Vossische Zeitung* stressed, due to any sympathy for the Jews, but purely because of a regard for law and order.

Prussia's Jewry was stunned. It was now clear that the deep distrust toward them at all levels of society had not abated and that the image among Christian Germans of the Jew as a destructive outsider was still intact. The granting of formal rights when the reformers were briefly in charge had evidently changed none of that. True acceptance and equality were still a long way off.

As always, there was more than one reason why they had again been caught between forces beyond their control. For one thing, enfranchising the Jews had been imposed from above without popular support. Nationalistic reaction to foreign humiliation was another factor, as was the onset of hard times. In 1816–17 bad crops had caused widespread famine and a trebling of the price of grain. Subsequent bumper crops led to gluts that hurt many farmers, while the demise of Napoleon's continental system of protective tariffs brought a flood of English imports and ruined many small manufacturers. When conditions were bad, blaming Jewish bankers and merchants was a time-honored reaction.

Last, but not least, there was also the weak and vacillating king, a monarch easily influenced to tolerate renewed pressure on a group of people he had never liked. Just as he had acceded to the wishes of the reformers a few years earlier, so now he was easy prey to the regressive counsel of the reactionaries he had chosen to take their place. As representatives of the *Junker* class, they were busy reversing the trend toward democratization, and he was not one to offer resistance to their policy of limiting Jewish rights, which was part of the process. Controlling intellectuals and students and getting rid of the freedom seekers and trouble makers was a lot more important. That was the policy that Prince Metternich urged from Vienna, and his advisers devoted their energies to it over the next two decades. For the Jews, forced to come to terms with their continuing status as second-class citizens, it was once again a bleak and disappointing time.

15

Following her marriage, Rahel had joined her husband in Vienna and accompanied him to Frankfurt and Karlsruhe, where Varnhagen served as the

Prussian Resident. In 1819, he left the diplomatic service and both returned to Berlin.

The capital city, now with more than two hundred thousand inhabitants, was calm on the surface, but this concealed unhealthy contrasts beneath. In many places, the stress of the early beginnings of industrialization was evident. The city teemed with beggars and thieves. There was much poverty in dreary structures called *Mietskasernen* (rental barracks), which housed factory workers whose children, often not much older than nine, worked twelve hours a day, seven days a week. The military remained omnipresent; one in ten Berliners was still a soldier. Among the middle class, Biedermeier culture pervaded city life. The focus was on respectable domesticity and middle-class comfort: stolid, conventional—and obedient. Since political discussion was dangerous and participation in political affairs foreclosed, the social life of the intelligentsia and the upper classes had turned toward more frivolous matters. In place of political debate, energies were absorbed by an exaggerated interest in music and the theatre, and by social gossip and minor scandals at the opera.

The more than four thousand Jews now in Berlin were back in their uncomfortable place between two inhospitable forces. In the streets and among Prussia's elite, anti-Semitic rhetoric was again in vogue. On one side, there was the government's policy to limit and undermine the Jews' status as citizens. On the other, they were confronted by a virulently nationalist opposition whose slogan was "Honor, Freedom, Fatherland," and who considered Jews un-German and wanted no part of them. Some carried their extreme and chauvinistic views a bit far. Turnvater Jahn, for one—the students' idol—preached physical fitness as a special Germanic virtue and advocated a total ban on spoken French and all foreign travel. To protect Germans from the outside, he seriously advocated a no-man's-land between Germany and France, populated by wild beasts and snakes. Jahn's whimsical ideas were a case of the German predilection for extreme ideas pushed to their ultimate, fanciful limit.

Rahel died in 1833. It is ironic that it was in these last two decades of her life—as a converted Christian with an aristocratic name—that her attitude toward Judaism should take a very different turn. It was precisely in these later years, under the impact of the capital's somber climate of chauvinism and renewed anti-Semitism, that the aging Rahel developed a new interest in her people, a more sympathetic understanding of their plight, and a deeper sense of her own connection with their destiny. In part, her many personal disappointments and her experience as a diplomat's wife had been a factor. Young Heinrich Heine, who became her friend and protegé after his arrival in Berlin in the early 1820s, also influenced her change of attitude.

In Vienna, Rahel had first begun to admire those who had chosen not to "cross over," growing particularly fond of a friend "who had remained completely Jewish (and been rewarded with) . . . great mental gifts and a rich life."[43] Because of her Jewish origins, it had at times been advisable to stay away from some of the diplomatic receptions. Often, she later confessed to Heine, she felt out of place, a stranger and impostor—"wie eine Pute auf fremden Hof "[44] (like a hen in the wrong barnyard). Outwardly she could, since her conversion and marriage, appear as someone else, but her inner soul would not let her forget the truth. Nor would the world around her. The reality of her Jewishness clung to her and would not release her. Gradually it had dawned on her that change of name and religion was not enough, that there was no escape, that denying herself was not, after all, the answer. The world might know her as Frau von Varnhagen, but in her heart she had remained Rahel.

The renewed climate of anti-Semitism, especially the Hep-Hep riots, had shaken her. More objective and analytical now, she had been deeply affected by the new mood, which made her look at her country more critically and see the Jewish plight with new understanding and sympathy. "I am boundlessly unhappy," she wrote to her brother, "in a way I have never been before. What is this multitude of expelled [Jews] to do?" In Germany, she concluded wistfully, their historic role was that of the eternal scapegoat, chosen perhaps because "they are the most civilized, good natured, peaceful, and obedient people."[45]

Later it was Heine who had much to do with her reassessment of past assumptions. When he arrived in Berlin from Bonn and Göttingen to continue his university studies, he was twenty-four years old, a slight young man, short, with unprepossessing looks, oddly dressed, extremely thin, pale, and with an oval face in which a high forehead and large mouth stood out as the most prominent features.

His family were Jews who had long been resident in Germany—there was a distant ancestral relationship to Glückel von Hameln—yet, when he was still very young, his mother had transferred him from a Jewish school to the Catholic lycée in his native Düsseldorf and raised him largely disconnected from his Jewish roots. Young Heine was entirely dependent on the reluctant financial support of a wealthy uncle, yet exuberantly irresponsible and spendthrift in his habits. He was also brash, arrogant, cynical, and irreverent. At Bonn, he had been expelled from the university for dueling and had departed anything but contrite—dropping personal cards inscribed *pour prendre congé* (on leave) on the very officials who had just turned him out.

He was, however, also a young man of wit and sharp intelligence, eager to be free and to live an unrestricted life to the fullest. When it suited him, he could be charming and amusing—the one person, a friend remarked, in whose company one could never be bored. In theory, he was in Berlin to study law. In fact, philosophy, literature, poetry, and the good life in Prussia's biggest city interested him a great deal more, and for those he had come well armed with introductions to the right people. Before long, Madame Beer, Giacomo's mother, included him in her musical soirées, where he formed a friendship with her youngest son, Michael, who also wrote poetry and was roughly his age. Before long he had also been introduced to the Varnhagens, who were once more receiving guests.

Young and impressionable, Heine was thrilled with his access to Rahel's salon. It was again a meeting place for a sprinkling of the intellectual elite, though now a smaller, older, and more homogeneous group, whose conversation was less free, unconventional, and exuberant than in former times. Rahel and Heine felt an immediate affinity for each other—she recognizing his exceptional mind and poetic talents, he captivated by her intuitive understanding of him. He eagerly accepted her as his patroness, and she took him under her wing, encouraged him, and scolded him gently when his tendency to act the enfant terrible got out of hand. She was one of the few people with whom Heine would not sooner or later have a serious falling out, and his admiration for her never ceased. "I should like to have engraved on my collar the words 'I belong to Madame Varnhagen,'" he wrote her. Years later he would still remember her as "the most gifted woman of the universe."[46]

At once cynical and clear-eyed, Heine never had any illusions and, unlike Rahel, required no noble motives to justify a decision to convert. Some
years later he would take the step—without in the least hiding the fact that
for him the baptismal certificate was nothing else than the "entrance
ticket" to wider endeavors, in his case a tenured university post. As it
turned out, the appointment never materialized, and Heine came to regret
what he had done almost as soon as the step was taken. In fact, the experience stimulated his interest in Jews and their problems. He too had to come
to terms with prejudice and discrimination. His response was to use biting
irony, sarcasm, and slashing criticism as his principal weapons and the
shield behind which to cloak the pain.

While Heine reaffirmed his Jewishness as soon as he had been touched
by the baptismal waters, Rahel's transformation took a lifetime and was not
completed until her waning years. Toward the end, she sometimes reverted
to the use of Hebrew when writing to her brother, occasionally addressing
him as *"Lieber Religionsbruder"* (Dear Coreligionist)—perhaps intending a
bit of pained irony, since both had converted to Christianity.

Yet, though she had retained her charm and wit, the older Rahel was a
woman much changed. Physically she had never been a beauty, but at fifty
she was already infirm and prematurely aged, a fat and unsightly woman
with a drooping chin and bent shoulders.[47] Yet it was Rahel's outlook that
had changed most of all, although her basic character remained the same.
She retained her interest in relationships, her seeking for truth, and
her empathy for others; she still held her admiration for Goethe and
Fichte, and her lifelong preoccupation with philosophic speculation, intermingled now with a heightened religiosity. Yet she was no longer the naive
romantic, the idealist who believed that she could be fulfilled through personal development or through communion with others. She had become
more reflective about herself, more insightful about Germany and Germans, and more realistic about the importance of the historical experiences
of both Germans and Jews as barriers to social and political progress.

Before she died a painful death in 1833, she had come to what must have
been for her the most surprising and unexpected insight of all: that her
lifelong struggle against her Jewish origins had been futile, that her Jewishness had in fact been the true essence of her being, the one thing that
had given her existence meaning. When she died, she had ceased to be at

war with her origins: "The thing that all my life seemed to me the greatest shame, that was the misery and misfortune of my life—having been born a Jew—this I should on no account wish to have missed," she said in the end.

Historical perspective has validated her final thoughts. As a major figure in the social and intellectual history of the Germany of her day, Rahel stands out not only because her salon was the meeting place for a cross section of Berlin's elite, the politicians, aristocrats, writers, philosophers, and reformers who shaped the thinking of her time but also because of her remarkable qualities, her magnetic personality, her special gifts of sensitivity and observation, and her not inconsiderable literary talent, reflected in the many volumes of letters she left behind. The ability of this unusual woman—homely, of modest means, and with little formal education—to attract and beguile so diverse and large a group of Prussia's intellectual elite remains a reason for the lasting interest in her.

Moses Mendelssohn believed that Jews, if given equal rights, would become as acceptable as Christian Germans, and still remain of "the Mosaic Faith." Rahel, for her part, was a prototype of cultivated German Jews of her time who were taking advantage of the crumbling ghetto walls to seek a new identity and personal freedom through assimilation. She had been too impatient to await the granting of civil rights and believed that her religion was a useless burden, that it could easily be discarded, and that acceptance in the German world would follow. Yet she, and those of her time who kept to their religion and counted on legal rights and accomplishment in business and intellectual pursuits for advancement, would find that this was merely the beginning of the battle. Nothing had really been solved. Citizenship—even recognition of individual accomplishment—did not mean an end to prejudice against Jews, or a beginning of their de facto equality among Germans.

Rahel's life story mirrors their experience and is a portent of what their descendants would confront later. To overcome prejudice, to come to terms with the world around her and to win her place, she walked down many of the roads later generations would travel repeatedly—and she was one of the first to find the same impediments they would encounter. In her attitude toward her Jewishness, and the evolution in her thinking over time, her trials stand out as a foretaste of what many Jews would experience as

Germany moved toward modernity. Over the generations, the range of their individual responses and reactions remained large and diverse, though they became increasingly predictable. Rahel discovered the consequences—and the pain and futility—of much of what was tried. Later generations would not fare better.

CHAPTER V

ACHIEVERS

Giacomo

Meyerbeer—a Jewish composer, whom good fortune endowed from birth with great sums of money, bribed the theatre to produce his medio-cre operas.

Wolfgang Menzel, a German critic

1837

Ninety-nine of a hundred . . . [of your readers] are Reschoim *[Jew hat-ers]. . . . What is to be done? No pommade de lion . . . not even the baptismal waters will grow back the piece of foreskin, of which they deprived us on the eighth day of our birth; and he who does not bleed to death . . . on the ninth day, will bleed from it all his life, even after death.*

Giacomo Meyerbeer to Heinrich Heine

1840

1

Giacomo Meyerbeer's life hardly resembled Rahel's. Though only twenty years her junior, he belonged to another generation, that of the children and grandchildren of the pioneers, for whom doors had been opened that were still firmly shut when Rahel was growing up. In almost every impor-tant respect, he had advantages she never enjoyed.

The eldest son of a close-knit and loving family totally supportive of his every endeavor, Giacomo was spared the agonies of Rahel's early years as the neglected daughter of a difficult father and dysfunctional mother, forced to educate herself and hovering between Jewish and secular worlds. The Beers were among the most respected and wealthiest of Berlin's Jews. They had already deeply assimilated into German culture and educated their eldest son with the finest tutors that money could buy. The family's wealth gave him lifelong freedom from financial concerns.

Most important of all, the scion of the Beers was a child prodigy born with a remarkable combination of gifts—a unique musical talent, a photographic memory, and the capacity for great bursts of energy and powers of creativity. Since his earliest years, there had been the certainty of a brilliant future in music. Whatever else would trouble him and fuel his pessimism and fears in later life—and there would be much of that—uncertainty about his talents or his calling was never a factor. Rahel had not been so felicitously endowed, and she had spent much of her time beset by doubts about herself and in search of a mission.

Yet there were elements of background and outlook that they shared. Both came from established Berlin Jewish families long resident in Brandenburg-Prussia, though Giacomo's was much the older and more distinguished, with roots going back to Jost Liebmann. For each, the consciousness of what it meant to be a Prussian Jew was a deeply ingrained and decisive element of their personalities. Both had early in life been wounded by anti-Semitic prejudice and neither could ever forget it. Though they dealt with it in entirely different ways, the experience would be a decisive influence on both their subsequent lives.

Rahel had suffered for years from anti-Jewish sentiments and struggled all her life to overcome them. While still a child, Giacomo had also been made keenly aware of anti-Semitic prejudice, and suffered no less from it. Grattenauer's attacks on him left a lasting impression. Other painful experiences had followed. When, as a young man, he had been rebuffed by "young lovelies" in an amorous advance, for reasons he assumed to be his Jewishness, he had confessed to his diary that they have "hurt me to the innermost regions of my soul. . . . When will I finally learn to resign myself calmly to the unavoidable?"[1] The Hep-Hep riots and the actor Wurm's hateful depiction of Jews had further wounded him, causing him to remind his brother of "das eiserne Wort 'Risches'" (unshakable Jew-hatred).[2]

Yet for Giacomo being a Jew was an equally unshakable fact of life.

Though he would later go to great lengths to advance his career, denying or abandoning his faith was never an option. He was proud to be a Jew, one of the chosen people. As a young man he had promised at his grandfather's deathbed never to convert and he never regretted the commitment in the slightest. From his parents, pillars of Berlin's Jewish community who were respected even by the royal family (in 1816 the king had accorded Madame Beer the singular honor of awarding her the *Luisenorder*,[3] a coveted Prussian medal), he had learned to regard anti-Semitism as a burden to be borne with dignity. His parents believed that anti-Jewish prejudice was the mark of the narrow-minded and the uncultured and that one best met it with patience and civility. The slights might hurt but one swallowed them silently, worked especially hard, used one's money wisely, and proved the bigots wrong by winning their respect through accomplishments and good deeds. From the beginning, it was this philosophy that Giacomo had adopted as his own.

By the early 1820s, while Heinrich Heine was discovering Berlin and Rahel was rethinking her life, Giacomo was in Italy, well removed from the problems of Prussia's Jews. The renewed wave of anti-Semitism at home was, of course, well known to him. It depressed him greatly, though it merely confirmed his innate pessimism about the depth of German prejudices. But Giacomo was now in single-minded pursuit of a goal he considered paramount—to complete his musical training and to win acclaim as an operatic composer. Family loyalties and filial duty meant much, yet even his father's pleading to come home had been to no avail, though it had clearly pained him. "You know that I have always considered familiarity with the French and Italian theatre to be indispensable. This is why I cannot . . . return to Berlin," he had answered his pleas, adding sadly, "It grieves me to realize how incapable I have recently been of pleasing you."[4] His parents had taught him the virtues of accomplishment, whether in business or in the arts. They had taught him well—nothing would now divert him from the quest for it.

Giacomo had first caused a stir as a child prodigy on the piano. In his teens, his parents dispatched him to Darmstadt for private musical training by the great Abbé Vogler, music teacher and organist par excellence. He was accompanied by brother Heinrich, a tutor, and a valet. The Darmstadt years were good ones for him, and he had formed a warm friendship with the young Carl Maria von Weber and several other of Vogler's talented students. They called themselves the Harmonic Society and, amply financed by Giacomo's liberal allowance, combined honing their musical skills with the pleasures of wine, women, and song.

Soon, however, Giacomo's interests shifted from the piano to composing, and by 1811 he had produced his first opus, a lyrical rhapsody entitled *Gott und die Natur* (God and Nature), which Amalie succeeded in having performed at the Royal National Theatre in Berlin. It was a youthful work of no lasting importance, but the story of its public appearance nevertheless provides a first glimpse of the "Meyerbeer system" of organizing the public presentation of his works, for which he would become famous and be much criticized in future years. Family and friends were mobilized in a full-court press to ensure maximum favorable publicity. His parents used their extensive connections to assemble the best singers and performers, important people were courted and flattered, and the Harmonic Society was enlisted to write favorable reviews under pseudonyms in the key musical journals. Giacomo took personal charge of the campaign and would repeat such an effort again the next year, when his first real operatic effort was nearing completion. He began with a direct request to Carl Maria von Weber: "My opera will be finished in three weeks. . . . Speak of me to Härtel [a critic] as someone whose essays would be very desirable."[5]

After the premiere, he hastened to inform Johann Gänsbacher, one of his Harmonic Society brothers who had established himself in Prague, of the "marvelous reception" and "flattering compliments from the Queen," adding that "I would be grateful if you put this in a [political] newspaper." For good measure he supplied Gänsbacher with the specific quote to be used.[6]

The challenge of composing operas now captured his imagination. He quickly composed two—and soon found that they were boring failures that not even a public relations campaign could salvage. Giacomo was disappointed, but he was learning and he remained undeterred. Mother and Father Beer now armed him with a fistful of introductions to the right people in Paris and London—Spontini and Cherubini among them—and Giacomo departed to sample the theatre and music scene in the two capitals, ending in Vienna where he waited out the war years. There he met the aging Antonio Salieri, Vienna's Court Conductor and composer, who advised him to leave the Austrian capital and move south. A serious effort to learn his craft, the maestro told him, required going to the source—to Italy, the land of opera and bel canto. Italian opera had reigned supreme for over a century, though its heyday was actually nearing an end. Only Rossini, the master of opera buffa, was still a great star, and he too would soon depart for Paris, where the latest trends in European opera were now being set.

In Italy a surfeit of stimulation awaited Giacomo. There was an opera house in every city. A never-ending output of new works was playing to full houses. There were Sicilian folk songs to absorb and Rossini's latest scores to study. The greatest singers were there. Giacomo arrived in 1816 and remained for eight years.

2

On October 29, 1824, while traveling in Italy, Karl Friedrich Schinkel went to the opera. He was Prussia's most important architect and arbiter of taste, whose unmistakable style of classical Prussian designs would leave an imprint on Berlin's major buildings for generations. Schinkel came to hear the latest, much talked about opera of Giacomo Meyerbeer, a fellow Berliner. But what he heard did not impress him, and he so recorded it in his diary: "In the evening a new opera was given at the Teatro della Pergola. *Il Crociato in Egitto* [Crusaders in Egypt] by the Jew Meyerbeer is a mad, indigestible, sweet-sour twaddle full of trivial sentiment and vulgar noise."[7]

The tenor of the comment is sadly revealing. For Schinkel, a Jew was a Prussian when he brought glory to the fatherland—when not, he was still a Jew. Was it because Giacomo was Jewish, as he had felt constrained to note, or were there other explanations why the opera had displeased him? Whatever his reason, in this instance Prussia's first architect was in a distinct minority. *Il Crociato,* premiered in Venice in March, was universally judged a major success; for Giacomo, it became the crowning achievement of his eight years in Italy. Over the next decade, the opera would be performed repeatedly in Paris, London, and Dresden and on virtually every stage of Italy, where the public could barely contain its enthusiasm. Heine, who later heard *Crociato* in Florence, reported that he had never witnessed such frenzy—that special *furore* that only Italian audiences are capable of.

The critics, too, had been unanimously enthusiastic, and it especially pleased Giacomo that this time, Schinkel to the contrary, even the Germans who had accorded his earlier efforts decidedly mixed receptions were definitely impressed. The correspondent of the *Allgemeine Musikalische Zeitung* wrote from Venice that impartial opinion could not praise the opera enough. While Schinkel had been quick to identify the "twaddle" as the work of a Jew, this critic noted that to have so much praise heaped on a native son was a special honor for Germany.

That Giacomo was a Jew was never in doubt. He was slight and short, with definite Semitic features, shortsighted, with a prominent hooked nose and large lips. He also had flat feet, and when he walked it was with an odd shuffling waddle. His dark eyes exuded sensitivity and intelligence, but there was a certain permanent sadness in them as well. He had a presence that commanded respect, and unlike Rahel he seemed at ease and unconcerned about his appearance. He spoke softly, was eternally polite and careful to avoid giving offense, yet he was proud to be a Jew and did not hesitate in the least to show it.

Crociato was the fifth and last opera Giacomo composed in Italy. Firmly establishing him as an important figure in the musical world, it was the principal factor in the realization of a long-cherished ambition: an invitation to compose for the Académie Royale de Musique, the new opera house that had recently opened its doors in the French capital. Paris was where Europe's operatic history was now being made—Rossini had already departed Italy to become the director of the Italian Opera there—and it was there, in the center of the musical world, that Giacomo wanted to reach for new heights. Now he would get his chance to do so.

Giacomo had worked hard and his growing reputation and final triumph in Italy with *Crociato* were no mere accidents. For eight years he had traveled the country, absorbed all he could, labored with great concentration, brought a total of five operas before the public, learned from each, and applied the experience to the next. He had engaged the best singers to perform for him, formed an alliance with Gaetano Rossi, one of Italy's foremost librettists, and courted the major impresarios. By all accounts, he was a rehearsal fanatic, working himself into a frenzy before each premiere, with nervous attention to the smallest details of score, libretto, and staging. At every turn, Amalie and the family were there with unstinting encouragement and assistance, sharing in each triumph and lamenting every setback. Giacomo's work was not only a source of their unbridled pride but also a kind of family enterprise in which all members of the Beer family eagerly played a part.

3

When Giacomo had first come to Italy in 1816, his second brother, Wolff— he now called himself Wilhelm—was his traveling companion. Later that year, Amalie personally journeyed south to check on his progress. When they were apart, a steady stream of letters flowed in both directions—Amalie providing the latest gossip from the home front's theatre and music scene, father Jakob reporting on business and sending letters of credit, and the brothers keeping their oar in with news on politics and assorted family matters.

It must have been no small task to keep up his side of this voluminous two-way family correspondence,[8] but Giacomo had been raised to take such responsibilities seriously and—ever the dutiful son—usually tried valiantly to comply. Some years earlier he had taken to combining his last two names into one and now, intoxicated with Italy and anxious to please his hosts, he adopted Giacomo as his given name and so signed even his letters home. For Amalie, however, he always remained "My dearest Meyer." When delinquent in his correspondence she would swiftly call him to account: "Do me the favor and write to Hans [Henoch/Heinrich]," she admonished him, "for otherwise he feels so hurt." Normally Giacomo quickly got the point, particularly if there were subtle allusions to a little guilt.

After almost two years of preparation, he scored an encouraging success with his first Italian opera, *Romilda e Constanza,* at the Teatro Nuovo in Padua. Rossi, perennially short of money and attracted by Giacomo's handsome fee, had written the libretto, and top performers for the major parts, normally poorly paid in Italy, had been induced to participate by equally high compensation. The local critics had been very positive, and even the Germans had taken note of his success. In Berlin, Amalie had wept so profusely, she said, "that my head hurts."[9] She insisted on receiving the score at once. Her dearest wish was to have her son's first Italian opera presented in the Prussian capital, but the style was not particularly pleasing to German tastes and nothing came of it. Two more operas followed in 1819 and again Madame Beer pressed hard to have them performed in Berlin. Be sure to send them to the king, she admonished him, and though Giacomo was concerned about adverse reaction to the Italian flavor and possible anti-Semitic prejudice, he had nevertheless obeyed.

As he had feared, his third opera, *Emma di Resburgo,* though favorably received in Italy, met with less enthusiasm at home. Nationalistic feeling was running high and anything foreign faced rough going. "How sad," the *Allgemeine Musikalische Zeitung*'s critic wrote, "that [his] native competence is drowned in Italian 'Rossinismus.' The composer must have been enamored of an Italian-Rossinic lady when he wrote the opera."[10] Even his friend Carl Maria von Weber grumbled that Giacomo was betraying the memory of the Abbé Vogler, their revered mentor. "My heart bleeds to see how a German artist with his own creative powers . . . lowers himself to [foreign] imitation," he wrote to a friend, later expressing the hope in Dresden's *Abendzeitung* that, having studied the best of what other nations have to offer, Meyerbeer might now return "to the German fatherland . . . to help erect the structure of a [uniquely] German national opera."[11]

These were the first muted rumblings of what would in time become a steady drumbeat of criticism of Meyerbeer's work—that he was too "cosmopolitan" and not German enough. It was the height of irony. On the one hand, as his fame grew the German musical establishment was eager to claim this Jew as one of their own and to shower him with honors. The king himself wrote to congratulate him for *Emma,* and on September 27, 1825, having attended the second Paris performance of *Crociato* and witnessed its huge success, he requested firmly that Giacomo adapt it for presentation in Berlin. Later, when the French and Brazilian governments decorated him for his achievements, Prussia quickly responded with the unprecedented step, for a Jew, of making him a full member of its Academy of Arts and awarded him its highest honor. On the other hand, the barbs against him grew steadily more pointed with each success in Italy and Paris. What elsewhere was hailed as his special genius for fusing the best of the great composers—from Gluck to Mozart and Rossini—into a unique blend, his enemies and critics in Germany denounced as mere plagiarism. Robert Schumann subsequently dismissed him as too "Frenchified" and incapable of originality, and eventually there would be those, led by Richard Wagner, who argued that these shortcomings were not merely un-German but in fact typically Jewish.

For the always cautious and fearful Giacomo, none of this was designed to encourage a quick return to Germany or, for that matter, ready assent to have his operas performed there. Yet he yearned to be appreciated in Germany, perhaps more than anything else, and so the attacks greatly pained him. All the same, in 1823, he politely ignored hints that he might be considered for the position of director of the Berlin Opera. Amalie, knowing her son, did her best to prepare and console him when she feared new attacks. "A full house watched your *Emma* [in Dresden] . . . and there was thunderous applause" she wrote him in 1820, ". . . but now the critics will come . . . do not fear them . . . they are nothing but a pack of dogs who leave no one alone. . . . They even reprimanded Rossini and Spontini like so many schoolboys." [12]

With his final Italian opera, Giacomo had firmly established his own personal style. Written in the manner of Rossini, *Crociato* was his most successful Italian effort, and the first to contain all the elements of his own unique contributions to the genre. Later, his special style would evolve further in his French operas and propel him to the top of musical Paris.

Giacomo wanted his operas to be grand. He specialized in what some called "optical" theater—spectacles in which libretto, music, ballet, stunning sets, and strong stage action were skillfully combined into a single dramatic whole. He pioneered new orchestration by greatly increasing the size of his orchestras and inventing unprecedented special instrumental effects, especially for the saxophone, clarinet, and bassoon. His scores were romantic and intensely melodic. He paid attention to the smallest details of music and staging; rehearsed, rewrote, and revised until the last moment; and insisted on the best performers for the most important parts. What he aimed for was *éclat*—to amaze, impress, and even to overwhelm with pomp and pageantry. He liked big character scenes, large choruses, dramatic vocal parts, and strong, melodic arias. Much of this appears overdramatic and sensational today, but Giacomo's audiences adored it, and it made his later French grand operas—*Robert le Diable*, *Les Huguenots*, *Le Prophète*, *L'Étoile du Nord*, *Dinorah*, and *L'Africaine*—intensely popular in their time.

Crociato, the story of religious crusaders cast adrift amid the oriental splendor of Egypt, was an ideal vehicle for him. There were massed choruses of slaves, crusaders, and emirs, great exotic tableaux and emotional arias with romantic themes—crusader valor, religious conflict, passion, love, and painful unresolvable tragedy. Later he would build on his success with *Crociato* and continue to develop themes of religious conflict, travelers stranded in foreign lands, and virtue confronting overwhelming forces. For Giacomo Meyerbeer there must have been a poignant symbolism in such themes. Tales of religious prejudice concerning small groups of powerless, yet noble people seeking refuge in alien cultures no doubt reflected his own experience. Perhaps it is even true, as some would later suggest, that his very love for grand opera with its larger-than-life scenes was for him a way to create his own world and escape the limits that prejudice imposed on him and his people in the real one.

Giacomo wanted success; indeed he craved it. His ambition was to be recognized and accepted for his accomplishments. Great achievements would validate him and prove his worth—in spite of the barriers, enemies, and prejudice lurking everywhere. Throughout his life, he exerted himself ceaselessly toward that end and sought satisfaction in public acclaim. Yet neither success, when it came, nor the pursuit of it made him a happy man. The joys were short-lived, there was little lasting satisfaction in the honors it brought, and a secure peace of mind eluded him most of his life.

It was not in his nature to feel happy, satisfied, and fulfilled for long. Ever fearful of giving offense, always expecting the worst, finely attuned to every slight, he saw enemies all around him, risks and dangers everywhere. He tried his best to coddle and influence the critics, but when they wrote unfavorable notices, he was greatly hurt and quick to suspect anti-Semitic bigotry. It was as if the centuries of Jewish suffering were imprinted on his soul and would leave him no peace.

The bombast of his works hid his personal fear of criticism and failure, and his polite manner reflected in some measure an innate timidity. A traumatic encounter with Beethoven in Vienna in 1813 has often been cited as an early illustration. Asked to join a mammoth orchestra for the premiere performance of the great master's "Wellington's Victory," the young Giacomo had been assigned to play the drums. But he incurred the composer's displeasure by hesitating momentarily to evoke the thunderous suddenness of the roar of the great cannons of battle. "Ha Ha, I was not satisfied with him," Beethoven is said to have declared to the general amusement of his friends. "Ha Ha, he beat them late. . . . He lacked the courage to beat them at the right moment!"[13] Giacomo never forgot the ridicule and the humiliation.

The tendency to worry and to expect the worst was deeply ingrained in him, and his family worried about it. "Dear Pessimist," Amalie had addressed her letter to him when his first Italian opera was in its Berlin rehearsal, attempting with humor and selective good news to cheer him.[14] Father Jakob had taken him to task more pointedly: "The Lord's gifts are wondrously given . . . and yours are one in a million," he wrote. "With your good fortune . . . it is very depressing for me to receive such morose letters from you. . . . If your illness is at fault, you should have gone to [the spa] Carlsbad. . . ."[15]

Giacomo was a hypochondriac from youth, his nervous afflictions, real and imagined, multiplying as he grew older. As deadlines approached or frustration over his work temporarily halted progress, they would steadily worsen and torment him greatly. "Finalmente . . . de' vostri Foruncoli?"[16] (Finally, how about your boils?) Rossi cautiously inquired in one of his letters. Much of the family correspondence is filled with concerns over medical crises. After each premiere, nervous exhaustion and all manner of stomach ailments, digestive problems, headaches, and painful skin rashes would force him to flee to "cures" to repair the damage. In the Belgian town of Spa, he became known as one of its most famous regulars.[17]

All this Giacomo endured with a fatalistic sense of inevitability, coupled with a tendency to allow lifelong superstitions to rule his decisions and the timing of important events. He believed that, for good luck, at least one beggar or indigent had to receive alms from him each day. Fridays he considered ominous, a day when no contract could be signed or decision taken. No premiere could unfold without receiving first a solemn blessing from his mother. Travels were carefully planned to avoid being on the road to anywhere on a Friday. To do otherwise, he feared, would enhance the chances for disaster en route or at his destination. Even if the premiere of an opera had been an enormous hit, he refused to utter the word "success" until at least after the third performance, fearing that otherwise failure might yet lurk in the wings.[18]

4

On August 28, 1831, the boatman Johann Wegner fell gravely ill in Berlin, and two doctors, summoned to his barge that evening, feared the worst. The next morning the unfortunate Wegner was dead, and when a team of eleven physicians completed the postmortem examination of his corpse, they confirmed the dread news: the Asiatic cholera had arrived in the capital city.

A year earlier, the disease had killed forty-five hundred Muscovites and thrown Russia's largest city into panic. By the following spring it had progressed to East Prussia and Posen, and in spite of efforts at quarantine and assorted other precautions, Berlin was now also afflicted. Before the epidemic ran its course, twenty-two hundred Berliners would be infected and more than half would die, often with extraordinary suddenness. A strapping young mason's apprentice had labored industriously in his workshop until, feeling slightly unwell at three in the morning, he climbed the stairs to his bed—only to be dead two-and-a-half hours later. In the streets, one of Berlin's numerous ladies of the night was said to have expired no more than a half hour after dismissing her last client.

In Prussia the first instinct was always to organize—even if, in this instance, it was restricted to the management of helplessness in the face of disaster. A special sanitary commission was appointed to manage the emergency in a more orderly fashion than in chaotic Moscow. Special cholera hospitals were set up, and teams readied to remove and bury the dead.

The blow nevertheless was severe. After the misery of an abnormally cold winter, the added dislocations from the epidemic led to a sharp escalation in the cost of food—potatoes doubled in price—and for months the city remained paralyzed and in the grip of fear. Before it was over, two of Prussia's senior generals had died, and the philosopher Hegel who, ironically, had fled in panic to the isolation of his country house and stocked it with a vast array of medicines and rumored cures had nevertheless also succumbed. His death, Varnhagen wrote, was like "a thunderbolt for friend and foe." [19]

It was a time when Prussia was still a backward country, in many respects far behind England and France in its development. Politically, there had been no loosening of autocratic rule and aristocratic supremacy and little progress in the rise of the bourgeoisie to positions of power. The country was still largely agricultural. Seven of ten Prussians continued to eke out a meager living on the land and industrial development remained in its infancy. Modern manufacturing, then making rapid strides in England, had hardly begun.

For almost two decades the country had remained firmly in the grip of the military and bureaucracy, much as the system had been conceived under Frederick the Great and his father. Foreigners marveled at this "nation of drillers and scribblers" and at the slavishness of its people. The governing motto was still *Suum Cuique*—to each his own according to class, rank, wealth, and estate. The king was the ruler, the nobility ran the military and the bureaucracy, burghers paid the taxes, and the peasants struggled on the land.

The system was designed to be held together by obedience and a code of conduct so rigid that a Chief of Staff was once forced to resign because he had the unacceptable habit of unbuttoning his tunic when seated at his desk.[20] The king personally dealt with such weighty matters as the question of whether an unmarried woman could call herself Fräulein (acceptable, if aristocratic), or merely Mamsell (if from the bourgeois classes).[21] The military was omnipresent, uniforms were everywhere, and everyone gave orders down and was expected to follow those from above. Berliners even complained that their thirty-six postmen, decked out in a uniform of tails with orange collars adorned with the royal insignia, acted more like top sergeants than state servants. City streets were filled with marching and drilling soldiers. Berlioz reported with amazement that instead of regimental musicians he had noted whole "regiments of musicians" with their marching trumpeters and drummers.

In spite of so much regimentation and a plethora of rules, Berlin nevertheless lagged far behind London and Paris, remaining a dusty, dirty, and unhygienic place. Paving of major streets and installation of gas lamps had only recently begun—much to the chagrin of the 112 night watchmen stumbling through the streets to enforce the locking of doors at night. Instead of shouting the hour, as in earlier times, they were now commanded to blow their whistles—an innovation that had done little to enhance their popularity. The city teemed with rats, and night soil still flowed through open sewers—some 200,000 buckets being collected nightly by a squadron of women fondly known locally as "night bucketeers" (*Nacht Eemas*—in Berlinese). Their job was to dump the stuff into the river each morning, and the permanent stench from it was so trenchant that most Berliners had taken to keeping their windows tightly shut even on hot summer days.

With cholera, economic problems, and political repression, 1831 was not a happy time for the citizenry, and to add to their miseries a depression in textiles had greatly enlarged the ranks of the city's poor. A full 20 percent of Berlin's quarter million people were forced to eat the free soup dispensed from public troughs. In fact, caring for the city's indigent had that year become the largest item in the municipal budget, and this was draining revenues from an ever-expanding array of levies and taxes. To help close the gap, Berliners were now assessed a greatly resented tax of three taler for each of their six thousand dogs, on top of the excises they paid for beer, milling, meat, and other food items and essentials. For a while, an imaginative official had even dreamed up a tax on nightingales, a popular pet among Berliners. That particular impost, however, was quickly abolished—having foundered on the owners' outrage on the one hand, and the paucity of the take on the other.[22]

Prince William, second son of the king and destined to rule one day as the first German Kaiser, shared the sour mood of Berliners that year, though not entirely for the same reasons. For him, the cholera was just one more in a string of worrisome developments and, as he saw it, hardly the worst.

He was tall, blond, blue-eyed, and handsome but, unfortunately, boring and bereft of sparkle or imagination. At thirty-three, he held conservative views that were as rigid as his ramrod-straight guard officer's bearing. More even than his father and his brother the Crown Prince, William was a firm believer in the virtues of military discipline and obedience, and strongly supported the prevailing policies, advocated by Prince Metternich in Vienna, to suppress all tendencies toward parliamentarianism and the popular franchise. If anything, he thought his father had not been vigorous enough in stamping out dissent, and he agreed with Metternich, who had prodded the king to use the recent spate of revolutionary troubles in Europe as a convenient excuse to root out liberal tendencies ever more firmly.

William had watched in dismay as a popular revolution had swept Paris in July of the previous year, forcing the Bourbon king, Charles X, to flee to

England and replacing him with the "citizen king" Louis Phillippe of Or-
léans who, it was said, walked the streets of Paris most unroyally clad in
bourgeois clothes, with a gray hat and carrying an umbrella. Worse yet,
the French nobility had been driven from power, and the new king was
permitted to take the throne only after swearing allegiance to a new bourgeois constitution. To add insult to injury, he had also been made to accept
the hated tricolor and Gallic cock in place of the royal white banner and
lilies as the new symbols of France. Was it the ghost of 1789 all over again?

As Prince William and Prussia's rulers feared, the July revolution had,
much like the cholera, inexorably spread beyond the national borders of
France. A people's revolt against the Russian occupiers of truncated Poland
had generated dangerous sympathies among Prussia's intelligentsia. In
Brussels, the censors unwisely allowed the performance of Auber's opera *La
Muette de Portici,* which was about a seventeenth-century revolt of Neapoli-
tan fishermen against the rule of the Spaniards. This tale of people struggling for their rights against oppressors so inflamed the audience that it
had actually precipitated a popular uprising and led to the splitting of Belgium from the Kingdom of the Netherlands. The spirit of unrest then
spread closer to home, and there had been bread riots and protests in a
number of German states, partly political and partly to demonstrate
against economic hardship. In the end, the rulers of Brunswick, Saxony,
and Hesse-Cassel were forced to abdicate, and new constitutions had been
introduced there and in Hanover.

Even in Berlin, tailors' apprentices had taken to the streets to protest
their harsh conditions—an unheard of provocation—though law and order were quickly restored by the loyal military. The prisons were full, but
on balance Prussia remained an island of relative calm and obedience amid
all the unrest; the censure and stern suppression of demagogues and trou-
blemakers were seeing to that.

Unsettled times such as these once again underscored the vulnerability
of the Jews—now nominally full citizens but in practice relegated to a distinctly second-class status. As long as Prussia and most of Germany remained politically and socially frozen, there was little chance for a more
normal Christian-Jewish relationship to emerge. Real integration of Jews
into German life was foreclosed while change was taboo, and while the
king and his ministers busily reinvented the past.

In England, France, the Netherlands, and America the introduction of constitutional government and the enfranchisement of the bourgeoisie had opened new doors for Jews. In Germany, that process had not yet begun, and so the vicious circle in which they had been caught for so long remained unbroken. The traditional restrictions still isolated them, and the isolation still fed and reinforced anti-Semitic prejudices. So long as that continued, progress toward real integration remained difficult or impossible, and Jewish exposure to the hazards of disliked outsiders and convenient scapegoats for popular resentments still prevailed.

Not surprisingly, the disturbances of 1830–31 had once more spilled over into familiar anti-Jewish excesses and new forms of Jew-hatred now that the Jews—better educated, more secular, and nominal citizens—were more in the public eye.

In Hamburg, handbills entitled DOWN WITH JEWS, THE POLICE, AND TAXES had appeared in the town center, along with the more novel public complaint that "Jew-boys who peddle during the week" throw their weight around and monopolize newspapers in the coffeehouses on their *Schabbes*. In Hessen-Darmstadt, a bread revolt in September 1830 led to sporadic attacks on Jewish merchants, in Karlsruhe synagogue windows were smashed, and in Breslau tailors' and carpenters' apprentices had staged a food riot and rampaged through Jewish shops. In Munich the chief of police reported that public complaints were focused on "lack of earnings, high food prices, the police, mechanical presses and . . . Jewish usurers." In sum, in the prevailing times of trouble and tension, Jews were still at risk as scapegoats. Even in orderly Prussia, Jewish windows had been broken and spasmodic attacks on their persons and property had occurred.[23]

Yet for the Jews there were also new opportunities alongside old risks. Even in Prussia's special environment of backwardness and order, political reaction and administrative efficiency, and aristocratic arrogance amid Biedermeier tranquillity, some change was inevitable, and the Jews were well placed to benefit from it. The world was changing and the Jews were changing even faster. Once again, the unintended consequences of anti-Jewish restrictions made themselves felt.

Beneath old thinking, there was also the welling up of new ideas in Prussia, and a flowering of art, literature, and scientific advance. Hardenberg's reforms had stimulated a zeal for education—soon Prussia's educational system would be the envy of the world—and the Jews, with their historic emphasis on learning, flooded in disproportionate numbers to schools and universities. As their absorption of European values progressed, their determination to be a part of the wider world became even stronger and their exertions to prove themselves through achievement more intense. In the process, they became more German in dress, habits, and general beliefs. A few had grown more assertive, self-assured, and willing to speak out. Yet their dominant sentiment remained one of nervous caution and a conviction that it was best not to call undue attention to oneself while quietly pursuing one's affairs. Industrial change brought new economic opportunities, and their historically enforced entrenchment in banking and commerce gave them advantages over their Christian competitors in these fields, and led to a disproportionate rise of Jewish prosperity and advancement into the middle class.

Their hope for political and social progress remained strong. Perhaps because there was no other choice, there reemerged even after the postwar disappointments an optimistic belief that the correct response to the setbacks was even greater effort and faster assimilation and that this would, in time, carry the day. Even Heine, hardly a dreamer, had during his Berlin period in the 1820s joined a group of young Jewish intellectuals whose avowed aim was to prepare young Jews for faster integration into the outside world. Their efforts were based on the idealistic belief that secular education—including entry into hitherto foreclosed vocations in agriculture and the trades—would more quickly overcome German resistance to Jews and make conversion unnecessary.

Among the upper strata, the spate of conversions continued, but for the majority of Jews for whom baptism was no option, the drive for assimilation led to a movement to modernize their religion, to move away from the old orthodoxy, to "scrape the barnacles off," as some put it. Giacomo's father was one of the movement's leaders, introducing choir singing, German prayers and sermons, the publication of a German-language hymnal, and the launching of a modern secular school for Jewish girls. It was the beginning of a movement of religious reform that split the Orthodox from the Reform wing of Ashkenazic Jews and has prevailed to the present day.

By the early 1830s, the number of Jews throughout Germany had risen to more than a quarter million, more than half of whom lived in the east-

ern part of Prussia, while in the old Prussian home province of Brandenburg there were still not many more than about six thousand. For these
Jews, and especially for the still small elite Jewish community of Berlin, life
involved considerable cross-currents and contradictions. On the one hand,
they advanced in business and intellectual pursuits, assimilated German
culture, achieved greater prosperity, and felt physically secure. In spite of
continuing barriers, Prussia remained a strong magnet for less fortunate
coreligionists from the East. On the other hand, there was no true equality.
Their greater visibility and the influx of the still unassimilated fed old anti-
Semitic resentments and bred a new social animus of the Jew as a pretentious show-off. Jewish advances and eagerness for accomplishment and
recognition were causing new resentment of the Jew as competitor and as
parvenu.

5

Living in Paris but a regular visitor to his native Prussia, Giacomo pursued
his quest for recognition and succeeded in rising to the top of the generation of achievers. No one attained greater prominence and honors than
he. No one would feel the anomalous status of the German Jew and the
bittersweet fruits of both the successes and the new resentments more intensely.

If 1830 and 1831 had been painful years in Prussia, they had for him been
the beginning of his greatest triumphs. *Crociato's* success had brought him
to the attention of Europe's operatic world. Rossini, the idol of Paris, personally conducted the premiere at the Théâtre Italien, and Giacomo's
brother Michael proudly reported to Amalie that "never before has there
been a more unanimous chorus of approval." Suddenly everyone was talking about the exciting new talent, and soon there was hardly an opera
house in Europe where *Crociato* was not being applauded. Even Goethe
wondered whether the young German Jew might not be the right person
to compose an opera based on his Faustian theme.

Giacomo, however, had come to Paris for a larger purpose—to compose
a new opera expressly for the recently completed opera house on the rue le
Pelletier, one that would meld the Italian style with French taste. It had
taken five years and endless negotiations, postponements, crises, and alter-

nating periods of hope and despair until *Robert le Diable,* the end product, was at last ready for its grand premiere on November 21, 1831. Its success was so unprecedented and extraordinary that French opera was permanently changed by it. Henceforth Giacomo would reign as a towering presence over the Paris operatic world, casting so long a shadow that, according to Berlioz, it made serious success "for anyone else virtually impossible" for the next three decades.

Giacomo's timing had been fortuitous. He had arrived in Paris when the general environment was particularly favorable and when there were soon no major competitors to challenge him. The great composers of the immediate past, Cherubini and Spontini, were aging and fading from the scene. The Paris favorite, Rossini, from whom Giacomo had learned so much, completed his last opera, *William Tell,* in 1829 and thereafter abruptly retired to the life of a country gentleman and the enjoyment of a new mistress. None of the others, such as Auber or Halévy, were ever able to mount a serious challenge.

Furthermore, Giacomo appeared when the clouds of the July revolution were gathering, and when the upheaval came, a new audience, and a bourgeois regime particularly hospitable to his work, came with it. The revolution sent bourgeois audiences into the opera with tastes that fit perfectly what he did best. Court opera and glorification of royalty had given way to themes more in accord with the sociopolitical climate of the times— revolution, the struggle against despots and oppression, and romantic tales of the contest between good and evil. Victor Hugo, the leader of bourgeois romanticism, and Dumas père were two favorites pursuing these themes in literature. In opera, Giacomo's *Crociato* had anticipated the trend, and Auber had proved its powerful appeal with his *Muette.*

Giacomo composed his first Paris work in the same genre. The new audiences wanted above all to be entertained and amused. They demanded stirring themes, but also spectacles, novelty, excitement, and grand action— and were more than willing to pay for it. That was important, for under the new regime the opera had become a decidedly commercial enterprise, no longer financed by royal subsidy and largely dependent for financial success on the sale of tickets. On the one hand, that suited Giacomo's desire for *éclat,* and on the other, as a banker's son, he well understood and appreciated the financial dimension.

Most importantly, Giacomo had joined forces with the right collaborators: Scribe, the librettist, and Véron, the new director of the opera. That
was equally critical, for Giacomo's grand operas, beginning with *Robert,* did
not depend for their success simply on his musical creations; they were
very much group projects cleverly promoted by an astute director with an
eye for what the public wanted and the public relations skills to sell the
final product.

In Augustin Eugène Scribe, with whom he concluded the libretto contract for *Robert* in 1827 and who would remain the librettist for all his subsequent works, Giacomo had found an ideal collaborator. A lawyer who
preferred vaudeville and opera to the courts, Scribe was a skilled and phe-
nomenally productive craftsman, a veritable factory who, with his collaborators, would write half the librettos for all the operas staged at the Opéra
Comique over a thirty-year period. His great strength was the speed of his
work, his uncanny knack for sensing public taste, and the ability to adjust
his librettos to Giacomo's musical style. That he was also an exceptionally
greedy and grasping man complicated the relationship but did not impair
it. Giacomo could—and did—pay well, and though much energy was devoted to tortuous contract negotiations, the operas made so much money
that everyone could profit handsomely.

The third of the triumvirate, Louis Véron, originally a doctor of medicine, was an equally felicitous partner. The Opéra was now a self-
supporting business, and about a year before *Robert* was ready, Véron had
successfully bid to become its director and put himself personally at risk.
He was a man with a golden touch and a master at managing for maximum
effect and profit. Vain, unscrupulous, and licentious—he once offered his
guests at a supper the "extra course" of a naked dancer from the corps de
ballet—he was a master at organizing and influencing critics and the ever-
present Paris claque, bribing and flattering where necessary. Proudly calling
himself the Bourgeois of Paris, he knew what the public wanted and invested shrewdly to produce the greatest thrills and excitement for the
middle class of the city. With the set designers and ballet masters, it was these
men who helped make Meyerbeer operas an enormous public success.[24]

Giacomo had prepared meticulously. He had purchased a five-hundred-
volume library of young composers' scores and scoured them for new ideas.
He revised and rewrote endlessly and would come to near despair over

changes in the direction and politics at the Opéra. Ever nervous, suspicious, and alert to impending disaster, he worried incessantly about intrigues, that others would beat him to the punch, or that Scribe might yet betray him with another Auber opera and steal his best ideas.

In the end, he practically lived at the theatre, working himself into a frenzy, constantly rehearsing and altering his complex *Robert le Diable*, a phantasmagoric tale of rebellion, protagonists allied with the devil, good and evil, and sin and redemption. Everything was done to heighten the drama, including trick effects galore—gas lights on stage, roller skates, and characters disappearing in clouds of sulfurous smoke.

For months there had been press reports throughout Europe on the opera's progress and a careful monitoring of rehearsals by the critics, the drama being heightened by Véron's feeding them sensational details. When, after no less than seven postponements, the curtain finally rose, Giacomo was in a state of nervous exhaustion, in mortal fear of failure and sustained by pills and medicines imported from Berlin by the anxious Beers. The demand for black market tickets had been unprecedented and *le tout* Paris—Berlioz, Balzac, Dumas, Cherubini, and the entire elite—was in attendance as Giacomo, bathed in perspiration, awaited the verdict.

He did not have to wait long. After the first act there was a thunderous twenty-minute applause and each new aria was greeted with ecstatic expressions of approval. Paris had seen nothing like it, and *Robert le Diable* and its composer were a sensational success. Over the next three years, the opera would be shown on seventy-seven separate stages, in thirty-one French and twenty-two German cities, in three Vienna opera houses simultaneously, and as far away even as Calcutta.[25] Heinrich Heine, writing from the French capital, concluded that Giacomo had achieved the impossible: "to fascinate the fickle Parisians for a full season."[26] As it turned out, he greatly understated the case. Over the next ten years, the opera would be presented 230 times in Paris alone, and in the next half century audiences around the world would flock to hear *Robert* at more than 900 performances.[27]

Overnight, Giacomo Meyerbeer had become a towering figure in Europe's world of opera. His reputation soared into the stratosphere. Whatever the critics thought (and their views were certainly not unanimous) the broad opera-going public adored Meyerbeer operas, and henceforth no

opera house could afford to omit them from its repertoire. Each new production became an eagerly awaited public event, though often years would
elapse before he completed a new one. *Les Huguenots,* his second Paris opera and as great a triumph as his first, was another tour de force, incorporating all the elements Giacomo and his collaborators had employed in
Robert. Berlioz thought the opera "encyclopedic" and praised it highly. The
theme—religious fanaticism and bloody deeds inflicted on a peaceful and
helpless religious minority—was well suited for the kind of stirring stage
action greatly in demand. Giuseppe Verdi later used it for his *Don Carlo;*
for Giacomo the story of injustice and religious intolerance no doubt had
special meaning.

In the next two decades there was *Le Prophète,* later on a patriotic work
with a martial theme composed expressly for Prussia, and in the 1850s, two
more operas. His last major effort, *L'Africaine,* on which he had labored for
well over a decade, appeared shortly after his death.

Not long after moving to Paris, Giacomo had, at age thirty-five, married
his cousin, Minna Mosson. It was a safe, semi-arranged, traditional union,
and there is no evidence that he was not a willing victim, as ready to assume the role of devoted husband and paterfamilias as he had been to be
the dutiful son. Yet such family bonds, though warm and solicitous, had
well-understood limits, and where his professional ambitions were concerned no one questioned his priorities. When his father died, Giacomo,
deep in Paris rehearsals, missed the funeral. Later, though there were visits
back and forth and a steady stream of letters to "my idol," "keeper of my
soul," or "my adored wife," he remained even after the birth of three daughters an absentee husband and father who rarely graced his family in Berlin
with a lengthy presence. Always anxious in matters of health, however, he
now readily included their well-being in his worries, once informing his
brother that Minna's illness had put him "in the blackest of moods,"[28] and
fretfully instructing a servant after a newborn had arrived to "send me daily
bulletins on the health of both mother and child."[29]

As the accolades accumulated, Giacomo had every reason to feel secure
and satisfied with his accomplishments. France inducted him into the *Lé-
gion d'honneur,* Austria honored him with a knighthood in the Order of
Francis Joseph, Europe's most prestigious academies of art and music proffered honorary memberships, universities bestowed doctorates *honoris*

causa, ministers flattered, and royalty asked for command performances. In England, the young Queen Victoria was entranced with his music, and when he crossed the Channel, she asked him to perform before her. There was even talk that he had politely demurred when her ministers discreetly inquired whether he might not take up permanent residence closer to Buckingham Palace. Yet when Victoria came to Germany on a state visit in the mid-1840s, there were no hard feelings, and Giacomo took charge of the concert in her honor.

He studiously avoided showing it, but it was recognition from Germany—and especially from his native Prussia—that meant most to him. There were medals from Hanover, while Württemberg went the extra mile and elevated him into its "personal nobility," an honor of which he chose not to avail himself. On the night of the *Robert* premiere, it was Alexander von Humboldt, Prussia's delegate to France and an old Beer family friend, who wrote to express his admiration, adding patriotically that he was one of those who "voyent grandir avec cette gloire celle de la patrie commune" (see in this triumph the enhanced triumph of the common fatherland).[30] For Giacomo, wounded by past anti-Semitic slights in Germany, it must have been a compliment tinged with irony.

Yet Humboldt was not alone in claiming him as one of Prussia's own. The king once again insisted that *Robert*'s next premiere be in Berlin and took the unheard of step, where a Jew was concerned, to appoint him *Hofkapellmeister* (royal conductor). Later he sent him a precious porcelain vase and saw to it that he was inducted into the Prussian Academy of Arts. Though the Prussian censors had banned his *Prophète* for six years, it was eventually the king's son and successor, Frederick William IV, who reversed them, personally attended the Berlin performance no less than three times, gave Giacomo the civilian *Pour le mérite* and, in 1842, appointed him *Generalmusikdirektor,* the top royally sanctioned musical job and honor. It was all quite unprecedented and astonishing.

6

For Germany's Jews, accustomed to discrimination and eager for achievement and recognition, it must have seemed that Giacomo had finally achieved it all. What they valued most was *Kultur* and *Besitz,* cultural stand-

ing and wealth—two assets they hoped would overcome prejudice and improve their social standing. Who could aspire to more than what Giacomo
had achieved? His operas added to his riches, and their popularity won him
honors and unheard-of prestige. Yet he remained unashamedly a Jew.

Giacomo, however, was finding that it was not that simple. Satisfactions
there had been, yet they had brought him little peace of mind. There was
no lasting fulfillment in his victories. He remained restless and anxious,
and the fear that insults, rebuffs, and failure lurked in the wings still had
him in its grip. The nervous apprehensions remained; if anything, success
had given rise to new concerns and insecurities.

Neither in the wake of *Robert,* nor in the years that followed, was there
an abatement in his lifelong struggles and preoccupations with his medical
condition. Some of it was no doubt genuine, yet much of what constantly
tortured him must have been psychosomatic. However many the honors
and successes, the chronic complaints—acid stomach, headaches, fevers,
rashes, and digestive crises—continued to make life miserable and to attest
to the absence of serenity. The visits to various spas to seek cures became
more frequent and prolonged; in time there were few the famous maestro
had not tried. Just as Rossi, his Italian librettist, had been forced to contend
with young Giacomo's *"Foruncoli,"* so Scribe had learned to commiserate
over his manifold medical complaints and to accept them as reasons why
the work proceeded slowly or not at all. The cold weather had aggravated
his gallbladder, Giacomo wrote him, and anxiety over the news that one
of his children had fallen ill had immediately sent him to bed. From Bad-
gastein, his mother was informed that headaches had made work impossible, and that the snow and cold had made him "drunk with pain."

Twenty years after his death, the memory of the celebrated composer
returning each year to Spa, his favorite Belgian resort for nursing his health,
was vividly captured in a revealing chronicle describing the annual appearance and daily habits of Giacomo and his "physionomie curieuse."[31] He
often arrived "wrenched with overwhelming and burning pains" caused
by worries from his work, the author reminisced, adding that "les fonctions
digestives étaient très irrégulières chez lui, et il en souffrait visiblement."
(His digestive functions were highly irregular, and he visibly suffered
from it.)[32]

The visits had commenced as early as 1829 when, accompanied by his mother and young wife, the Meyerbeer entourage had first taken up residence at the Hotel du Portugal. In later years, he would limp back alone with only a valet and a personal barber to shave him each morning and attend to his hair. Always in black, with ill-fitting frock coat and overly large gloves, carrying a black umbrella even on bright sunny days, he was remembered as a man with the air of a "melancholy bird," ambling on his daily walks with a *va-et-vient de pendule,* the famous Meyerbeer waddle.

Though he was often tense and would, for fear of the cold, pace his room wrapped in a thickly lined greatcoat, nervously tapping his fingers against the window, the locals appreciated his concern about not offending anyone. He was "le plus doux et modeste . . . un homme grave avant l'âge . . . doué de la politesse la plus exquise . . . ne contradisant jamais." (The softest and most modest of men, serious beyond his years, with the most exquisite politeness and never contradicting anyone.) On his walks, the famous man would often be besieged by petitioners and supplicants, but though visibly bothered by them, he maintained at all times the same air of politesse and calm.

Supplicants, to be sure, were now many—and not merely on his daily walks in Spa. The greater his prominence, the more it had become one of his worries: how to satisfy and not offend the growing legion of *demandeurs* as well as the critics, journalists, and others in the worlds of music and politics whose ill will he feared and suspected for reasons probably having to do with their "*Risches.*" Some would use this extreme sensitivity to criticism as a weak spot to be played upon for their own advantage—and none would do it more effectively and with less shame than Heinrich Heine.

Heine had arrived in Paris just as *Robert* was approaching its premiere. Since leaving Berlin, he too had made a name for himself, as a poet and author of brilliant essays skewering without mercy falsehoods, political repression, and societal foibles. His travel books and the lyric poetry of his *Buch der Lieder* had earned him the admiration of some, and the enmity of the German establishment and censors because of their attacks on the established order. Now, like a growing number of others, he was a refugee from Hohenzollern Prussia in Paris, even more alienated from his fatherland than Giacomo. Unlike him, however, he was an exuberantly independent spirit, wearing the outrage his writings engendered as a badge of honor and drowning the pain of the outsider in the torrent of irony and wit that poured from his pen. Unlike Giacomo, he was also poor and constantly in need of money.

Heine quickly discovered how to flatter the composer while feeding his fears—and raiding his purse. Giacomo was the *maestro divino* and "the triumphant one," the poet assured him, but with his prominence and *Risches* everywhere, too many were eager to harm his reputation. He, Heine, would spend judiciously to thwart them—five hundred francs, or perhaps one thousand, would do wonders.[33]

"Heine's protection is more dangerous than his enmity,"[34] brother Michael warned from Berlin. Yet Giacomo knew that the poet was reporting on the Paris music scene for German papers, and so he flattered him—and paid up. There were choice tickets for the opera, invitations to vaudeville, dinners, and even the high compliment of an inquiry about as yet "musically unmarried" verse the admiring composer might utilize. Always there was the money, and when he met resistance, Heine knew how to hint and signal that paying up was the better part of wisdom. His pressure increased with his financial problems and growing envy of Giacomo's wealth and fame. Eventually the composer balked when Heine's demands for help became too distasteful, and Heine retaliated with gusto. As happened frequently, Giacomo would find that buying goodwill could be a double-edged sword.

Heine was, however, only one of the many whom Giacomo tried to keep on his side. Another was a starving young composer named Richard Wagner. When he first wrote to Giacomo in 1837, the twenty-four-year-old was so destitute that he had been forced to borrow the few taler to travel to Königsberg—musically, a Prussian Siberia—for employment at the local opera house. Nothing had worked for him in his private or his professional life, and he was frustrated and impatient. No one of significance had as yet taken the slightest note of Richard Wagner.

He had composed his first opera, *Rienzi,* in the Meyerbeer style, and now he dreamed of Giacomo's sponsorship as the key to its success. Sending him some early drafts, Wagner took pen to hand and did his ingratiating best: "Can I deny that it is precisely your work that has shown me the new direction?"[35] More obsequious notes followed, but when creditors again closed in, Wagner was forced into an undignified nocturnal escape to France under an assumed name. Soon thereafter, he appeared in Boulognesur-Mer, where the *Hofkapellmeister,* his great hope, was spending the summer.

The gulf between the two could hardly have been wider—one a culti-vated, transplanted German Jew, wealthy from birth, Europe's premier composer at the peak of his career; the other a young, petit bourgeois of modest and uncertain origins, speaking heavily accented Saxon German, unknown, unsuccessful, and desperately in need of financial and profes-sional support. Giacomo thought the young man talented, but a bit strange, and did his best with letters and money. His diary shows seventeen separate Wagner entries for the last three months of 1839 alone, as the in-creasingly tedious and fulsome petitioner continued to beg and flatter: "My gratitude to you, my noble protector . . . knows no limits," he wrote, and in the most extravagant and pathetic of all pleas he enthused in 1840 that "Goethe is dead—he was moreover no musician; now we are left with no one but you!"[36] The punch line, to be sure, was a request for a twenty-five-hundred-franc "loan," which, as always, Giacomo provided.

Scribe and Véron were not interested, but eventually Giacomo's interces-sions led to *Rienzi*'s acceptance in Dresden, and Wagner was thrilled. When in 1840 yet another Meyerbeer recommendation of his just completed *Fly-ing Dutchman* led to an opening in Berlin, Wagner's effusive thanks poured forth once more: "I sat in my little room with my poor wife. . . . Then I read those heaven-sent words. . . . May God fill each day of your marvellous life with joy."[37]

For a while, the requests for money and help continued, but gradually greater self-confidence and a heightened sense of independence devel-oped, and as Wagner's circumstances changed, so did his deference toward the maestro. In Paris, where Giacomo reigned supreme, no one had taken Wagner seriously. The rebuffs and the bitterness over his failure there would rankle for the rest of his life. Giacomo, more than anyone, would soon feel the effects of Wagner's venom, and be shocked by them even though he had never been burdened by great illusions. "Anti-Semitism is like love in the theatres and novels: no matter how often one encounters it in all its shapes and sizes, it never misses its target," he once wrote Heine.[38]

For Giacomo, the pervasive suspicion—and the fear—of *"Risches"* was everywhere. For any problem or difficulty, his first instinct was to assume that Jew-hatred was at its core. When mistakes in a copy of one of his scores had led to annoying problems, he wrote his brother Michael that "it smells of *Risches*,"[39] and when Minna reported that *Robert* had been received rather coldly in Frankfurt, he replied that in his opinion the "*Risches*-public"[40] was at fault.

Such pessimism was extreme, yet no farther off the mark than the contrary view that Jew-hatred was a fading anachronism. He was right that anti-Semitism remained deep in the German mind and that neither wealth nor honors was a guarantee against its painful sting.

On the one hand, his achievements, earnings, and family wealth had opened many doors, and his cultural refinement and generosity had won him favorable notice. Yet the same successes and attention had also generated new jealousies, envy, and antipathies. It was a vicious circle—the reverse side of Jewish achievements and wealth.

There were legitimate substantive grounds to criticize Giacomo's music. When Felix Mendelssohn-Bartholdi said that "he produces effects but I can't find the true music there,"[41] it was a professional judgment of Meyerbeer, the composer. When Robert Schumann questioned his operas on grounds of their overemphasis on titillation and thrills and their lack of originality, that too was acceptable critique. Others, such as Stendhal, who wrote that he disliked Giacomo's "barbarian French musical tastes,"[42] and even the otherwise often sympathetic Berlioz, who noted the limits of Giacomo's capacity to innovate, offered equally understandable comments.

The hypersensitive Giacomo sometimes mistakenly ascribed such critiques to anti-Semitic prejudice alone. Yet, in an important sense, the root of his fears was justified, and until long after his death there were those in Germany who would envy, hate, and attack him not merely for his music but for his origins. Schumann, indeed, had been one of the first to shift the argument with thinly veiled allusions to his alien Jewishness. He hated *Les Huguenots,* he wrote, because "a good protestant is outraged to hear his dearest airs profaned," and "virtuous German maidens [should] shut their eyes rather than view so much sacrilege—pretense, immorality in churches, seducing nuns—all stitched together as a cheap speculation for profit and for public approval bought with bribery." Giacomo's operas mixed many styles; they were cosmopolitan and offensive to a true German, he said. There was only one "original" element he had detected, and that was a "bleating unstable rhythm"[43] (meckernde unständige Rhythmus), the distinguishing mark of all of Giacomo's themes.

Schumann might not have realized it, but it would be this passing com-

ment that became the heart of the subsequent anti-Semitic attacks on Giacomo's work—and eventually on the artistic work of Jews in general. More
than ten years later, Schumann's words inspired a series of openly scurrilous articles in Leipzig's *Neue Zeitschrift für Musik*, in which it was said that
Giacomo's operas reflected a special quality common to all Jewish composers—bleating: to wit, melodic tone sequences and metric structures
resonating the sing-song of the Jew-German language. The baptized
Mendelssohn-Bartholdi, the writer claimed, showed traces of it; in the
work of the Jew Meyerbeer it was especially prominent. It was alien "judais-
tic music." The critic named it "Hebraic taste in art" (*Hebräischer Kunst-
geschmack*).[44]

This was the phrase that would inspire Richard Wagner, and become the
centerpiece in his subsequent polemic, *Das Judentum in der Musik* (Jewry in
Music), his best-remembered and most notorious contribution to German
anti-Semitic literature, later frequently cited by his ideological heirs. For
anti-Semites, the idea that Jews inevitably had a special "Hebraic" taste was
proof that they were un-German, alien, and therefore unworthy. A hundred years later, a Nazi minister named Joseph Goebbels would triumphantly adopt the concept and carry its meaning to its ultimate extreme.

7

When Frederick William III died in 1840, after forty-three years on the
throne, he is said to have muttered "ça va mal" (it's going badly), before
expiring. He no doubt referred to his own in extremis condition, yet the
comment might just as well have applied to the unsettled state of his country, the restless mood of the people, and his own mediocre record as a ruler.

On his deathbed he gave a last and, under the circumstances, rather odd
instruction to his wife to adjust the clocks: "Make sure they don't run
ahead," he is said to have whispered. If true, it was yet another parting comment with appropriately symbolic meaning. The misfortune of Prussia,
and ultimately of the larger Germany of which Prussia became the heart,
was not merely that a rigid absolute monarchy had retained power for too
long. It was also that the Hohenzollerns who followed Frederick the Great
were neither very competent nor well suited to their task. Too often they
chose narrow-minded and reactionary *Junker* as ministers and advisers and

were more concerned with preserving the past than devising policies in tune with the times in which they lived.

The earlier Hohenzollern rulers had been intelligent, determined, and innovative leaders who built Prussia into a strong nation with a powerful army and an effective bureaucracy. Their successors demonstrated few of these qualities. They were rigid and pedantic, narrow-minded, backward-looking, erratic, and insecure—and most were not particularly bright. They chose to cling to the worst and most outmoded features of what they had inherited—overblown militarism, bureaucratic inertia, stubborn protection of feudal privilege, and a refusal to countenance any kind of meaningful parliamentary institutions.

The dead king's son, Frederick William IV, had all these failings. He differed from his father and from William, his rigid brother and eventual successor, in only one respect—not a guards officer type, he was decidedly unmilitary in his bearing and interests. He was short and fat, with weak and womanly features. He was also an impetuous romantic who liked building castles more than barracks, and who harbored opinions that veered erratically between liberal ideals and reactionary stubbornness. He would often get caught up in his own considerable, though essentially empty, powers of oratory, making promises freely and telling all sides what they wanted to hear. At heart, however, he believed even more deeply than his father and brother that he ruled by God's grace. He hated revolutions as much as they, and in the Christian-Germanic faction of *Junkers* who surrounded him, he had chosen as reactionary and backward-looking a group of advisers as any of his predecessors.

What saved Prussia from decline and disaster and made it so special a place is that its situation was never completely one-sided. In spite of the dubious quality of its kings and frozen sociopolitical landscape, Prussia had important offsetting assets. What counterbalanced the reactionary nature of its politics and worked powerfully to its advantage was, first, an obedient and hard-working people, and, second, that at key moments there were those who succeeded in instituting farsighted reforms, in spite of the rulers. Stein, Hardenberg, and others had laid the foundation for progress with one of the best administrative and educational systems in Europe. Finally, the loyalty and honesty of the Prussian bureaucracy provided an environment of stability in which invention, science, and the arts could flourish and in which the delayed industrial development, once it began, could proceed with astonishing speed.

In spite of the underlying hostility against them, it was this that continued to attract more Jews to Prussia and facilitated their advance and assimilation into German culture. By midcentury, their quest for success and accomplishments was gathering powerful momentum. Later, when a skillful new political figure appeared on the scene and propelled Prussia toward leadership of a unified Germany in the forefront of European political and economic power, it would be this Jewish "yeast" that played a not insignificant part in the country's rise to preeminence.

That, however, still lay in the future. Frederick William IV ruled for seventeen years, and his oratory and a few palliative moves to the contrary, he tolerated no easing of repression. Censorship actually was tightened under him. From Paris, Heine unmercifully satirized the results by skewering "the oceans of platitudes" that it spawned. Throughout the 1840s, discontent continued to bubble below the surface. The liberals formed "reading circles" and applauded any challenge to the tottering Metternich system. They devoured foreign journals in Berlin's cafés and loudly cheered reports of rebellion—in defiance of a police ordinance which expressly ordained that "any loud expression of opinion, applause, or criticism while reading" was *verboten*.[45] Social discontent among the working classes was also on the rise. A revolt of Silesian weavers was brutally repressed, artisans were being hurt by new factories, while poor harvests in 1846 and a world trade crisis a year later led to more unemployment and sporadic disturbances.

Yet Prussia could not isolate itself from the larger forces sweeping continental Europe, making it a powder keg ready to explode. Bourgeois populations everywhere were no longer prepared to tolerate their lack of rights, and they demanded government responsible to the people, universal suffrage, freedom of expression, and fiscal reform. In the Austro-Hungarian Empire, national minorities clamored for independence. The rise of factories pitted artisans against owners and led to demands for social reforms, better working conditions, and the right to form unions and cooperatives. On the land, peasants chafed under the domination of large landowners and wanted protection against impoverishment from recurring agricultural and fiscal crises.

Finally, in February 1848, the fuse was lit in Paris. A single pistol shot had ignited the revolt, the "citizen king" Louis Phillippe was overthrown, and a nephew of Napoleon was elected as president of France's Second Republic. Three years later he proclaimed himself Emperor Napoleon III. His opponents would call him Louis le Petit, but for the moment at least, republicanism had triumphed.

French revolutionary spirit spread quickly. There was insurrection in Vienna, the Habsburg Empire tottered, and Metternich, camouflaged as a woman, was forced to flee the angry mob. There were uprisings in Hungary, Bohemia, and Italy, and by the middle of March the disorders had spread to southern and western Germany and to Silesia and East Prussia.

Prussia was not to be spared either. In the early decades of the century, the prerequisites for industrial development had still been missing. But since about 1830, the population had risen rapidly. A customs union (*Zollverein*) under Prussian aegis had powerfully stimulated intra-German trade and commerce. Agricultural productivity was up and the building of railroads had exploded. In 1842, the king proudly took a forty-two-minute train ride across the twenty kilometers from Berlin to Potsdam. Eight years later there were already more than three thousand kilometers of track, providing cheap transport and greatly stimulating the manufacture of iron, machinery, and ancillary products. Berlin now had a large working-class proletariat. Its bulging population had doubled to 330,000 over thirty years, and with the rapid changes there had come the speculators and crooks, the ups and downs of industrial cycles, the miseries of factory work, and unemployment.

With the news of revolt everywhere, Berlin too was ripe to erupt. On March 15, Guard officers were stoned, and three days later an effort at brutal military suppression of a crowd gathered before the palace led to several deaths. The excitable and insecure Frederick William IV, wavering between repression and appeasement, was thrown into a near panic. To placate his people, he sent his brother William to London, in civilian clothes, his beard shaved, only a step ahead of angry crowds who saw him, more than the sovereign, as the symbol of past repression. The king, for his part, was forced to make a humiliating public apology and to join in a march to pay homage to the slain victims of the riots.

For a while, it seemed as if fundamental changes were finally on the way, yet within little more than a year the tide once more receded. A National

Constituent Assembly, reluctantly convened by the king, drafted a new constitution, but in the end counterrevolution carried the day. The final version still preserved the dominant role of the aristocracy and the absolute power of the sovereign. Most significantly, it is this document that remained the charter under which Prussia—and all of Germany—would be governed for the next seventy years.

Meanwhile, the eight hundred delegates to an all-German Parliament had assembled with much haste in the Paulskirche in Frankfurt am Main in 1849, and after much debating they drafted a bill of the people's rights. It provided for political freedom, civil equality, an uncensored press, trial by jury, and the protection of workers. The Parliament's purpose was to unite the separate German states under this charter, and for that they had offered the Prussian king the imperial crown, which he had disdainfully refused. A crown proffered by the people was not worth the having. And so, after much factional wrangling the Paulskirche Parliament adjourned in failure.

Yet another ten-year period of reaction would follow, until there would finally be progress toward German unity under Otto von Bismarck, with strong leadership and real change. But 1849 and its aftermath were an important milestone, and Germany and Prussia would never again be quite the same. A period of explosive economic growth was beginning, and far-reaching political and economic change would go hand in hand with it. Major advances in science and technology and their application to industry would fuel the economic upsurge and provide the basis for Germany's rise as a major European power. The population—well educated, disciplined, and obedient—would work diligently to contribute to this remarkable forward march and would experience major changes in their lives.

For no group in the population, however, would the impact be greater than for the Jews. In all of Prussia there were, in the late 1840s, about sixteen million inhabitants. Among them about 1.3 percent, or a little more than two hundred thousand, were Jews. The greater part of them still lived in Posen and the other eastern areas of the kingdom. In the countryside of Brandenburg, growth had been slow, but in the capital the number of Jews had doubled to more than eight thousand in less than two decades. They now accounted for more than 2 percent of all Berliners. As others were drawn to the booming and burgeoning capital, Berlin's Jewish community was poised for a further tripling over the next twenty years. By the late 1860s more than 4 percent of Berliners were Jewish.[46]

The days when the authorities had fought a losing battle to restrict their numbers were now largely a thing of the past. There had been rapid natural growth, because Jews still tended toward large families, and always there were new arrivals attracted by Prussian order and opportunity. They were among the most aggressive and adventurous entrepreneurs, and Jewish manufacturers and merchants were now contributing substantially to the booming growth. Long experience in finance had thrust them into key positions as providers of capital, and now that the doors were more open, the younger generation flooded the universities and the professions in disproportionate numbers. A remarkable push into the modern world and an accelerated process of assimilation were under way.

Throughout the various German states and cities, the four hundred thousand Jewish residents were also forging ahead. Yet everywhere their position remained uncertain and anomalous. As a group, their image among Christians remained distorted by centuries of prejudice, and these had left deep, though sometimes invisible, scars. As nineteenth-century Jews advanced and assimilated with extraordinary rapidity, they developed a keen sense of their insecure status and unfavorable group image. Each, in his own way, tried to distance himself from it—striving to make his place as an individual, a distinct person of value recognized and respected for his personal attributes and accomplishments, and anxious to separate himself from the unfavorable collective image of "the Jew."[47]

Like Rahel, there were always a few who came to believe the Christians' distorted view of Jews, and chose to escape it through denial and conversion. But they were never many. The far greater number, whether in business or intellectual pursuits, tried to prove themselves in their work, as Giacomo had done so brilliantly. As their self-confidence rose, some also stepped forward to become fighters for social justice, rebels speaking out and battling back not merely against Jew-hatred but against injustices toward all people. Heine had taken on this role of poet as social and political critic. Other young Jews mounted the barricades in the revolution of '48, as delegates to the Frankfurt parliament and as fighters for better conditions for workers and the poor. Who, after all, had a keener understanding and greater sympathy for humanity's mistreated and downtrodden than a Jew? Some moved into the forefront of the nascent socialist movement and a few became disciples of its most radical wing. In fact, a young baptized Jew from Germany, banned from his homeland and living in England, was just about to issue a call for nothing less than a world revolution to correct these injustices. Karl Marx, who disliked Jews, was laying the groundwork for a totally different religion that would one day reshape the world.

All this still remained far removed from the little country towns of Brandenburg, where small Jewish communities were continuing to flourish quietly. There the pace of change was slower; sometimes it seemed that not much had changed there at all. For one thing, the inertia and ingrained habits of the provincial bureaucracy remained very much in evidence. In spite of their nominally full and equal citizenship, country Jews remained the subject of an enormous flow of reports and paper up and down the bureaucratic ladder. As late as 1846, local scribes were still laboring over their *Judentabellen,* the statistical reports on the Jews in their midst. In the town of Freienwalde, not far from Oranienburg, a local bureaucrat had, at last, screwed up his courage in 1846 to put a bold question to higher-ups in Potsdam: Was it truly essential, he inquired, that these reports still be submitted with no fewer than eighty separate copies?

The familiar warnings to monitor Jewish behavior and to guard against infractions still rained down on the locals. There was, on June 27, 1844, the circular advising watchfulness concerning the old problem of Jewish peddling, particularly from Polish itinerants surreptitiously renting local rooms from which to sally forth illegally to sell their wares. The loss of franchise taxes thus incurred was evidently of particular concern. Whether or not even the legal Jewish residents were law abiding and truly operating in "open stores" was another subject of intense interest and frequent inquiry. From time to time, there would come special warnings to be alert to the "strained anti-Jewish atmosphere" elsewhere in the kingdom: "The experience of the past teaches that such a mood can be infectious, and anything nourishing it is to be avoided," a senior Potsdam official sternly advised the towns in 1844.[48]

In general, Brandenburg's small-town Jews lived peacefully and prospered slowly. In Oranienburg, there were in 1849 still fewer than twenty families—not quite a hundred persons in all—seven merchants, four junk shop owners, one dealer in horses and cattle, a few artisans, and the rest old folks and community retainers.

Just then, however, there was a new addition to their ranks. Levin Blumenthal from Wittstock who had recently taken the German name of

Louis, had claimed Regine, the daughter of the Simon family in Branden-
burg/Havel as his bride. The match had met with universal approval. His
parents and grandparents before him had been well-known to the Simons.
Zippora, his paternal grandmother, had been an established resident in
these parts since 1765, and on his mother's side there was that prideful distant relationship to Rahel Levin on the one hand, and to the Beers of Berlin
and to Giacomo, their famous son, on the other.

When the old Blumenthal house in Pritzwalk burned to the ground in
1821, the entire family had moved to Wittstock when Louis was just two
years old. His father and his uncle Isaac Nathan still lived there. Uncle Nathan, it was said, was a pious and productive man—as evidenced not only
in his success with textiles but by the ten children he had fathered.

Louis, however, was a placid and peaceful man. The textile business was
good now, there was as yet no competitor in Oranienburg, and the town
was not particularly antagonistic toward Jews. It was, by all accounts, a
good opportunity for a knowledgeable and honest textile Jew, and the Simons had faith that their young son-in-law would make a success of it.
They would not be disappointed.

8

Giacomo's entire life was marked by a painful, unrequited love for the
country of his birth. In spite of many foreign honors and international acclaim, he never forgot the attacks on him in Germany as a child. He wanted
approval in Germany above all else, and it was German criticism of his music and denigration of his talents that cut most deeply. Paris embraced him,
provided a refuge, and lionized him for his accomplishments, yet his emotional attachment to his native Germany remained unbroken. However
profound the disappointments there, he could not turn his back on his
countrymen nor, for that matter, would they ever truly let him go or cease
to claim him as one of their own.

Thus the mutual love-hate relationship continued to the end, and Giacomo and Germany remained locked in their ambiguous embrace with its
uncomfortable mixture of respect, antipathy, and need. Not even death itself would change that. Louis Napoleon wanted him enshrined in the Panthéon amid the heroes of France. It was the highest honor the French could

grant but Giacomo politely declined it. When he died, he said in his will, he wanted to be returned to Berlin and to be buried in the place that, in spite of everything, he still considered home.

Ill and weak, yet intent on one last great success, he exhausted his waning energies on the preparations for his new opera, *L'Africaine,* persisting against the advice of family and doctors until he no longer had the strength to leave his bed. Even as he lay dying, the lifelong habit of courtesy and fear of giving offense remained intact. His last words were to thank everyone for their efforts and to wish them a good night before, in the early morning hours of May 2, 1864, he finally breathed his last.

With banner headlines—"Meyerbeer n'est plus"—Paris announced the death of its musical favorite. The Emperor declared an official day of mourning, eulogies poured forth from all sides, and the elite of the Académie, led by the eighty-year-old Auber and followed by Gounod and other members of the Directoire, accompanied the hearse through the streets of Paris to the Gare du Nord, which was draped in black for the occasion. Rossini, too distraught to attend, wandered disconsolately around the Parc Monceau and sent a religious meditation to "my dear friend Giacomo Meyerbeer." Black banners inscribed in gold with Giacomo's initials fluttered in the wind. There were personal wreaths from the Emperor and Empress, and the imperial guard played musical excerpts from Meyerbeer compositions as the special train returning him to Berlin slowly pulled out of the station. It was a solemn and impressive occasion, but there was also some irony in the arrangements. Giacomo would certainly have objected that the funeral train departed on a Friday—the one day on which he had adamantly refused to travel anywhere while alive. With his deeply rooted pessimism he would have been struck by the poignant paradox that his final journey should have been scheduled for so unlucky a day.

There were other contradictions. In France the grief was genuine, widespread, and without a discordant note. In Germany the reaction was more nuanced. At one level, officialdom was determined to claim the famous composer for itself and to profit from his international renown. The Prussian ambassador in Paris was one of the first to present his condolences and to insist on taking charge of the arrangements for the transfer of the casket. As the train carrying Giacomo's body crossed the border at Aix-la-Chapelle, all French insignia, flags, and wreaths were removed and German ones substituted in their place. There were elaborate arrival ceremonies in Berlin staged to surpass those in Paris, the king sent a relative and assorted ministers, and a half dozen royal carriages led the funeral procession past ten thousand Berliners lining the streets.[49]

Yet while Berlin's premier musical journal gave a reverential account of these royal honors, the familiar voices that had caused Giacomo so much grief in life persisted even in death. At lunch in Dresden, Richard Wagner and his friends toasted with unabashed glee the news that the detested Jew was dead. In Leipzig, the *Allgemeine* could not resist criticizing him yet once more for focusing on "life's negatives" and for failing to stress more uplifting heroic and patriotic themes. Though born in Germany, its obituary noted, he had not been a real German but a cosmopolitan without the capacity for originality or true art in his works.[50]

His Jewishness was not directly mentioned but the implication nevertheless was clear. Even in death, Germany's posthumous homage to a famous native remained muted by the familiar reservations toward a member of the Hebrew minority. If the world honored him, it was appropriate that it was as a German. Yet for all his accomplishments, in German eyes Giacomo Meyerbeer remained an outsider—uncharacteristic, different, and not fully acceptable. He was, after all, not only a German but also a Jew.

For the thousands of Berliners who turned out to witness his final journey, the occasion, though noteworthy, was somewhat of a novelty. It wasn't every day, after all, that the authorities organized so much pomp and pageantry for a composer of operas who, albeit a famous *Hofkapellmeister,* was neither an aristocrat nor a soldier. Prince George of Prussia was in personal attendance, there were court carriages to be admired and the muffled cadence of an elite musical corps to lend solemnity to the occasion. Berliners came to watch because they loved any kind of parade, though in truth they much preferred military *défilés,* with soldiers and cavalrymen in smart uniforms, plenty of cannon, and brass bands and flags to stir their patriotic hearts. The Jewish composer's funeral had been interesting enough. Soon, however, there would be abundant opportunities to enjoy the real thing and to cheer the martial spectacles they liked best.

CHAPTER VI

PATRIOTS

Louis

Our German fatherland must be protected from socio-political Juda-ization.

Wilhelm Marr

1880

The Jews are our misfortune.

Heinrich V. Treitschke

1879

For now I have stepped on German sod,
A magic sap steals through me;
The giant has touched his mother again,
And her love and her strength renew me.

Caput I

The Works of Heinrich Heine

translated by Charles Godrey Leland

1

At the beginning of the 1850s, William I had found himself mired in a seemingly insoluble political dispute with the Prussian Diet. The Diet was at best a pseudoparliament with limited powers, but it was capable of causing trouble—which is precisely what the bourgeois moderate-reformist majority was doing by stubbornly refusing to go along with the monarch's cherished plans to reform and strengthen his army. At wits' end, frustrated enough over the impasse to have come close to abdication in favor of his son, he had as a last resort reluctantly turned to a formidable figure in his civil service, a man whom paradoxically he neither much liked nor entirely trusted but who was his last remaining hope.

Otto von Bismarck was a typical representative of Prussia's ruling aristocracy, a landed *Junker* from Pomerania with strong views, firmly conservative instincts, and a reputation for decisiveness. He had only recently arrived in France as Prussia's ambassador when the desperate king called him to the rescue and offered him the one job Bismarck had long wanted— *Ministerpräsident,* Foreign Minister and head of the Prussian government.

For king and country it was a felicitous choice, and for the rest of Europe a fateful one. Over the next twenty years this powerful *Junker*—tall, broadly built, with a face dominated by a large drooping mustache, and cold, piercing, yet somewhat doleful eyes—would dominate the politics of the Continent, unify Germany, elevate his king to emperor, and transform the medium-sized kingdom of Prussia into the most powerful continental power. It would take three quick wars to do so, but Bismarck was tough and determined, and his timing was always good. Luck was on his side and he planned well. Under Bismarck, Berliners would get more than their share of victory parades.

Bismarck's great strengths were that he was a cold realist not easily ruled by emotion and that he never lost sight of his two principal goals—to preserve at all costs the supremacy of the monarchy against parliamentary encroachment and to push aside tottering Austria, unifying Germany under Prussian leadership. He was also highly intelligent and a superb judge of human character. Ruthless and devious in maneuvering others to do his bidding, he knew how to bide his time when necessary and was ready to resort to the selective use of force when the odds were in his favor.

The 1860s were the years of his greatest triumphs. He quickly resolved the standoff over reforming the army, with obfuscating maneuvers laced with conciliatory proposals of compromise, and then finessed further arguments through the simple expedient of proroguing the Diet and sending it home, which, under Prussia's constitution, the king had the right to do.

Before the controversy could flare up anew, he permanently changed the subject by leading Prussia into three quick, stunningly successful wars, first against Denmark, then Austria, and finally against France. "It is not by speeches and majority resolutions that the great questions of our times are decided. . . . It is by blood and iron," he had declared before the Diet.

He later came to regret these words, which would remain associated with him forever. At home his opponents howled in protest that the "Blood and Iron" *Junker* had shown his true colors, and statesmen abroad sat up and took notice. Yet when he sent Prussia's soldiers to do battle for the fatherland and the highly nationalistic majority in the Diet saw its long-cherished dream of Prussian-led German unification moving closer, everyone rallied to the cause. The successes stirred even the opposition's patriotic fervor and other considerations were, for a time at least, swept aside.

In 1864 he took the duchies of Schleswig and Holstein from the Danes in a brief war and two years later, having defeated the Austrians, incorporated both into a new North German Federation under Prussian control. Once the nominal leadership of Austria in German matters was ended, only one more step remained to secure Prussia's position of power in Europe and to bring the southern states of Germany under Prussian control.

The opportunity came in 1870 and Bismarck did not hesitate to seize it. Taking advantage of an emotional spat with France over succession to the throne of Spain, he skillfully maneuvered the weak and insecure French Emperor to declare war on the militarily stronger and better organized Prussians, who were well equipped and ready for the encounter. The decisive battle was fought at Sedan on September 2, 1870. The French were roundly defeated and thereafter their fate was sealed. Within a few months, Prussian soldiers captured Paris and paraded down its main boulevards. Bismarck exacted a heavy price in money and territory to make peace, and French hegemony on the continent of Europe came to an end. Prussia had triumphed and Bismarck made the point by arranging to have William crowned emperor of a newly constituted German Reich in—of all places—the mirrored halls of Versailles.

The date was January 18, 1871, and united Germany under Prussia was at the height of her power in Europe. It was also Bismarck's greatest personal moment. Henceforth, the canny, powerful *Junker* in the uniform of the Seventh "Yellow" Grenadiers would stand as the symbol of jackbooted Prussian dominance. His mournful eyes peering out from behind an old-fashioned lorgnette, and his oddly high-pitched voice would be both feared and respected in European councils of state for years to come.

As for William I, Bismarck's sovereign, he had left his palace as King of Prussia, a medium-sized kingdom of twenty-four million. Now the aging monarch was returning to Berlin from Versailles as the Kaiser of the Second German Reich, a conglomeration of twenty-five federated states under Prussian control, comprising four kingdoms, six archdukedoms, five duchies, seven princedoms, and three Free Cities. His domain was half again as large as before, with a population of more than forty million, and in most respects it was the strongest and most important continental power.

The new constitution of the German Reich was strange, convoluted, and unprecedented in its complexity. Cobbled together by Bismarck, it was the product of a tortured compromise between Prussian centrism and the separatist leanings of Bavaria and other southern German states. All the legal niceties of decentralized power sharing had been observed, yet appearances disguised reality and nothing was quite as it seemed.

In principle, domestic sovereignty was lodged not in the Kaiser but in the Reich's twenty-two separate ruling monarchs and the three senates of its Free Cities. In fact, however, Prussia was so dominant in population and size that the Kaiser and Reich Chancellor, who were simultaneously Prussian King and Prime Minister, could generally impose their will if they wished. Though the constitution provided that foreign affairs were the Kaiser's responsibility, at least four of the German states retained the legal right to separate diplomatic representation abroad, and Bavaria, for one, availed itself of the privilege for the next half century. There were numerous other anomalies. The army was unified only in times of war, though the Kaiser was nominally the Reich's commander-in-chief even in peace. The constitution guaranteed certain basic rights, yet implementation lay with the separate states, and differences in interpretation were tolerated and continued.

The Kaiser's expanded domain was still far from a democracy. He retained the sole power to appoint the heads of the government—Reich chancellors accountable only to him, who faced a two-chamber Diet with important though clearly circumscribed powers. The central administration remained firmly in the hands of the same narrow class of bureaucrats and soldiers recruited from the landed aristocracy, who had long dominated key positions of power in Prussia and whose hidebound views and prejudices had changed little. The intelligentsia and bourgeoisie might be clamoring for more parliamentary rights, but the king's conservative advisers under Bismarck were determined to ignore them and to keep his power—and theirs—intact and unabridged.

2

A vital war had been won, and for the French foe the price for peace was substantial: the enormous sum of five billion gold francs in war reparations and loss to the Reich of the provinces of Alsace and Lorraine. It was a harsh settlement with the seeds of future trouble in it for both sides. For the moment, what mattered to the people of Prussia was not that the new constitution was full of anomalies, that the hope for greater parliamentary democracy remained unfulfilled, that archconservatives retained much power, nor that new problems might lie ahead. What they saw was a stunning victory, greater even than any under Frederick the Great. With Germany united and dominant in Europe, the prevailing sentiment was one of nationalistic fervor and pride.

Berliners, in particular, were in high spirits and rejoiced that the victory parade for the newly crowned Kaiser's return to his capital city from Versailles, on June 16, 1871, was to be by far the biggest yet. The impressive sum of 150,000 taler was allocated to cover the cost of the celebrations, and another sum was set aside to mete out a one-taler cash gift for each and every of the thousands of soldiers expected to march. It promised to be an occasion Berliners would one day be telling their grandchildren about.

For weeks the city's artists and artisans had labored over the decorations for the parade route from the fields of Tempelhof through the Brandenburg Gate to the inner city. The soldiers were to march through three commemorative arches, past no fewer than five separate clusters of monuments, dozens of victory columns, and several giant canvases erected in strategic spots. Thousands of flags, banners, and garlands would greet them, and virtually every house, shop, or stall was festooned with arrays of patriotic ornaments. The theme was Prussia's glorious past and its rise to power, with allegorical representations of former kings, generals, and heroes, in celebration of the unification of Germany under their monarch.

A huge downpour three days earlier soaked and partially dissolved the plaster and papier maché materials and threatened to wreak havoc on the decorations, but feverish activity to repair the damage saved the day at the last moment. Berlin was bursting at the seams with thousands of visitors from the provinces waiting in specially erected stands along the route of the marchers. The seating was arranged strictly in accordance with status and rank—aristocrats and senior officials in the best spots near the Crown Prince's palace, important merchants and higher bourgeoisie a bit farther out, and the crafts, tradesmen, and working classes, each with their own distinctive dress, insignia, and brass bands, farthest from the center.

In Prussia, the people were accustomed to fancy uniforms and martial displays but the spectators had never seen anything like this. There were rousing cheers as the advance contingents made their appearance, led by the venerable eighty-seven-year-old Field Marshall Wrangel astride his horse, a hero of long-ago Prussian victories resurrected from retirement for the honor of heading the parade. The "Hurrahs," "Hochs" and "Heils" reached their crescendo as the major figures came into view—von Moltke, the top general; Bismarck, architect of the political triumphs and recently rewarded with the title of *Fürst* or Prince; and Minister of War von Roon— followed by the Kaiser, riding alone, and behind him Prussian princes and endless columns of guards, riders, infantry, and regiment upon regiment of every sort. Even the newly organized field railroaders were loudly cheered.[1]

It was an unforgettable sight and Oranienburg Mayor Kahlbaum, Town Councillor Louis Blumenthal, and their families were elated. Many weeks earlier Louis had surprised Regine and their five children with the suggestion that they travel to Berlin to witness the historic occasion. He had invited the Kahlbaums to be their guests, and proceeded to pull strings for good seats and hard-to-get reservations. A successful businessman in small Oranienburg, Louis had connections among Berlin's growing community of Jews, which he had used to good advantage. Ensconced in excellent seats, Mayor Kahlbaum and family were visibly impressed and grateful to their Jewish neighbor for the invitation.

Among the more than eight hundred thousand inhabitants of expanding, sprawling Berlin, the Jews remained a small minority, though a
prosperous and important one. For at least a decade, the influx from the
provinces had been rapid, and the Jewish community had grown quickly.
It now numbered some thirty-six thousand. Additional arrivals were being
registered almost every week. More than three-quarters of Prussia's people
still lived on the land or in towns of less than five thousand inhabitants.
But by the 1850s industrialization, though late in coming, had finally taken
off—a process more compressed and disruptive, and more quickly changing and dislocating traditional life, than in countries where it had begun
earlier and evolved more slowly. Railroads were spreading out across the
land at a rapid pace. The small net of thirty-five hundred kilometers of
Prussian track built by 1850 had increased fivefold and expansion continued at a feverish pace. In the larger Reich almost thirty thousand kilometers
were already in place. Iron and coal mining were greatly stimulated by the
explosion of railroad construction; joint stock companies were sprouting
like mushrooms and being listed on the booming Berlin stock exchange.

Ironically, patterns of past occupational discrimination now provided
special advantages for Prussia's Jews and attracted them to the capital in
large numbers. Exclusion from land ownership, the bureaucracy, and the
crafts had kept them out of those sectors faced with the most difficult problems of adjustment to the industrial age, while centuries of honing their
skills in finance and commerce were now a major advantage. Berlin was
where entrepreneurs came with ideas, where risks were taken and deals
made. It was where new enterprises were started and financed and where,
with hard work, skill, and luck, an ambitious man had the best chance for
business success and education for his children. A generation earlier, a large
majority of Berlin's Jews was still struggling near the bottom of the economic ladder. Now they poured in from the provinces to take advantage of
the city's manifold opportunities, moving into the middle classes or advancing to comfortable wealth.

Throughout the Reich, the pull of the bigger cities was urbanizing Germany's Jews at an even faster rate than the population in general. This was
the major reason why the Jews in Oranienburg remained a small and static
community, even though most were comfortably established. Louis and
Regine's family was a case in point. Minna, the eldest, was already engaged

to a young Berliner and her two younger sisters also had their eyes open
for suitable matches and would not be far behind. The capital was full of
eligible and ambitious young Jewish men—some traders on the stock exchange, others working in the many Jewish-owned private banks, or starting new businesses of their own. Now that admission to the universities
was no longer a problem, many were in pursuit of the coveted *Doktortitel*
and promising careers as doctors, lawyers, or accountants. Since government jobs remained closed to Jews, they flocked to the "free professions"
as the next best alternative. Academic degrees carried high prestige among
the more assimilated who valued the visible evidence of German *Bildung*
along with the economic security of the professions. Below the university
level, sending their sons—and daughters—to the *Gymnasia* and classical
high schools was also very much in vogue. Fifteen-year-old Emil, the older
of the two Blumenthal boys, had already been dispatched to a boarding
school on the outskirts of Berlin. One day, he too would leave Oranienburg
for the big city. Only Martin, the youngest, would stay to take over the
family business. At the moment, however, the family's junior was still a
child of thirteen and a great deal more interested in brass bands and military displays than in his future career.

The Kahlbaums had with alacrity accepted Louis's invitation to see the
parade. They were eager not to miss the great day, and the mayor knew that
his Jewish friend, with his lines into Berlin's Jews, was well placed to make
the right arrangements. Like most of the town's gentiles, the mayor normally had only limited Jewish social contacts. His relations with them were
nevertheless friendly and included the occasional shared beer at the *Gasthaus* or a holiday drop-in to offer the town's best wishes to the community
and its leading members.

Louis, however, was different in Kahlbaum's eyes. He had brought his
bride to the town in the mid-1840s, and it hadn't taken long before he established himself not only as a successful businessman but also as a trusted
citizen and adviser on their finances. In time, he had become one of the
mayor's closest advisers in managing the town's affairs. Kahlbaum especially admired him for his knowledge and cautious good judgment in matters of money. It was what Jews did best and the mayor saw no reason why
he should not avail himself of this sober and honest townsman's special
talents.

What was different—though not unusual in a small town like Oranienburg—was that a kind of cautious friendship reaching beyond pure business issues had actually developed between the two. It was not a truly close
social intimacy across the traditional Christian–Jewish divide, but some
time ago they had taken to bowling together on Thursday nights, and occasionally they shared confidences about family matters and personal finances. True, when Kahlbaum had first floated the idea of Louis's candi-
dacy as Town Councillor, some eyebrows had been raised. Jews were not
normally elected to such positions—in earlier days it would have been
unthinkable. But times had changed. There were no longer any legal impediments, and though Louis was a Jew he was appreciated as a substantial
citizen and town booster. When the time came, a comfortable majority
voted him in, and Louis was actually elected as one of the five members of
the *Magistrat,* the top municipal governing body of the town.

That morning, as General Wrangel and the advance guard were coming
into view, the Mayor noted the evident enthusiasm and patriotic pride of
his Jewish hosts. Like most Christians, he had only the sketchiest knowledge of Jewish problems, and if Louis had not talked at length on the way
into Berlin about the significance of the recent political developments for
his people, Kahlbaum might have been excused for finding their fervor a
bit excessive. But the reserved and sober Louis had talked with unusual
feeling and given the mayor new insight into Jewish thinking.

The normally frugal Louis had been uncharacteristically extravagant for
the occasion. Avoiding Oranienburg's cheaper but unreliable postal coach
service, he had rented a large private carriage for what was still a four- to
five-hour journey into Berlin. While they were bouncing along, frequently
slowed by heavy traffic from Berlin-bound visitors, Louis had mentioned
Jewish hopes for a secure future in the Second Reich, and explained why
the new constitution was a turning point for the more than half million of
his coreligionists in the expanded borders of the Reich.

The new constitutional language was music to Jewish ears, Louis said. It
guaranteed every citizen, regardless of his religion, the right to full civic
equality without any of the restrictions and roundabout limitations of the
past. Twice before in Prussia's history—once at the time of Napoleon and
again after 1848—Jews thought that the goal of full equality had been
reached, only to discover that subsequent interpretation of qualifying

paragraphs were legal cover for continued discrimination, especially where employment in state positions was concerned. He had quoted—from memory—the defiant comment in the *Allgemeine,* Prussia's principal Jewish paper, when in 1850 religion was once more made a barrier to unfettered civil equality: "You do not emancipate Jews, yet they have long ago emancipated themselves," the paper had written. "From the time they left the ghetto, joined in all industrial and intellectual endeavors, sent their children to [German] high schools and universities and participated in science, art, business, and the professions, when their women acquired general *Bildung* . . . they have been emancipated, and do not have to wait for a few constitutional words!"[2] Louis then concluded: "We have lived here for centuries and are as German as you. We speak the same language and have the same loyalties. Our soldiers fought and died for Prussia . . . and there were seven thousand young Jews among our troops who beat the French at Sedan and marched into Paris. Yet it took two more decades since 1850 until Bismarck's constitution finally made clear that religion would no longer be a hindrance to full equality. Government service and the officer ranks are now a constitutionally guaranteed right for all of us. Assimilation and emancipation go hand in hand. From now on we will be accepted and treated as full Germans like everyone else!"

The mayor had listened intently, somewhat astonished at his normally sober Jewish friend's highly emotional and optimistic view of the future. Would Jews, with all their peculiar habits and special traits, actually become senior officials or higher officers—heretofore the exclusive preserve of the traditional aristocracy? Kahlbaum kept his own counsel, though he found the idea hard to accept. He was an open-minded man but this vision simply did not accord with his view of the Jews' place in society. Was it really the wave of the future, the mayor wondered, or merely a Jewish pipe dream?

Louis's respect and admiration for, of all people, the Iron and Blood Chancellor, had surprised Kahlbaum no less. He now realized that it reflected the changed attitude of a large number of Jews. The young Bismarck, after all, had been the spokesman for the most aggressively reactionary faction of the *Junker* class and had vociferously opposed the completion of Jewish emancipation because he considered it incompatible with his oft-expressed views of Prussia as a Christian state. It had been a pleasant surprise for the Jewish minority, therefore, that Bismarck in power was not the same as Bismarck on the outside looking in. As the head of government he had shown himself to be the ultimate practitioner of real-politik in domestic as well as international matters. He now viewed Jews strictly from the viewpoint of what they might contribute to the achievement of his principal aim: to make Prussia strong and to unify Germany. Gerson Bleichröder, the rich Jewish banker and close associate of the mighty Rothschilds, was his principal financial agent and adviser. He consulted Ludwig Bamberger, a highly intelligent Jewish Reichstag member, as an expert on French law and used him as a bridge to the National Liberal party. In many other ways his attitude toward Jews had become more flexible. His opponents, in fact, were now attacking him for his reliance on Bleichröder, but this appeared not to faze the Chancellor, and the surprised Jews were grateful and admired him for it.

To be sure, Louis had made it clear that he, like most thinking German Jews, had few illusions that Bismarck or others of his class had shed their fundamental prejudices. It would take more time for the old attitudes and social barriers to fade, and Louis knew that even his friend, Kahlbaum, still harbored many of these reservations. Yet, Louis had assured the mayor, with the legal basis for fully equal treatment established, the day when the remaining barriers would fall was no longer far away.

3

In Oranienburg, the Jews were still a tiny handful among the town's thirty-five hundred inhabitants, though a more prosperous and important group than in the past.

The past ten years had been good ones, there was plenty of economic opportunity, and most had advanced nicely. No one among the twenty-two member families of the local community was needy or poor. Certainly not *Herr Doktor* Lebin, perhaps the town's most successful lawyer, who had arrived from the university with his *Doktortitel* in hand and had hung out his shingle only twenty years ago. Now he had the dubious distinction of ranking as the third highest among the town's 350 taxpayers. Few important legal matters were decided in Oranienburg or its surroundings without his involvement. Gossip had it that the *b* in his surname had once been a v, though Dr. Lebin—without denying it—avoided the subject. His father had been a minimally educated Brandenburg trader whose German still bore traces of the Yiddish he used as a child. The son, however, had left Berlin's university adorned with the telltale dueling scars of Prussian students, and he occasionally fell into speaking the peculiar clipped German favored by officers and aristocrats as smartly *zackig,* or taut. Now Levin-Lebin was dispensing legal advice to the same farmers and locals to whom the father had once peddled his wares, and the respectful *Herr Doktor* with which they addressed him had been a source of immense pleasure and pride for Lebin senior.

Lebin was not the only prominent Jew in town. Salomon Neisser, number five on the tax rolls, owned a distillery. Hennoch Ehrlich and Moses Crohn were prosperous local merchants, ranked among the top twenty-five taxpayers, and Dr. Bernhard Weiss, Oranienburg's busy general practitioner of medicine, was not far behind. Louis Blumenthal, president of the Jewish community, was eighth on the town's tax rolls. Louis's rising fortunes mirrored those of Prussia's Jews in general. He was born at a time when his family still had modest means and expectations. Yet in spite of all the wars, troubles, and barriers, and the back-and-forth of the fight over Jewish rights, Louis had persevered and advanced. As recently as 1857, more than a decade after he brought Regine to Oranienburg and opened his piece goods store, he still paid only a rather modest forty-nine taler in taxes. But with improving economic conditions in the 1860s, his business had expanded, and what at first was a small sideline—financing credit for his customers—had become a significant added source of profit. It had brought him into contact with the many Jewish-owned private banks in Berlin and his reputation for reliability and hard work led to his appointment by the prestigious Berliner Handelsgesellschaft as its official local agent. Recently launched as a joint stock company with the support of the formidable Gerson Bleichröder and other Jewish banking powerhouses, including the privately owned Mendelssohn & Co., the Berliner was one of several at the center of the feverish pace of new-enterprise founding and the booming stock market. Even in little Oranienburg and surroundings everyone wanted to get in on the act, and Louis was finding that his financial sideline was rapidly overtaking in scope and profits his basic business.

In the lower house of the Prussian Diet, Bismarck was supported by the

National Liberals, the moderate party favored by the patriotic rising bourgeoisie. Like most Jews, Louis was an ardent National Liberal. He especially admired Eduard Lasker and Ludwig Bamberger, the party's two most prominent Jewish legislators who stood for liberalism, progress, and Jewish rights in the Reichstag.

Louis and his friends took their hard-won voting rights seriously. They exchanged political gossip and closely followed Prussian Diet and Reichstag debates, always alert to renewed evidence of anti-Semitic agitation. They worried especially about the *Protzer,* vulgar showoffs and extravagant spenders among the Jewish nouveaux riches of Berlin, throwing their money around and overly anxious to make an impression. *Wir Juden sollten nicht zu sehr auffallen* (We Jews shouldn't attract too much attention), Louis was fond of telling his Jewish friends.

There was, after all, a lot to be thankful for in their improved condition. They were leading solid middle-class lives, at ease with the middle-class German values they had adopted, and thoroughly in tune with German culture. The academic achievements of their children in German schools and universities were an immense source of pride. Good relations with their neighbors and involvement in Oranienburg's public affairs were no less a source of satisfaction. The only trouble was that, in the process, commitment and interest in their own community, the local *Synagogengemeinschaft,* were decidedly on the wane.

For Louis, who had reluctantly agreed to be reelected three times as community president, the matter was becoming more than a small annoyance. The last time in 1869, when Police Constable Schulz issued the formal notice of election—all religious affairs being an official matter—only an embarrassing total of six votes were cast. In the end, the same little group of reluctant "volunteers" agreed to stand for reelection, and Louis was forced to continue as president.

It was not that the Jews were turning away from their religion. The bonds were still there, though for many of the younger ones they were now as much sentimental as religious. Twenty years earlier, when Louis brought his widowed father, Israel, to Oranienburg from Wittstock, it was still quite different. The old man was an observant Jew, walking to the synagogue every Friday night and Saturday without fail. Out of respect for him, Regine had done her best to observe the dietary laws, and even for those younger

Oranienburg Jews whose interest in strict religious observances had flagged, life in and around their synagogue—first inaugurated with much fanfare in 1837—remained a central focus. But now most people were busily climbing the economic ladder. Being a good German was at least as important and rewarding as participation in Jewish affairs. In fact, getting enough of them into the synagogue on Friday night was a real problem, and kosher Oranienburg kitchens had become the exception rather than the rule.

With their children attending Christian schools, Louis and Regine had some time ago yielded to their insistent pleas and allowed Christmas and Easter to be celebrated alongside the Jewish holidays. At first, the tree in his living room seemed oddly incongruous to Louis. He was glad that his parents were not there to see it, but now he no longer minded, the children expected it, and his only preoccupation was getting Emil and Martin to take the Hebrew lessons for their bar mitzvahs seriously. It was a common problem for many emancipated Jewish families and Louis frequently discussed it with his friends in Berlin where the loosening of Jewish bonds was even more acute than in his small town.

Only recent arrivals from the East remained truly close to their religion. Established, rising Jews were now more interested in their economic and social status as Germans. The sentimental and emotional bonds to their Jewish past remained intact but were expressed more often than not in material rather than religious forms. The wealthier ones made generous contributions to the elaborately decorated new synagogue with its impressive gilded dome, recently inaugurated on Oranienburgerstrasse, in the old Jewish district of Berlin. They gave for the Jewish poor and collected relief funds for the victims of pogroms in the East, but the old religious and communal connections that had been their primary bond were no longer strong.

4

Technological progress, unbridled optimism, and financial speculation were feeding a powerful economic boom in the Reich and in much of the Western world.

The industrial revolution had transformed England, where iron and steel manufacturing was exploding and the economy was in a period of sustained expansion. William Gladstone spoke of prosperity advancing "by leaps and bounds,"[3] while Benjamin Disraeli said the phenomenon was nothing less than "a convulsion of prosperity."[4] On the other side of the Atlantic, America was in the midst of a post–Civil War reconstruction boom, railroads were snaking their way westward across the continent, and waves of immigrants were bringing fresh energy and creating new wealth.

In nearby Austria, rapid growth and the good life quintupled the consumption of beer in five years, and the hope of more prosperity to follow a world's fair planned for Vienna in 1872 was pushing a booming stock market into the stratosphere.[5] The inauguration of the Suez Canal in 1869 had shortened trade routes and was stimulating international commerce. Everywhere new technologies were raising horizons and creating unbounded enthusiasm about the future. In the process, prices were rising rapidly, squeezing some, enriching others, and encouraging speculators. There were new winners and losers, and inevitably, stable societal patterns of the past were being upset.

In the Reich, special factors were generating an enormous speculative boom and overheated growth. For one thing, the industrial revolution came later and the pace of change was more compressed and convulsive than elsewhere. For another, Bismarck's extraction of five billion francs in war reparations from the French greatly contributed to manic investment activity and unprecedented market euphoria in the years 1870–73—and sowed the seeds of the collapse that followed. Ironically, the money was an unintended French revenge for the humiliation at Versailles—a revenge that was destined to take much bloodier forms over the next half century.

The problem was that France had floated a big loan and paid off its debt to Germany early, in three years rather than the agreed-upon five. Because of misguided monetary policy, most of this flood of gold francs was allowed to wind up in the hands of German businesses, consumers, and speculators, setting off a spree of ill-considered investments and consumer spending. To make matters worse, new gold coins were issued before the silver already in circulation was called in. This mishandling of the reparations and an indiscriminate threefold expansion of the money supply led to rapid inflation and fueled much of the speculation and excess spending.

Louis's business prospered substantially from all the money coursing through Prussia. As agent for the Berliner Bank, he had become one of the many small cogs in a rapidly growing network of large and small banks throughout the Reich, mobilizing capital for the industrial expansion and new railroads. His occasional announcements in the local paper for selling shares, redeeming coupons, and providing help with investments yielded increasing fees from local citizens no less eager than big-city folk to get in on the get-rich-quick bonanza. Innately conservative and cautious, he remained prudent and careful in his own investments. When Oranienburg's town fathers, carried away by the enthusiasm of the day, voted to raise a substantial ten thousand taler from among its anything-but-wealthy citizens to buy shares in the Nordbahn rail line, Louis was openly skeptical and refused to support the idea. In the end, overwhelmingly supported by the rest of the *Magistrat,* the investment nevertheless went forward.

Louis admired Ludwig Bamberger and Eduard Lasker, the two most prominent Jewish members among the National Liberals in the Reichstag. Possibly he was influenced by the warnings of Bamberger, a banker and skilled financial expert. The university-educated son of a banker and a committed liberal, Ludwig Bamberger was one of that first generation of thoroughly assimilated young Jews who had become politically active on the national scene at midcentury. He had acquired his financial acumen, an understanding of French law—and considerable personal wealth—while a refugee in Paris and London after the collapse of the 1848 revolt. Condemned to death in absentia for his revolutionary activities, he had fled abroad and when pardoned returned to Prussia to make common cause with Bismarck. The alliance between the liberal Jew and the conservative *Junker* was somewhat of an anomaly, but the Chancellor was willing to work with anyone who could further his purposes, and he respected the Jew's talents and political credibility with the liberals. As a German patriot, Bamberger, in turn, favored Bismarck's policies of unification and, as a Jew, hoped that they would lead to the cementing of firm and full legal rights for his people throughout the Reich.

When Bismarck called Bamberger to his headquarters during the war and sought his expert advice on the financial aspects of the peace settlement, the Jewish financier had warned against the risks of flooding Germany with the reparation cash. Unfortunately, however, his recommendation that the last installment of the indemnity not be accepted before the end of the stipulated five years was ignored and virtually none of the money was kept out of circulation. There were generous gifts to officers and bureaucrats, debts incurred during the war were paid off in one fell swoop, and most of the five billion francs were allowed to find their way into the hands of a public happily bent on a spree of spending and dubious investments.

In economic history, there are many examples of periodic speculative mania, feeding-frenzied booms followed by panic and busts. The object of speculation has varied from a rush to gold or silver, to stocks and bonds, land, real estate, and even, in seventeenth-century Holland, simple tulip bulbs. In all such booms there is a pervasive air of hysteria, and a mass psychology of wild get-rich-quick schemes. Always, moreover, the speculative bubble attracts not only legitimate businessmen but also the corner cutters and outright swindlers.

The German boom of 1870–73 was no different, and it focused first and foremost on the shares of joint stock companies. The pace of company formations was fast and furious and all the classic characteristics and excesses common to boom periods were present. Subsequently, the era would become known as the *Gründerzeit* (time of the founding of enterprises). In North Germany, 265 joint stock companies with a total capital of more than one billion marks were organized in 1871 alone. The following year the pace accelerated, and almost five hundred firms with a nominal capital of one and one-half billion marks were newly listed on the Berlin *Börse*. In the first quarter of 1873, two hundred additional companies appeared. Even when, later that year, the signs of an impending crash multiplied, dozens of new enterprises were still being registered.[6]

It was the banking and railroad sectors, however, that expanded at an especially frantic pace. The two banks that remain Germany's largest today, the Deutsche Bank and the Dresdner, have their origin in those years. Other large mixed banks—the Berliner, Darmstädter, and Disconto—were organized somewhat earlier but grew mightily during the *Gründerzeit* boom. These were the banks that financed the Reich's industrial growth and the many new rail lines at the heart of the frantic pace of economic activity.

The big banks were critical, but the greatest boom was in the hundreds of smaller public and private ones. These became the major source of cash fueling the spending and speculation. In Berlin and throughout the Reich, most of the population was caught up in one way or another in the frenzy of stock speculation. With the rural population flocking to Berlin and the other large cities, there was also much homelessness, overcrowding, and widespread hardship from rising prices, as well as grumbling from those on fixed incomes and the bourgeoisie, who deplored the visible decline of morals, the shady operators, hucksters, and outright crooks, and the vulgar ostentation and conspicuous spending of the nouveaux riches. Even those—aristocrats, bureaucrats, and others—who grumbled most were caught up in the speculative fever, lending their names to decorate boards of directors, investing their savings, and borrowing money to speculate on the exchange.

Some, of course, like Louis Blumenthal in Oranienburg, were legitimate businessmen who flourished with the times. Only a few years earlier, Louis had made a modest living running his dry-goods store. Now the larger part of his growing income came from his association with the Berliner bank.

Not surprisingly, a substantial, highly visible number of Jews were prominently active in the *Gründerzeit*'s frothy economy. By background and tradition, they were among the most skilled in finance and commerce and inevitably, as bankers, brokers, traders, and entrepreneurs, they participated energetically in the boom. For years, law and custom had kept many near the bottom of the economic ladder. Now they had full legal rights, and the economic expansion was opening the doors to new business opportunities for them. By exerting themselves in the pursuit of business success and wealth, they manifested their eagerness to contribute to the Reich's economic growth and achieve at last that precious recognition and respectability denied them for centuries.

It is hardly surprising that the Jews' traditionally dominant position in German banking would grow yet further during the boom years. The numbers are astonishing. In 1860 there were already twice as many Jewish as non-Jewish banks in Prussia. A decade later, the total number of banks in the Reich had risen to 580, of which an extraordinary 40 percent were owned exclusively by those of Jewish origin, another third or more were under mixed Jewish and Christian control, and only a quarter were exclusively in gentile hands.[7]

When the major banks were formed, big Jewish bankers invariably played leading roles. As they extended their networks into the Reich's smaller provincial towns, Jews like Louis in Oranienburg were their preferred business partners—an important factor in the rapid growth of the many small Jewish country banks during the period.

To the envy and chagrin of many of the traditionalists, it was the Jew Gerson Bleichröder, grandson of a gravedigger, who stood at the top of the pyramid as the undisputed powerhouse banker during the *Gründerzeit* years. His father's foresight in assiduously courting the powerful Rothschilds had elevated him as their preferred agent in Berlin, thus parlaying a small exchange shop into a significant banking business. When Gerson took over from him, he was as fortunate in his timing as his father had been in making the right connections. The Prussian economy was emerging from the doldrums and gathering steam, and Bismarck was the kingdom's most important politician. There were wars to finance and new enterprises to sponsor and that meant opportunity for an ambitious banker.

Timing is critical in business, and Bleichröder was lucky as well as smart: he was the right man in the right place at the right time. Even before Bismarck had risen to head the government, Baron Meyer Carl von Rothschild in Frankfurt had recommended him to his powerful Prussian friend as a reliable confidential financial adviser in Berlin. Thus began a long, profitable, yet always ambiguous association between the ambitious and acquisitive *Junker* and the no less aggressive and enterprising Jew. Bismarck was not above mocking Bleichröder behind his back as a pretentious, social-climbing "money-Jew." Yet he respected Bleichröder for his acumen in financial questions, treated him courteously, and relied heavily on his advice in public and personal money matters. For Bleichröder, the association with Europe's dominant politician was a source of immense psychological satisfaction and pride, quite apart from the opportunity for substantial power and great profit.[8]

By the early 1870s, there were few major financial questions or deals in which Gerson Bleichröder's name did not figure prominently as the Chancellor's counselor and agent. His involvement occasionally extended to broader political issues. The relationship was important to both, yet Bismarck's intimacy with the rich Jew also became grist for the mill of the lengthening list of his enemies and opponents, no less so than for the ever-present traditional anti-Semites. Bleichröder had helped to finance Bismarck's wars and advised on the settlement with the French at Versailles. He played a leading role in most of the great public financing syndicates and was prominent in underwriting the founding of the Reich's major rail and industrial ventures. He was, in a sense, the classic "Court Jew" close to the seat of power. Bleichröder became rich and important, and the wider the swath he cut in Berlin, the more he was both courted and feared for his power—and also resented as the most visible symbol for the excesses of the new capitalist age.

Once there had been talk that Giacomo Meyerbeer might be rewarded with a hereditary title for his achievements, but this had never been done for a Jew with living heirs, and nothing came of it. In 1872, on Bismarck's recommendation, Gerson Bleichröder became the first to be so honored. Henceforth he would be Baron von Bleichröder, proud as a peacock, anxious to act the part and to be accepted in the nobility. But it was not that simple. For Prussian society, he remained a disagreeable parvenu, the abhorrent metaphor for the rise of the Jewish minority to an elevated status in a capitalist world they instinctively feared and disliked. Bleichröder and those like him would never be acceptable as social equals.

There were others, of course, who played prominent roles on the economic scene during the boom years—major Jewish bankers in the key provincial centers, like the Oppenheims in Cologne, Warburgs in Hamburg, and Arnholds in Dresden, and the important gentile pastor's son, Adolph Hansemann, who was Bleichröder's closest banking associate in Berlin. Together these men founded the big banks, financed the railroads, underwrote the new industrial enterprises, and had their fingers in every new deal. Elsewhere Jews prospered alongside their gentile counterparts in railroad building, textiles, breweries, and chemicals. They were especially dominant in the establishment of the new fashion houses, and in retailing, in publishing, as wholesalers and middlemen, as country bankers and—most visibly—as brokers on Berlin's booming stock exchange.

There were Jews and non-Jews in all of these fields, but since the Jewish minority was disproportionately represented, it was their activities and their wealth and success that stood out in the public perception. Until recently the Jewish community in Berlin had been small. Now it was growing even faster than burgeoning Berlin's population as a whole. New arrivals from the eastern provinces were arriving daily, mixing with the city's long-established and more assimilated old-time Jewish residents. In dress, speech, and custom they were markedly different, a highly visible group active at all levels in the city's hectic economic expansion.

So Jews became the symbol in the public mind of the changes and dislocations of traditional life, and of the shadow side of the age of raw capitalism. If there was grudging admiration and respect for their enterprise and success, there was at least an equal measure of barely concealed resentment and envy from those who disliked the atmosphere of material striving and were unwilling or unable to adapt to it.

5

In the 1860s and 1870s Berlin, the central stage for these developments, was a growing city of stark contrasts. On the periphery, there were sprawling tent cities overcrowded with rural people and Polish immigrants looking for work. Next to these were dreary, hastily built and overcrowded structures, the *Mietskasernen,* which housed Berlin's growing array of workers who labored long hours for little pay in factories where abominable working conditions were common. For this underclass, the new age meant hardships, rising criminality, and declining morals. On the streets the ubiquitous beggar, often a one-legged veteran still in uniform, had become a common sight.

At the other extreme, ostentatious spending was the order of the day. Rents skyrocketed, theatre tickets went for prices greater than a year's pay for a worker, and champagne flowed freely. On weekends, the city's affluent paraded up and down the major boulevards, decked out in their finery and eager to show off the visible evidence of their prosperity.

For the small number of super-rich gentiles and Jews, there was indescribable luxury and a sumptuous lifestyle that surpassed anything seen before. In Essen, Friedrich Krupp, the iron and steel magnate, built himself an estate, the Villa Hügel, containing no fewer than two hundred rooms. In Berlin, the banker Hansemann lived in a palace surrounded by dozens of footmen and servants.

It was this vulgar flaunting of new wealth and possessions that deeply offended the traditionalists. Many had not benefited from the boom and were under great pressure. New technologies undermined the security of artisans, small shopkeepers were hurt by larger retailers, and landowning aristocrats were caught in a squeeze between rising taxes and falling agricultural values on the one hand and the escalating cost of living on the other. These were the elements of the German population most affronted by the showy upstarts, and most open to anti-Semitic agitation.

Gerson Bleichröder and the most public and flamboyant of the new entrepreneurs, a baptized Jew named Henry Bethel Strousberg, whom everyone called "the king of railroads," were the best-known actors in this changed world. Ambitious and fabulously wealthy, they were the new plutocrats, eager to impress with their money and power. Their sumptuous lifestyle became the talk of Europe. At 63 Behrenstrasse, the freshly minted Baron von Bleichröder lived in a magnificent home amid Berlin's finest mansions, not far from the Crown Prince's palace. Outside the city, he owned a country estate more resplendent than that of any landed *Junker*. In season, he entertained royally and gave balls "that were great events, Lucullan feasts."[9] Even Disraeli, writing to Queen Victoria, could not resist telling her of his stunned perplexity at seeing the banker's "palace, and his magnificent banqueting hall . . . very vast and very lofty, and indeed the whole of the mansion . . . built of every species of rare marble, and where it is not marble, it is gold . . . with . . . splendid saloons, and picture galleries, and a ballroom fit for a fairy tale."[10]

Bleichröder was a proud and ambitious man who saw wealth, influence, prominence, and well-publicized good deeds as the key to respectability and social status. In time there would be many others among Germany's Jews, although at much less lofty levels, who harbored similar beliefs. Like him, they would discover that the greater their success and the harder they tried to impress with accomplishment and wealth, the more they would be resisted and resented.

Henry Bethel Strousberg, for a while reputed to be the richest German, would make a similar discovery. When he fell from grace and his empire

collapsed, not only his hapless investors but all who had flattered and petitioned him for the favors and money he had dispensed liberally would turn
to cursing him as the prototype of the conniving Jew. He too lived in great
Gründerprunk style, and there was a time when not even Bleichröder and
his circle could equal the showy opulence of his mansion on Wilhelm-
strasse. Some said he held court there in the manner of an Oriental poten-
tate. With its renaissance facade and precious contents, it was reputed
to have cost an unheard of one million marks. The skylighted vestibule
was adorned with Corinthian columns and had a fountain at its center.
An elaborate winter garden contained an artificial lark as its pièce-de-
résistance, and visitors were led over lush red carpets to his private quarters,
past a gallery containing one of Berlin's finest collections of paintings.

Strousberg, who loved landed properties, was an inveterate purchaser of
real estate. In time, he bought large country homes for each of his seven
children and several more for himself, including a Bohemian estate of more
than sixty thousand acres, with four hundred separate buildings and a
castle at its center. Some called it a miniature kingdom.[11] When he traveled,
it was by private train or in a four-horse carriage with liveried coachmen
and a large staff of retainers. A publicity hound who had acquired his own
newspaper in Berlin, he made sure that everyone knew of his exploits. *Klad-
deratsch,* Berlin's humor magazine, awarded him its *Bürgerkrone,* the mock
crown of an emperor, and Engels derisively wrote to Karl Marx that he is
"Europe's biggest man. Next, the fellow will be Kaiser of the Germans.
Wherever you turn, people talk about him."[12]

Strousberg's extravagance was constant fodder for the rumor mills. Like
most Germans and many of his Jewish friends, Louis was impressed by his
business success, yet he viewed the drumbeat of publicity about this larger-
than-life Jewish magnate with a mixture of distaste and concern. The man
was noisy and vulgar and that, Louis suspected, could spell trouble. In a
day of unrestrained capitalism, he was a classic corner cutter whose business ethics left much to be desired. Louis was right, of course, but in the
end Strousberg's importance lay not in his lifestyle, his business ethics, or
his spectacular bankruptcy but in his lasting imprint on German industrial
development. For, apart from his many foibles and failings, he was also a
far-sighted and gifted innovator whose contributions to the German economy were permanent—and a fascinating counterpart to two others of Jew-

ish origin, Ferdinand Lassalle, founder of the German Labor Movement, and Karl Marx, the father of communism, who were capitalism's most vociferous social critics.[13]

He was born Baruch Hirsch Strausberg into an impoverished Jewish family in East Prussia in 1823. Orphaned at age twelve, he was sent to live with an uncle in England. As a young boy, his name had been Germanized to Barthel Heinrich, and in England it was anglicized as Bethel Henry. What is known of his ensuing years in England and America, until he reappeared in Berlin a quarter century later, remains uncertain and comes from his own not always reliable telling.[14] Self-educated, baptized into the Anglican Church, at times a trader, at others a journalist, newspaper publisher, and statistician, he claimed to have studied political economy, and added a *Doktortitel* to his name.

Returning to his native Germany, still full of ambition and still in search of his niche in life, he was led almost by accident to his real calling—the organizing, financing, and building of railroads—by a fortuitous connection with English investors anxious to share in the German boom.

Most towns wanted a railroad in the 1860s, yet lack of funding and a complex web of financial regulations had brought construction to a virtual standstill. The creative and agile Strousberg was not to be deterred. His solution brilliantly combined innovation and creative financial engineering. First, the "System Strousberg" he invented—and whose mystique he fostered—introduced the novel English concept of the general contractor with responsibility for all aspects of a project from planning to funding and turnkey construction. Next, to lower costs, he bought land early and cheaply and pioneered the ideas of vertical integration and economies of scale, acquiring mines, fabricators, and suppliers, and running several projects at once to lower overhead. Finally, to hurdle the financing roadblocks, he bypassed traditional bank lenders and sold securities directly to the public with techniques that observed the letter, though hardly the spirit, of the law—often by issuing watered stock exceeding the value of the underlying assets.

For some years, Strousberg succeeded brilliantly. He was the talk of Europe and his success in garnering new concessions and rapid building became legendary. Within eight years, he raised eighty-four million marks in capital and completed the construction of a record seventeen hundred kilometers of track for seven separate rail projects from East Prussia to Brandenburg and Hanover. They remain a part of Germany's rail network to the present day.

The more he succeeded, the more feverish and daring the style of his operations, and the more frantic his purchases of landed estates and industrial properties. At the peak, he owned mines from Bohemia to the Ruhr, locomotive factories in Hanover, and machine shops and iron and steel works all over Germany. He even bought Berlin's wholesale market and a part of Antwerp's harbor.

With an intuitive understanding of psychology and public relations, he knew that in business the appearance of success, as much as the reality, works wonders and can open doors to yet further successes. The greater his reach, the more the anterooms of his mansion on Behrenstrasse were filled with the high and mighty from all over Europe bidding for his money and his investments. Prussian officials probably suspected some of his methods, yet because he succeeded—and treated them generously—they blinked at them. In turn, he made sure to decorate the boards of his enterprises with counts, dukes, and assorted influential aristocrats.

Always at risk, rushing from one project to another, it was inevitable that he would eventually come to grief. Hurt by the war and then by the spectacular failure of a rail project in Romania, his luck finally ran out. Deeply in debt, he was forced into the progressive sale of his properties and his position quickly grew precarious. Lasker's exposé of his cozy relationship with Prussian officialdom and questionable methods of finance was the last straw. His overvalued rail shares plummeted and many investors were ruined. The king of railroads had become the king of bankruptcy.

Now he was no longer the brilliant investor with the golden touch, but the Jew responsible for the collapse of the boom. Traveling to Russia on business, he was—probably unfairly—accused of fraud and imprisoned in Moscow for over a year. He never recovered after he returned to Berlin. His properties, mansions, and landed estates gone, he retired to two furnished rooms and died poor and discredited.

6

The good times abruptly came to an end in October 1873. The speculative bubble burst, stock prices collapsed, bankruptcies multiplied, unemployment rose, and Germany entered a prolonged period of economic depression. For many who had counted on comfortable wealth, there was instead ruination and hard times. For the discontented and disaffected, it was proof that the system had been rotten all along and that the solid values of former years had been undermined and subverted by those they had long suspected of it.

Louis's worst nightmare had come true, and in 1874, he spared Oranienburg's town fathers none of his fears and frustrations: "In my opinion," he wrote them, "bankruptcy of the *Nordbahn* is unavoidable. The town has ten thousand taler invested in obligations bought at 100, and now they are worth no more than 20–22 each. We should sell all or part of our holdings. . . . In bankruptcy they may be worth nothing. . . . Greatest speed is of the essence!"[15]

In the boom years, he had worried about the inflated value of railroad securities and counseled against the investment. When overruled, he refused to sign the purchase resolution. Now the bottom had dropped out of the market, but the town was still not ready to throw in the towel. No one could believe that the dream was really over. The financial disaster was worsening daily but instead of selling out, Kahlbaum was dispatched to Berlin on a final rescue mission to see what could still be saved. The mayor managed exemplary frugality, spent only two taler and two groschen on a cheap coach seat, and contented himself with a single seven-groschen cab in the capital.[16] Yet it was all to no avail. No one was willing to bail Oranienburg out, and even this minimal expense, duly recorded in meticulous detail by the town cashier, proved to be a poor investment—a case of throwing good money after bad. The town would have done better to listen to the advice of its dissenting counselor.

Germany's great boom had given way to the great bust. In the market crash of the previous October the value of railroad obligations collapsed and the Nordbahn was no exception. When Oranienburg finally sold, the price was down to eleven and one-half taler. Only about a tenth of the investment was saved.[17]

The town's loss was bad enough, but to Louis's dismay it was two of Berlin's best-known, most ego-driven, and publicity-prone Jews who were now being accused of responsibility for the crash. One was Eduard Lasker, the fighter for liberal causes in the Reichstag, whose charges of corruption in the granting of railroad concessions had been a factor in bursting the bubble and sending the Berlin market into its precipitous decline. Worse yet, it was the activities of Bethel Henry Strousberg that had been at the core of Lasker's revelations. Now, with thousands ruined, unemployment mounting, and misery everywhere, these two prominent Jews—accuser and accused—were being assigned a heavy share of the blame. Just as Louis and many of his friends had feared, when any one Jew stood out, let alone two, all Jews were vulnerable.

It was the other side of the coin of the Jewish advance in German life. With success came greater prominence, public exposure, and a normalization of their status. Yet, they remained "special," and the old stereotypes and traditional prejudices against the Jew still prevailed. If a gentile was under the gun it was an individual matter. When a Jew got into trouble, all were at risk.

In fact, however, the panic of 1873 and the depression that followed were a worldwide phenomenon. Lasker and Strousberg were hardly the fundamental causes of the collapse. With advancing technology and more trade, financial centers had become interconnected, and the causes of ups and downs were no longer purely domestic. Germans had exuberantly invested in the booming stock market of Vienna and in the railroad expansion of America. The vulnerability to a crash was due to many factors rather than the result of a single local event, such as Lasker's revelations or Strousberg's recklessness.[18]

The storm clouds, in fact, had been gathering for some time. In the summer of 1872, rail and textile shares started falling in Vienna, and only a concerted government rescue operation had saved the day. When Strousberg's far-flung empire began to rock dangerously at about the same time, it took a complex bailout maneuver by Bleichröder and Hansemann to prevent major investor losses. Lasker's subsequent attacks on corruption in high places and on Strousberg's business practices had further shaken confidence, though in the immediate aftermath the German market shrugged off the news and for a while prices had continued to rise.

It was the total collapse of the Vienna market in May, and the failure of a major American investment house followed by the closing of the New York exchange, that eventually brought the *Börse* to its knees. When Berlin's Quistorp bank declared itself illiquid, the panic there became unstoppable.

Burning of Jews accused of desecrating the Eucharist in Berlin during pogroms in 1510. Nineteenth-century woodcut by Ludwig Bürger.
[Bildarchiv Preussischer Kulturbesitz, Berlin]

Representation of a wandering Jewish peddler, from an early nineteenth-century engraving.
[Bildarchiv Preussischer Kulturbesitz, Berlin. Orig.: Leo Baeck Institute, New York.]

Jude.

Jost Liebmann in his later years
as Court Jeweler and protected Jew.
Portrait (1702?) by Anton Schoonjans
(Antwerp 1655–Vienna 1726).
[Courtesy Leo Baeck Institute, New York.
Orig.: Verwaltung der Staatlichen Schlösser
und Gärten, Schloss Charlottenburg, Berlin.
Photograph © W. Gregor.]

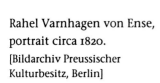

Rahel Varnhagen von Ense,
portrait circa 1820.
[Bildarchiv Preussischer
Kulturbesitz, Berlin]

Giacomo Meyerbeer as child prodigy. This portrait (1802), by Friedrich Georg Weitsch (1758–1828), hung briefly in Prussia's Royal Academy but was removed because of anti-Semitic protests.
[Aufnahme der Landesbildstelle Berlin]

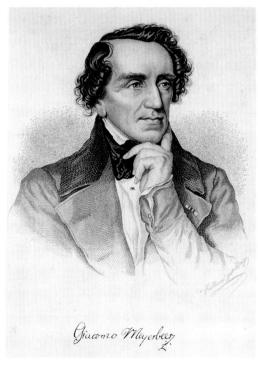

Giacomo Meyerbeer, portrait engraving (1852), by M. Lämmel, Leipzig.
[Landesbildstelle Berlin]

Caricatures of Jews were not uncommon in the nineteenth century. This one is called "Studies in Physiognomy." From the the periodical *Die Fliegenden Blätter*, 1869. [Bildarchiv Preussischer Kulturbesitz, Berlin]

„Herr Baron, der Bub' stiehlt Ihnen Ihr Sacktuch!"
„Lassen sen geihn, mer hab'n aach klein angefangen."

Caricature depicting the alleged dishonesty of Jewish stock exchange traders. The legend reads, "Baron, the boy's stealing your handkerchief!" "Never mind, I started young too." From the the periodical *Die Fliegenden Blätter*, 1851–52.
[Bildarchiv Preussischer Kulturbesitz, Berlin]

The young William,
first Kaiser of Prussia,
portrait sketch by
Franz Kruger.
[Ullstein Bilderdienst,
Berlin]

Willliam I of Prussia
with Crown Prince
Frederick III during the
Franco-Prussian War,
1870–71, from a paint-
ing by C. Wagner.
[Ullstein Bilderdienst,
Berlin]

Otto von Bismarck (left) presents Prussia's harsh peace terms to Jules Favre and Adolphe Thiers (in armchair) at Versailles, 1871, from a painting by Karl Wagner.
[Ullstein Bilderdienst, Berlin]

Victory parade: Kaiser William I and Bismarck return to Berlin, June 6, 1871.
[Ullstein Bilderdienst, Berlin]

In the wild 1920s Arthur Eloesser would remember the days when policemen were a respected presence in the streets of Berlin. Photograph circa 1900.
[Ullstein Bilderdienst, Berlin]

Anti-Semitic caricature from 1920. The heading reads, "For the Friends of the German Republic," and the legend reads, "Come on in, gentlemen! Even if Germany's sons go hungry, *you* will not perish." From the periodical *Deutsches Witzblatt* 4. [Bildarchiv Preussischer Kulturbesitz, Berlin]

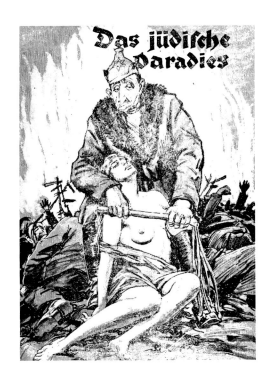

Anti-Semitic caricature from 1922. The heading reads, "Jewish Paradise." From the periodical *Deutsches Witzblatt* 45–46. [Bildarchiv Preussischer Kulturbesitz, Berlin]

Hyperinflation in 1923. People carried vast amounts of the greatly devalued paper money in suitcases and laundry baskets. [Ullstein Bilderdienst, Berlin]

Arthur Eloesser, February 18, 1930. Photograph by Abraham Pisarek.
[Ullstein Bilderdienst, Berlin]

Arthur Eloesser with Thomas and Heinrich Mann on Heinrich Mann's sixtieth birthday, 1931, at the Academy of Arts, Berlin. (Left to right: Dr. Adolf Grimme, Eloesser, Heinrich Mann, Thomas Mann.) [Ullstein Bilderdienst, Berlin]

Hermann Göring in Nuremberg in 1929. Photograph by Heinrich Hoffmann.
[Bildarchiv Preussischer Kulturbesitz, Berlin]

The Nazi's anti-Semitic hate campaign was in high gear by 1932. This drawing is captioned, "The 'German' citizen of Jewish faith." [Bildarchiv Preussischer Kulturbesitz, Berlin]

Nazis confiscating books for burning in Hamburg, May 1933. Photograph by Joseph Shorer. [Bildarchiv Preussischer Kulturbesitz, Berlin]

Book burning, 1933, with students attending in full regalia. Photograph by Shorer.
[DHM, Berlin]

Nazis with boycott placards in front of a Jewish business in Berlin, April 1, 1933.
[Bildarchiv Preussischer Kulturbesitz, Berlin]

Berlin, 1933: Nazis use terror tactics against Jewish shopkeepers. [Bildarchiv Preussischer Kulturbesitz, Berlin]

Persecution of Jews as an official function, 1933. In Munich, attorney Michael Siegel had protested to the police when one of his clients was arrested. He was paraded on the street with a placard hung around his neck that read, "I will never again complain to the police." [Ullstein Bilderdienst, Berlin]

"The air in Buckow is
unhealthy for Jews." Such
postings were common at
the entrances to towns all
over the Nazi Germany
of the late 1930s.
[DHM, Berlin]

Jews cleaning up the
debris after *Kristallnacht*,
November 10, 1938.
[Ullstein Bilderdienst,
Berlin. AP photo.]

The main synagogue of Berlin after *Kristallnacht*. [Landesbildstelle Berlin]

By 1939 anti-Jewish propaganda was everywhere. This poster by Hans Stalüter announces a major exhibition in Dresden, "The Eternal Jew." [DHM, Berlin]

A Jewish girl arrives in London on a children's transport, December 1938.
[Bildarchiv Preussischer Kulturbesitz, Berlin]

A room in a *Heim.*
[Leo Baeck Institute, New York]

Refugees in Shanghai ghetto offering clothes for sale. [Leo Baeck Institute, New York]

A postwar cry for help: Who will admit a Jewish D.P.? Shanghai, 1947.
[Leo Baeck Institute, New York]

Within weeks, twenty-seven banks suspended payments, industrial firms collapsed all over Germany, output plummeted, prices and wages fell, the unemployed rioted in the streets, and thousands of small savers were ruined. In the first year, sixty-one banks, four railroads, and more than a hundred industrial companies went bankrupt. Germany entered a deep economic depression. The flimsier enterprises quickly disappeared, and a few unscrupulous promoters and shady operators got their comeuppance, but many more fundamentally sound smaller companies were ruined as well. Thousands of honest citizens were impoverished. Yet some of the largest enterprises founded during those years survived and became the foundation of Germany's future industrial might. As to the railroads, the public lost heavily but the network remained in place. Eventually it was reorganized, taken over by the state, and after a hiatus of some years, continued its growth into one of Europe's finest systems.

It had been a time of dynamic change, when the old world of feudalism clashed with the emerging liberalism of the new capitalist age. In many other countries of Europe this process led to the emergence of a politically strengthened bourgeois middle class, the expansion of private enterprise, and more democratic political institutions. In Germany that did not happen. Bourgeois society in 1873 was still in its infancy and the *Junker,* aristocrats, and ultraconservatives had remained strong and resentful over the loss of their privileges.

Following the collapse, the conservatives eventually reassumed power and instead of a greater bourgeois liberalism they perpetuated a tightly controlled, highly authoritarian, and nationalistic politico-economic system heavily dominated by the state. The dislocations of rapid industrial growth, followed by hard times, gave democratic liberalism a bad name and discredited it for many years. The values of the *Junker* class remained dominant and the evolution of a liberal middle-class society was greatly retarded. Germany became what one historian has called a "Faulted Nation," a kind of industrial feudal society, dominated by large enterprises with heavy state influence, politically authoritarian and socially intolerant.[19]

The conservative power elite held firm to its nostalgic attachment to the old order and hated the messy, often chaotic world that had taken its place. They despised the new arrivals and the nouveaux riches, and a wave of

hostility welled up against all minorities—foreigners, labor unions, socialists, and even against Catholics. New restrictive laws against these groups
were enacted, but the greatest hatred was directed against the Jews. A new,
more virulent and aggressive version of Germany's age-old anti-Semitic
heritage, destined to prevail with ultimately disastrous consequences into
the next century, was born.

7

The collapse ushered in half a decade of decline and stagnation, followed
by a halting and uneven recovery. The first serious crisis of bourgeois society was underway, and it crystallized deep fears and resentments. What had
happened, people asked, and who was to blame?

It was not long before those convinced that it was all the fault of the Jews
appeared on the scene. Bleichröder, Strousberg, prominent Jewish bankers,
and newly enriched large merchants were convenient and ready symbols
for what Judeophobes claimed was corrupt Jewish power. Lasker, Bamberger, and others of Jewish origin among the Chancellor's National Liberals
favoring bourgeois democracy also became the focus of their attacks. Indeed, the finger was now being pointed at all Jews. The complaint was that
they had been allowed to become a powerful alien and corrosive force on
the national scene. Unless a fight to the finish against the Jews was engaged, the public was told, the prospects for a strong, moral, healthy Reich
looked dim.

One of the first in a steadily expanding phalanx of anti-Jewish polemicists making these arguments was a skilled political agitator named Wilhelm Marr who, soon after the economic collapse, aroused public interest
with a pamphlet destined to go through twelve editions in the span of six
years. Marr never became a major figure on the political scene, and many
considered him uncouth and vulgar. Yet he occupies a lasting place as a
pioneer of sorts in the history of Judeophobes. For one thing, he is credited
with being the inventor of the term *anti-Semitism,* the first to use it and to
introduce several other pejorative concepts into the standard vocabulary
of future generations of German Jew-haters. *Verjudung* (Judaization), a favorite word of Hitler and the Nazis, was another of his coinages.

Most importantly, however, the avowed atheist Marr was one of the first to shift anti-Jewish agitation to a novel and fateful plane by attacking Jews on politico-racial rather than religious grounds—not as un-Christian, but as un-German. In his pamphlet, entitled *Der Sieg des Judenthums über das Germanenthum* (The Victory of Judaism over Germanism), and in several later writings, he argued that Jews were Orientals stranded in a Western world "as alien to them as they are to it." A thousand years of discrimination, he wrote, had sharpened their innate racial characteristics, honed their skills for ruthless survival, and transformed them into a powerful bloc posing a deadly threat to German society. Marr claimed that Jewish power had grown overwhelming under Bismarck, and he took to calling the Second Reich a "New Palestine" dominated by Jews who corrupted standards of decency and were devoid of all ideals. The question was whether Germans would rise to defend themselves, lest—as the title of his pamphlet implied—Jewry would defeat them and emerge forever victorious.

Marr remained in the limelight for some years. In 1879, before he faded from the scene, he founded a "League of Anti-Semites" to unite Germany's by then numerous anti-Jewish groups, parties, and assorted activists into a single force dedicated to fighting Jews. Meanwhile there were other voices at least as influential as his who had joined in the scapegoating and the anti-Semitic agitation. In 1874, a series of inflammatory articles in the *Gartenlaube,* a popular, widely read middle-class magazine, accused Jews as the prime movers behind predatory capitalism. In the next year, the organ of the archconservative opposition to Bismarck, the *Kreuzzeitung,* kept the pot boiling by linking Jews to the Chancellor's policies of social reform.

By then, the campaign had widened steadily and become hopelessly intertwined in broader political intrigues against the Chancellor. The poor economic climate and social dislocation favored the spread of anti-Semitism, and various political factions found capitalizing on it an excellent way to gain public support for their fight against those of his policies they especially disliked.

Bismarck's main goal had always been to strengthen the authority of the state, while modernizing its institutions without impinging on the Crown's prerogatives or surrendering power to parliament. Archconservatives on the right opposed him bitterly because they resisted any change at all and wanted to give up nothing. On the left, Progressives and Socialists were in opposition because they wanted more democracy and an end to

aristocratic privilege. The National Liberals had been Bismarck's main supporters, and when he embarked on a campaign of bringing Germany's
Catholics under secular control—a policy that became known as the *Kulturkampf*—it was they who stood behind him in the Reichstag.

The issue was highly inflammatory and drove the infuriated Catholics
to make common cause with Bismarck's opposition on the right. The alle-
gation that he was subject to undue Jewish influence proved the glue for
the alliance. Archconservatives blamed Jews for the loss of their economic
power; their Catholic allies argued that it was Jews who wanted to secular-
ize German society and that the *Kulturkampf* had been their idea in the first
place. Even Pope Pius IX in Rome issued an encyclical protesting Bismarck's
policies and joined in thinly veiled allegations that the Jews were at fault.

Meanwhile there were political developments that further worked
against the Jews. In 1878, two attempts on the old Kaiser's life were cited as
evidence of a loosening of public discipline, for which some blamed the
Jewish minority. The worldwide recession led to the dumping of agricultural and industrial products in Germany, and open trade, favored by the
National Liberals, came under severe attack. Agrarian interests joined
heavy industry in opposing Bismarck's free-trade policies with vociferous
demands for more protection, and when the Liberals lost ground at the
polls, Bismarck—ever the pragmatic realist—quickly drew the conclusion
that the time had come for a change. In 1878 he abandoned the Liberals,
outlawed the increasingly more numerous Socialists to please the right,
raised protective tariffs, and switched to a conservative-center alliance in
the Reichstag. As a result, the pro-liberal Jewish minority was left isolated
and exposed, the Chancellor's protection was temporarily muted, and em-
boldened anti-Semitic agitators grew louder. By the early 1880s, the Jewish
Question was once again a central issue of public debate.

Many joined the fray. Some were crude rabblerousers playing on the
fears and grievances of the public. Others were more sophisticated orators,
and some held positions that guaranteed them prestige and a large audience. The best known of these was Court Preacher Adolf Stoecker, an influential, monarchist, antidemocratic theologian who especially hated
Socialists. He had founded a rival Christian Social Workers Party to enlist
the masses for the conservatives with an amorphous program of social
reform. As Stoecker's star waxed and waned, anti-Semitism became an

increasingly strident part of his position. He blamed the Jews for the rise of the Socialists, formed a Berlin Movement to unite all anti-Semites, and argued that Germany was a Christian nation where no Jew should hold a position of power and that "the capital of the German Reich . . . [cannot] be permitted to remain in democratic, Jewish, un-German hands."[20]

Though noisy and important because he spoke from his pulpit at the Berlin Dom, with what seemed at times the implicit blessing of the court, Stoecker was less radical than others who cared little about religion and attacked Jews on racial grounds. One of these was Otto Böckel, who stirred up the peasants, wanted to repeal the emancipation laws, and argued for the total exclusion of that "tough old alien race which cannot be subdued by baptism or intermarriage."[21] Having won election to the Reichstag on this platform, he was the first to organize one of its avowedly anti-Semitic factions, and astonished his colleagues with imaginative statistical projections to prove that Jews would eventually outnumber gentiles in all the major cities, with a million of them in Berlin alone.[22] Not to be outdone, another of the polemicists stepped forward to cite crime statistics to prove conclusively that Jews were much more likely to commit criminal offenses than non-Jews. Another activist, Eugen Dühring, a bitter contrarian who hated all symbols of success and power and blamed Jews for his failure as a journalist and his dismissal from an academic post, exceeded everyone with his outpouring of unabashed vitriolic rhetoric and hatred.[23]

As time passed, there were dozens of others spanning a wide range of views and motives who joined in the campaign of hate. Some were Christian zealots, others conservatives, agrarians, spokesmen for the disaffected petit bourgeoisie, or simply malcontents and rabblerousers enthusiastically adding fuel to the flames. Some labored on the fringes; others formed political movements, lectured to the public, or organized "anti-Semite" days where they outdid each other in anti-Jewish diatribes. All in all, though a noisy and worrisome minority, they lacked the status and respectability to become a true mainstream force.

All, that is, except one prominent academic who stepped forward to lend his considerable prestige to the anti-Semitic movement and provided it with respectability, an intellectual rationale, and some of the vocabulary that would remain a part of German thinking and anti-Jewish agitation for generations to come. He was Henrich von Treitschke, one of the best-known and widely read historians of his time, a scholar with considerable influence on German ruling circles. Treitschke occupied the senior history chair at Berlin University where he was the favorite of the students immersed in the prevailing romantic nationalism. His lectures were amongst the most popular and heavily attended. Long after his death, the legacy of the ideas he imparted to them in his passionate lectures and writings would remain a permanent part of German anti-Semitic theories.

As much a political publicist and active politician as a pure academic— he served in the Reichstag for some years—Treitschke was above all a supreme nationalist with profoundly undemocratic ideas and exaggerated notions of the superiority of Germanic virtues. He was also a racist who believed that it was the destiny of inferior Slavs and Baltics to live under the superior Germanic race. He supported aggressive colonial expansion and spoke of war as a justified means to a glorious end. In his accounts of German history, he glorified the rights of "Prussia, strong in arms and with the colors of a mighty fleet,"[24] exulted in conquests as the nation's most magnificent moments, and prophesied that "the white race will rule the earth."[25] The young Emperor William I was to him "blond, Germanic, and ramrod straight" (blonde Germanische Reckengestalt).[26] The summoning of English doctors to consult on the ruler's final illness he condemned as a national affront and a threat to the dying monarch.

Treitschke especially disliked the Socialists and thought that inequality of the classes in Germany was proper and unavoidable. Some are born to lead and others to serve, he proclaimed, observing that "there can be no Kultur without servants."[27] Treitschke published voluminously and his theoretical arguments and views were complex and evolved over time. Read today, they seem outlandish and extreme, and it is difficult to understand his enormous popularity, the idolization of his students, and the great impact he had on the intellectual circles of his time.

Almost from the start, his strong nationalism was tinged with criticism of Germany's Jews, whom he considered a group incompatible with his heroic German ideals. In his view, they were by nature too individualistic, too arrogant, and a negative influence on German culture. Their disappearance through total absorption was the only answer. There were, however, "good" and "bad" Jews. He especially disliked the un-German recent arrivals he called the "Kaftan-Jews." In the realm of culture, he condemned Jewish intellectuals, such as Heine, for introducing "rootless, radical, and abstract ideas into German life." Giacomo Meyerbeer was subjected to the familiar criticism that he was a cosmopolitan who had shown no evidence of "that simple German art," while Felix Mendelssohn-Bartholdy was that rare exception, a true German "from head to toe."[28] Jewish businessmen, in his view, were mostly hagglers and usurers and the financial power of international Jewry was to be feared. There was, he wrote, a justifiable "silent anger of the masses" that so large a part of German money had fallen into Jewish hands. He even objected that Berlin's "largest and most magnificent church is a synagogue" and attacked Jewish "press barons" for stifling public exposure of Jewish sins. German "aryanism" is the antithesis of a Judaism corrosive of German culture, he maintained, coining a slogan that would become the favorite of all future German anti-Semites—"Die Juden sind unser Unglück" (The Jews are our misfortune).[29]

The Jews were stunned, perplexed, and confused. They had considered the issue of their place in Germany settled. Now, to their dismay, the "Jewish Question" was once again being debated, and this time they were caught by complex political forces playing the anti-Jewish card with novel arguments about international economic power, cultural subversion, and an unbridgeable gulf based on race and ethnicity.

What were they to think? The polemics of the agitators were painful, and Treitschke's support vexing and highly unfortunate—but was it merely a passing aberration brought on by economic hard times, or was it something more fundamental and permanent? The evidence was by no means clear. Only a vociferous minority of gentiles seemed to agree with the onslaught against them, even when it came to Treitschke's intellectual arguments. True, not many non-Jews came forward to mount a defense, but the respected historian Theodor Mommsen vigorously rejected Treitschke's ideas with strong counterarguments, and a group of seventy-five academics joined him in signing a public manifesto of support. What, then, was the proper response?

For want of a better idea, the Jewish establishment counseled caution and suggested lying low. The principal Jewish paper thought that official complaints would merely publicize the views of a few fanatics, and at Erfurt a group of leaders passed a resolution pledging to "maintain a contemptuous silence."[30] Most Jews agreed, and when Heinrich Graetz, a scholar

whose focus on Jewish history Treitschke had singled out for special criticism, answered him aggressively, a bitter exchange ensued. But Graetz remained a lonely voice, and he was attacked for striking back. Bamberger
called him a zealot, the Jewish counterpart to the intemperate Stoecker.
Others apologized for Graetz's outbursts. One Jewish historian went so far
as to inquire of Treitschke what guidelines there were for his ideas of promoting the disappearance of the Jewish minority through total absorption.

In time, as the attacks continued, there were a few cautious efforts to
counteract them. Hermann Cohen, a respected philosopher who actually
held a tenured faculty position at Marburg, protested to Treitschke in an
open letter that loyalty to the Jewish religion in no way compromised one's
commitment to the state. The Jewish establishment formed a Committee
of Elders who counseled self-improvement, explanation of Jewish values,
and acts of loyalty to Germany. One or two student groups tried to counter
the anti-Semitic propaganda at universities, and the largest community
organization sent a petition for help to Bismarck, which, however, remained unanswered.

Yet these were isolated efforts. The majority of Jews remained silent and
passive before the attacks. They could not understand why their German
Kultur counted for nothing and why their Jewishness should be seen as incompatible with their status as citizens. Thousands of Jews had fought and
died for Germany in times of war, and all around them there was evidence
of Jewish contributions to the fatherland in times of peace.

The new wave of attacks was a shock; still, there was also evidence of
progress. Germany's Jews had their civil rights, and the great majority was
doing well. Their children were flocking to the *Gymnasia* and universities
and advancing to promising careers in the professions. Here and there a
Jew won a previously unheard-of tenured faculty position at a university,
and a few Jewish judges had been appointed to lower courts. If the influx
from the East was continuing unabated, it was because compared to the
viciousness of pogroms in Galicia, life in Germany was rewarding and rich.

For the bulk of Germany's assimilated Jews in Berlin and in the smaller
towns like Oranienburg, there was a strong attachment to Germany and to
German *Kultur.* In truth, they were locked into a kind of love affair with
Germany, stronger than the accusations and insults of their enemies. Heinrich Heine, who had been scathing in his criticisms of German foibles, had

expressed it in his poetry. Most assimilated German Jews felt it more than ever in their hearts. They were deeply attached to their country, and they were determined to prove it with their accomplishments and deeds.

The 1860s and 1870s had been a watershed in two important ways. The Jews had progressed fast and far, and their optimism for the future was great. But the period also witnessed the rise of a new and virulent form of anti-Semitism, with novel arguments and rhetoric based on pseudoscientific theories of race, mixed with a particular brand of extreme nationalism.

These elements would play an important part in the German-Jewish relationship of coming years.

CHAPTER VII

DREAMERS
Arthur

*We stand firmly on the foundation of patriotic German ideology . . .
our bonds are inseparably united with the German fatherland!*
Founding statement of the Jewish National Student Federation
1896

Our desire is for races to become homogeneous and to expel foreign elements.
Founding statement of the Pan-German League
1893

1

On June 25, 1888, speaking softly and visibly nervous, but otherwise in a
buoyant mood, the third Kaiser of the Second Reich flung back his crimson
mantle and rose to open the Reichstag in the Great White Hall of his Berlin
palace. To make this a brilliant, dramatic occasion, William II had chosen
the resplendent uniform of the Order of Black Eagle Knights. Court pages
were outfitted in new black knee breeches adorned with crepe, and palace
guards were dressed as in the days of Frederick the Great to symbolize the
link with his illustrious forebear.

The new Kaiser liked to be the center of attention and to strike theatrical
poses in fancy uniforms amid military trappings. This was his great mo-

ment, the first time when the world would see him as the Reich's powerful new sovereign. He had ordered that internal dispatches must henceforth refer to him only as "The Most High" or "The All Highest," and that his commands be conveyed on distinctive blue stationery, unmistakable as emanating from the All Highest. Nor would he tolerate any argument about his orders—only a bow and a humble "As Your Majesty commands" were appropriate.

William II had reached the throne unexpectedly and suddenly. He was a young man, unevenly educated and with a personality poorly suited to the task. By temperament, he preferred activity and motion to thoroughness and careful thought and was given to quick changes in mood, flights of oratory, and grandiose talk. For years his parents had despaired of their eldest son's posturing and his unfortunate manner, his overestimation of himself, and his guard officer tone and barracks-room thinking. Only recently his father had described him as still "inexperienced, immature and presumptuous."[1]

No matter. At the time of his birth he was merely the third in succession to the throne yet now, not thirty years old, he was the Kaiser of a Continental power, and he stood proudly erect, surrounded by members of the royal House, lesser German kings, princes, and archdukes, his ministers, foreign dignitaries, and the nobility, as the aging Chancellor—forty-four years his senior—stepped forward and bent to kiss his hand. It was a traditional gesture of obeisance, and Bismarck had performed it twice before when a new Emperor took the throne. Each time the sovereign had quickly lifted him up and embraced him in a reciprocal sign of cordiality and respect. William II, however, remained straight and immobile as the older man bowed before him. He believed he had inherited divinely endowed powers and wanted everyone to know it.

True to form, he chose an address to troops taking their oath of allegiance as the occasion for his first public proclamation, telling them that "I and the army . . . we are bound to one another, and so we shall hold together indissolubly whether, as God wills, we are to have peace or storms." This odd, warlike initial pronouncement had a predictably jarring effect on foreign ears. Though he quickly followed it with a more peaceful statement to the public at large, senior officials in St. Petersburg, Paris, and London were not favorably impressed and wondered what he meant to say.

It was the first, though not the last, occasion when William II's loose talk would rattle them. Eventually they came to realize that there was more boastful rhetoric than carefully worded messages and well-defined intent in what he said. In an age when preserving an uneasy continental status quo was much on European minds, his reputation for aggressive words and unpredictability was being established early.

His parents had wanted to give their "Fritz" a broad liberal education and had sent him to a regular high school and, briefly, to Bonn University, but he had learned little there. On the other hand, his grandfather, Kaiser William I, had made no secret of his dislike for Fritz's exposure to all that modern thinking. Bismarck, for his part, suspected the young man's English mother of scheming to infiltrate into the Reich the same detested notions of parliamentary democracy with which his grandmother, Queen Victoria, ruled in England. Kaiser and Chancellor had, therefore, insisted that William be made a lieutenant in a Potsdam guard regiment at an early age, where his companions could be counted on to be free of liberal ideas. In the final analysis, it was this arch-Prussian milieu, with its martial atmosphere and mindless guard officer demeanor—and not the public schooling—that shaped William's character. He could be charming if he wished, but more often than not his manner was domineering and arrogant and his talk rash, loud, barking, and grammatically stilted in the nasal style popular among the Prussian officer elite.

William II was a profoundly insecure man who compensated for his self-doubt with bombast and an overbearing manner. A largely useless left arm, damaged at birth, contributed to his sense of inadequacy and his need to impress. His bruised ego craved the posturing of the commander and the deference and flattery of those below him. The army gave him a sense of power, and taut procedures, quick action, unquestioning obedience, military dress, and snappy salutes provided comfort and security. Now that he was Kaiser, he wanted his court organized strictly along military lines, and he let it be known that everyone around him was expected to be in uniform at all times.

He lost little time in showing how he expected to rule. Within days of the Berlin ceremony, without observing even a minimum period of mourning for his father, he departed for Kiel, dressed in an admiral's uniform, to review the fleet. Then he sailed across the Baltic to greet Czar Alexander III in St. Petersburg, appearing there in the uniform of a general in the Russian regiment named in his honor. Returning home, he donned his favorite tightly fitted hussar's tunic and began to force his personal stamp on the conduct of the Reich's domestic and international affairs to a degree that none of his predecessors had done. Often there were unintended and unfortunate results. Even that dominant statesman of European politics, his wily old Chancellor Otto von Bismarck, soon discovered that it was impossible to stop him.

Many Germans had hoped for liberalizing changes after the passing of William I. Yet, with the conservative grandson rather than his more liberal son Frederick III on the throne, 1888, the year of the old Kaiser's death, became a different kind of turning point in German history. Later it would be known as the *Dreikaiserjahr,* the year of the three Kaisers, when circumstances conspired to rob the country of its best opportunity to move away from authoritarianism toward more democracy. By a quirk of fate, three different Emperors occupied the German throne that year in a span of less than six months, and within four months two of them had died. It was Germany's misfortune that one had lived too long and the other not long enough—and that the third, who remained Kaiser for thirty years, was the wrong man for the job.

In 1888, the Reich was the strongest Continental nation. Its science and industry were the admiration of the world. Yet German society was still marked by advances in science, learning, and the arts on the one hand and a stubbornly undemocratic and militaristic sociopolitical system on the other: a love of *Kultur* alongside the veneration of soldiers—the spirit of Weimar opposite the spirit of Potsdam.

The Reich, virtually alone among major countries (Russia excepted) had withstood revolution and popular demands for personal freedom and more democracy. During the long reign of William I and under Bismarck's stewardship, Germany remained as authoritarian as ever, an *Obrigkeitstaat* in which those above gave the orders and those below were expected to follow them. The constitution Bismarck had conceived gave the sovereign unchallenged final authority where it mattered and delegated only limited and circumscribed powers to the Reichstag. The Prussian three-class voting system was based on income and wealth, and the leaders of its traditional stratified society continued to monopolize the key positions of power. Servility, obedience, and respect for the ubiquitous uniform remained the order of the day.

Among the bourgeoisie and intelligentsia, there were those who chafed under this state of affairs and impatiently awaited a change at the top to unfreeze the political landscape. For years it had been their dream that once the ancient Kaiser was gone, Crown Prince Frederick would free the political institutions from their straitjacket. Frederick's distaste for Bismarck's authoritarianism was an open secret, and his more moderate views on a wide range of domestic issues had been known for years. Liberals and progressives could barely contain their impatience for him to take the throne. They knew that he was an unusual Hohenzollern, different in outlook from his predecessors, the first with democratic instincts and openly out of sympathy with his father's conservatism. Like his ancestors, he was a soldier, and he had proved himself in battle. Yet he was also a man of culture and peace who had made it plain that he wanted greater freedom for his people, more democratic political institutions, and a loosening of social restrictions. It was later said that if his paternal ancestors represented Potsdam militarism, his mother personified Weimar culture, and that it was she and Victoria, his strong-willed wife and the daughter of the English queen, whose influence had been dominant in shaping his views.

He was, however, a tragically unlucky monarch, and fate intervened against him at several critical moments. As far back as 1862, his frustrated and rigid father had offered to abdicate in his favor. But Frederick feared the precedent and had successfully argued against it. Nine years later, at forty years of age, he returned a hero from the war against France, ready to claim the throne and determined to nudge Germany toward a more liberal road. His father was then already well into his seventies, a ripe old age for the times. Yet circumstances conspired against Frederick once again. The older man defied the actuarial odds and lived another seventeen years, while his son watched impotently as the Iron Chancellor pursued an intricate power game of realpolitik abroad and resisted all efforts to liberalize political life at home.

The third and worst blow came when, at age ninety-one, William I at last passed from the scene. "Why are the heavens so cruel to me?" the unfortunate Frederick lamented as his father lay dead in March of 1888. His own tragic illness had begun in January of the previous year with no more than some hoarseness attributed to too many speaking engagements and the winter weather. The old Kaiser was visibly declining and the country expected a smooth transition. At his father's ninetieth birthday, Frederick's voice had failed altogether, but few attributed much significance to it. It was said that springtime and rest in warmer climes would take care of the problem. Here and there, the first rumors that something more serious was afoot began to circulate but his supporters refused to worry. A liberal newspaper breezily dismissed such talk with a clever doggerel to reassure the faithful:

> Und ist der Fritz auch heiser,
> So wankt das Reich noch nicht;
> Man hört den deutschen Kaiser,
> Auch wenn er leise spricht.[2]

In the summer, astride his white horse at Queen Victoria's Golden Jubilee in London, Frederick still impressed many as the most striking figure among her numerous sons-in-law. Only a few perceptive observers noticed his sunken eyes and pallid complexion. It was in the autumn that persistent rumors of a serious illness had arisen. Finally, on November 12, an official court bulletin announced that "the illness is the result of a malignant cancerlike growth" and it confirmed the worst.[3] He had wanted to do great things for his country but instead now faced his own imminent death from a cancerous larynx. At age fifty-six, he outlived his father by only ninety-nine days.

Suddenly the prospects for a more open and democratic Germany were in doubt. Industrialization had come much later than elsewhere. Democratization, it now appeared, would still not follow. There was despair among Liberals and Progressives while Frederick's archconservative opponents openly rejoiced. For the rest, there was the dread of uncertainty: "The Kaiser ancient, the Crown Prince mortally ill, decisions of the most fateful significance ahead," one of Prussia's senior diplomats close to the court noted in his diary.[4]

None, however, were as dismayed as Germany's Jews, for whom Frederick and his wife had been the bright lights at the end of a very long tunnel.

Their distaste for the anti-Semitism movement and the fact that they had been the only ones in court circles willing to take a public stand against it was well-known. Frederick, an ardent Freemason, had insisted that Prussian lodges, which excluded Jews, open their doors to visiting Jewish Masons from England.[5] Later, to demonstrate his disapproval of Treitschke's attacks, he made it a point to attend a synagogue service in the full regalia of a Prussian field marshal, and he publicly condemned anti-Semitism as a "shameful blot on our time."[6] When Frederick and his wife appeared at a synagogue concert in Wiesbaden at a particularly sensitive moment in the public debate of the "Jewish Question," Jewish hopes that he would defend their cause as Kaiser had soared.

The Jews had expected him to sweep away the remaining impediments to their full equality. But the transition to his untried son, who had little sympathy for his father's liberal ideas, was deeply troubling. How would Germany fare under this erratic young monarch? Would there be a further shift toward authoritarianism and greater militarization? Was there still a chance for liberal ideas or would reactionaries remain in control? As to the Jews, would their integration into German society be allowed to move forward, or would William's conservative friends succeed in halting or perhaps even reversing it?

No one knew the answers. In 1888, as William II unexpectedly became Kaiser, there was nothing to do but hope for the best. No one could say with certainty where it would all end.

2

As soon as he read the announcement of the Crown Prince's fatal illness, Arthur Eloesser knew that it was bad news for the cause of German liberalism and especially for the Jews. He was not yet eighteen years old, a senior at Berlin's Sophiengymnasium, and optimistic about his future. The hurdle of his final exams remained before him, but he was a superior student and expected to do well. Arthur was the youngest and most intellectually gifted of five Eloesser children. In the autumn he expected to enroll at Berlin University to begin what he hoped would be a lifelong academic career.

The Eloessers were long-established Prussian Jews and Arthur was a firm nationalist, who, after three wars and victories "had been raised in a noisy patriotism."[7] In fact, he admitted to a somewhat foolish yet palpably real pleasure to have been born a few months prior to the end of the war against the French and the birth of the Second Reich, "to have come into the world in time to be present at so significant an event"[8] as he would later say. He felt fortunate to be a citizen of a powerful and important country, a *Kulturstaat* with a rich tradition in literature and the arts, where education, learning, and culture were valued as nowhere else.

Arthur saw himself first of all as a German and only secondarily as a Jew, or—as it had become customary to say—"of the Mosaic Faith." With Stoecker's Berlin Movement and the rest of the anti-Semites railing against Jews, the word had acquired an unpleasant pejorative ring in assimilated Jewish German ears. "Mosaic" was, after all, as descriptive and sounded a great deal more refined. Whatever one called it, however, Arthur had no illusions that it was the best thing in the world to have been born a Jew in Germany, and the official discrimination and socially prejudiced attitudes of some gentile teachers and classmates were uncomfortable and hurtful. Yet, he had come into the world a Jew, and though he and his family were no longer close to their faith and had abandoned religious practices, he had no intention of denying his Jewishness or of converting. Some of his friends had done so, but Arthur and his family, like many Jews, considered that futile and dishonorable. Besides, he believed in the inevitability of progress and was full of youthful confidence that it was only a matter of time before the remaining restrictions would disappear and anti-Semitic biases fade away.

In Berlin, Arthur's friends were a mixed group of gentiles and Jews. In elementary school, in fact, his playmates had mostly been non-Jewish, and he had grown up thinking of that as entirely normal. It had taken time, he later reminisced with evident satisfaction, even to be aware that he was part of a minority.[9]

Arthur belonged to that generation of youngsters born in the Second Reich who were the children of financially comfortable, educated, and assimilated middle-class Berlin Jews. His mother and father had come to the city as part of the great influx from the east in the early 1820s—she from Pomerania and he from East Prussia. On his father's side, the Eloessers had earned their living as tanners around Ortelsburg in East Prussia since the mid-sixteenth century, and Arthur was certain that this made him a real

Prussian—an *Urpreusse,* so to speak. East Prussian and Brandenburg Jews considered themselves genuine Germans, superior to those from the sometime Polish province of Posen, who were thought to be less steeped in German history and culture. He had been made aware of his deep German roots from early childhood and accepted them as an unquestioned fact. The fortuitous happenstance that his father had been born somewhere in Posen while Arthur's grandmother was visiting there changed nothing. The family dismissed it as an embarrassing accident of history, a slight blemish not worth mentioning to others.

When Theodor Eloesser, Arthur's father, first came to Berlin, he brought some small capital with him and, like many Jewish arrivals, invested it in the heavily Jewish textile industry, where he could count on his connections with family and friends. The Eloessers had settled into the respectable, though modest, Prenzlauerberg section of central Berlin. It was one of the capital's oldest districts, a quiet neighborhood where Christians and Jews lived side by side in general harmony, though Arthur once noted that the Jews typically occupied the better apartments at the front of the buildings. By the late 1880s, as he was finishing the *Gymnasium,* Eloesser Wholesale Linens was flourishing, and the family had advanced to solid middle-class status. For Arthur, Prenzlauerstrasse 26, where he grew up and spent his early life, always remained the place he associated with the real Berlin and where his lifelong affair of the heart with the city was born. Later, older and wiser, and with the Great War having swept away many of the illusions of his youth, he would still reminisce warmly about life in Prenzlauerberg streets.

As Arthur turned eighteen, his parents had grown immensely proud of their talented youngest son. For generations, they had been merchants because it was the only calling open to most Jews. Intellectual achievement and renown, however, had long been their much admired and cherished ideal. Even Arthur's grandfather, an East Prussian tanner of Russian skins at the turn of the 1800s, had sacrificed to send his sons to a "higher school" at Insterburg. But Arthur's father—to his lifelong regret—had been obliged to go to work at age sixteen. All the more reason to value the advanced learning he had missed and take inordinate pleasure that his youngest son had the gifts and ambition to embark on a full-fledged academic career.

Arthur wanted to study history, and during the autumn of his senior year he discussed these plans with his *Gymnasium* principal, who had taken a benevolent interest in him. "Why history?" the older man inquired of his precocious student. Arthur answered with the certainty and conviction of a seventeen-year-old unburdened by doubt. There had been much progress in science and the accumulation of general human knowledge, he replied, and Germany was much the better for it. Yet it was evident that everywhere in the world the capacity to govern with wisdom and justice remained deficient. If properly understood, history surely held the lessons to improve on that situation and to move mankind forward. Was that not an excellent reason, Arthur asked, to choose history as the discipline in which to contribute to German progress?

At the Sophiengymnasium, as at virtually every "higher school" for boys in Berlin, more than a quarter of the students were Jews, and at the equivalent girls' schools almost one in two students was Jewish. These were astonishing numbers, considering that the Jewish minority made up less than 4 percent of Berlin's total population. Beyond age fourteen, education still cost money, but the Eloessers were not alone among upwardly mobile Jews eager to invest in advanced schooling for their children. Respect for learning and culture was a widely shared Jewish value both for its own sake and because it was seen as a key to a more honorable social position than that of trader or merchant. Many in the older generations had started out as peddlers and had been imbued with the spirit of traders who "knew nothing except how to make money," as Arthur put it. Yet many had long hungered for more refined pursuits, and now they were eager to support their children's quest for intellectual advancement and more prestigious careers, particularly in the professions.

The principal, a non-Jew, was an enlightened and tolerant man. He admired the Jews' praiseworthy commitment to higher education, yet he worried about the lopsided enrollment statistics, and the grumbling and resentment that the disproportionately large number of Jewish *Gymnasium* students was causing in some gentile circles. In the prevailing climate of anti-Jewish agitation and Court Preacher Stoecker's anti-Semitic tirades, it was becoming quite a problem. The fact that a number of his teachers openly harbored anti-Semitic views did not help. In any event, the choicest careers for academically trained Germans were in the bureaucracy—tenured university posts included—and such positions remained firmly closed to an unbaptized Jew. Berlin University's history faculty, where Heinrich von Treitschke thundered against the Jews as "Germany's misfortune," was a particularly inhospitable place. No Jew had ever been appointed to a regular professorship there.

With a smile at Arthur's earnestness and a compliment for his ambition, the Principal nevertheless felt it necessary to issue a cautionary warning. He chose his words with care. Had his young charge considered the "special difficulties" of an academic career in history, he inquired? Speaking in this sort of code was common, and Arthur immediately understood the thrust of the question. "Special difficulties" did not deter him, he confidently replied; on the contrary, he was determined to confront and overcome them. In modern Germany, and with goodwill, such difficulties would surely soon become a thing of the past! "Well my good fellow," the Principal replied, still smiling, "nevertheless I see your future as a journalist." Arthur, however, insisted firmly: "I shall be a Professor of History!"[10]

There was defiance, youthful naivité, and hope in his stubborn optimism. An unbaptized Jew had heretofore had no chance for an appointment to a regular professorship. Two decades after all formal barriers had fallen, the de facto exclusion of Jews from any meaningful positions in the bureaucracy and the military still remained virtually complete. For years not a single Jew had been accepted even as a reserve officer in the Prussian military.[11] A lucky few had won appointments as lower-level judges, but Jews, still considered socially beyond the pale, were systematically excluded from all prestigious public appointments. Even the powerful Baron Bleichröder's strenuous efforts to win a place for his son in the diplomatic service had been unsuccessful. The diplomats, mostly titled aristocrats, resisted accepting even a converted Jew in their midst, let alone the unbaptized kind, and in this matter Bismarck, who respected Bleichröder as banker and financier, agreed that Jews simply lacked the grace and manners required for diplomacy.[12]

Arthur knew all this, yet he shared the hope of most Jews that once the old Kaiser was gone, discriminatory abuses would gradually come to an end under his more liberal son. He was as shocked as anyone to hear of Frederick's illness. Yet the full impact of what it might mean had become clear to him only the following January on a visit to Oranienburg, where Ida, the elder of his two sisters, now lived. It was there that he heard the matter discussed ad nauseum among the local Jews, and it had left Arthur worried and concerned.

Both Eloesser sisters had made what the family considered good matches. Fanny, the younger, was married to a prosperous young man who was already an impressive top-hatted figure as stockbroker, with his own seat on the exchange. Ida had done even better, marrying a prosperous Oranienburg banker's son. The only drawback was that her marriage involved moving from Berlin to the small town's more limited provincial environment. Still, Martin Blumenthal, her husband, and Louis, her father-in-law, lived in one of the town's most stately houses near the *Schloss* the Great Elector had built for his homesick Dutch wife.

Louis and Theodor were business acquaintances, and though their children's union was ostensibly a love match—Martin and Ida met on a hayride—there had been a fair amount of surreptitous behind-the-scenes matchmaking, a leftover relic from the days when virtually all Jewish marriages were openly arranged. The Blumenthals had been carefully vetted as acceptable—solid, prosperous, old-established Prussian Jews. Like the Eloessers, they were traditional National Liberal voters now leaning toward the *Freisinnige,* a recently formed left-liberal splinter group more clearly in favor of full Jewish rights. Their relationship to the famous Beer family, however remote, hadn't hurt either. Ida's mother had a habit of slipping this impressive little fact into her accounts of her daughter's family and her happy and prosperous Oranienburg marriage.

Arthur had found the mood among Oranienburg's Jews somber and concerned. The consensus was that Frederick's imminent death was a calamity, a serious threat to the further evolution of Jewish rights. The pessimists argued that it would take another quarter century before Jews achieved true equality. Others were more hopeful that the logic of modernity and industrial development and the German sense of morality and belief in the law made liberalizing changes inevitable even under this Kaiser. The debate had raged back and forth, and Arthur—remembering his talk with the Principal—argued the optimistic line with some passion.

Now he was returning to Berlin in a pensive mood. Visits to Oranienburg were not his preferred pastimes, and he avoided them whenever possible. This time, however, there had been no choice. The occasion was the fiftieth anniversary of the building of the local synagogue—a major event, presided over by Martin Blumenthal, who had recently succeeded his father as community president. It had been an elaborate affair, with a solemn religious service and much ancillary patriotic speechmaking and feasting. Even the gentile city fathers had been in full if somewhat self-conscious attendance.

Arthur usually felt ill at ease in Oranienburg because the atmosphere was quaintly provincial and slightly alien, and this time had been no exception. In Berlin he was rarely exposed to religious matters or Jewish community affairs, and being caught up in the still clearly bifurcated social life of Jews in little Oranienburg made him feel guiltily uncomfortable. It underlined what he expected would soon be a thing of the past—the separate identity of Jews as a distinct minority and social group. In Berlin, Arthur's self-image was that of a true German in every sense. In Oranienburg such assimilation was still not so clear, and so Arthur was relieved to climb back on the Nordbahn for the return trip home. The political debate had left him concerned, but he remained as determined as ever to prove the pessimists—and his Principal—wrong.

3

In 1888, more than a half million Jews were living in Germany. Toward the end of the decade, there were fleeting signs that the wave of anti-Semitic agitation might have crested. After the Reichstag elections of 1887, the National Liberals had joined in an alliance with Conservatives in support of Bismarck's policies. There were plenty of anti-Semites among the rightwingers in this so-called *Kartell* coalition, but open display of animosity toward Jews was temporarily muted in deference to their political partners. Moreover, Stoecker's shrill demagoguery had become a sufficient embarrassment to force him out of politics and, subsequently, to retire him from all official court positions.

But hopes that the anti-Semites were permanently sidelined proved premature. William II could not bear to reign in the shadow of Bismarck's overwhelming presence and in 1890 he peremptorily dismissed him. At the same time, the *Kartell* suffered a heavy defeat at the polls, and a new government coalition under Leo von Caprivi, his weaker and more pliable successor—and an unknown quantity where Jewish affairs were concerned—

took his place. With Bismarck gone, national confidence declined and public uncertainty about the future rose. Moreover, the Kaiser's policy of placating labor with favorable social benefits proved a failure, and the now legalized Social Democratic Party, anathema to the Crown and Conservatives, polled a million and a half votes and struck fear in the hearts of the right, who cast around for an issue to woo workers to their side. Worst of all, the economy turned unfavorable, industrial activity was stagnant, and Caprivi's policy of lowering agricultural protection led to hardship in the countryside and disaffection among agrarian interests.

All this was a ready-made formula for a renewed flare-up of anti-Jewish sentiment. As always when times were bad, agitators blamed the Jews for every conceivable problem, and right-wing politicians seized on the issue to win votes for their side. Freed of earlier political constraints, anti-Jewish agitators were again active and, if anything, more visible than before. In 1887, the first avowed anti-Semite split from the Conservatives and won a Reichstag seat. In the next election he was joined by four others, and three years later a quarter million voters seated no less than sixteen members of anti-Semitic parties in the Reichstag—a sufficient number to form their own parliamentary group.

Historically, anti-Semites had come to active Jew-baiting from widely different directions and for many reasons. Some were religious zealots, others political opportunists, and some primarily saw a chance for material gain. The most unrelenting and extreme, however, always were the single-minded fanatics and pure haters, the near psychotics who viewed the world through a distorted prism in which alleged Jewish crimes became the central focus of their lives, and all of society's ills were due to Jewish depravities and cunning.

From the very start, the racial anti-Semites were like that. In the last great wave of the early 1890s it was Hermann Ahlwardt who was one of their most active and poisonous leaders preaching race hatred. He had served in the legislature for ten years and authored a three-volume diatribe entitled *"The Desperate Struggle of the Aryan Peoples with Jewry."*

"Berlin no longer has brothels, but it has its *Konfektion*,"[13] he had shouted, referring to Berlin's largely Jewish ready-to-wear industry. His rhetoric was violent and extreme, and linking alleged Jewish sexual immorality with accusations of exploitation in business was standard fare for the racists. In Ahlwardt's feverish mind, "the Jew" was a mythical figure of evil, and individual Jews were cheats, usurers, and race polluters of pure German blood.

For a while a surprising number of people had listened, and Ahlwardt was riding high with his calls for righteous Aryans to rise against mongrelizing Jews out to destroy them. But people lost interest, particularly as the economic situation improved and Ahlwardt overplayed his hand. A few years later he was gone, disgraced and out of sight. So also was his soulmate Otto Böckel, who liked to write articles under the pseudonym "Dr. Capistrano," and specialized in whipping up the restive peasantry with his extreme fulminations. Almost all anti-Semitic agitators, in fact, who in and out of the Reichstag had kept the pot boiling one more time had become irrelevant after 1893.

By the mid-1890s, the latest crisis had eased. At Heilige Geist Strasse 40, in Berlin's largely Jewish textile district, "Theodor Eloesser, Linens, en Gros" flourished enough to finance family support of Arthur's budding academic career. His father, however, with fewer illusions than the idealistic Arthur about the problems his son would face in the eventual choice of a career, prevailed on him to accept the counsel of an eminent, prize-winning Jewish scholar and family friend.[14] His recommendation for Arthur was to include public and constitutional law courses in his studies. If becoming an academic historian proved impossible, a career in the law—a "free" profession open to Jews—would be a second-best alternative. Arthur continued to count on a professorship, but to keep the peace, he dutifully acquiesced.

In fact, his first year at Berlin University's faculty of history turned out to be a bittersweet experience and Arthur soon realized that hedging his bets was sound advice. On the one hand, there was the thrill of the university life he had long dreamed of. On the other, there was also something new and—for him—unexpected: a pervasive atmosphere of reaction and anti-Semitism among a large number of faculty and students. As employees of the state, the faculty vigorously supported official government policy, including strong opposition to Social Democrats and Progressives and to liberal ideas in general.

In public law, the two most respected authorities did little to hide their anti-Semitism. At the history faculty, Treitschke, aging and almost deaf, was still the dominant personality—a thunderous academic orator espousing theories of state power, nationalism, and the sword as the *"ultimo ratio"* of the German nation. His hatred for English "Manchesterism" was undiminished, as was his contempt for Queen Victoria—that "old lady drinking her tea at Windsor"—and her effrontery to impose a Jewish Prime Minister on Anglo–German relations. Treitschke especially abhorred Social Democrats, at one moment railing against Germany's Jews as "oriental leaders of this chorus of revolutionaries" and at another castigating them as the incarnation of detested Manchester commercialism. Recent Jewish immigrants from the east incurred his special wrath because he considered them irretrievably alien.

Sitting in the overcrowded lecture hall amid Treitschke's rapturous student supporters must have been profoundly distressing and disturbing for Jews like Arthur. "We tolerated it," he recalled later, because "we had convinced ourselves that . . . one had to accept it, to listen to such an intellectual giant."[15]

In fact, Arthur could bear the strain for only a year before he switched from history to the study of literature. Perhaps it was the more benign atmosphere of a summer semester along the shores of Geneva's Lac Léman that turned him in a different direction. Or perhaps, filled with an ethical idealism about the future of his homeland, he had simply met in Treitschke and his supporters a contrary reality too distasteful to face and too painful to tolerate. But the change in direction came when he encountered an irresistible magnet at the faculty of literature, and a rarity at Berlin University—a liberal professor without social or racial prejudices who selected his students for their ability and invited them to think for themselves.

Erich Schmidt was only thirty-six years old when Arthur enrolled to study with him. He had recently arrived at the university as an up-and-coming German scholar of Romantic literature (for which he would soon be inducted into the Academy of Sciences). Arthur and other young liberals quickly flocked to Schmidt and made him their idol. Once accepted in his seminars, students were treated as equals—another rarity—and he encouraged open discussion of major social questions and their treatment in literature. In Schmidt's circle, there was no room for anti-Semitic diatribes, no undertone of prejudice, and no closed minds to critical thinking and progressive ideas. His humanism and enthusiasm for literature as insight into human affairs and guide to intellectual thought was exciting and deeply appealing, exactly what Arthur had been looking for. Here was German *Kultur* and *Bildung* at its best—the sort of tolerant progressive view of society he believed in. Writers and poets, he now realized, were as good a source as historians for thinking about the betterment of human affairs. Studying literature under Schmidt, and philosophy and sociology under like-minded young teachers in Schmidt's orbit, was irresistible. Schmidt, in turn, readily recognized Arthur's talents. Arthur had found his lifelong calling.

Arthur had come face-to-face with a discouraging dual reality from which even the most gifted and German-feeling Jewish student could not escape: the stubborn anti-Semitism that pervaded academic and student life, and the full implications of the bureaucratic rigidities of Germany's closed society for their future careers.

Many professors and students made it painfully clear that they resented the prominent presence of so many Jews in their midst, and the most prestigious student organizations systematically excluded them. After completing their studies, the chance for a regular professorship or position in state service was virtually nil. For non-Jewish university graduates, the lesser yet respected career of *Studienrat,* or *Gymnasium* teacher, was a viable option, yet here too academically trained unbaptized Jews had little or no chance of employment. The statistics spoke volumes: in 1890, there were 6,247 "higher school" teachers in Prussia, yet only 62 of these were Jews. In primary schools there were even fewer.

But the Jewish drive for the coveted academic degree continued undeterred, and the disproportionately large number of Jews at the universities grew steadily. Though they accounted for only a fraction more than 1 percent of the German population, Jews constituted more than 10 percent of all university students. For every 100,000 male Protestants, 58 were studying at universities in 1890; for Catholics the corresponding number was 33—but there were ten times as many Jews—518 university students for each 100,000 Jewish males.[16] Many chose mathematics, the natural sciences, the law, and technical or medical fields, because in these disciplines a career in a "free profession" was an alternative to service in the bureaucracy. For those who, like Arthur, studied at the social sciences or philosophical faculties, future professional prospects were much more limited.

Journalism, the theatre, or the arts were possibilities. Nevertheless, an academic degree, even in these impractical disciplines with limited employment opportunity, remained an irresistible lure. If there were limited prospects of earthly rewards from a *Doktorat* in philosophy or literature, then so be it. The older generation was willing to support their "academic" sons nonetheless, proud of the enhanced status in German society they expected it to guarantee them.

Arthur loved the university. The degree would be a great prize, and in its quest there was the joy of intellectual discovery and the pleasures of Berlin's cultural life. Yet it was in the practices and traditions of student life outside the lecture halls that his ambiguous and uncertain status as a second-class outsider was made most plain to him. No institution, in fact, reflected the prejudiced, closed conservatism of Wilhelmine Germany more than the student fraternities, which dominated university life.

Their stated purpose was "to guard against the softening of the male senses"[17] and their favorite pastimes were raucous bawling and brawling in student *Kneipen* (pubs), guzzling beer and engaging in the officially banned though widely practiced sport of defending their honor in elaborately staged, ritualistic fencing duels. Dueling was a bizarre, peculiarly German student tradition, and the telltale scarred face of a university man was thought to be a badge of valor. Outside Germany it was seen as one more evidence of the oddities of the Teutonic mind.

The practice began early in the century when German students felt deprived by the loss of opportunity to prove their courage in war. Thus dueling was a by-product of the militarism that pervaded German society. Fraternity members were easily recognizable by the distinctive colors of their caps, and each fraternity (*Verbindung*) had special rituals and conventions—the stiff-armed toast with a mug of beer in hand, clicking heels, clipped military speech, the formal bow from the waist, and the erect, standing salute of junior to senior or fencing victor to a valorous vanquished opponent.

What went on in most fraternities did not appeal to Arthur. He had little taste for the brawling, dueling, militaristic rituals, and general inanities. His patriotism was strong but took a less aggressive form and found its expression in love for the German language, pride of German accomplishment in science, and an enthusiasm for German theatre and music. He

shared with many Jewish students "the family tradition of a common respect for a 'higher culture' and a peculiarly German-Jewish literary and artistic inclination."[18]

Yet the fraternities were at the very heart of German student life and to
stand apart or be rejected was one more painful reminder of their "otherness" for many Jews. As a result, how to structure life off campus and
come to terms with the fraternities presented them the same "dilemmas
and helpless uncertainties as . . . the choice of a career."[19] Many fraternities,
especially the socially most prestigious, totally excluded Jews. A few maintained a small *numerus clausus* for a handful of specially chosen ones—
generally those most "un-Jewish looking." There were also the "reform
fraternities," which admitted Jews freely but were considered less desirable.
Many Jews shunned them. Some, not to be outdone and too proud to be
rejected, formed their own Jewish "fighting fraternities," and made it a
point of honor to confront the slightest gentile provocation with unrelenting dueling challenges. It was their way not only to counter the insults but
also to prove that the common image of the unmanly Jew interested less
in his honor than his pocketbook was off the mark. Their eagerness to make
the point actually led to the conviction of proportionately four times as
many Jews as Christians for illegal dueling. "More cut-up and scarred faces
than among this 'guard of Maccabeans' were not to be seen anywhere,"
Arthur later recalled.[20]

The alternative to the dueling fraternities was strictly professional asso-
ciations. Some gentiles and a large number of Jews, whether by inclination
or faute de mieux, joined these, though it was clear that it confirmed their
status as *Fink,* the derogatory name for the nonjoiner or unacceptable outsider. For Christians, standing apart may have been a matter of choice; for
Jews it was more often than not a painful necessity. Arthur remained a *Fink*
throughout his university years.

4

Being a *Fink* may have been an embarrassment, but Arthur wanted to enjoy
life to the fullest and Berlin provided plenty of opportunity for stimulation
and excitement. The lively cultural scene of the Berlin of the 1890s was

marked by a high level of controversy and ferment in art, literature, music, and architecture, reflecting what were essentially two quite different Germanys.[21]

One was the imperial Germany of the Kaiser and its narrowly conservative and nationalistic society with the court and nobility on top a stratified, socially exclusionary, heavily militaristic, and implicitly anti-Semitic elite. It found its artistic expression in what one historian has labeled "Knackfuss" culture,[22] after a court painter by the same name who immortalized Wilhelmine values with large, rather ugly canvases, depicting Pan-German, historical, and folk themes. In the theatre, its principal protagonist, and the Kaiser's favorite, was the illegitimate grandson of a Prussian prince, who wrote platitudinous pieces in which acts of heroism, patriotic songs, pious Protestants, and scenes of solemn public praying tended to predominate.[23] Though the Kaiser admired his plays, most critics snickered at their modest intellectual sophistication. Even the *Vossische Zeitung,* hardly a counterculture publication, observed dryly that "psychology and logic are not, and never will be, his forte."[24]

The other Germany was that of the educated progressive intellectuals. Critical of traditional German society, concerned with the suffering of the working class, and at once exuberant at the possibilities yet worried about the inherent contradictions of modern life, its outlook was more liberal, its horizons more open to the world, and its interests more focused on contemporary social problems and the need for change and reform. The artists of that time were eager to innovate and to experiment with new and unconventional forms of expression. Much of the ferment and vibrancy in Berlin's cultural scene came from this other Germany, led by Theodor Fontane in literature, Gerhart Hauptmann in drama, Max Liebermann in painting, and many others. The great majority of Jewish intellectuals were naturally drawn into this circle, though its adherents were a mixed and eclectic group spanning a range of backgrounds and religions. Fontane was a descendant of French Huguenots, Hauptmann a Protestant from Silesia, and Liebermann the son of wealthy Jews with deep Berlin roots.

Many of these writers and artists had become fascinated with the naturalist movement, which substituted realism in depicting ordinary life and modern social conditions for the pseudoidealism of mythical and romantic themes. Many also were interested in the social application of Darwin's theory of evolution in nature, and Liebermann and others were beginning to experiment with a German version of impressionism in painting.

In spring 1892, Hauptmann's new play *Die Weber* (*The Weavers*), concerned with the plight of Silesian weavers in an 1844 revolt, was ordered closed as too radical. In response, the naturalist rebels organized private performances beyond the censor's control in a theatre of their own that they named "The Free Stage." A Prussian deputy who shared the Kaiser's views thought a more appropriate epithet was "intellectual brothel." Some in the Kaiser's circle suggested that Hauptmann deserved to be put behind bars.[25] Yet the rebels prevailed, and four years later a judge once more cleared the play for public showing at the Deutsche Theater, where it played to overflow audiences. The Kaiser was outraged. He publicly excoriated the judge who had signed the order and peremptorily canceled the royal box. The judge, mortified at so public an imperial rebuke, abjectly retired at the end of the year.[26]

In the visual arts, there was even greater controversy and turmoil. William II, who considered himself a connoisseur in the field, liked "elevated subject matter" portraying "the noble, beautiful and true" from history and legend.[27] Public depiction of nudity in art was banned. His great pride was "Victory Avenue," just beyond the Brandenburg Gate, with its thirty-two monster statues of German heroes. For the square in front of the palace, he commissioned a giant thirty-foot statuary likeness of William I.

Berlin's avant-garde painters and sculptors had fundamentally different interests. In 1892, an exhibition of the Norwegian expressionist Edvard Munch under the auspices of the official art association aroused the special displeasure of the censor and was ordered to close forthwith. The Kaiser thought Munch's work was nothing more than "audacious daubing" and the paintings of impressionists and expressionists he considered nothing less than "socialist-anarchist agitation." Once more, however, the authorities failed to contain the rebels. They formed a rival private association where they continued to exhibit their counterculture works. From it, in time, grew the Secessionist movement in art, with Liebermann, Max Slevogt, and Lovis Corinth in the lead, and such popular Berliners as Heinrich Zille and Käthe Kollwitz as particularly active members.

For Arthur, a student in Berlin amid so much controversy and excitement, and with the world of literature now as his chosen métier, it was a wonderfully stimulating time. Progressive theater was a particular thrill. From the beginning, he had been drawn to literature with contemporary social themes, and he passionately debated naturalism and the works of Zola, Ibsen, and Dostoevski with like-minded friends until late into the night. A parallel interest in romantic and classical literature led him in 1893 to write a highly regarded dissertation on the first German translations of Molière, which more than justified his mentor's faith in his special talents.[28]

His ambition for an academic career remained undiminished. To advance it, Arthur now began an ambitious four-year project for a book on the bourgeois drama.[29] It was to be his *Habilitationsschrift,* the first publication required of all aspirants for professorial status in Germany. When it was published in 1898 it was unusually well received in professional circles as a significant effort by a promising young scholar. The twenty-seven-year-old Arthur had worked tirelessly on it and produced a noteworthy first work for one so young. In spite of all the warning signals, however, he remained optimistic that his success would open the doors to the academic world. But he was about to experience his greatest disappointment. What came next was not the hoped-for call to a university but the realization that as an unbaptized Jew there was not, and never had been, a chance of realizing his impossible dream.

Many years later, Arthur was able to look back on the episode with wry amusement: "My benefactor, Erich Schmidt, received [the book] with positive benevolence and engaged me in a friendly warning interview [on the critical issue of a possible conversion to Christianity]: 'The whole matter . . . [of your job chances] would be simplified—I must pose this question to you—if you could see your way clear to . . .' 'No, Herr Professor,' I told him, 'that I cannot do!'[30]

"Whereupon he shook my hand—and the professorship idea was finished."

The rejection was a painful blow, and he was deeply disappointed. He should have anticipated it because a first book, however brilliant, meant nothing in the face of a policy of exclusion as rigidly observed as it was technically contrary to the law. Not even a Nobel Prize would have sufficed to overcome it.[31]

Resigned to the inevitable, Arthur had to confront the issue all academically inclined Jewish university men faced—what next? Had his old *Gymnasium* mentor been right after all? Was the only solution a "free" occupation—journalism or the uncertain prospect of earning a living as an independent writer? It was not an easy choice, yet at least he had the moral and financial support of his parents and the time to ponder the question at some leisure.

Many times before, talented German Jews, stung by anti-Semitic rejection in their own country, had gone abroad to lick their wounds. For want of a better idea, Arthur made the same choice: "I decided to travel, as a sort of literary journeyman, certain that paper and ink were to be found anywhere,"[32] he later wrote. He chose France as his first destination. From there he planned to continue to London, America, and Japan. He wanted a long trip, long enough to try to forget, and to gather new ideas and impressions.

In fact what had been planned as a trip around the world ended abruptly with a telegram at his first stop, in a Basque village of the French Pyrenees. The principal theatre critic at the *Vossische Zeitung*—a prestigious position once held by Theodor Fontane—had just been named dramatic director of the Burgtheater in Vienna. The impression Arthur had made with his book was greater than he realized. Not yet thirty years old, he was now offered the critic's job. To take over so influential a position was an extraordinary opportunity and honor. Arthur could hardly believe his good fortune. He accepted at once. "I 'have habilitated' myself," he triumphantly wrote his father, "not at the University—but at the *Vossische* instead!"

5

On October 25, 1899, the *Vossische* carried an initial review by its new drama critic, a report of Alphonse Daudet's *L'Arlésienne* at the Royal Opera House. It was the first of his regular columns over the next fourteen years. Arthur signed it A. E., and the theatre-going public soon recognized the initials as those of a thoughtful and dependable new observer of the Berlin stage. A few months earlier, Arthur had left, despondent and uncertain about his future. Now suddenly he was back, an important direct participant in Berlin's cultural life.

Years later, his friends would still remember him in those early days—a precocious young man, honest and incorruptible, enthusiastic and, at age thirty, imbued to the bone with German culture, a sensitive aesthete, "already old and wise beyond his years."[33] Slight of stature and of less than medium height, clean shaven and with thinning dark hair, he had as his most notable features lively soft brown eyes and the characteristically prominent, bulbous Eloesser family nose. Carefully groomed in conservative dark suits, "Elo" became a familiar figure at theatre openings or in the favorite haunts of the literati—the Schwarze Ferkel restaurant downtown; the Victoria at the busy corner of Friedrichstrasse and Unter den Linden, with its marble floors and a dozen fine paintings; or the Romanische Café in West Berlin, where actors, writers, and artists gathered to debate latest trends in art and drama or to gossip about confrontations with the censor's efforts to enforce the Kaiser's ossified cultural standards. There was lively conversation, good food, drink, and for Arthur the ubiquitous cigar, in spite of the beginnings of a lung ailment that would bother him throughout his life.

The Berlin of Arthur's years had grown helter-skelter into a major world city of two and a half million souls. New technologies had quickened the pace, and life was hectic. Almost a million foreigners now visited Berlin each year and filled the many new hotels and smaller rooming houses. They mixed with the inhabitants in elegant shopping streets, in Berlin's center, and in nearby cafés and restaurants. The novel stand-up eating places—a new rage—were busy until late into the night. Traffic was dense and chaotic. By the early 1890s, the authorities registered almost 17,000 individual horse transport vehicles, 3,187 taxis, and 255 horse buses. The year before Arthur's return, horse-drawn tramways transported a record 250 million passengers through Berlin's crowded streets, but the conversion of the public transport system to electrical streetcars was already under way. The Berlin subway was under construction and the first automobiles were making their appearance.[34]

A new century was dawning, and Germany was in the midst of another period of sustained growth. With a rapidly growing population of fifty-six million and a rail network that had tripled over the previous thirty years, industrial production was expanding fast. The Reich's steel output was now greater than Britain's; coal production surpassed that of France and Belgium; and German chemical, electrical, and precision engineering industries were among the world's most advanced. Germany's foreign trade doubled between 1870 and 1890, and in the next ten years it doubled yet again, surpassing France and challenging Britain with an aggressive invasion of her traditional overseas markets.

Economic advances translated into new prosperity for many. During the ups and downs of the previous half century, almost five million Germans had left the country for a better life elsewhere. Now the flow of overseas emigration slowed to a trickle, personal incomes rose, urban bourgeois society expanded, and a new class of wealthy entrepreneurs and industrialists was gaining at the expense of the landed aristocracy.[35]

The Kaiser had announced that "Full Steam Ahead" was the watchword for the new century. The slogan was meant to symbolize latecomer Germany's bid for recognition as a power on the seas as well as on land. No one had much difficulty understanding that the nautical metaphor was a not very subtle allusion to the major naval shipbuilding program recently launched to rival Britain's mighty fleet, which the Kaiser linked to an aggressive drive for colonial expansion overseas.

Yet the bourgeois classes, while larger and more prosperous, were not gaining commensurate political influence. The social structure remained rigid, Germany remained a militarized society, and the same restricted group of aristocrats and top bureaucrats were in charge. The constitution was still only pseudodemocratic, at best.

The military continued to dominate public life. In the fifty levels of precedence at court, field marshals outranked German princes, a colonel came ahead of the Lord Mayor of Berlin, and even a lowly army captain preceded the rector of the university, who was relegated to the third rung from the bottom.[36] No one enjoyed greater prestige and respect than the smartly dressed guard officer, and nothing was more important to the Kaiser than his uniform and that of his men; so important, in fact, that in the first sixteen years of his reign, he ordered their dress altered no fewer than thirty-seven times.[37] Berlin was home to the Ministry of War and the General Staff, and it was garrison for twenty-two thousand active soldiers comprising fourteen guard regiments and scores of other regiments, battalions, and specialized units. Uniforms were everywhere. Guard officers were punished for wearing civilian dress except on specified occasions.

Though Berliners had a justified reputation for irreverence, they none-

theless shared the prevailing public ethos of militarism mixed with patriotic devotion. In a turn-of-century poll, they voted Field Marshal von
Moltke "the greatest German thinker," overwhelmingly above Kant and
Schopenhauer. By more than seven to one, Bismarck was selected as the
greatest German of the century and the old Kaiser William I as the greatest
hero for presiding over the Second Reich's rise to Continental preeminence. Along similar lines, Richard Wagner, the prophet of Germanic superiority, was voted the greatest national musician. Even Beethoven lost out
to him, with Mozart, Liszt, and Meyerbeer being considered next in importance.[38] (Wagner died in 1883. Cosima Wagner, who detested Giacomo
Meyerbeer as much or more than her late husband had, must have
shuddered that the cosmopolitan Jew still ranked as one of Germany's
greatest.)[39]

As the first day of 1900 dawned, Berliners noisily celebrated the night
away, undaunted by arguments over whether the new year was the last of
the old century or the first of the new one. As usual, the official celebrations
were military in nature. Concentrated volleys of the Kaiser's field artillery
greeted the new century and on New Year's morning his soldiers paraded
in front of the Zeughaus military museum, followed by a solemn dedication of regimental banners and flags. The presiding field chaplain exhorted
the troops to have faith in their "sword and shield under the crucifix," and
the sovereign, for his part, pledged that in the new century the navy would
have his unwavering support, so that "the German Reich may reach its yet
to be attained [proper] place in foreign lands."[40]

For Arthur and the majority of Berlin's Jewish community, soldiers, parades, and uniforms were a normal part of the daily scene. They were less
directly involved with the military than others, yet they were equally patriotic and shared in the general satisfaction that Germany was strong and
that her accomplishments were widely recognized and admired.

Still only 1 percent of the German population were Jews, though their
numbers were, as they had always been, proportionately greater in the big
cities. Berlin, as always, was a particular magnet. In the first decade after
1900, the one hundred and fifty thousand Jewish residents made up about
5 percent of the capital's population. They had grown into a small but disproportionately important minority, more visible and influential than anywhere else in the Reich. Many were joining the migration of the middle

and upper bourgeoisie to the new residential areas in the western suburbs, and gradually there were entire sections in "Berlin W" with a conspicuous presence of well-situated Jews from the business and professional classes. Meanwhile, the capital's still substantial less assimilated Jewish proletariat, fed by a steady stream of new arrivals, remained much in evidence in the traditional Jewish quarters of old Berlin.

With better times, the wave of anti-Semitism had subsided and there was steady personal progress for many Jews. There was plenty of opportunity for everyone; Berlin's ambitious and well-educated Jewish minority was well placed to seize it, and many did so with gusto. The next years were their best, a time when Germany prospered, and the Jews prospered more than most. Many advanced to respected positions in virtually every area of national life outside the bureaucracy. It was a time they would later remember with longing and nostalgia as their happiest days, when the world appeared at peace, and it seemed that Christians and Jews were finally at peace as well.

For the Berlin Eloessers and the Oranienburg Blumenthals, and in Arthur's circle of sophisticated friends, the feeling of optimism was strong. Removed from their religion, many were happy to forget or to ignore that there was still a German-Jewish question at all—or, at worst, to believe that there would soon no longer be one.

For the moment, the Kaiser's motto for the twentieth century—for all its aggressive connotations—seemed appropriate. Life was prosperous and comfortable, Germany was modernizing, and the Jews were a vital part of the process. Like Arthur, a disproportionate number of them were involved in Berlin's cultural life, playing important and influential roles. Their self-image was no longer that of the outsider. The way they saw it, being a Jew now mattered less.

Many Jews were among Berlin's most enthusiastic patrons of the arts, and Jews made up a conspicuous part of audiences at concerts and in theatres. In the media, in literature, art, and on the stage, Jews were also among the most prominent movers and shakers. The generally liberal and avant-garde Jewish elite was putting its stamp on Berlin culture to a degree far greater than their numbers implied.

It was the logical result, or the unintended consequence, of past patterns of social and professional discrimination. Highly educated, but frozen out of the academic world for the time being, Arthur was one of many Jews pushed into a "free profession" where the most talented now occupied key positions. Even at the *Vossische,* Arthur was not the first Jew in his influential job. His friend, Otto Brahm, who had shortened his name from Abrahamsohn, had preceded him and started the rebel "Free Stage." Now he was one of the capital's best-known drama directors at the Lessing Theater, where another Jew, "Iron Oscar" Blumenthal had once ruled. Brahm, in turn, brought the young Jew Max Reinhardt to Berlin, and no one was having a greater influence on the Berlin stage. Elsewhere, Jews were among the founders of Berlin's Deutsche Theater, and Jewish playwrights, dramatists, actors, and critics in Arthur's circle were influencing the theatre scene and making their presence felt.

The Jewish presence was even more pronounced in the exploding newspaper and publishing industry. The day was long since past when there was only a handful of dull, semiofficial publications, mostly conservative mouthpieces of the aristocracy. In the thirty years preceding the turn of the century, the number of newspapers more than tripled, and Berliners now could choose between no fewer than thirty morning dailies, ten evening papers, and some fifty others in the suburbs.[41] Berlin had become a true newspaper city. Jewish entrepreneurs had been the first to see the possibilities for profit and influence in catering to the demand for real news and entertainment of a better-educated population.

Journalism was a natural field for Jews, for it combined business sense and daring with intellectual interests. They seemed to have a talent for tailoring newspapers to the public's taste. Rudolf Mosse, a committed liberal and the son of a Jewish country doctor from Posen, was one of its earliest pioneers. He had already made a small fortune in publishing when, in 1871, he saw opportunity in linking advertising with the news business and founded his first paper, the *Berliner Tageblatt.* By 1900, his genius for organizing the selling of ads and for hiring talented collaborators had led to a vast family news empire, comprising a half dozen or more morning and evening papers, in addition to ownership of several "prestige" publications, including the Jewish *Allgemeine Zeitung.* In the process he became enormously rich—Berlin's third richest man in 1911—surpassed only by the Kaiser himself and by the ennobled Jewish business magnate Fritz von Friedländer-Fuld.[42]

Leopold Ullstein was another politically engaged Jew who built a no less important press and publishing empire. In time, he owned even more newspapers than Mosse, including Berlin's major photo weekly, the *Berliner Illustrierte,* and he extended his reach vertically by moving into printing and book publishing. Like Mosse, he was not only an astute businessman and talented organizer but also a committed liberal. When the perennially unprofitable *Vossische* got into financial difficulties, Ullstein, eager to control so prestigious a publication, readily added it to his stable of publications—much to the dismay of Arthur who feared that quality would be sacrificed to Ullstein's eye for the bottom line.

In fact, only one of the Berlin's "Big Three" media barons, August Scherl, was not a Jew. Scherl controlled a number of important dailies, among them the *Lokalanzeiger,* a paper tailored to appeal to the broad masses. All three houses competed vigorously, Scherl's papers being the more conservative and apolitical. Many of the journalists, writers, commentators, and critics were Jewish, with social and political views on the liberal side.

The fact that so many Jews were active in the nonofficial media world was a cause for considerable annoyance to the Kaiser and the official establishment. William's own reading habits rarely went beyond the perusal of a weekly devoted to news of the military and to reports on the princely Houses.[43] There was, to be sure, no shortage of apple-polishing journalists eager to shower him with worshipful flattery and interpret even his most questionable pronouncements in the best possible light. The monarch gloried in such hero worship, just as he feared and detested the more liberal press. Its journalists, he once said, were nothing more than "starvation-candidates" and "degenerate High Schoolers."[44] Anything resembling criticism of his person was a particular taboo. Each year there were as many as six hundred separate instances of individuals being hauled into court for allegedly committing the unpardonable sin of lèse-majesté against the Kaiser's person. The standards of what was acceptable or not were vague; sometimes the censor would confiscate entire editions, and not infrequently editors and writers were summarily jailed. Failure to convict them infuriated the Kaiser, and once, when a judge acquitted an accused, he promptly had the judge dismissed.

Guard officers were under strict orders not to read any of the liberal press. The Kaiser once boasted to his uncle, England's Edward VII, that "the press here has no influence because I am the only master of German politics."[45] He was only partly correct, for although the Berlin press was never entirely free and was often ignored from above, his officials could neither really stifle journalists nor effectively control the art scene or the stage. Contrary to the Kaiser's boast, some newspapers and individual journalists had considerable influence; none was more unstoppable, more widely read, and more influential than Maximilian Felix Ernst Harden (né Witkowski). No account of Berlin journalism of the period would be complete without him.

Harden was a fiercely independent, immensely talented polemicist, the most noteworthy of the Wilhelmine era, a natural orator and political essayist. If there was anyone who drove the Kaiser to paroxysms of fury with relentless attacks on the monarchy and William's friends, it was he. In one outburst, the Kaiser called him "a loathsome, dirty Jewish fiend" and "a poisonous toad out of the slime of hell."[46]

In his widely read paper, *The Future,* where he was at once publisher, chief editor, and most prolific contributor, Harden took aim mercilessly at the Kaiser's Chancellors and court clique, giving no quarter in exposing their shortcomings and foibles with sharp sarcasm and wit. Yet as a typical figure among assimilated German Jews of his day, his persona transcends the significance of his role as a journalist.

Harden's family had prepared him for a career in business, and like Heine he had rebelled and gone his own way. As a young man he had joined a troop of actors. Later he was baptized, and he redefined himself with a new name. His love of the theatre led him to a stint as drama critic, and he had a hand in the founding of the Free Stage and the Deutsche Theater. But he was eager to play a political role, and so he offered his services to the Kaiser. When he was rudely rebuffed, he became a confidant of the dismissed Bismarck and turned to a lifelong fight against monarchical privileges and for parliamentary rule.

Through his newspaper, which he founded in 1892 and which eventually made him a wealthy man, he attacked and roared at one and all—not only the archconservative upper classes but equally the liberals—many of them Jews—whom he considered too conciliatory to the establishment. He was unsparing in his criticism of the Social Democrats, Zionists, and any number of others. Some even accused him of being an anti-Semite. More than once he was jailed for his attacks on the Crown, but he remained undeterred, and he rose to his greatest prominence with an exposé of moral laxity and homosexual escapades among some of the Kaiser's closest friends.

For a good many years Harden was the most prominent, unrelenting, and most exposed among those journalists and writers who were willing to take on the establishment. To some, he was a hero, a fearless, independent fighter against the abuse of privilege. For others, his name became the symbol for the presence of far too many Jews in the press, and of a troublesome media more interested in tearing down tradition than in glorifyng it.

6

Even in good times, insecurities and worries were never far below the surface for the Jewish leadership. "What makes *Risches*?"[47] the *Allgemeine*'s lead article asked once again as the virulent anti-Semitic wave of the early 1890s was finally coming to an end. It was a familiar question, endlessly discussed and debated, and the paper frequently returned to it.

The answer, the writer suggested, lay not in the unapologetically open practice of one's faith. Those leaving their religion or too embarrassed to admit their Jewishness were misguided, as were those too frightened to join in a vigorous defense against outrageous anti-Jewish slanders. However, making big waves in daily life was quite another matter. Readers were warned against "pushy behavior" and ostentation; a more modest profile was best. In this, Maximilian Harden was clearly not the model to follow.

Louis Blumenthal had been fond of saying the same thing a generation earlier—a Jew would do well not to attract too much attention. Many shared this view, yet in practice maintaining a low profile was proving difficult for the Jewish minority regardless of how hard an individual might try. Their growing presence in the cities, their preeminence in art, theatre, media, and business was now as obvious as it was significant. Around 1870, four out of five Jews were still to be found scattered in small towns and rural areas. Thirty years later, 60 percent lived in the larger urban centers where their presence was unmistakable. In Berlin the Jewish population had tripled over forty years, and past restrictions had led to the concentration of Jews in limited, yet important and visible, areas, enhancing public perception of their power and influence—as well as envy and resentment. It was, as one historian aptly put it, their "burden of success."[48]

Arthur's career was a case in point. His reports on the Berlin stage were widely read and his name was well known in the media world. He reported on all that was happening in the theatre, yet it was obvious that his heart was with the newer, more progressive plays focused on the dilemmas of modern life, of which officialdom still greatly disapproved—and he also happened to be a Jew! "The Berlin stage is a bad influence on the city's morals. It has become fashionable to emphasize all that is decadent and perverse," one of the conservatives complained in the *Berliner Illustrierte*. In Otto Brahm's Lessing Theatre, the writer pointed out, the locale of the current *Die Herren vom Maxim* was actually a house of ill-repute. What was worse, he lamented, there had already been more than a hundred performances, and all were playing to full houses![49]

Thus the tension between traditionalists and progressives persisted, and Arthur was in the thick of it, but he was not the only one. Many young Jews his age had grown up with the same reservation toward making money and had been encouraged by their families to look elsewhere than, as Arthur put it, at "the only thing that Jews had once been trained to do." As a consequence, he was one of no fewer than eleven Jews among Berlin's thirteen best and most widely read stage critics. With so many Jewish newspaper owners, many of them liberals, the grumbling in official circles about Berlin's "*Judenpresse*" soon ceased to be an isolated event.

In law and medicine, the situation was the same. As the most sought-after professions, there was so heavy an overrepresentation that the *Allgemeine* felt called upon to defend it regularly as "the only safe harbor of the Jewish intelligentsia."[50] The numbers were striking. With one in ten German law students a Jew, and the barriers against admitting them to all but the lowest levels of the judiciary tight, the number of independent Jewish attorneys had grown impressively. At the beginning of the 1880s, 7 percent of all Prussian lawyers were Jews; a quarter century later the Jewish proportion had risen to 27 percent, and in the major metropolitan areas it was even greater. Before Hitler forced all of them out, Jews would account for almost one of every two Berlin lawyers. In Franfurt am Main and Breslau the situation was much the same.[51]

With a lower birthrate among Jews than Christians, their percentage in the overall German population was actually declining, to below 1 percent after the turn of the century—which made Jewish overrepresentation in medicine, as in the law, all the more startling. Ten percent of German doctors were Jews, but in Berlin they eventually made up 30 to 40 percent of all practicing physicians. Some achieved world renown. Though few were allowed as full-fledged professors in schools of medicine, a good many worked as medical scientists in laboratories and research institutes, and their contributions to the advancement of German medicine, one of the world's most advanced in the prewar years, were well known,[52] as were, in time, the envy and resentment of some of their non-Jewish colleagues and competitors.

In certain highly visible and concentrated areas of business and commerce the driving force of Jewish entrepreneurship and enterprise was especially evident. The main example was the overwhelming Jewish presence in retailing and in the closely related Berlin *Konfektion,* the ready-to-wear clothing trade, the city's largest industry. A revolution was under way in these fields, and Jews were spearheading it. The giant new department stores—shiny architectural marvels to which Berliners flocked by the thousands to shop and gape at elaborate window displays—were all the rage. For Wertheim's on Leipzigerstrasse, or the Tietz brothers' imposing establishment at Alexanderplatz, a low profile was not in the cards. Nor for N. Israel, whose founder had started a business of silks, embroideries, lace, and French fabrics as far back as the days of Frederick William III, and whose heirs developed it into one of Berlin's biggest and best-known emporia, where more than two thousand tailors were kept busy sewing clothes.

Many Berliners probably neither knew nor cared that the owners of Berlin's most important department stores were Jews. Yet thousands of the many small storekeepers and merchants, finding the going increasingly difficult, certainly did, and for those who had missed the point, there were always the agitators pointing fingers and blaming the big Jewish houses for the squeeze on small business.

The Berlin *Konfektion* industry was an almost totally Jewish domain. The streets around the city's center, where the Eloesser business flourished, were dominated by hundreds of large and small Jewish manufacturers, wholesalers, jobbers, and traders supplying the department stores and a large export market.[53] The coat business alone, according to the *Berliner Illustrierte,* employed fifty thousand workers in its 300 factories, and more than two thousand foreign buyers were said to visit the city on buying trips each

year.[54] Berlin style and enterprise were fine, the paper said, yet in so successful a business, why were a few getting so rich while so many workers toiled
for hours for so little pay? The prevalence of Jewish owners was, in this
instance, not mentioned, yet it was a theme to which those less favorably
inclined frequently returned.

There were other areas, old and new, where a prominent Jewish presence
was equally unmistakable. Almost half of Germany's private banks were in
Jewish hands. Among the big public ones, hardly any were not under Jewish ownership or at least without several Jewish directors. And at the very
top there was the highly visible elite of a handful of Jews who were among
the country's most prominent and influential industrialists: Emil Rathenau, a friend of Thomas Edison, whose AEG Company was helping to elec-
trify Germany; Albert Ballin, a leader in building the Reich's shipping fleet;
James Simon, a wealthy banker, art patron, and philanthropist; Carl Fürs-
tenberg, the banker who sat on more corporate boards than anyone else;
and a handful of others. These were the *Kaiserjuden,* the few whose accomplishments and knowledge even William recognized and respected, and
whose company and advice he would occasionally seek.

Though German living standards were rising, they still remained below
those of Britain. In rural areas and in the working-class districts of Berlin,
the proletariat continued to live poorly, and often in squalor. For artisans,
tradesmen, and petty officials on limited incomes, the pinching of pfen-
nigs remained a frustrating part of daily life. Among Jews there were similar
pockets of poverty, yet on average they were clearly better off—and visibly
so. In Berlin, and in other big cities, the new class of Jewish professionals
and prospering businessmen made up an important part of upper-middle-
class income earners. In Hamburg 27 percent of Jewish taxpayers were in
the highest tax brackets, in Breslau it was 15 percent, and in Berlin the Jews
paid a third of all taxes collected. More and more upwardly mobile Jews
were settling in the handsome, turn-of-the-century apartment houses rising in the leafy western section, often in close proximity to each other, thus
making the more concentrated Jewish presence in Berlin a geographic as
well as financial reality.

While many Jews were now comfortable and prosperous, a few had become extraordinarily rich. Joining the heirs of "old" Jewish money from
preindustrial days, a group of super-rich Jews accounted for an unmistak-

ably significant share of the wealthiest Germans in the prewar years. In Hesse-Nassau, twelve out of the twenty largest taxpayers were Jews. In Berlin, the Mosse family had amassed a fabulous fortune of fifty million marks from its publishing empire, and the Tietzs and Wertheims were worth close to ten million marks each. The estimates are that among the twenty-five wealthiest Germans in 1909–11, 44 percent were Jews or of Jewish descent, and that more than a quarter, or fifty-five of Prussia's two hundred richest citizens, were Jewish.[55]

On the surface, the progress many were enjoying was cause for optimism. Beneath that, however, other forces were growing that put the Jewish position at risk. The peculiar appeal to Germans of the distorted theories of race was one crucial factor. German imperialism, and the militarism and chauvinistic nationalism that helped to foster it, was another.

7

Another change had occurred. The Jews had learned to fight back, and their self-confidence had risen. When the attacks against them first began in earnest in the 1880s, most had been too stunned and frightened to respond, and the Jewish establishment had largely remained passive. One of their papers had advised "contemptuous silence," arguing that any public answer would merely inflame the spirits further. Eventually, however, Jewish leaders moved to a more active policy to defend Jewish interests. In 1893, they founded the Central Union for German Citizens of the Jewish Faith (known as the CV, for *Centralverein,* or central union), and made it the official voice for stating Jewish positions and affirming their loyalty to the state. "We want to be Germans, yet remain Jews," the organizers explained, "true and loyal citizens and unflinching believers in Judaism."[56]

In parallel, Jewish dueling fraternities at universities united into the Kartell Convent (KC), a national federation dedicated to prove the students' patriotism and to defend their honor against the claim that Jews were too cowardly to fight. "We stand firmly on the foundation of patriotic German ideology . . . our bonds are inseparably united with the German fatherland. We will always be ready and able to defend the political and legal rights of the Jews," the KC promised. As to the claim that they were insipid weak-

lings, the students would show that "every member of our association is
equal to every Christian fellow student in physical exercise and chivalry."[57]

The founding of an "Association to Repel Anti-Semitism," organized
by a group of Christian political activists, was a further welcome development, yet for most Jews basic nervousness and insecurities remained. Years
of denigration had taken their toll and left psychological scars too deep to
be easily healed. In spite of good times and growing self-confidence, most
remained uncertain about their identity, even as they pursued their various
individual strategies for gaining respect and status.

Outright baptism remained relatively rare in the first decade of the new
century, though the number of mixed marriages was rising. The leadership
worried about it and made it a frequent subject of discussion. We can't win,
the *Allgemeine* complained bitterly: "Deserters from the Jewish camp harm
us doubly, because their contributions to German life are no longer seen
as Jewish, while their alleged misdeeds remain characterized as such!"[58]
Among the young, formal resignations from the community were becoming more common and even for those not formally "crossing over" or
resigning, the loosening of their links to Judaism remained a matter of concern. Because of insufficient funds and the lack of students, rabbis and
teachers sometimes had to be dismissed. Yet there was at least the consolation that there were still "the full hearts of noble-minded Jews who contribute for welfare . . . and for orphanages, hospitals and the aged."[59] All the
same, "on Saturdays the synagogues are empty" and "participation of the
Jewish population [of Berlin] in community matters exists in only a minor
degree," the *Allgemeine* lamented.[60]

Whatever their lack of interest, the great majority of Jews remained
nominally Jewish. Some did so with pride, others more with embarrassment. A good many simply ignored the whole issue and tried to live as
Germans, adopting German attitudes and values and doing their best to
blend in with their Christian neighbors by emulating their manners and
speech, and even by adopting some of their most obvious preconceptions
about "unfortunate" Jewish traits. There were those, for example, who worried about looking too Jewish. The blond, blue-eyed Nordic type was widely
taken by them as the preferred ideal of beauty, and Semitic features—the
hooked nose, darker complexion, and large lips—were considered less desirable. Most eschewed Jewish names for their children and preferred clas-

sic German ones like Siegfried, Hellmuth, Werner, Elfriede, and Ursula. Children were admonished to avoid "Jewish manners," by which was meant ostentation, loud talk, heavy gesturing, and a general lack of self-control.

In the same vein, German Jews feared and disdained their more recently arrived Polish and Russian coreligionists, precisely because they thought that their manner and speech conformed too closely to the stereotyped negatives they tried so hard to avoid. When the popular humor magazine *Simplicissimus* depicted distorted caricatures of a "typical" Jew—unattractive and pushy, Semitic face with hooked nose, money hungry, and socially ambitious—many Jews smiled along with the public while inwardly they winced. Not uncommonly, they made the image their own with self-conscious deprecating jokes, always anxious to put distance between themselves and their un-German and unassimilated cousins.

Most were hardly aware of the trap they had fallen into. When Arthur, a sensitive man of subtle intelligence, recalled that Jews had been taught to do nothing more than make money, he chose instead a noncommercial profession focused on German culture. It was a turning away from a "Jewish occupation" and an echoing of gentile values and prejudices deeply embedded in his own psyche. Late in his life, when he was ostracized by the Nazis, unable to publish anywhere except in a Jewish paper and much more aware of his Jewishness, he reminisced about his favorite uncle and characterized him warmly as a man "as beautiful as the king of Bavaria," and a proud, chivalrous, and courageous fighter full of bravura, who could "brawl and drink" in the best East Prussian manner, he was still reflecting the same attitude.[61]

Values and attitudes were one thing, specific patterns of behavior to win approval in a Christian world were another. Many German Jews tried hard—some too hard—to do it right. At the very top there was the wealthy elite, who sought to gain access to the highest strata of society with lavish entertainment showered on prominent Christian guests. Some gentiles accepted their hospitality because of genuine friendship or interest. Others did so in part because of the hope for a useful financial connection or to make use of the host's influence and power, or perhaps just because they were curious and enjoyed the good food, the champagne, and the fine art on the walls. But this did not mean that they were willing to accept Jews on equal terms; after all, even the Kaiser found it useful to have his *Kaiser-juden* to tea from time to time and saw no harm in tapping them for contributions to his pet projects.

Whether the Jews realized it or not, the social gulf and the contradictions remained even in good times. Just as the Kaiser dealt with his *Kaiserjuden* but enthusiastically endorsed tracts glorifying the German race and denigrating Jews, so the aristocrats frequented Jewish drawing rooms as slightly uncomfortable yet curious visitors, all the while retaining their basic anti-Jewish bias. "One has to apologize to other gentiles to accept a Jewish invitation," Charles Huret, a French journalist reporting on Berlin's social scene, quoted one of them as telling him. Another explained that he went—but made it a point to refrain from removing his gloves.[62]

In Germany's hierarchical society, and especially in Prussia, nothing counted more than a title. For virtually all Jews, the hereditary nobility was out of reach, but for prominent bankers and businessmen, the non-hereditary honors of *Kommerzienrat* (KR), and the higher level of *Geheimer Kommerzienrat* (GKR), were much sought-after prizes. These titles were an honor and they opened doors to business opportunity. They were a sign of a significant level of achieved wealth, which assured one of a respectful hearing anywhere and deferential treatment from associates and lesser mortals, such as hotel owners and headwaiters. Above all, it gave what many Jews wanted most—status and recognition. Thus many pursued them with especial fervor and tenacity. They did this so avidly, in fact, that ministers and senior officials regularly complained that the greatest and most unrelenting pressure to be included in the official lists invariably came from Jewish claimants. The fact that by the early 1900s 15 to 20 percent of all KRs and GKRs were given to them is evidence not only of their hunger for recognition but also of their prominence in many fields.

In the years before World War I there were many outward signs that Germany's Jews were finally being integrated into German life. Yet beneath the surface, the basic problem of the Jew as outsider remained. "German anti-Semitism," the keenly observant Huret noted in his reports from Berlin, while no longer officially sanctioned "is indirect, passive, and below the surface—but remains no less real." He concluded that the place of the old ghetto had been taken by "'moral barriers,' taking different forms at different levels, depending against what group [of Jews] they are directed against."[63]

The political anti-Semites focused on the contrast between German nationalism and Jewish internationalism. The economic animus of others derived from Prussian agrarianism's distrust of Jewish capitalists and bankers, while the petit bourgeoisie resented the competition of Jewish merchants. The complaints against them, Huret marveled, ran the gamut. Some said they smelled, their skin was dark, and they were morally inferior. Others were bitter about their flooding the free professions and said they lacked tact and style. Some insisted Jews were tightfisted and avaricious; others resented them as showoffs and overly lavish spenders.

Huret thought that there was a far deeper and more pervasive dislike of Jews in Germany than in England and in France. It struck him as quite puzzling and contradictory, and the views of the most outspoken critics seemed particularly surprising and impractical because the Jewish minority had become so visibly beneficial and important in German life. If, as some advocated, Jews were removed from their positions of influence, then "nine-tenths of Berlin's wealth would be lost," he concluded.[64]

8

There is little evidence that Arthur gave a great deal of thought to the "Jewish Question" or realized the risks for Jews. Two or three times each month during the season, the *Vossische* carried his reports on the new and the noteworthy in the theatre, leaving him enough time for his own literary efforts. In 1904, a second book, *Literary Portraits of Modern France,* won approval for its careful scholarship, followed a year later by a biography of Heinrich Kleist and the start of a major project to edit a five-volume edition of Kleist plays, as well as a biographical review of the nineteenth-century dramatist Otto Ludwig.

Arthur had married Margarethe Nauenberg, a young Jew with cultural interests like his own. Eleven years his junior, she was beginning to try her hand at writing children's plays. Max, their eldest son, arrived just as they were joining the familiar exodus to the western suburbs, where their second child, Elizabeth, was born a few years later. At Dahlmannstrasse 29, near the newly fashionable Kurfürstendamm, Arthur had rented quarters in a modern building, home to several other Jewish families who, like the Eloessers, had recently arrived from old Jewish neighborhoods. The rents were high and the *Vossische's* salary modest, but Arthur liked his work, and there were the odd small honoraria for a speech or special article. When all else failed, they could count on gifts from their families who basked proudly in his accomplishments and fame.

He still made his infrequent visits to Oranienburg, where his sister had long since put down roots and presided over a growing family. Though comfortably settled, Ida still complained about her isolation from the capital's bright lights and cultural stimulation. Reading was a family passion, and her main consolation was the monthly arrival from Berlin of a consignment of specially ordered books. Her brother, for his part, never arrived without bringing his own selection for her. This time (it was the fall of 1906) he had chosen Sudermann's *Frau Sorge,* also the script for *Elga,* Hauptmann's latest play, and to add some spice, Arthur Schnitzler's sexually daring *Reigen,* or *La Ronde.*

The pièce de résistance, specially requested by her, was a new book everyone was talking about in Berlin—Georg Herrmann's *Jettchen Gebert.* It had a Jewish theme—the story of a Berlin Jewish girl of the 1840s in love with a gentile but forced into a traditional marriage with another Jew. Jettchen's dilemma, caught between love and duty, desperate to break out to modern life, had struck a responsive chord with the older generation. Its relevance to everyday problems appealed to Christians and Jews alike, and everyone was reading it. The *Vossische* was serializing the book, and Arthur had recently reviewed it.

Louis and Regine had died and Martin had stepped into his father's shoes at the bank and in local affairs. Like his father, he had been elected town councillor and gave advice on municipal finances. In an expanding economy, the Blumenthal bank was strong, and the family lived in considerable comfort. There was even the thought of hiring a chauffeur and buying one of the new-fangled automobiles. It would be one of the town's first. Martin was greatly tempted but he worried that it might kindle local anti-Semitism. What did Arthur think, he inquired?

During the height of the anti-Jewish agitation, Oranienburg's Jews had been subjected to their share of unpleasantness, and in the small town there had been no escaping distinctly uncomfortable embarrassments. Several farmers and tradesmen, perennial malcontents, and a few rather unexpected sympathizers, had passed around Böckel's pamphlets and made nasty remarks about Jewish bankers and lawyers. Ida said she was comforted that the town's leadership made known its disapproval—some not as decisively as one might have wished—but now all of that, thank God, seemed to be over.

She had joined the local Vaterländische Frauenverein, a patriotic ladies society devoted to Prussian history and the planning of celebrations for the Kaiser's birthday and similar national events. Eventually the members had elected her chairwoman. During the height of the troubles, a few women members stayed away from the Blumenthal house, but the majority nevertheless continued to appear for the monthly meeting. Maybe they were secretly anti-Semites, but "they like to inspect our furniture and they enjoy my *Kuchen*," Ida thought. "Several of their husbands also owe the bank money," Martin had added with a wry smile.

There were now three Blumenthal offspring, spruced up and waiting to be presented for their Uncle Arthur's inspection. In 1906, at age seventeen, Ewald, the eldest, was the apple of his mother's eye. Hellmuth was a little boy of eight and their sister, Edith, was three. Ewald had recently finished his studies at a local high school, and soon his mother would greatly miss him, Martin having apprenticed him for a three-year stint at a small private Jewish bank in Berlin, where he would learn the rudiments of the family business. Ida adored and spoiled him. His performance at school had been mixed but one hoped he was growing up. The plan was that he would return and join Martin at the bank. His mother was counting on Arthur and the Eloessers to keep a watchful eye out for him in Berlin.

He was still an unfinished young man, though rather handsome and pleasant in appearance. Clean shaven, he had dark hair against a pale complexion and prominent brows emphasizing friendly brown eyes. His soft features bore an unmistakable resemblance to his mother's side of the family. Slim and of medium height, he had unusually small feet and an odd manner in his stride; his toes turned outward in a manner uncannily similar to the oft-noted waving waddle of Giacomo Meyerbeer, his ancestor.

In Berlin, there was the incessant noise of big-city bustle, streets choked with horses and carts, automobiles adding to the din, electric streetcars clanking, and sidewalks full of businessmen, brokers in bowler hats, street vendors, shopgirls, soldiers, and assorted unique Berlin types. At night, there were the cafés, the bars and dives, the easy girls, and dance music on that sensational new invention, the gramophone disc.

Ewald knew little and cared less about Jewish affairs and problems. Jettchen Gebert's conflict between Jewish heritage and German modernity still had its special appeal for his mother and her contemporaries. For him, it had little meaning. Moreover he had a natural tendency, often demonstrated in later years, to avoid dwelling on the unpleasant. Of course, he was well aware that he was a Jew—living in small Oranienburg had made that inevitable. Yet he had been raised by his parents to be a German, had attended Christian public schools, made gentile friends, and learned more about Prussian history than Jewish traditions. What some called "the Jewish Question" frankly bored him.

As far as he was concerned, the old Jewish travails were history, or soon would be. William was his Kaiser, far out of reach and larger than life, yet a sovereign to be admired, followed, and joked about. As with most Germans, whatever interest he had in public affairs was primarily directed at the Kaiser, his family, and court life. He also enjoyed watching Berlin's frequent military parades. The interesting new weaponry the Kaiser was promoting made him proud of German technological skills. Just recently the first submarine had been launched at Kiel, for instance, and the potential of the new-fangled Zeppelin balloons seemed unlimited. He knew that some day he too would have to do military service. Perhaps, with the right connections, he would be a one-year volunteer in one of those fancy guard regiments, he thought, though not as an officer, of course.

Parades of soldiers in fancy dress were a thrill, but there were those who maintained that the prevailing passion for the military had its less appealing side. In Wilhelmine Prussia a man in uniform represented higher authority, and the public was accustomed to blind obedience of his commands. Some condemned this as dangerous and foolish, others merely laughed, yet everyone toed the line. Complaints about potentially troublesome consequences had little impact—until, that is, a striking incident finally gripped the public's attention.

A forty-seven-year-old unemployed shoemaker—one Wilhelm Voigt with three prior criminal convictions, it later developed—had donned the uniform of a captain in the Kaiser's First Regiment of guards and, "in the name of higher authority," taken command of seven soldiers and a sergeant marching home from their post as guards at a military swim club. Brandishing what he claimed was a cabinet order, he commandeered two horse taxis, transported the entire complement to the town hall of Köpenick, a Berlin suburb, arrested the badly shaken mayor, and confiscated the municipal cash box. Having receipted its contents and left the soldiers to guard the captive, he then promptly disappeared into thin air, four thousand marks and all.

He spoke, the hapless mayor said in his defense, in the authentic tone of a military man, and under the circumstances, his wife had counseled obedience. So, for that matter, had the local police recruited by Voigt to keep order during the arrest, as well as the coachmen whose only complaint was that they hadn't been paid. As to the soldiers, they worried about missing their lunch, but the bogus captain barked the right commands and his uniform seemed entirely proper. Only the small quirk that he wore a cap rather than the regulation spiked helmet aroused momentary suspicion. Later it was revealed that the used-clothing store outfitting the imposter had lacked a helmet big enough for his large, oddly shaped head.

The affair was headline news for days. The *Berliner Zeitung* observed that neither the appointment of Clemenceau in France nor yet another failed attempt on the life of the Czar had aroused as much interest among Berliners. The consensus was that it was an embarrassing joke and a fitting commentary on the German awe for the "hallowed coat." Quoting the Italian *Corriere della Sera,* the paper noted that even the foreigners were laughing and concluded that for the average citizen a uniform was more important than a man's accomplishments or his intelligence.

The Köpenick caper was a farce but in a deeper sense it was no laughing matter. Germany's hierarchical society, where orders were given and followed without question, was being Prussianized, and in Prussia the veneration of the uniform was only the visible manifestation of a progressive militarization and cult of obedience with deep historical roots and unfortunate consequences.

Bismarck's inflexible constitution was poorly suited to the twentieth century. It gave the sovereign extraordinary powers without protective checks and balances. He alone chose his Chancellor, who remained responsible only to him and whom he could dismiss at will. Under William II there would be four of them, each unimpressive and deficient, chosen more for a willingness to comply with his master's wishes than for wisdom and judgment.

The caste system remained in effect right up to the First World War, and its conservative beneficiaries in the military and the bureaucracy solidly supported the Kaiser's policies. The elaborate system of titles and honors—so integral a hallmark of German society—tended to fortify and confirm the existing structure. The three years of military service where blind obedience was drilled into every recruit were a seminal, unifying experience for the men. The unquestioning obedience learned as soldiers continued to guide their behavior and to define the national ethos of respect for authority.

Above all, it was the Kaiser himself—a man with a strong personality and a weak character—who was responsible for the worst excesses of the system. Under his leadership, in a vicious circle of bluster and blunder, Germany followed policies in the prewar years that frightened her neighbors, led to her growing isolation, and in turn bred a national sense of insecurity over imagined threats from abroad. Foreign resistance to the Kaiser's boasts that Germany would be a world power produced fears among the German leadership and people of the risk of encirclement and led to an ever greater military role in society. A docile public, trained to obey, was goaded into a spirit of national fervor to be militarily strong so that Germany could take its "place in the sun" even in the face of hostile forces. No one as yet realized that the ultimate result would be the greatest war the world had ever seen.

Bismarck had been a master of international politics, cautiously building, step by step, a complex system of treaties and alliances aimed to avoid offending England while keeping Russia and France from uniting against him. His successors, supported by the Kaiser, blundered into destroying this system almost from the start. Germany was committed to a Triple Alliance with Italy and the Austro-Hungarian Empire, whose interests in the Balkans often collided with Russia's. A secret Russo-German treaty of "reinsurance," meant to comfort the Russians, was allowed to lapse, thus driving the Czar into a pact with the French, whose revanchist sentiments Germany feared. German hope for support from Britain was undermined by the Kaiser's love-hate attitude toward his mother's country, and his boastful, ill-considered speeches and initiatives led to a progressive estrangement. While the British were embroiled in the Boer War, William sent a supportive telegram to the Boers' leader, "Oom Paul" Kruger. His loud support for the German-built Baghdad railroad managed to offend both Russia and England, which feared a threat to their interests in the Middle East. As to the French, the Kaiser's two ill-conceived and ultimately futile attempts to challenge their preeminence in Morocco further exacerbated tensions and deepened mutual resentments.

His subjects good-naturedly liked to call the incessantly junketing William their *Reisekaiser* (traveling Kaiser).[65] Unfortunately, he had a tendency to appear in the wrong places at the wrong time and to lose himself in foolish and damaging oratory. One of the worst examples was his famous "Huns" speech, destined to haunt him—and German soldiers—for a generation. "Have no pity. Take no prisoners," he shouted to soldiers embarking to put down the Chinese Boxer rebellion. "Just as a thousand years ago the Huns made a name for themselves, so must the name of Germans be known . . . that no Chinese, for a thousand years, will dare even to look at a German!"

Beneath his oratorical swagger and the missteps there were hard policies—German colonial ambitions in Africa and Asia and, in a drastic break with the past, the challenge to Britain's preeminence on the seas. This was the most damaging to the German position. The Royal Navy had long been the Kaiser's envy, and nothing was more designed to threaten Britain than the Reich's drive, after 1900, to challenge it on the high seas with an unbridled arms race in the building of ships. The Kaiser put naval affairs on a par with other ministries, made Admiral von Tirpitz, the most enthusiastic proponent of naval expansion, his Secretary of State, and exuberantly backed him as he steadily increased the pressure. At first the goal was to commission two naval squadrons with sixteen ships; in the end, the Reichstag authorized dreadnoughts and heavy cruisers and no fewer than sixty ships, in a direct challenge to the British policy of having twice as many ships as any potential foe.

Step by step, Germany found itself more isolated and feared while the naval race continued and her neighbors cemented their alliances. More and more, the view was being fostered at home that the Reich was surrounded by hostile forces, and the spirit of national fervor and defiance grew.

Germany's Jews were caught up in the same spirit. Yet for them, there were other consequences. In the prevailing national mood, it was the patriotic organizations that emerged as key engines of Germany's imperialism. As they grew in importance, the problem was that they favored the rhetoric of German racial superiority to justify their imperialist cause. Step by step, racism and nationalism were being merged. It was a dangerous mixture for the Jewish cause.

9

In 1906, Reich Chancellor von Bülow heightened the national paranoia, further bolstering the military's ever-larger hold on German life. A deliberate policy of encirclement is being fostered against the fatherland, he informed the people. To meet the threat, Germany must be militarily strong and pursue its national goals of colonial expansion and naval power "with a free hand."[66] The public cheered, but the policy proved to be only another step in the growing isolation of the Reich.

It would be eight years before a disastrous war engulfed Germany and much of the world. Not many could see the connection between the national mood, militarism, and the cult of obedience on the one hand, and unquestioning public support for policies leading to armed conflict on the other. The greater part of the citizenry— Jews, aristocrats, bourgeoisie, and proletariat—supported the government, shared the enthusiasm for Germany's colonial claims, and were ready to follow orders.

Yet for Jews the problems being raised by Germany's imperialism and feverish nationalism were serious. They bolstered the influence of precisely those elements and institutions most prone to anti-Semitic prejudice.

The Pan-German League was one of the most important of these. Founded in 1893, league membership grew quickly as the pressure for imperialist policies rose, and so did its access to those in power. One-third of the members were conservative academics, the others were prominent reactionaries from business and the upper bureaucracy, and many of the leading members were unabashed racists and open anti-Semites. The league's avowed purpose was, first and foremost, to influence public opinion in favor of the all-out pursuit of imperialist expansion. Its emphasis in pressing for overseas expansion was based on Germanic values, closer ties between all people of "Germanic stock" and the need for "racial solidarity." It was a racial ideology, expressed in aggressive rhetoric, and it automatically left Jews out in the cold. The stated desire "for races to become homogeneous and to expel foreign elements" had clear anti-Jewish overtones.[67] "Our future lies in our blood," they exclaimed.

The Colonial Society, the Army League, and especially the Navy League were similar authoritarian, patriotic organizations with overlapping memberships,[68] riding high in the years before the war. They generally excluded Jews who, anxious to show their patriotism, were left wondering what to do. For the *Kaiserjuden,* it was a special problem, but at least one of them, the shipping magnate Albert Ballin, a friend of Chancellor von Bülow and a man with strong monarchical leanings, thought he had solved his problems. He was a leading factor in the Kaiser's shipbuilding program, and though the navy steadfastly refused to accept any Jews in its ranks he simply joined the Navy League anyway.[69]

The language and influence of the patriotic organizations, closely resembling that of the racial anti-Semites, should have alerted Germany's Jews that underlying anti-Semitic sentiments were still dangerous and widespread. Instead, many preferred to focus their attention on the Dreyfus trial in France. They followed it avidly and congratulated themselves that this dangerous incident had occurred in another country. At the same time, reports of bloody pogroms in Kiev and Odessa led them to take comfort in their own safer circumstance.

For those few willing to open their eyes and acknowledge it, there was certainly clear evidence that the anti-Semitic virus remained much alive. As late as 1899, there were accounts of several Jews in the West Prussian town of Konitz having been charged with ritual murder, although they were later acquitted. On another occasion, Christmas fliers distributed in downtown Berlin alleged that their religion allowed Jews to cheat Christians and suggested they were racially "lower than cattle." Elsewhere, several *Gymnasia* had blackballed Jewish applicants while, in an omen of wartime troubles to come, an army captain had circulated a list of thirty-eight alleged incidents of cowardice among Jewish soldiers.[70] On a further ominous note, rumors that on a visit to London in 1907, the Kaiser had openly made hostile anti-Jewish remarks proved to be correct. "There are far too many of them in Germany and they want stamping out," he told Sir Edward Grey, the Foreign Secretary.[71]

Most Jews preferred to look the other way. They believed in progress and their place in society and wanted to prove their patriotism. None but a handful were open to the Zionist ideas of the Austrian journalist Theodor Herzl, and most rejected his assertion that they could never be truly secure outside a Jewish homeland. Herzl's solution—emigration and return to a Jewish Palestinian state—seemed to them outlandish and impractical. For the Eloessers and Blumenthals and the many assimilated Jews with deep German roots going back generations, the idea was not only unthinkable but embarrassing and dangerous. They feared that such proposals coming from a Jew might give comfort to those who had claimed all along that Jews were a race and nation apart, and not to be trusted.

In ignoring or belittling the evidence of continuing anti-Semitism, their biggest mistake was to fail to appreciate the dangers of the racial theories that were becoming standard fare in the rhetoric of their enemies and the degree to which these penetrated German thinking. It was, to be sure, a relatively recent development. The earliest versions had originated in mid-nineteenth-century France, where Joseph-Arthur Gobineau first theorized that blond, blue-eyed Aryans, or Teutons, were a superior race and, conversely, Jews a race apart and vastly inferior. Wilhelm Marr, Eugen Dühring, Hermann Ahlwardt, and others had eagerly picked up the French import and popularized it in Germany.

Why these ideas took hold so much more in Germany than elsewhere remains a mystery. Perhaps it was their pseudoscientific, theoretical trappings that had a peculiar appeal there. Yet, for whatever reasons, it was in Germany that race ideas achieved their greatest appeal. No one, for example, espoused the glorification of a superior Germanic race more fervently than Richard Wagner, and no one was a more enthusiastic proponent of "Gobineauism's" view of Jewish inferiority. Wagner's influence in spreading the race doctrine in Germany was considerable, and eventually the English-born naturalized publicist Houston Stewart Chamberlain, Wagner's son-in-law, carried the torch yet further. Over time, anti-Jewish racism evolved into an organized, integrated, purportedly scientific theory justifying the total rejection of Jews as Germans. "Jews are a mongrel race

which will always retain its mongrel character," Chamberlain flatly as-
serted.[72]

Wagner, Chamberlain, their predecessors, and their followers spawned
a vast literature of anti-Jewish racial hate. Respected scholars dismissed
them as a lunatic fringe, and their claims of a biological basis for Jewish
inferiority as scientific humbug. But that did not deter them. The tracts
multiplied, and there were those—traditional Jew haters or the discontented and disaffected in search of a cause to give meaning to their lives—
who accepted the ideas and made them a central focus of their lives. Only
a few were as yet being heard; most were still obscure and insignificant outsiders.

Some, however, would not remain unnoticed. At the very time when
Germany's Jews were enjoying their best years, a bright but poorly educated
young man in Vienna, leading an idler's life and smarting from repeated
rejections and disappointments, nourished his hatred of bourgeois society
by devouring *Ostara,* a nondescript magazine that was one of the many
specializing in theories of Germanic racial superiority and slogans of blood
pollution and mongrelization through Jews. For Adolf Hitler, still in his
twenties, dissatisfied, restless and in search of a cause, *Ostara's* stories lit a
spark that led him to more books and pamphlets of the same genre—and
finally "to the greatest spiritual upheaval. . . . I ceased to be a weak-kneed
cosmopolitan and became an anti-Semite."[73] It had all become quite clear
to him and it was the literature of race and Jew hatred, abundantly available in Vienna, that had, he said, revealed the truth: German salvation lay
in a true Pan-Germanism. That was the answer—and the Jewish purveyor
of filth and defiler of race was the problem. "By defending myself against
the Jew, I am fighting for the work of the Lord," he explained.[74]

When World War I broke out, Hitler was in Munich, a confirmed racial
anti-Semite caught up in the war fever gripping many Germans. The war
would be short and glorious, everyone believed. As for Hitler, "overpow-
ered by strong enthusiasm, I fell down on my knees and thanked heaven."[75]
Pan-Germanism's ideas of the historic mission of those with Germanic
blood had done much to influence his imagination.

He was not alone. In a village near Düsseldorf, the Catholic son of a
bookkeeper, a sickly boy of sixteen, too young and unfit for military service, felt the same national euphoria. Someday Joseph Goebbels would

share Hitler's race hatreds and become his master's most assiduous propagandist in spreading the theories of Gobineau, Marr, Ahlwardt, Wagner, and Chamberlain. In the prewar years, he and similar fanatics were dismissed as an insignificant fringe group. When they reached power their views became official doctrine, and every German would be told that they were true. In the wake of the disappointments of a lost war and the years of hardship that followed, it would not be difficult to convince many others to join them as true believers.

Thus, with militarism, avid nationalism, and the sense of a historic mission for the special race and blood of Germans, the seeds of a special German Jew hatred were sown, even as the Jews' good years continued. There was ever more persistent talk of war, and Arthur was too intelligent not to understand the calamity of an armed conflict. But he was also a patriot, he too thought that the war would be brief, that the Reich's cause was just, and that Germany would certainly prevail.

Many Jews shared his view. Ewald, his young nephew, had not the slightest doubt. He had done his military service as a one-year volunteer in 1912, fortunate that his father's connections had opened the doors to the Kaiser's Second Regiment of guards, one of Berlin's best. For a year he had paraded before the Kaiser and the Crown Prince, stood guard at the Brandenburg Gate, and saluted royalty passing by his post. He was proud of that, and the one-year volunteer soldier's life had not been too bad.

He returned to the bank in 1913, and when war broke out, he hurried to his unit and marched off to the conflict. In time, his much older Uncle Arthur would put on a German uniform and follow him.

CHAPTER VIII

SURVIVORS

Ewald

If there were a Nobel prize for a German attitude, German Jews would win it.

Alfred Wiener
June 26, 1930

Bear in mind the devastations which Jewish bastardization visits on our nation each day.

Adolf Hitler, in *Mein Kampf*

1

The sensational murder in Sarajevo of the heir to the Austrian throne on June 28, 1914, hit Berlin like a thunderbolt. The *Berliner Tageblatt* reminded its readers of Julius Caesar's unfortunate demise at the hands of a political assassin, commenting that while senseless acts had always been a part of human history, in modern times the Balkan powderkeg was particularly prone to them. Recently, King George I of Greece had been the victim of an assassin; before that Alexander I of Serbia, Bulgarian Premier Stambolov, and the Turkish leader Mahmut Shevket Pasha all had been dispatched to an untimely end by fanatics.[1]

The assassination of Austrian Archduke Francis Ferdinand and his wife Sophie was nevertheless a serious matter, the paper said, noting the risk of grave political consequences. Together with Italy, Austria-Hungary was Germany's principal ally in the Triple Alliance. Serbian nationalists would not have acted without the clandestine support of the Pan-Slavs backed by Russia, and Austria would certainly now move vigorously against the pesky Serbians. The question was how Russia would respond, how their French allies would react, and what wider repercussions Germany's support for Austria might have.

There were banner headlines and much initial excitement, yet at first no one seriously expected a general war. The Balkans were a faraway place and their problems arcane and hard to understand. The assumption was that the Serbs would be suitably dealt with by Austria and that the crisis was fundamentally a local affair. Early signs, in fact, seemed to confirm that the matter was being brought under control. The Kaiser, having assured Austrian emissaries of Germany's full backing for whatever action their country might take, left for his customary summer naval junket in northern waters, and most ministers and senior officials departed on their normal summer leaves.[2]

For days, a lingering barometric depression over the Atlantic had produced unusually hot weather in much of Western Europe, sending many in the capital to seek relief in the woods and lakes dotting the periphery of Berlin, away from daily news bulletins. On July 3, a report of yet another change in army uniforms was taken as further evidence of a return to normalcy, and Berliners joked that even the French had caught the disease. Reports from Paris were that the traditional red pants of French infantry were to be phased out, and that soldiers modeling new grays for foot soldiers and yellows for chasseurs had been paraded before a commission of deputies to solicit their opinion on so important a matter.[3] If both sides were more concerned with the color of their soldiers' tunics and trousers than with assembling armies and armaments, the people reasoned, then the risk of general war must surely be receding.

As the month progressed, however, the early optimism faded. Throughout July political tensions rose, and inexorably the Serbian affair drew the major powers toward an armed confrontation. On July 23, Austria sent a stiff ultimatum to Serbia, and over the next several days one country after another mobilized its forces. A war, Berlin newspapers concurred, was becoming virtually inevitable, and while the Socialists continued to demonstrate against it, Conservatives openly agitated for taking up arms. It would be a short and glorious war, they argued—six to eight weeks at most. The Austrian ally deserved full support and the Reich was strong and well prepared to show its enemies bent on encirclement that it would not be denied its rightful place as a major power.

The public mood vacillated wildly. At times the atmosphere was almost carefree with groups parading through the streets and singing patriotic songs in an outpouring of national fervor. Then, with ministers hurrying back from their leaves and mobilization expected momentarily, an anxious quiet replaced earlier exuberance and tensions rose to the breaking point.

Saturday, August 1, was a beautiful warm and sunny day. Ewald Blumenthal, a young man of twenty-five, had refused to give up his weekly trip to Berlin in spite of the prospect of imminent mobilization and war. During the week he labored dutifully in the Oranienburg family bank, but on his free days Berlin with its theatres, cabarets, and late-night eateries was a strong magnet. There was, moreover, an additional reason for frequent visits, though he had not yet had the courage to mention it to his family. He had recently become involved with a young woman, a non-Jew, and they were secretly contemplating marriage. Lucy, blonde and very attractive, had just graduated from school. She was barely nineteen years old. That was one of the problems. Another was that she was the daughter of an ennobled Prussian officer, and it was a question which family would take the greater exception—her parents at the prospect of a Jewish son-in-law, albeit a prosperous one, or his own family asked to accept his unconventional marriage to a Christian. Mixed marriages were no longer uncommon, yet it was still a touchy matter, and for the moment neither was ready to break the news at home.

Like thousands of others, Lucy and Ewald wandered the streets all weekend, observing the hectic activity in the city gripped by frantic preparation for war. On the previous day, they were at their favorite café, the Kranzler, when officers in open cars raced by and officially proclaimed a "state of imminent danger of war." Later they had followed excited crowds to the palace where at 6 P.M. the Kaiser appeared on the balcony to announce that Germany's enemies had "thrust the sword into our hand" and that, if war came, the enemy would learn "what it means to attack Germany." The crowd responded with cheers and singing, and even Ewald and Lucy were for the moment swept away by the enthusiasm, though the somber implications of war were certainly not lost on them.[4]

Saturday morning, "extras" announced mobilization in Austria, Russia, and Belgium, while France had put its border guards on high alert. Only one last step remained. Everyone knew that mobilization meant war but Germany had not yet taken the final plunge.

The town was rife with rumors until at midday a complement of guards appeared at Unter den Linden on its way to the palace, flags waving and its band playing stirring marches. The milling crowds, assuming that the critical moment had arrived and released from the tense waiting, again exploded with songs and enthusiastic *Hochs*. As it happened, the soldiers were from Ewald's own Second Guards and he knew that after mobilization he would at once be joining their ranks. He would go, of course, yet to be back with his regiment in a war did not thrill him. In Oranienburg, people were saying that young Jewish men had a double reason to fight—first, for the fatherland, and second, for the Jews, to prove the anti-Semites wrong and to show that they were as loyal and brave as anyone in standing up for country and Kaiser. Ewald didn't disagree, yet risking his life to show up the Jew haters did little to ease the depressing thought of being back in uniform. At least, he consoled Lucy—and himself—it would be a short war. Germany's enemies could not stand a long struggle.

Final certainty came a few hours later. At 5 P.M., staff officers hurried by waving their handkerchiefs, and in front of the palace a gendarme officially announced German mobilization. The Reich had declared war on Russia, and ninety minutes later the Kaiser once more stepped onto his balcony to address a giant crowd clamoring to hear him. "In the impending struggle," he shouted, "I no longer know any parties; I only know Germans." The crowd roared its approval. "Hearts were full," the *Frankfurter Zeitung* reported the next day, "and ecstasy knew no bounds!"[5]

In light of the disastrous and bloody four-year conflict that followed, the exuberance with which the war was greeted in most European capitals is hard to comprehend. In virtually all countries, people cheered as volunteers crowded recruiting stations and soldiers marched off to battle. In Germany there was an especially wild frenzy of excitement, banners were flying, music echoing, and tumultuous crowds celebrated the prospect of certain victory. Frenzied patriotism gripped the nation and lifted spirits to

an emotional high. No one was immune from the intoxication of the moment. Even the writer Arnold Zweig, who dreaded the conflict, would later
confess that "there was a majestic, rapturous, and even seductive something in this first outbreak of the people," and that "in spite of all my hatred
and aversion for war, I should not like to have missed the memory of those
first days."[6]

The Kaiser had called for a *Burgfriede*—a truce to political quarrels and
closing of ranks among all elements in society. He had even held out his
hand to the detested Socialists, and for a moment everyone took him at his
word. Right and left, north and south, Protestants, Catholics, and Jews vied
to show patriotism and cooperation. Strangers embraced in the streets, and
suddenly differences in class and rank no longer seemed to matter. Overnight strikes and lockouts ceased, and the Socialists lined up behind the
war effort. A right-wing newspaper that only a few days earlier had used
thinly veiled anti-Semitic rhetoric to assail Socialist leaders as "those former Galicians, now Germans" abruptly ended its attacks, and the Socialist
parliamentary leader in the Reichstag, who had strenuously argued against
war credits, rose to pledge his full support. The always obstreperous Maximilian Harden announced that "at such an hour, it is everyone's duty to
end all criticism. Now the issue is Power and Fatherland!"[7]

In time, there would be much soul-searching and pondering this initial
ardor for war. No one stopped to ask what the possible price and risks might
be. People only thought in positives, and their image of conflicts was still
fashioned by the memory of nineteenth-century battles—brief struggles
with cavalry charges, banners flying, bugles sounding, and acts of heroism
in a "cleansing bath of steel." Few realized that new technologies would
transform modern battles into a bloody struggle without real winners,
fought with giant cannons, airplanes, tanks, and machine guns, not on
horseback but in the mud and misery of the trenches.

The Kaiser had proclaimed August 5 as a day of prayer for "innocently
attacked Germany." In the synagogues, rabbis asked for God's blessing of
the fatherland and exhorted their congregations to fight harder than anyone for German honor and culture. "Especially we Jews," the *Allgemeine*
commented, "want to show that the blood of heroes pulses through our
veins!"[8] Even the small band of German Zionists who had always argued
Herzl's view that Jews belonged in a country of their own signed a ringing

joint appeal of the national leadership: "German Jews!" it read. "In this hour we must once again show that as 'proud members of our lineage,' we belong among the best of the fatherland's sons. . . . Service to country with all our hearts, souls, and ability is in accord with that special Jewish sense of duty." Jewish student and athletic groups added their own challenge— the young, they said, must give "special proof of Jewish manly strength and martial virtues."[9] Do not wait to be called, they urged, go and volunteer!

More often than most cared to remember, Jewish hopes for equality had been raised, and quickly disappointed. "Past history does not lend itself to optimism but this time we can truly hope that it will be different," the CV wrote in a September editorial. "Wartime unity," the article concluded, at last is "that liberating force that will create equality for all—hopefully forever!"[10]

2

No war plan was ever more carefully honed in all its details than the German High Command's long-standing Schlieffen Plan for defeating France and Russia in a one-two punch based on surprise and overwhelming force. None ever went awry as quickly and totally as this one.

Stage one involved a quick blitzkrieg in the West, with a lightning thrust through Belgium to envelop Paris from the north and force the French to their knees in eight weeks or less. Weaker Russia was to be held at bay by Austria and limited German forces, to be easily defeated in stage two of a short and decisive war. "Home before the leaves fall," as the Kaiser had pledged, was not to be an idle promise.

At first, all seemed to be going according to plan. When Ewald reported to Company Seven, Second Battalion of his guards regiment, he was one of millions of reservists carrying a card with detailed instructions on what to do, where to go, and how to get there within twenty-four hours of the order to mobilize. When, scarcely a week later, his fully equipped unit boarded a troop train at Berlin's Charlottenburg Station to join Colonel-General von Bülow's Second Army in Belgium, his was one of 11,100 transports moving some three million men and 860,000 horses to the western front at record speed.

Three days later, still seemingly on plan, and with the roar of cannons from besieged Liège in the distance, Ewald's regiment was advancing on forced marches deep inside Belgium. Though the men were tired and foot-sore in the intense summer heat, their spirits were high. On August 22, Seventh Company registered its first casualty—a bicycle messenger car-rying the order to engage the enemy retreating at Namur. From the next day forward, they were engaged in an almost continuous series of bloodly battles with determined French defenders, and before long the vicious fighting and heavy losses had sobered their early exuberance. All along the front, progress slowed to a crawl, and by the time Ewald's unit had fought its way across the Marne and reached Epernay on September 1, less than a hundred miles from Paris, there were no reserves left of either energies or supplies—just as the French launched a furious counterattack through a gap in the German lines. Less than a week later, after murderous hand-to-hand fighting, Ewald was among what was left of his unit staggering back across the Marne to seek cover in hastily dug trenches near Reims.[11]

In less than three weeks, the regiment had lost more than three thou-sand officers and men. Fighting desperately to hold on while waiting for badly needed replacements, there was no longer talk of an early victory celebration in Paris and not much evidence of a superior German fighting spirit. In a clear, albeit understated departure from his earlier confident en-thusiasm, the regimental scribe—noting general exhaustion and a lack of bread—observed drily that "by virtue of losses, compounded by heat, mud, and rain, the troops have lost some of their freshness."[12]

Something had gone dreadfully wrong. Everywhere on the western front the German advance had first been slowed and then halted. The Schlieffen Plan had failed, and the confidence of the German military was badly shaken. The German High Command's detailed plans had proved inflex-ible when faced by unforeseeable contingencies of actual modern combat. Coordination was poor, supplies failed to arrive in time, the Belgians fought longer and inflicted heavier losses than expected, and the French had not crumbled under the initial onslaught. Worse yet, no one had counted on England's quick entry into the war, and the Austrians proved too weak to hold back a surprisingly strong Russian attack. In September, two German army corps suddenly had to be shifted east to avoid disaster in Galicia and East Prussia.

Losses in men and materials in the early weeks of fighting had been extraordinarily heavy, yet this was only a foretaste of things to come. The dream of German superiority and quick victories was over, replaced by the reality of a two-front war in the trenches with four years of bloodletting ahead for the soldiers, and hardship and deprivation at home.

In the early weeks, morale on the home front could not have been higher. Everywhere there were promises of unity, sacrifice, and cooperation. From one day to the next, as if by magic, all anti-Jewish attacks ceased, and even extreme anti-Semites were not heard from. German Jewry was elated; finally their moment had come, and Jewish eagerness to show devotion to the fatherland knew no limits.

Jews were in the forefront of those subscribing to war loans and in glorifying Germany's righteous cause. A Jew named Ernst Lissauer, carried away by the enthusiasm of the moment, composed a "Song of Hate against England" that was so popular that the Kaiser decorated him forthwith with the Order of the Black Eagle. From the battlefront there was no end of glowing reports of Jewish heroism and sacrifice. A young Jew named Eugen Schleyer, not yet fifteen years old, talked his way into a Königsberg regiment and participated in the capture of five hundred Russians.[13] In Bavaria, a certain Paul Spiegel volunteered at the age of sixty-two, and Ludwig Stern, an elderly veteran of the 1870 war, insisted on rejoining his old regiment, though the exertion led to a heart attack before he saw actual fighting. When Ludwig Frank, a prominent Jewish member of the Reichstag, volunteered and was among the first August casualties, his final letter from the front was widely admired in Jewish circles: "I go as all others—full of joy and certain of victory . . . glad to let my blood flow for the fatherland." Another Jewish volunteer tersely noted in his diary just before being killed in battle: "to die for hundreds—magnificent!"[14]

In Oranienburg, Town Councillor Martin Blumenthal, having sent his eldest son off to war, stepped forward to help organize a local war relief committee for needy families, and when the first Red Cross drive got under way he led the town's Jews with generous contributions.[15]

Gradually, however, as the fierce fighting continued, casualty lists lengthened and shortages at home multiplied. Within months, the public mood had sobered, and the reality of a long war began to intrude on people's lives. First it had been merely price controls on flour and salt and the inevitable shortages that followed. Then, step by step, food grew scarcer, there was more rationing, prices rose, and lines at foodstores lengthened. Grumbling increased and spirits grew truculent and bitter. Who was to blame for their losses and deprivation, Germans were asking?

Perhaps the Jews should have anticipated that with setbacks and disappointments, it would be they who were blamed. Yet during the early weeks' enthusiasm, few of them had thought to acknowledge that possibility, and even now they still clung to the *Burgfriede,* protesting to the authorities when the first voices blaming them for Germany's problems were being heard. At first any renewal of anti-Semitic attacks was vigorously censored, but gradually the traditional Jew haters grew more active, officialdom was less inclined to impede them, and a widening segment of the disillusioned public was willing to listen.

The war had turned sour, and once again the Jews were the scapegoats, a convenient lightning rod to divert public discontent from those responsible for the unfolding disaster. To their acute distress, all their efforts and sacrifices failed to satisfy their enemies. When, at the end of 1914, it was reported that 710 Iron Crosses had already been earned by Jewish soldiers and that several dozen had won battlefield promotions to officer rank, the censor quickly squelched scattered efforts to belittle the Jewish contribution. Eighteen months later, when close to seven thousand such decorations had been awarded and almost three thousand Jews had died at the front, the anti-Semitic press was less inhibited. There were twice as many medals for Jews as battlefield deaths, they jeered, while for others the proportions were exactly reversed. That was proof, according to one of the Pan-German organizations, that Jews were in control behind the front and used their influence to win undeserved honors.[16]

Two principal anti-Jewish claims now circulating were widely believed. One was that Jews were cowards and avoided service in the trenches. The other was that they were war profiteers benefiting from artificially engineered shortages.

It was the military and the bureaucracy who had failed at the front and in not preparing for a longer war. Yet, rather than take responsibility, they welcomed holding up the Jews as the guilty ones. When war broke out, Walther Rathenau, son of the founder of the giant electrical company AEG, was among the first to criticize the lack of planning for a war economy. When his concerns proved justified, it led to his appointment as head of a

War Raw Materials Board, where he organized separate public companies for coordinating war production and the flow of supplies to the front and for home consumption. The Jewish Rathenau was a fiercely loyal German nationalist who rendered a vital service with his organizational skills. The military backed him strongly, even insisting that men with skills needed to staff his efforts be ordered back from the front. Some were Jews, though not many, and at home Jewish businessmen, academics, and scientists joined in volunteering for Rathenau's organization, with about 10 percent of the staff Jewish and a few in visible positions of leadership.

During 1916, a British naval blockade tightened the noose around the Reich, living conditions worsened, and more Germans went hungry. Rathenau continued his strenuous efforts, yet for anti-Semites the widening misery was fertile ground for singling out his supply organization for their attacks. Jews, they claimed, were hiding under Rathenau to escape front-line service, and they were responsible for the general suffering. Other right-wing conservatives joined in to further their own political agenda. They feared that Reich Chancellor Bethmann-Hollweg favored a negoti-ated peace and that after an indecisive or lost war their traditional privi-leges were at risk. To turn public sentiment against him, they eagerly played the anti-Jewish card by calling him "Chancellor of the Jews," and suggest-ing that it was Jews such as Rathenau—more interested in commercial gain than German honor—who controlled him.

Under the pressure of a long war, the old anti-Semitism was back stronger than ever, though isolated reports of Jews accused of price-gouging and profiteering had appeared almost at once. By the end of 1914, one Jewish paper ran a regular column it called "War Anti-Semitism," to record such incidents. In one report, schools were still refusing to hire Jews as replacements for departing reservist teachers; in another, Jews were be-ing branded as foreign spies,[17] and there were stories of wounded Jewish war veterans being accused of cowardice while on home leave. If they wore Iron Crosses, it was said, they had probably bought them.[18]

There was dismay and a sense of panic and helplessness in the Jewish community. The Zionists argued that they had been right all along: anti-Semitism was permanent, and there was no hope for Jews without a country of their own. At the opposite end of the spectrum, the fiercest as-similationists urged yet greater sacrifices and proof of patriotism. Most others simply remained silent—saying little, suffering the insults, looking away, and hoping for better times.

By July 1, 1916, Ewald had been at the front for two years. The year before, on the afternoon of March 13, 1915, he had been among those to whom the Kaiser personally distributed Iron Crosses after bloody fighting in the Champagne. Now, the Allies were launching a major effort to break through German lines at the Somme, and once again Seventh Company was ordered into the trenches at Maurepas-Cléry to help hold them off. On the opening day of the campaign, a quarter million shells were fired by the attackers in the first hour, massed machine guns mowed them down, giant cannons chewed up the earth, and for four months thereafter, the daily struggle for small bits of territory continued. When it ended in October, 165,000 Germans had died, and the Anglo-French attackers had lost 146,000, but nothing decisive had been accomplished by either side in what Rathenau, in his diary, called that "dance of death."[19]

For soldiers on both sides, mere survival was now all that counted. Boredom and fear had replaced the taste for battle, and apathy about home politics was common. When Ewald had heard that, at age forty-four, his uncle Arthur had volunteered, it seemed incomprehensible to him—whatever the arguments for a special Jewish effort. On learning that Arthur had been sent home from Alsace with a lung ailment a year later, Ewald's reaction was envy at his uncle's good fortune.

There were a number of Jews in his unit, but apart from the occasional crude joke there was little direct anti-Semitism in the trenches, where common dangers were faced, and Jewish soldiers bled and died like Christians. Victor Cohen, the battalion's Jewish field surgeon, was widely admired, and when his assistant, the Jew Sally Beer, fell in battle, there was genuine grief among all.

Thus, when at the end of October 1916 Ewald's unit received the order from higher headquarters to conduct a special census of Jewish soldiers at the front to uncover statistical evidence on possible shirkers, it was greeted with embarrassment by his superiors, and with a mixture of outrage and resignation by the Jewish troops. The irony of the insult was galling, to say the least. Each day they faced death, yet still they remained "special." Most took the news stoically, though some wrote home to protest the affront. Yet the authorities had ordered them counted and that is what happened everywhere in the German armed forces on the prescribed day.

If any further proof of the deterioration of the Jewish position was needed, this *Judenzählung*—the counting of Jews at the front—was the clearest and most worrisome evidence that the war had raised German anti-Semitic sentiments to a new high. The War Minister was plain enough in promulgating the decree:

> The War Ministry is continually receiving complaints from the population that large numbers of men of the Israelite faith who are fit for military service are either exempt from military duties or are evading their obligation to serve. . . .
>
> In order to examine these complaints and, should they prove unwarranted, to be able to refute them, the War Ministry respectfully requests that the pertinent information be supplied in accordance with the two attached forms.[20]

While Jewish soldiers in the field reacted bitterly or with quiet fatalism, the dismay of Jews at home could not have been greater. Jewish leaders protested that the order was a vile, officially sanctioned defamation. Accusations against Jews as crooks and war usurers were bad enough, but now even their soldiers were insulted and singled out, in spite of the thousands who had already given their lives.

No protests mattered; the census went forward. On November 1, 1916, Second Battalion counted its Jews, and Ewald, the other Jewish soldiers, and Dr. Victor Cohen were duly recorded as serving at the front. One month later, the field surgeon was killed on the battlefield. In the official history it was recorded that the regiment "owes much to his devotion."[21]

Then came the winter of 1916–17, the hardest war winter yet and one Germans would long remember as their "winter of turnips." Plagued by poor harvests, grain prices escalated. Bread and even potatoes were in short supply. Without coal, school children stayed at home to scrounge for fuel, public bathing facilities closed, and in Berlin the street lamps remained unlit. The next year brought more bad news—failure of German submarine warfare, peace feelers coming to naught, and worst of all, America's entry into the war. Peace with Russia temporarily raised hopes, yet the blood-letting and the stalemate in the west continued.

Meanwhile, domestic political divisions deepened. War weariness was spreading, and the center and left looked for ways to bring the fighting to an honorable end. On the right, the "bitter enders"—seeing their hopes for territorial gains dissolving and in fear for their privileges—responded with shrill accusations against peace advocates, whom they called weak-bellied defeatists and traitors. Their noisy campaign against Jews as the true culprits scheming to sell Germany escalated, and more converts among an embittered public joined their cause.

Once again, Germany's Jews had been mistaken in their hope. The roots of German anti-Semitism had proved deeper and stronger than anyone had understood. The war had heightened anti-Jewish feeling and neither time nor accomplishments nor contributions to German life had changed anything. In peacetime, their rapid rise to prominence in business, the professions, and German cultural life had caused unexpected new resentments. In war, their greater role in political and public life made them more visible targets for blame. The hope that their Christian countrymen would finally accord them an equal place had once more proved an illusion.

3

On the morning of November 9, 1918, Field Marshall Paul von Hindenburg; General Wilhelm Gröner, the Chief of the General Staff; and several advisers met the Kaiser in his conference room at the Villa Franeuse in the Belgian resort town of Spa to tell him that the troops would no longer follow him and that his abdication was unavoidable.

The historic scene was grim and tense. Hindenburg was in a state of high emotion, and on the way to the Kaiser he had several times broken down in tears. Unable to speak when finally in the monarch's presence, it was left to General Gröner to convey their baleful message. The war was lost, sailors had mutinied in Kiel, the country was on the brink of revolt, and with the impending armistice a change of political regimes was unavoidable. The specter of a Russian-style revolution hung over Germany. The Kaiser must go at once so the soldiers could return home to save the country from Bolshevism. There was no other way out.

One day later, William II crossed the Belgian-Dutch frontier at Eysen and handed a stunned border guard his sword.[22] The third and last Kaiser of the Second German Reich was gone, and with it the Hohenzollern dynasty. Defeated and exhausted, Germany was at the mercy of her enemies. At II A.M., her representatives signed an unconditional surrender in the woods near Compiègne. At noon, all along the western front, the guns fell silent.

For months, the writing had been on the wall. The great German spring and summer offensives at the Somme and Aisne rivers had collapsed with huge losses on both sides. Then, on August 8, the forces of the Entente, reinforced by fresh American troops, counterattacked and went on the offensive, forcing the Kaiser's troops to retreat all along the front. The Triple Alliance was in a state of collapse with Turkey and Bulgaria finished and Austria's army in disarray. In September, Hindenburg and Ludendorff finally conceded defeat and frantically urged an immediate armistice.

Until the bitter end, the Kaiser remained incapable of facing the full reality of the disaster and the hopelessness of his own situation. Almost from the first day of the war, in fact, the pressures of the conflict had revealed his weak and unstable character and his concern more with his own image than with steadfastness and leadership. When the first shots were fired, he had stood tall as the Supreme War Lord of a united people, but within weeks, as the Russians advanced in East Prussia, he became despondent and accused his staff of shunning him with unspoken blame.[23] With the war dragging on, his mood swings worsened. After each success he prophesied imminent victory; each setback threw him into despair. Incapable of crisp decisions or coherent action, he lost all relevance at the top of the chain of command and Hindenburg had long since been forced to step in to fill the void.

As for his people, they no longer cared about their Kaiser. For many he had long since become a somewhat ridiculous and pathetic figure. Coping with daily living took up all their energies and except for supernationalist extremists, most wanted nothing so much as an end to the war. Yet when it did come, they were as unprepared for the totality of the defeat and humiliation, and for the chaos and turmoil that followed, as the Kaiser had been for his own downfall.

In Oranienburg, as everywhere else, there was increasing war weariness throughout 1918. Longer than he cared to remember, Martin Blumenthal and the rest of the town's food-rationing committee had been obliged to sign a steady stream of bad-news announcements. Everything was in short supply, and prices were constantly on the rise. With most barbers in uniform, it had even been necessary to fix the maximum price for a shave.

That there were no traditional "Berliner" doughnuts, a sacred requirement for New Year's Day, was bad enough. The news, on January 27, of a reduction in the weekly meat ration to 250 grams along with new restrictions on jam and cheese was much worse. The announcement that there was virtually no milk and that mothers were to feed their babies a semolina gruel instead had been the worst blow and nearly caused a riot.

With the outlook so bleak, tempers were short and allegations of black-marketeering were reaching alarming proportions. For several months on end, nothing had worried Martin more than the flood of nasty complaints that the local mill's flour was virtually inedible while quality product was being sold under the table at sky-high prices. Investigation proved the rumor false, yet the local supplier in question was always cited as "Cohn's Mill," and even in normally calm Oranienburg, such stories were fuel for grumbling about alleged Jewish war cheats. Reports of arrests for profiteering—whenever the alleged culprit was a Jew—simply reinforced the Judeophobes' tendency to blame Jews for everything.

Worse even than the deprivations of daily living, the horrible losses at the front had affected more and more families. Casualty lists had grown frequent and long. At the war's beginning, Oranienburg had often been spared for weeks, but now there were constant reports of losses. On June 9, while the local paper triumphantly reported that the enemy's attacks in France had been repulsed with heavy losses, Casualty List No. 1157 showed that the price had been heavy.[24] A record twenty locals were listed as dead, wounded, or missing, and this time the Blumenthals had not been spared either. Though Ewald was on temporary duty in Berlin and out of harm's way, Hellmuth, his younger brother, had entered the army in January and reached the front in the spring. Reported in the latest list as heavily wounded with his right leg amputated, he now lay near death in a field hospital somewhere in France. For Ida and Martin the blow was heavy.

It was high time for the war to end. Germany had lost 1.8 million dead and had over 4 million wounded. Ever since early October, when Prince Max von Baden had taken over as Chancellor, it was clear that the horrible carnage must stop. Most people hoped for it fervently, yet few understood how total the defeat would be when it came. All were ready for disappointments, yet until virtually the day the armistice was signed, the news from the front had been mixed, reports of victories and enemy failures had continued, and no one expected a military disaster.

Suddenly it was all over, but the collapse and confusion that followed was shocking. Germany was left sick and deeply split politically. The monarchy and its supporters were discredited. Rival factions on the left and right were vying for power. There was chaos everywhere.

4

The Kaiser was gone, his champions were in disfavor, and the bloodiest conflict in European history was over. Millions of German soldiers had been lost or maimed, and another three-quarter million civilians had died of starvation. More than fifty billion marks had been spent on the fighting but in human terms the cost of the war was incalculable.

On November 9, at three o'clock in the afternoon—even before the Kaiser had crossed the Dutch border—the Social Democratic leader Philipp Scheidemann hurried to the balcony of the Berlin Reichstag to proclaim Germany's first republic. He was attempting to forestall a rival group of Communists and dissident leftists—the Spartacists—who, virtually at the same time, appeared on the balcony of the nearby *Schloss* to announce a "Free Socialist Republic" of their own. Meanwhile, in Munich, leftist idealists were establishing a Soviet-style people's government of councils, the "*Räte*" republic. To add to the confusion, a forty-three-year old Catholic mayor of Cologne named Konrad Adenauer was calling for a Rhineland state, independent of Berlin. Other provinces and cities were in equal turmoil, and in the capital there were constant clashes and streetfighting between competing political factions vying to fill the vacuum left by the fleeing Kaiser.

The typical German citizen, however, had more pressing preoccupations. Under the terms of the armistice, the Allied blockade continued, and hunger and starvation were worse than ever. Agriculture was at a virtual standstill, the livestock was totally depleted, there was no feed for the animals, and no horses to pull the plows. Millions of soldiers were returning home and had to be fed.

Adding to the overall misery, a disastrous outbreak of the Spanish flu had swept Europe and reached pandemic proportions just as the fighting ended. In Britain, 150,000 fell victim to the illness, in Budapest 100,000 succumbed, and it was the same in Paris and Vienna. More American soldiers died from influenza than were killed in battle—20,000 in two months alone[25]—while in Germany the general undernourishment greatly exacerbated the effects of the scourge. By mid-October, 25,000 cases were recorded in Munich, and in Breslau some 15,000 had already died. In Hamburg, the telephones stopped functioning for lack of operators, and in Berlin 3,000 new cases were being recorded in a single day.[26]

For weeks the pain and the political turmoil continued, but gradually the fledgling November republic, defended by remnants of the military, gained the upper hand. The Spartacists were defeated after bloody fighting and the brutal murder of their leaders by street gangs led by rightist former officers—the Free Corps—who feared and hated them. In Munich, the *Räte* republic and its leaders suffered a similar fate. Finally, in the summer of 1919, a national assembly of elected representatives adopted Germany's first democratic constitution, chosing Friedrich Ebert, a former saddle maker and leader of the Social Democrats, as President.

Berlin, the heart of Hohenzollern Germany and Prussian militarism, was neither particularly safe that spring nor an appropriate meeting place to turn over a page in German history and create something entirely new— a true parliamentary democracy. Weimar, on the other hand, the city of Goethe and of poets, philosophers, and humanists, held the right kind of symbolism. Hence it was there that the meetings were held and the constitution adopted.

It was not an auspicious beginning for the fledgling Weimar Republic, and the first years were the most difficult. The economic situation was terrible, and the country was divided and shaken by abortive revolts and political assassinations. Without a tradition of parliamentary rule, the new government lacked experience to deal with enormous economic and political pressures and was sorely tried to maintain itself against enemies on the left and right. On one side were the Communists and Independent Socialists, the latter a dissident group of Marxists who wanted a true proletarian revolution and bitterly opposed the pragmatism of the majority Social Democrats, who were more interested in trade unions, wages, and social benefits than ideological purity. At the other extreme stood the rightist reactionaries of the *Kaiserreich* who refused to acknowledge that anything had fundamentally changed, loathed the new republic, considered it merely a short interlude, and plotted incessantly to bring it down. Between them, fishing in troubled waters, were any number of ex-officers, disappointed nationalists, malcontents, unemployed cranks, and adventurers scheming against those in power.

The greatest burden, however, was the intransigence of the victors. Brushing aside all appeals for understanding and reason, they summoned the republic's representatives to Versailles in June 1919 and forced them to sign the draft of a calamitous treaty destined to cause enormous economic and political damage in Germany—and to sow the seeds for an even greater world war two decades hence. To the French, the treaty was revenge for their own humiliation at Versailles a half century earlier. In Germany, it was deeply resented as the Versailles *Diktat,* and it critically undermined Weimar's effective functioning and ultimately its survival.

The harsh territorial losses and the crushing burden of reparations imposed on Germany were bad enough. Psychologically, Allied insistence on the fateful Article 231, in which Germany had to admit its sole responsibility as instigator of the war, was even worse. For years the German people had been told of their encirclement and of being unfairly attacked. Unprepared for total defeat and convinced that all parties had contributed to the disaster, they felt their dignity and honor offended by Article 231. Nothing served better to fuel national outrage, fan the flames of resentment and hate, and win recruits for Weimar's opponents on the right than the battle-cries of "November criminals" and "Versailles traitors" leveled constantly at those who, under the threat of military occupation and worse, had assumed the heavy burden of signing the treaty.

Always there were the believers—liberals, centrists, and moderate conservatives—who remained dedicated to Germany's first experience with parliamentary democracy. They worked earnestly and hard, and that they survived the early years and prevailed as long as they did is in itself a miracle. Equally remarkable is that in the midst of the constant political and economic pressures, the Weimar years also saw the flowering of an extraordinarily vibrant and creative cultural life.

It was as if the end of the war and the demise of the Wilhelmine era had released long-suppressed energies and a hunger for artistic experimentation and expression. There was a pervasive sense that the past had been an abomination, the present was insane, and the future uncertain or hopeless. Simple everyday existence was a struggle, yet these very sentiments stimulated feverish activity and the desire to live with abandon, to taste life to the fullest and to reject the old for the unconventional and the new. Strangely, for painters, composers, architects, writers, and poets the most difficult years between 1919 and 1923 were also the most productive.

Berlin was the center of this new Weimar culture, and almost overnight the capital became the mecca for kindred souls from all over the world. The stage was alive with new offerings of every kind, from Erwin Piscator's "Proletarian Theatre" to the new five-thousand-seat Grosse Schauspielhaus, which had opened its doors in 1919. There were sensational silent films by Ernst Lubitsch and Fritz Lang, with Pola Negri and the sultry young Marlene Dietrich the glamorous female leads. In the visual arts it was the expressionist scene and the outpourings of the dadaists ridiculing rationalism and bourgeois values. There was Walter Gropius's revolutionary Bauhaus architecture and the literature of social criticism, such as Heinrich Mann's bestselling novel The Underling, and the antimilitarism of Arnold Zweig, or the expressionist poetry of Else Lasker-Schüler. There were pacifist playwrights, the atonal compositions of Arnold Schönberg, and virtuoso musical performers, notably Fritz Kreisler and Artur Schnabel.

For those from abroad, the German currency was cheap—and getting cheaper by the day—and Berlin's frenzied nightlife was as much a magnet as more serious cultural offerings. Outside, there were constant strikes and a widespread breakdown of law and order. The streets were dark, the houses dilapidated from wartime neglect, and the people hungry, undernourished, and angry. In the midst of all this, the capital appeared to have gone quite mad. George Grosz, the sometime dadaist and expressionist painter who did his best work during those years, called it that "mad, degenerate, fantastic Berlin."[27] Political cabarets proliferated, nightclubs and cellar dives never closed, and the rage was American jazz and nonstop dancing of the tango, foxtrot, and the wild shimmy. Nothing was sacred and moral restraints had vanished. A wave of pornography swept the city and there was free love, girls and boys of easy virtue, garish homosexuals, transvestites, and open consumption of drugs.

The war had robbed people of their illusions. In the nightclubs, Grosz recalled, the dominant attitude was "the war is over and the world is going to hell. '*Je m'en fous.*' Let's live a little!" People drank champagne they couldn't afford, traded gossip and contraband—and stopped just long enough to check the latest exchange rate for the declining mark.

Foreigners flocked to Berlin for the art scene, the fun, and the round-the-clock partying but appearances were deceiving. For Germans, much of the cultural life and all of the frantic celebrating were not so much signs of joie de vivre as of pessimism and despair. It was, as Grosz put it, a negative world enveloped in an outer layer of brightly colored foam, and Berlin's dadaists were its perfect symbol. Their nihilist antics and penchant for tearing down all that had once been sacred came across as a joke, but it was really a cry of pain and despair. The revelers drank and danced because they thought everything was rotten and the world a black hole where nothing mattered.

Postwar Germany was in deep psychological crisis. The cultural scene was vibrant, but Berlin's excesses and modernist culture disgusted the traditionalists, confused the masses, and was fodder for counterrevolutionaries who blamed the leadership of the hated republic for the breakdown in public order, even while busily fomenting more unrest. Most Germans were still in shock over the totality of the military debacle and resented the national humiliation. The political chaos dismayed them, and the loss of the stable and familiar patterns of prewar life was deeply disturbing. Consumed by the daily struggle for bare essentials, people were asking how it had come to this and who was to blame.

At the street corners, there were many answers. The left insisted it was the capitalists, and the right blamed the Communists; some said the fault lay with the *Junker,* others pointed at the military, the politicians, department stores, the Allies, or the godless. But those who preached it was all the fault of the Jews were the most violent haters, the ones who shouted the loudest. The confused postwar climate was proving a fertile environment for the spread of intense anti-Jewish feeling. To the dismay of the Jews, a virulent form of postwar anti-Semitic agitation had emerged and become a permanent and inescapable part of their lives.

5

When Ewald returned to Oranienburg after the war, he found the town somber and the public mood bitter and strained. Sad-faced women in black stood in line outside stores where supplies were scarce and prices high. The streets were drab, electricity and fuel scarce, and people shivered in the winter cold. In shops and pubs, there was angry talk about the economy, political disorder, and the *Diktat* at Versailles. The old neighborliness was missing, and there were bitter arguments about who was responsible for Germany's woes.

Christians and Jews had peacefully coexisted in the town for many years. Overt anti-Jewish agitation was rare, and even under the strains of war, the long-established cordial relations between the two groups were generally preserved. Yet now there was a nervous and less friendly atmosphere that the Jews easily detected.

Some were openly talking about "the Jew" as the cause for their grievances, and others repeated the crude, inflammatory slogans of Germany's newly energized Pan-German Judeophobes and nationalist extremists. Their number was small, but for Oranienburg it was something unaccustomed and it worried and confused the Jews. Some said it was only a passing phase in troubled times, and that the few agitators were best ignored. Others said it was serious and ominous and required a strong response. Ewald, for his part, had a taste of it soon after he returned. As a front-line veteran, he had been warmly greeted at the *Gasthaus* by classmates and old friends. A small group, however, remained distant and cold, and several beers later he heard them noisily discoursing about Jew cowards and usurous bankers. As was his customary reaction to situations of this kind, he pretended not to hear the remarks obviously meant for him, but the experience unnerved him, and now he avoided the place whenever he could.

In reality, though Oranienburg's Jews were on average better off than the rest of the town, they suffered no less than anyone else. Neither Christian nor Jew had been spared by the war and even privileged citizens like his own family had received their share of blows. For one thing, the bank was gravely at risk. Business was down, farmers were in trouble, and borrowers were unable to service their debts. All over Germany, small private banks were failing or being forcibly absorbed, and the bank was barely hanging on.

Financial worries were bad enough, but the calamitous condition of his brother was worse. First Hellmuth's wounds had stubbornly refused to heal. When he finally came home he was in terrible shape, hopelessly addicted to painkilling drugs. Months later, he still lingered in his room and refused to wear his awkward wooden leg. He was always in pain, drug-dependent, demoralized, and unable to lead a normal life.

Ewald counted himself lucky to have come through the war without a scratch, yet he was not untouched by it because days before the fighting ended, his fiancée had become violently ill with the Spanish flu. She was one of thousands of victims in Berlin, where hospitals were full and medical supplies scarce. Like many others, she had little resistance to the high fever, and less than a week after falling ill, Lucy had died a miserable death.

Throughout the long years of the war, they had hoped to marry once peace was restored and their families had become reconciled to the unorthodox match. Her death was a heavy blow and the first serious personal setback Ewald ever faced. He belonged to the generation that reached adulthood in the comfortable, placid years before the war—"the good times," many Jews called them. His parents prospered, life was orderly, and anti-Semitism was low. The town's generally harmonious Christian-Jewish relations and his family's privileged status had largely insulated him from exposure to serious anti-Jewish tensions and prejudice. Whatever barriers there were against Jews, he had accepted as inevitable relics of a less enlightened time. No one in his circle had ever been exposed to pogroms or direct physical violence. To Ewald, such excesses were unfortunate outbreaks restricted to the big-city *Ostjuden* quarters of the very poor, or to less cultured and primitive countries elsewhere.

His values were those of his parents with their deep German roots, and his dual self-image was that of the majority of better-educated and well-established Jews. First and foremost, Ewald considered himself a loyal and patriotic German. He loved his country, respected its institutions, and felt special pride for its culture. What mattered to him was not so much his Jewish roots but his identity as a member of the German *Volk* (people). Divorced from his religion and indifferent to Jewish traditions, he acknowledged his Jewish extraction as nothing more than a secondary historical fact and an inconvenience to be played down. He avoided membership in Jewish organizations and shunned anti-Semitic unpleasantness and provocations. Where he encountered prejudice, he endured it with resignation and minimized its significance. What he cared for was a solid business and

pursuing the good life. In his political views he was a moderate. Radicalism—in any form—was not in his nature.

Like many Germans, Ewald remembered the Kaiser's Reich with nostalgia and shared the interest and respect of the bourgeoisie for royalty and
the upper classes—while taking it as a given that it was a strongly elitist
and exclusive society, and that its barriers and social reservations against
Jews were regrettable and unfair. Yet like most Jews, he welcomed the new
constitution with its promise of complete equality, and he favored the ruling coalition of moderates and their commitment to parliamentary democracy and universal suffrage.

The postwar wave of anti-Jewish extremism of the Pan-Germans worried
and repelled him. He feared their crude rhetoric, resented their wild accusations of Jewish cowardice, and shuddered at their distorted labeling of Weimar as the "Jew Republic." He hated their distorted image of "the Jew,"
which equated assimilated, long-standing Germans like him with the *Ostjuden* who had recently come to Germany as war workers or refugees from
eastern pogroms. He had first encountered these unassimilated coreligionists as a soldier during the Galician campaign, and they had struck him as
alien, uncultured, and vaguely distasteful. To be sure, he was sorry for their
plight, but he felt little affinity for them. Their unattractive Yiddish patois,
their distinctive medieval dress, and their un-German ways estranged him,
and he worried that they were one reason why anti-Semitism was on the
rise. If they were poor, they needed help, yet he agreed with those of his
Jewish friends who argued that it was surely in everyone's interest to limit
their influx, lest their presence poison the climate for all.

The change of atmosphere in his town was in fact only a weak echo of
the wave of anti-Jewish feeling sweeping the country. Within a month after
the armistice, the CV had noted with alarm that "in Germany, the wind of
pogroms is in the air."[28] Jews had become everyone's favorite scapegoats for
the collapse—beginning with the Kaiser, who had railed about losing his
throne "because of 100 Jews and 1,000 workers."[29] The Pan-Germans had
led the parade, and in February of 1919 organized a "German-Völkisch
League for Defense and Defiance" to promote "the moral rebirth of the
unique German Volk," which, they announced, required "eliminating re-
pressive, corrosive Jewish influence." The league's membership grew steadily, eventually reaching some 30,000–40,000 members, with several thou-

sand joining in Berlin within the first two years. In a single year, they boasted of having distributed 7.6 million flyers and as many pamphlets and propaganda stamps to educate the German public to the Jewish danger.[30]

The league was merely the largest and best known among many groups, parties, and political movements opposed to the republic or fighting to restore the prewar status quo. Many were small, poorly organized, and internally divided, yet all resorted to anti-Semitic rhetoric to win converts to their side. Antirepublican and openly anti-Semitic generals, such as the unscrupulous former Chief of Staff Erich Ludendorff, were anxious to shift the blame for military failures and joined those who accused Jews of having stabbed the troops in the back and stirred up defeatism and revolt at home. Supernationalist students and their professors, opposed to democracy and resentful of Jewish competition in academia and the professions, made common cause with the military and denounced Jews as "November criminals" and "Versailles traitors." And everywhere racial ideologues reappeared with warnings about the mongrelization of German blood, quoting Houston Chamberlain, Richard Wagner, and the gamut of prewar racist literature including the spurious but widely believed "Protocols of the Elders of Zion," a crude forgery alleging a Jewish conspiracy to dominate the world.

The capital was the center for much of the agitation, but Munich, where the leftist *Räte* republic had briefly ruled before being overthrown, was another hotbed for all sorts of obscure clubs and parties advocating a fight to the finish against Weimar and the Jews. One group of rightist racist conspirators called itself the Thule Society, admitted only members "of Aryan blood," and urged that the hated *Ostjuden* be put into concentration camps or, better yet, driven out with whips.[31] Their members included a young Rudolf Hess; Alfred Rosenberg, a Baltic-German student with fanatical racist views; and an ambitious anti-Semitic lawyer named Hans Frank. Among others, they maintained contacts with an ex-lieutenant and former schoolteacher, Julius Streicher, an avid student of the writings of Mehring and Dürr with his own minuscule party specialized in violent anti-Jewish rhetoric laced with pornographic images. Another tiny group called itself the German Workers Party (DAP) and met intermittently in the cellar of a rundown restaurant to give vent to their hatred of Weimar and alleged Jewish misdeeds. An obscure corporal named Adolf Hitler was a recent addition to their ranks, practicing his oratory and urging more active public agitation while maneuvering to assume leadership of the group.

Hitler had wept over Germany's defeat as "the greatest villainy of the century."[32] He was already a confirmed anti-Semite and the war had fortified his view of Jews as a polluted race devoid of a capacity to strive for "higher things" except money and power. Later, elevated as the party's leader, or Führer, he would change its name to National Socialist German Workers Party (NSDAP), the Nazis; push through a twenty-five-point program, including the demand for removing all Jews from German public life; and organize "storm troopers" to battle opponents in the streets. For the moment, however, Hitler's party and the Thule group remained local phenomena unknown outside their narrow Munich orbit.

For the Jewish leadership, there was no escaping the shocking reality that, for the first time in German history, anti-Semitism in its worst forms had become an integral part of its politics. "Reaction is in full swing,"[33] one of their papers warned at the end of 1919, yet in casting around for an effective response, there was wide disagreement on what should be done. Veterans were especially dismayed at the persistent charges of Jewish cowardice and shirking in the war. Almost one hundred thousand Jews had served, two-thirds of them at the front, twelve thousand had died in battle, and many more had won battlefield decorations and promotions. Yet one of the *Völkisch* propagandists had leaked statistics claimed to be the unpublished results of the infamous 1916 soldier's census and purporting to prove that only a small number of Jews had actually been active at the front.[34]

With their honor at stake, a few Jewish ex-soldiers were determined to react to these charges, and in 1919 they founded their own organization, the League of Jewish Front Soldiers (the RJF), to set the record straight, pay homage to those who had died, and stand ready to defend Jewish areas threatened by mob attack. Ewald found it prudent to wear his Iron Cross ribbon when visiting Berlin, yet the RJF was the subject of heated controversy among his friends, and he declined to join it. An instinctive assimilationist, he had little taste for a strictly Jewish organization, even if he approved of its purpose. His uncle Arthur and he agreed that it risked underlining rather than bridging the gulf between Christians and Jews, and that in the present heated political climate too prominent a political Jewish presence might be provocative. Their viewpoint was shared by many, and

the RJF's active members remained limited. In Berlin it took two years before one thousand veterans had enrolled.[35]

It was hard to know what to do in these troubled times and Hindenburg's
official blessing of the "stab in the back" legend with its anti-Jewish overtones left even Ewald impatient and angry. For years he had fought in the
trenches, many Jewish comrades were dead, and his brother lay shattered
at home. It was the generals who had been enthusiastic about war, caused
untold suffering, presided over the military defeat, and urged an immediate armistice when the front was about to collapse. Now these same men
were rewriting history, inverting cause and effect, and denying their responsibility by blaming the Jews' defeatism at home.

What an irony, Ewald thought, that after so much bloodshed, the public
was still filled with adulation and awe for Hindenburg, their hero. When
he was called to testify before a committee of the National Assembly on
November 18, 1919, large crowds had cheered him along the way, chrysan-
themums and ribbons with the imperial colors decorated his witness chair,
and when he repeated the claim of a stab in the back and spoke of "failure
and weakness" (behind the front) and an "undefeated army," he was loudly
applauded. The fact that the committee challenged him with contrary evidence and that two of its members were Jews only hardened the lines.
Ewald was one of many Jews who winced when the *Völkisch* press jeered
the "Jew Committee" conducting a "Jew inquisition," and expressed outrage that members with names like Cohn and Sinzheimer would dare to
question the integrity of so hallowed a German hero.

6

Germany continued in crisis. In March 1920 a conspiracy of military officers and rightists mounted the first serious counterrevolutionary challenge
against the republic. For a while, the danger seemed real, and the government fled the capital, but the takeover attempt, led by a Pan-German
named Wolfgang Kapp, was amateurish and poorly conceived. Even the
bureaucrats joined the workers in a general strike, the Kapp Putsch collapsed, and the government returned to Berlin. The Jews were greatly relieved, but the domestic turmoil continued and the Allies' enormous reparations demands weighed heavily on the public and the republic's

harassed guardians. In the streets there were protest marches and fighting so bitter that in a single bloody incident, forty-two workers lost their lives outside the Reichstag.

In the summer, the situation destabilized further when left and right radicals swept to victory in the Reichstag at the expense of the SPD-led coalition of moderates. Thereafter, one weak government precariously allied with either the left or right followed the next, in a climate of instability and the progressive polarization of political forces.

The voters were abandoning the middle. Hurt by inflation, angry at Allied intransigence, and repelled by immorality and confusion in the cities, more bourgeois voters were lining up with supernationalists, archconservatives, and rebellious students against the republic. At the opposite end of the spectrum, the working classes suffered from the poor economy and rising prices and turned from the moderate Social Democrats to the more radical Socialists and Communists.

For the Jews these were dangerous developments, leaving them isolated in the middle, with no place to go and faced with an uncomfortable and paradoxical dilemma. The war had propelled them into positions of greater prominence in German life, opening many previously closed doors. The Weimar constitution confirmed and codified their rights, and for the first time all official discrimination against them had ended. The bureaucracy was open to them, and some were winning regular university appointments. There were many leading Jews in cultural affairs and in the media, business, and the professions. A few occupied high positions in government and political life. As many as one-third of all Jews were still poor, but the majority was solidly middle-class and their economic situation was above the average for all German citizens. In absolute numbers, moreover, open anti-Semites were a minority. Most voters did not support them. The majority parties disavowed the hate campaigns, and some prominent Christians regularly spoke out against them.

Yet the anti-Semites were growing in number and had never been more vocal. Ironically, it was precisely the more visible, equal, and prominent role of the Jews that enabled Judeophobes to exaggerate the extent of Jewish influence, and to hold up "the Jew" as symbol of a threatening modernity and of the problems of a parliamentary democracy many Germans disliked.

It was especially ominous that in the climate of adversity the worst racial

anti-Semites could make common cause with those motivated by economic distress and envy or religious prejudices, and win additional adherents by capitalizing on long-standing social prejudices. Split among
themselves, these disparate groups had at least one thing in common: their
willingness to blame "the Jew" for the war's outcome and for Weimar's ills.
The litany of their complaints was long and demeaning. During the war,
they argued, "the Jew" had been a disloyal coward and profited financially,
and his machinations had helped "stab the military in the back." The supernationalists said it was Jewish influence that had caused Germany's signing
of a dishonorable peace. Those who hated the new constitution polem-
icized that Weimar was a *Judenrepublik,* in which Jews were pulling all the
strings. The racists, meanwhile, never tired of asserting that evil and betrayal were innate to the Jew, and that it was in his nature to spread a decadent culture, pollute German blood, and seduce the German soul.

That their enemies painted an image of "the Jew" as a leftist revolutionary out to undermine and destabilize traditional German life was especially
ironic. In fact, the opposite was true. Three-quarters of Germany's Jews
were, like Ewald and Arthur, bankers, businessmen, and middle-class professionals, whose every instinct and interest drew them to the moderate
center. The last thing they wanted was to stand out as provocateurs. They
prospered in a climate of stability; extremism frightened them.

Yet the Jewish minority was never a homogeneous group. While most
were moderate liberals, there were always some overcompensating supernationalists who stood as far to the right as possible, and others who sym-
pathized with the radicalism of the left. The fact that there were Jews, long
the subjects of oppression, among the idealists determined to fight all injustice on behalf of society's disadvantaged was, after all, hardly surprising.

Jewish radicals were always in the minority, but that mattered little. Rosa
Luxemburg, one of the two Spartacist leaders murdered after their failed
attempt to seize power, was Jewish but the other, Karl Liebknecht, was not.
Kurt Eisner, the head of the short-lived Bavarian *Räte* republic was an idealistic Socialist Jew; several Jewish Communists and anarchists had been at
his side, yet many non-Jews were also involved. But it was they and the
Jewish presence in Communist revolutions in Russia and Hungary that the
anti-Semites seized on to brand all Jews as revolutionaries and exaggerate
their influence in leftist movements.

The role Jews such as Walther Rathenau and Albert Ballin had played in the war economy was proof to anti-Semites of Jewish responsibility for betrayal on the homefront—even though Ballin, in despair over the lost war, had died from an overdose of sleeping pills.[36] The presence of two Jewish bankers, Warburg and Melchior, among the German delegates at Versailles sufficed to brand the treaty "Jewish treason." The facts that a Jew had been among those appointed by Ebert to the provisional government and that two Jewish SPD leaders headed the provincial governments of Prussia and Saxony were enough for the claim that Weimar was a "Jew Republic." The fact that Hugo Preuss, a constitutional expert who had helped draft the constitution, was Jewish provided confirmation.

In reality, most Jews were intensely loyal Germans and only a few had been leftist radicals. Far more Christians than Jews had been convicted of profiteering, and while it was true that Jews were important in intellectual and cultural life, their most important contributions were in traditional and mainstream fields rather than in the most exotic modernist areas. Where Weimar culture's most acclaimed achievements in music, literature, and science were concerned, it was often Jews who were winning the Nobel Prizes and enhancing Germany's reputation.

Strenuous Jewish efforts to cite this contrary evidence had only limited impact against all the shouting. German anti-Semitism had shown itself to be deeply entrenched. Germany's Jews were under more constant and distressing attack than ever before.

7

Then came the ultimate disaster of hyperinflation. There is a story about a wealthy, best-selling Berlin author who grew despondent in 1923, withdrew his entire life savings—an amount in six figures—and spent it all on a single subway ticket for a last ride through the city. Thereafter he returned home, locked the door, and starved to death.[37] At about this time, the concert pianist Artur Schnabel carried a suitcase full of bills home as his fee for a concert. Because the many bills were heavy, he spent half of them on two sausages, but the next day he found that the other half would not buy him even one.[38] Earlier in the year, a noontime cup of coffee cost "only" 300,000 marks, yet when settling the bill an hour or so later, the price might well have risen to twice that amount. Before the mad carnival of devalued paper money and exploding prices ended, Berliners were paying 10 billion marks just for their daily newspaper, and 320 billion for one egg!

At the end of the war, a single press at the Reichsbank sufficed to print the country's entire stock of banknotes. When the inflationary spiral peaked at the end of 1923, 132 private firms were running 1,723 presses round the clock, and thirty factories were working at full capacity merely to keep them supplied with paper more valuable than the banknotes themselves. A conscientious clerk kept track of the Reichbank's losses—a dizzying 32,776.9 trillion marks![39]

Between 1922 and 1923, Germany was in the midst of an inflationary frenzy unlike any previously known and never experienced since. The deterioration of the currency began during the war and gradually accelerated thereafter but it was not until the latter part of 1922 that a combination of domestic policy errors and international events led to the money machine spinning utterly out of control. At its peak, people were being paid twice a day, with time off at noon to spend the worthless paper on whatever was available in stores, where shelves were perennially empty. Merchants did not sell because restocking invariably involved heavy losses. People rushed to buy because money held even for hours was worthless. Salaries of ordinary workers—and prices—escalated into the billions and trillions.

Foreign currency was king, and the mark–dollar exchange became the fever chart for the inflationary sickness. In 1914, the rate stood at 4.2 to 1, and by the end of the war the mark had lost somewhat less than half its prewar value. By mid-1923, the dollar bought 414,000 marks, and thereafter the decline sped forward at an unimaginable rate, first into the millions and then billions. On November 20, 1923, a foreign visitor exchanging a single dollar would have been handed a bewildering 4.2 trillion marks!

There was more than one cause for the disastrous collapse. The gradual decline in the mark's value during the war was closely related to faulty fiscal policy—borrowing instead of taxing to finance the war and failing to adjust the money supply to the inevitable shortages of a war economy. When peace was restored, the shaky republic's fear of public unrest led it to finance a false boom with easy credit and large government deficits intended to keep the people employed. For a while, it worked and postwar unemployment in Germany paradoxically stayed substantially lower than in the victors' countries. But the inflationary cost was heavy, and much worse was to come when the final downward spiral was triggered by a series of international blows.

The Allies' "reduced" reparation demands of an impossible 132 billion gold marks gravely impaired what little confidence in the German economy had been preserved. Then, in January 1923, inevitable payment arrears were used as a pretext by Franco-Belgian forces to occupy the vital industrial area of the Ruhr. The nation seethed with anger, and the government reacted by ordering a policy of passive resistance to the occupiers. Production of coal and steel declined, and shortages were financed by a flood of yet more paper money, with even more calamitous results.

The social and political consequences of this hyperinflation were enormous, leaving a deep imprint on German attitudes and politics. Not everyone, though, was a loser. Cheap money and cheap exports unleashed a large but highly inefficient splurge in investment, enriching big manufacturers and accelerating a major concentration of German industry. Debtors could wipe out their obligations virtually overnight, mortgages were redeemed for nothing, and some property owners prospered. Large and small speculators, the unscrupulous and those quick on their feet or with access to foreign exchange, had a field day though the population hated them and called them *Raffkes*, unsavory crooks. For those who did well, it was a time of high living, great luxury, and waste. Berlin's theatres and operas were full, there were elegant women in jewels and fur coats, and expensive cars passed through streets where the undernourished and helpless stood at street corners begging for handouts.

Many more suffered than gained. Savings were wiped out, pensioners starved, and wage earners' real incomes plummeted. Much of the bourgeois class was impoverished overnight, and with their savings gone many found themselves on relief, full of shame and resentment over a situation they could not understand. There was a widespread sense of indignation, a hatred for those doing well, and anger at a system held responsible for their woes.

The environment was ready-made for political demagogues, and Weimar's rightist enemies were busier than ever, railing against the infamy of Versailles and calling for a reawakening of Germany's greatness. With growing frustration over their impoverishment and the immorality and chaos around them, the number of those listening to their shouts of "Der Jude ist schuld" (it's the fault of the Jew) was steadily on the rise. By 1922, official membership in the League for Defense and Defiance surpassed two thousand. In Munich, the once tiny NSDAP had enrolled six thousand members, and Adolf Hitler, its new leader, was beginning to make a name for himself outside Bavaria with mass rallies and shrill anti-Jewish oratory.

In the Jewish press, agonized reports of anti-Semitic incidents lengthened. In the little town of Zippnow, a memorial plaque for fallen soldiers excluded Jews because townspeople "wanted nothing to do with them."[40] In Oldenburg, gangs attacked Jews in the streets, and much the same occurred in Nuremberg and Breslau, where Jewish shop windows were smashed. In Munich, Hitler's storm troopers fell upon Italian fruit sellers because "they looked Jewish," and an American complained to police of being roughed up in broad daylight for the same reason.[41] Even Albert Einstein, awarded the 1921 Nobel Prize, was attacked for his "Jewish science." He was one of Germany's foremost physicists at the Kaiser Wilhelm Institute, but that mattered less to ultranationalist students than the fact that he was a "dirty, internationalist, pacifist scientist-Jew." Neither his supporters nor his detractors understood his work, but many Germans were intensely proud of his accomplishments. Yet there were also enough threats on his life from extremists on the right that he required bodyguards to protect him.[42]

Such threats were not idle. *Völkisch* radicals regularly used inflammatory language to incite violence against those they hated, and there were any number of attempts to kill or maim those with whom they wanted to settle political scores. Finance Minister Matthias Erzberger was murdered for signing the armistice, and in several provinces other politicians were assassinated. Philipp Scheidemann, the prominent SPD politician, was wounded in an acid attack, and Maximilian Harden suffered the same fate.

The favorite target of violent extremist rhetoric was Walther Rathenau, the man who had organized the war economy and became Foreign Minister in January 1922. To *Völkisch* conspirators he was doubly the devil's incarnation: first, as architect of a policy of accommodation with the Allies and signer of the Rapallo Peace Treaty with Communist Soviet Russia; and second, as a Jew. On June 24, 1922, at 10:30 A.M., Rathenau left his villa in the elegant Grunewald section of Berlin en route to his Foreign Ministry office.

He was a proud and vain man, but one given to bouts of melancholy and a brooding pessimism, and he had steadfastly refused the bodyguards who should have protected him. That morning, as his driver rounded a curve, an open sports car with three young men drew up alongside. One rose and emptied his rifle at him at point-blank range, and for good measure, another followed up with a grenade. Rathenau died almost instantly. That night *Völkisch* groups throughout Germany celebrated, and students lit bonfires and sang *Deutschland, erwache* (Awake, O Germany). Immediately, however, an even greater wave of revulsion and outrage swept the nation. Rathenau was given a state funeral, and the Reichstag enacted a new law aimed at the conspirators and their friends.

Walther Rathenau typified better than anyone the dilemma confronting Germany's assimilated Jews in the 1920s. Heir to an industrial empire, he was a leading member of the business elite, and his company's reach and power were enormous. In business he was powerful, and in the open environment of Weimar politics he rose higher than any Jew could have hoped. Yet in German society he remained an outsider, flattered and courted when needed but forever second class, disliked for his origins and humiliated by an invisible wall behind which those who mattered most to him kept him at arm's length.

Even on his lofty perch, this highly intelligent and sophisticated intellectual, author, and man of business and world affairs could not break through to a world he knew to be unjust and unfair, but one to which he desperately wanted to belong. From childhood, his character had been split between a fatal attraction for those who rejected him and stubborn, painful pride for a Jewishness he would not deny or abandon, and which no one would let him forget. Because of family influence, he had served in a regiment of guards, but as a Jew was not promoted, and he suffered from being shunned by the blue-eyed Germanic officers he admired.

Like many of his coreligionists, he felt thoroughly German and once wrote: "I am a German of the Jewish lineage. My people are the German people, my native soil is the German land, my faith is German faith, which is higher even than religious confession."[43] And like many, it took him time to deal with his Jewishness, and his attitudes changed and softened over the years. As a young unabashed Germanophile he published a critical tract urging Jews to conscious self-education away from the "typically Jewish" habits and traits of their "darkish-skinned, enslaved and fearful race" toward emulation of the "blond and brave" race he so admired. "Look in the mirror . . . with your poor build, high shoulders, awkward feet, the soft contours of a shape [that is] the sign of physical decay."[44] Later he came to regret these intemperate words full of self-hate, yet his struggle and ceaseless striving for honor and acceptance continued, and so did the suffering over the unjust dislike of his countrymen. In a final, tragic irony, the conspirators who killed him were precisely the blond, blue-eyed officers he adored.

Rathenau confronted his demons openly in his writings and speeches. Others, less reflective or courageous, simply ignored them. Ewald was among the many who went about their affairs, and looked away. Arthur, more thoughtful than many, was prominent in Weimar's world of the stage, but he chose to do much the same. His book on the Berlin of his youth, written in the midst of feverish anti-Semitic strife, reminisced charmingly about an idealized world where German-Jewish life was in harmony with its surroundings and free of strain. His columns in the *Frankfurter Zeitung* reporting on the Berlin of the early 1920s say nothing about anti-Jewish tensions. To his readers, he remained the perfect cultured German bourgeois, moderately conservative with monarchist leanings, and pining for the lost values of another day. Studiously avoiding controversy, he wrote instead of his tender love for things German, of "old neighborhoods and chestnut trees to dream under and read by" when Frederick William IV, "the last romantic," sat on the throne. His "black and white [monarchist] soul" deplored the decline of law and order, and "republican lack of discipline"[45]—without the slightest allusion to the Jew hatred swirling all around.

In a Berlin theatre, Arthur Schnitzler's *Der Reigen* had been the scene of a nasty anti-Semitic riot. *Völkisch* gangs appeared en masse, thrown stinkbombs, and screamed their abuse at the play's "Jewish decadence and obscenity." The authorities' response was to appoint an expert committee to render an opinion, with Arthur one of its members. In a later column, he explained his view at great length (mediocre play, but not obscene), yet there was not a single word about the anti-Jewish aspects. Nothing, it seemed, could deter him from avoiding the unpleasantness of which he was so much a part.

Thus 1923 drew to a close amid deepening crisis. Rathenau was dead, Franco-Belgian forces were in the Ruhr, political agitation was rampant, and inflation was out of control. In the wake of the violent attacks and murder, the anti-terrorist Law for the Protection of the Republic was in effect, and it was being enforced against extremist inciters to violence. Even in Munich, the weak conservative government was under pressure to rein in the mass rallies and wild rhetoric of the extremists, and Adolf Hitler was feeling the heat.

The NSDAP was now a sizable organization with a membership of fifty-five thousand. More than half its members had joined in just two months, and its storm troopers numbered an impressive fifteen thousand. The party had become the largest and most active of the many rightist organizations, yet the threat of restrictions worried them, and to counter it, Hitler had struck an alliance, the Kampfbund, with other like-minded *Völkisch* and paramilitary groups. In early November, they thought that their time had come, and on the night of November 8, at the Bürgerbräukeller in central Munich, they took government hostages and proclaimed a revolt to seize power in Bavaria. On the morning of the ninth, they set out to march to the town hall, intent to install their government and to seize power in Berlin.

Hitler was leading the march, surrounded by Hess, Göring, Streicher, and other Thule members, along with ex-officers and the ubiquitous Ludendorff. But their reach was greater than their grasp. Out in the square, they were confronted by Bavarian government forces and loyal police, and the revolt collapsed in a hail of bullets and confusion.

Weimar had survived yet another challenge. Inflation was about to end with a stunningly successful reform. Hitler and most of the conspirators were safely behind bars. The tension eased, and for a brief moment Germany relaxed.

8

A period of relative calm, economic revival, and international progress followed. Some later called them the "golden years," but that was always an exaggeration. Even in the good times, serious problems continued to fester below the surface, and many Germans remained disillusioned, financially strained, and psychologically adrift.

For the time being, the country relaxed, and 1924 began on an upbeat note. Rathenau's murderers were hunted down and committed suicide when cornered. Hitler and his putschists were tried and sent to prison, only Ludendorff having somewhat inexplicably been acquitted. The threat of further military coups receded, and power was in the hands of a coalition of centrist bourgeois parties.

As if by a miracle, there was a stable new currency and the comforting presence of the man credited with its creation, *Reichswährungskommissar* (Currency Commissioner) Dr. Hjalmar Schacht. The final exchange rate of the old currency to his new *rentenmark* had been an incredible 4.2 trillion to 1. He had pegged it to the price of gold, and by using the largely semantic ploy of pledging all of Germany's physical assets against the new money, he had achieved the near impossible. The rentenmark remained stable, economic life returned to normal, and the focus shifted to recovery and trade. Employment and productivity rose and by 1925, unemployment dipped to between 5 and 6 percent. Imports were up and store shelves were once again full.

Even the sudden death of *Reichspräsident* Ebert and the election of the seventy-seven-year-old Hindenburg to succeed him caused only a brief ripple of concern. During the war, when the Emperor faded from view, many Germans had become used to the Field Marshall as substitute Kaiser and comforting father figure in the familiar uniform. Given a choice between the venerable, strongly conservative old soldier and a centrist civilian, the voters had intuitively opted for the uniform over morning coat and top hat.

Liberals and moderates worried nervously that Hindenburg as *Reichspräsident* might lead an assault of rightist reactionaries against the constitution. One observer noted sarcastically that if war was "politics by other means," with Hindenburg's election the republic had reverted to the "continuation of the Kaiserreich with other persons."[46] To everyone's relief, however, the fears of reaction were not realized and, if anything, the Field Marshall's presence proved to have a calming effect on the public mood.

In Berlin, artistic and intellectual life flourished as never before. The standards were high, the offerings wide-ranging, and the mood innovative, irreverent, and exciting. Audiences were large and sophisticated and—whether as artists, critics, or appreciative connoisseurs—Jews were more prominent among them than ever. For a few short years of freedom, the Berlin of the '20s was one of the world's great cultural centers, and its reputation for richness and vibrancy would have been unthinkable without the large Jewish presence.

With its Philharmonic Orchestra and three major opera houses, Bruno Walter presiding at one and Otto Klemperer and Erich Kleiber at the others, the capital was a muscial mecca for stars from around the world. When the seventeen-year-old Rudolf Serkin played the *Goldberg Variations* in his musical debut before a select Berlin audience, only a handful of people attended, but Einstein and Artur Schnabel were among them, and their approval was enough to establish Serkin's reputation. Rising young soloists like Claudio Arrau and Vladimir Horowitz found Berlin no less exciting and rewarding, and when the twelve-year-old violin prodigy Yehudi Menuhin made his debut under Bruno Walter at the Philharmonic, his triumph was hailed as a major world event.[47]

Berlin's numerous literary cafés were celebrated meeting places where people came to be seen, exchange ideas, trade stories, and make deals. Even the Lord Mayor, proudly conscious of the cafés' importance to his city's reputation as a cultural center, made it a point to drop in at the Romanische, one of the most famous, to get a feel for the "unique milieu."[48] On the right afternoon, he might well have met in one corner Berlin's enfant terrible, the eccentric Georg Grosz, dressed as a cowboy and regaling his friends with his latest exploits ridiculing thick-necked Prussians and monocled aristocrats. In another, Max Reinhardt, the undisputed king of the Berlin stage, might have been in earnest conversation with the young actress Elisabeth Bergner, his recent discovery, and the talk of all Berlin. Perhaps Erwin Piscator, the leftist Proletarian Theatre impresario would have been there to argue and debate with Berlin's numerous theatrical critics. They were the acknowledged arbiters of dramatic taste, and the biting commentaries of Alfred Kerr, the best known, and the more benign yet thoughtful opinions of Arthur Eloesser, his friend and competitor writing for the *Weltbühne's Blaue Heft*, were must reading for stage cognoscenti.

Arthur was in his element in the Berlin of the 1920s. Yet unlike Kerr's sharp pen, or the bitter sarcasm of Kurt Tucholsky, one of the republic's unrelenting leftist critics and Arthur's journalistic colleague at the *Welt-bühne,* his own writings were noteworthy for their avoidance of any overt political engagement. He seemed to feel his special vulnerability as a Jew more keenly than his colleagues, and he remained determined to give the enemy no ammunition for attacks. The unstable politics of Weimar were swirling around him and the "Jewish Question" was always present, but Arthur took no notice of it in his professional work. Conservative by tem-perament, he believed deeply in German culture and its civilizing influ-ence, and his faith in his country—and of the Jews' place in it—was strong. He treasured the great literature of many countries, yet German writing and drama remained his special pleasure and pride. Steeped in the world of literature and drama, he wrote his weekly columns and worked on his books—a Thomas Mann biography in 1925, and one on Elisabeth Bergner three years later.[49] Thereafter, he launched what would be his life's work—an ambitious two-volume critical survey of German literature after the Ro-mantics.[50]

His love and loyalty for the established order and for things German re-mained unshaken, much to the chagrin of some. Piscator complained that he was "the voice of a reactionary clique intent on dismissing political the-atre as either damaging or worthy of comment only from a technical point of view," and that people like Arthur had "a longing for the mindless vagueness of the prewar theatre life of a generation . . . whose cowardice pushed us into the foxholes of war."[51] The criticism was cruel, yet Piscator had a point. Life in the middle years of the '20s was quieter and better for Jews than it had been in a long time, and Arthur was glad to forget the fearful past and eager to avoid fanning new flames.

The vicious hate campaign had been a big scare, but now there was less of it, and Jewish optimists were once again out in force. In Oranienburg the situation had greatly improved, agriculture was back on track, stores were busy, and people were working. With greater liquidity and a stable currency, the bank was thriving, and enjoying some of its best years.

A year after Lucy's death—faster than had seemed possible—Ewald had married Valerie Markt, the daughter of a family friend. Like his first great love she was, at twenty-two, a pretty Berliner, the blonde Germanic type he liked. This time, however, there were no cultural complications. Valerie was Jewish, though no more connected to Judaism than he, fully acceptable to the family. With boundless energy and drive, she had quickly taken her place alongside the heir to the town bank. Her family were relatively recent arrivals of modest means from Posen, which put them lower down on the Jewish social scale, but for Ewald her humbler origin was only a slight blemish and, with her good looks and charm, easy enough to overlook. The birth of a daughter in 1921 cemented her place in the family, and it was followed five years later by the arrival of a son. Settled in a comfortable house staffed with servants, no one in the family was complaining.

Life was pleasant and Ewald and Valerie were not disposed to notice that in spite of the good times there were contrary signals of future trouble. "What we ardently wish, we soon believe." Ewald believed easily and without much reflection. Arthur's love affair with Germany was more intensely intellectual and romantic. For both, their German ties were stronger than their Jewish ones, and hope came easily. A more skeptical observer might have worried about unfavorable political developments even during these "golden years," yet under the circumstances it was easy for Jews to be complacent. In this they were not alone, yet the stakes for them were exceptionally high and the consequences especially calamitous.

Below the surface the ideological divisiveness and stress of a flawed political structure continued to erode and weaken the republic's foundations. There was, for one thing, the rapid resurgence of the same undemocratic rightist elements that had been briefly discredited at the end of the war. They were back in force, the election of Hindenburg had strengthened their hand, and most of them were openly anti-Semitic. The Field Marshall was more than eighty years old, there was no obvious successor, and the coterie of antirepublicans surrounding him was anything but reassuring. Nor was the general political structure particularly solid or secure. None of the parties near the center had a large or stable enough base to govern, and one weak coalition followed another. By 1928, fifteen cabinets had come and gone, all within fewer than ten years.

The progressive polarization of the electorate, leaving the Jews isolated and vulnerable in the middle, should have been equally worrying. In 1919, the German Democratic Party (DDP) had been the third strongest, with

seventy-five seats in the Reichstag. It was the only centrist party that unam-
biguously rejected anti-Semitism, and the largest number of Jews supported it. Yet a year later, the DDP had lost more than half its parliamentary
seats, and thereafter it faded into irrelevance, leaving the majority of Jews
without an obvious political home.

The underlying problem was that large elements of the German bourgeoisie had grown embittered by their impoverishment from inflation. Dis-
enchanted with the failures of parliamentary democracy, they were steadily
shifting their political allegiances to the right. Some rightist parties were
openly anti-Semitic, and even in the others Jews were less than welcome.
The left, on the other hand, was split, poorly led, ideologically hidebound,
and politically inept. For middle-class business or professional Jews there
was no logical haven, and the DDP was seen more and more as a Jewish
party, a *Judenpartei*—which did neither it nor its Jewish partisans much
good.

Finally, for those willing to see it, there was still plenty of evidence of the
depth of German anti-Semitism in many quarters, and of the willingness to
tolerate it even if many Germans were not themselves active Jew baiters.
The courts, army, and police were open centers for anti-Jewish feeling. Radical rightist sentiments among students remained strong, 77 percent of
them having voted in a 1927 Prussian student poll against admitting Jews
to their organizations.[52] Meanwhile, the RJF continued to record anti-
Semitic incidents such as the one in Liegnitz, where local ex-soldiers had
voted to exclude Jewish veterans from their memorial service for fallen
comrades.[53]

Often Jews were comforted that Germans took little notice of such matters and that their personal relations with Christians were friendly and un-
contentious. Even though more Germans now voted for the right, there
was little evidence that anti-Semitism had been the main reason. Yet every
Jew knew that in spite of individual friendships, a "genteel" kind of animosity toward the stereotypical "bad" Jew remained widespread. When all
was said and done, what should have been of concern was that few groups
or influential non-Jewish voices could be counted on to defend them. Their
Christian friends assured them that the uncouth rabble did not matter, and
the Jews were only too ready to believe them.

9

The good times ended abruptly in the autumn of 1929, and no one was prepared for the catastrophe of the world depression and its disastrous consequences. Everyone would be deeply affected but none as gravely as the politically and socially vulnerable Jews.

Of Germany's 63 million inhabitants in 1925, some 568,000 were Jewish. In absolute terms, they were few, yet that does not tell the whole story. Though limited in numbers, they were a highly visible part of the German population, strongly concentrated in Berlin and a few urban centers. Their socioeconomic status was on average far above that of most Germans, and many occupied positions of wealth and prestige.[54]

The Jews were an urban people. One in three was in Berlin, half in the country's seven largest cities, and two-thirds in urban centers over one hundred thousand. Mostly they lived in Prussia and in Berlin, where they made up 4.3 percent of the population and were heavily concentrated in a handful of the city's many districts. The prestigious western Wilmersdorf was 14 percent Jewish, and in the top areas in and around the Kurfürstendamm—the "Park Avenue" of Berlin—there were entire apartment buildings where wealthier Jewish families predominated. The upper-middle-class Charlottenburg was 10 percent Jewish, and in Berlin's poorer central district, there was a sizable and highly visible presence of non-German Orthodox immigrants from the East.

As had long been the case, Jewish concentration in certain occupations was as pronounced as their geographic clustering. One in six German lawyers and one in nine doctors was a Jew, and in Berlin their presence in these professions and in journalism and the arts was much higher.

In business, Jews dominated such fields as textiles, department stores, retailing, private banking, and certain areas of trading. There were four thousand Jewish textile firms, and 60 percent of textile wholesaling was in Jewish hands. Virtually all the big department stores and half the country's private banks were Jewish. Half of all working Germans but only 9 percent of Jews were wage earners, while virtually the reverse was true in the self-employed and professional categories.

It was this pattern of concentration in key places and occupations that accentuated the Jewish minority's exposure to public envy and resentment.

Politically isolated and without powerful groups to speak for them, it was a formula for trouble in times of stress.

New York's Wall Street crash on "Black Friday," October 25, 1929, was front-page news in Germany. At first the public was slow to grasp its significance, though there were signs of domestic trouble well before the crash. In the spring, unemployment topped 3 million, and over the summer business failures began to rise. In the countryside there was a growing restiveness, and lengthening newspaper columns announcing forced auctions of farms. Few people, however, paid much attention to these early signs of trouble.

The underlying reality was that the German economy of the Golden Twenties was structurally unsound. Its affluence was artificial, fueled by foreign capital and short-term debt—"prosperity on the cuff," the cynics called it. Total foreign indebtedness was close to 30 billion gold marks. In one year alone it had soared by 7 billion, most of it from America. Some of the dollars flowed right back for reparations payments, but the rest financed an unhealthy investment boom and underwrote dangerously lax bank credit. Farmers were heavily in debt and, with farm prices dropping, many had trouble meeting their interest payments and tax obligations.

There was also a serious structural imbalance in the pattern of wages and employment. Under pressure from organized labor and the SPD, worker benefits had steadily expanded. The middle class and peasantry benefited little from these improvements, although the tax burden to finance them hit them hard. Finally, a wave of industrial rationalization had led to considerable excess capacity and the loss of traditional jobs, causing especially high unemployment among women and the young.

After the U.S. stock market collapsed, the influx of American dollars stopped, capital grew scarce, investment spending ceased, exports dried up, overextended banks failed, consumer demand plummeted, and unemployment soared. The weak coalition government deadlocked and was unable to cope with the emergency. Domestic politics and the structural anomalies exacerbated the problems. Month by month the crisis deepened.

In early 1929, less than 6 percent of the German work force had been unemployed. By December, 8 percent were out of work; 12 months later it was 16 percent. In 1932, the worst year of the depression, 6.3 million Germans were idle and untold more had simply given up looking for work.

Almost one in four wage earners was unemployed, and many others were working short hours for real wages that had declined by as much as a third.

Germany was in deep economic trouble, and the social and political consequences of the world depression were especially serious there because virtually no one—workers, middle class, businessmen, or bankers—was spared, and the democratic underpinnings were fragile. The middle class was particularly hard hit and deeply demoralized. With unemployment funds running dry, almost one-third of all Germans was on the dole by 1932, and suicides soared. On Berlin's outskirts there were tent cities of the homeless, the unemployed marched in the streets, and bloody riots erupted between political factions of the radical right and left.

It was an environment in which demagogues and extremists had a field day. Seizing on the widespread despair, they were out in force, casting blame in all directions and peddling their pet theories for radical solutions. The Communists were gaining on the left, but many more Germans at all levels were listening to the radical right, and none were more active and vociferous than Hitler's surging Nazis, who were better organized, more ruthless, and more single-minded than any others in taking advantage of the situation.

No one had expected the regeneration of the NSDAP and the rise of Adolf Hitler from discredited putschist to leading player on the German political scene in the span of a few short years. At the end of 1924, he had left prison in a depressed mood, and found his party reduced to a pitiful seven hundred members. In the Reichstag, the entire *Völkisch*-racialist bloc held only fourteen seats and had just suffered its worst defeat at the polls. Hitler was banned from public speaking, the "golden years" were beginning, and his fortunes were at a nadir. Most people thought he was finished.

Yet by 1926 he had reunited the party, recruited a total of 27,000 new members, organized it in twenty-three national *Gaue* (Districts), and become its undisputed leader. Over the next three years, his progress was slow, and there were many ups and downs, but Hitler battled on with messianic zeal. In the Reichstag elections of 1928—the last of the good years—800,000 people voted for him. It was still a relatively small number, and without the impending economic collapse it is doubtful that it would have grown much. But a year later, with the economy stalled, the Nazis began to score impressively in several provincial elections, and for the first time one of them became a minister in a provincial government.

Not even Hitler himself had anticipated so quick and complete a change of fortunes. In prison he concluded that the attempted coup had been a mistake and that, though his contempt for the Reichstag was undiminished, it was easier to gain power through the ballot box than to seize it by force. His strategy now was to use the very institutions of democracy to destroy them.

Starting out broke and with few supporters, his chances seemed poor, nor were they enhanced by the appeal of any comprehensive program for change or concrete proposals to deal with Germany's ills. *Mein Kampf* (My Struggle), the book he had written at a feverish pace while in prison, was muddle-headed and confused. Few who voted for him had read or understood it or, if they did, took seriously what he said. As to his speeches, they were noteworthy mainly for the specificity of what he denounced and the generalities he extolled. In the list of his hates, there was Versailles, internationalism, Bolsheviks, bankers, democracy, and—always—the conspiracy of the Jew. On the positive side, there was little except evocations of the destiny of a superior Germany and ritual appeals to patriotism, leadership, and strength.

Yet in the politically weak environment of Weimar, Hitler drew on substantial strengths: shrewdness and skill in sensing the public mood, a capacity for messianic oratory, a tightly organized party machinery of fanatical followers and—at the right moments—extraordinary luck. Other parties were burdened with ideological baggage, but Hitler's Nazis had none of that. Opportunistic and flexible in their propaganda and ruthless and violent in advancing their cause, they directed their appeals toward anyone who would listen—workers and farmers, the old and the young, the middle class, students, and academics. The internal contradictions of their slogans worried them little, and noise of oratory easily drowned out the faulty logic.

As long as the economy held up, their progress had been slow. But with collapse and economic despair, Hitler's formula was just right, and millions of Germans were suddenly ready to support him. He gave them reasons to blame and to hate, promised them jobs and relief from the very disorder his storm troopers were fomenting in the streets, and talked of rejuvenating German society, which especially appealed to the idealism of the young.

Central to what he told the voters was his abiding hatred of Jews, and the public attention he gained by pounding them incessantly ideally served this purpose. In his very first speech after leaving prison, he set the pattern, declaring "all that is beautiful is Aryan; all that is ugly is Jewish."[55] In *Mein Kampf*, speaking of the war and its aftermath, he repeated it: "If we pass all the causes of the German collapse in review, the ultimate and most decisive remains the failure to recognize . . . the Jewish menace."[56]

For Hitler, the Jew was a Marxist who misled workers to exploit them, and at the same time an international capitalist out to control the world. In politics, democracy was the Jew's Trojan Horse, in business he was a cheat, and culturally "he contaminates . . . and makes a mockery of natural feeling . . . and of the noble and the good."[57] Above all, there was always the staple of the Jew as racial polluter, presented in images bordering on the pornographic: "With satanic joy in his face, the black-haired Jewish youth lurks in wait for the unsuspecting girl whom he defiles with his blood."[58] In sum, the struggle for German rejuvenation, according to Hitler, was in its essentials a fight against Jews, and Germany would not be saved until they were eliminated from German life.

The Jews had taken no more notice of him in the early years than had the rest of Germany. Fringe elements of extremists had always existed, and Hitler's small band of fanatics seemed no different. In Berlin, it was a minuscule splinter party operating out of a dingy back room. When, on November 7, 1926, Joseph Goebbels came to take charge of them, he was appalled by their disarray and deeply disappointed that the media hardly took notice of the man Hitler had just appointed Berlin *Gauleiter*, the head of the capital's Nazi party, and national chief of propaganda. "Only one Jew rag," he later recalled, mentioned that "a certain Herr Göbels [*sic*] had arrived from the Ruhr and dispensed the familiar rhetoric and fables."[59] Hitler's first appearance in Berlin the following May was reported on an inside page under "Miscellania," and the next day his speech merited no more than two lines.

Goebbels was Hitler's most recent convert and a fanatical hero-worshipping follower, yet hardly the prototype of the Aryan superman idealized by the Nazis. Berlin's twenty-nine-year-old new *Gauleiter* had arrived there with a single suitcase, no money, and few other assets, but he was a smart and cynical fanatic, and he had a clear plan for building the Berlin party into a force to be reckoned with. He moved them into a new, more visible headquarters, stressed organization building, and insisted on tight discipline and obedience. Above all, he was a talented speaker and a clever and unscrupulous propagandist. He believed that, in modern propaganda, "anything that works is good."[60] What impressed the masses, he believed, were dramatic images conveyed through action and the spoken, rather than the written, word. Truth was secondary—the bigger the lie, the more likely that it would be believed. There was a Nazi paper, *Angriff* (Attack), but his main thrust was to engage the enemy in the streets, confronting Communists on their own turf and using SA storm troopers to precipitate street fights, so that Berliners would begin to take notice. "The street is where the battle takes place" and "attackers are stronger than defenders" were his guiding principles.[61] His main enemy was the police chief, and as a special target for vilification he chose Dr. Bernhard Weiss, the Jewish deputy. Goebbels dubbed him "Isidor" and his Semitic looks made him the perfect foil for the image of Jews as "that parasitical body which flourishes in the swamps of a dying culture."[62]

Hitler seized the opportunity of economic hardship with full force, and the results were spectacular. From one year to the next, support for the NSDAP exploded, and an astounding 6.4 million Germans voted to seat 107 Nazis in the Reichstag of 1930, making them the second largest party and Hitler the undisputed leader of the German right.

Even when he overplayed his hand and lost decisively in his race for President of the Republic against the venerated Hindenburg, he polled a yet more impressive 11.3 million votes. The year was 1932, and the depression was worse than ever. The German people were desperate for decisive leadership, and Hitler had promised to give it to them.

For Jews the old complacency was gone. The dimensions of the Nazi surge and the vehemence of their hatred shocked them. A major effort had to be mounted to counteract the danger. Yet from the beginning, their efforts suffered from internal divisions and disagreements over strategy and tactics, the lack of strong outside political support, and the choice of ineffective argumentation in an environment of severe public distress and ruthlessly emotional Nazi propaganda.

The principal role in the campaign of political action and publicity fell to the CV. With 60,000 members, it was the oldest, largest, and most active of the Jewish organizations, and Goebbels called it "the Jewish General Staff" and the "High Command of the Jewish Conspiracy." Its views mirrored those of the majority of assimilated Jews who felt strongly about their identity as Germans and wanted to defend their place in German society. In their newspaper and in speeches the CV leadership exerted all their energies to protest Jewish loyalty to the country. "If there were a Nobel Prize for a German attitude, German Jews would win it," one of them wrote in 1930.[63] If the anti-Semites denigrated the Jewish role in society, the CV's answer was to disseminate statistical data to cite contrary evidence of Jewish accomplishments. If Jews were accused of cowardice, they responded with data on Jewish war dead, and occasionally there would even be a resort to the sophistry of arguing that anti-Jewish and world anti-German prejudice had much in common, in that both were rooted in envy of talents rather than faults.

The CV's stepped-up campaign of publicity, or "enlightenment," was conducted through a welter of books, pamphlets, newspapers, flyers, and speeches emphasizing Jewish patriotism and loyalty to Germany, countering accusations of collective guilt, debunking pseudoscientific theories of race, and citing Jewish contributions to the fatherland. Their arguments, however, had only limited effect. Few Germans heard them, and the weakness of liberal parties and lack of a political base limited their impact on voters. The CV also suffered from internal dissension and debates among those who thought direct political action was best, those who preferred enlightenment as the major thrust, and those who thought that contemptuous silence was best of all.

Some Jewish groups strongly disagreed with the CV's approach. The small but growing Zionists preferred to focus on their Jewish, rather than their German, identity. They opposed, on principle, the CV's efforts to fight Judeophobia, arguing that anti-Semitism was inevitable in the diaspora and that a clear Jewish consciousness combined with a national Palestinian state was the only answer. The RJF, on the other hand, had long been preoccupied primarily with defending the honor of ex-soldiers, and there was an even smaller group of supernationalistic right-wingers who flirted with

Völkisch-German ideology and thought that an accommodation with the Nazis might be possible.

Stunned by the rapid deterioration of the Jewish position, a brief effort had been made to unite these disparate forces into a joint working committee for the crucial election of September 1930, yet the cooperation collapsed in disagreement and recrimination once the disastrous results were in.

Separate efforts continued. The CV organized a special office to fight Nazi propaganda and there was a *White Book* on Nazi terror and diverse publications to expose the lack of a scientific basis for the widely accepted theories of race. In the Jewish press, the fight against the persecution and attacks remained front-page news in every issue. Each election was a call for action and reports of anti-Semitic outrages alternated with appeals for calm and assurances that everything would still turn out for the best. The Jewish leadership was desperately worried, even if their faith in the fundamental goodwill of the majority of their Christian neighbors remained unshaken.

10

"Who is Adolf Hitler?" one of Berlin's major dailies asked in the summer of 1930. It was a moment when it was still an open question. Many Germans had just begun to take serious notice of him. The article concluded optimistically that his fervent nationalism might well be put to constructive use in a cooperative effort with the center and moderate rightists.[64]

Four months later, after the Nazi landslide, the question no longer needed asking, and the idea of peaceful collaboration with the center was the height of naiveté. More than 6 million Germans had voted for him, and in the two and one-half months between the election and the end of the year Nazi party membership quadrupled to almost 400,000. Hitler's brownshirts were everywhere in the streets, battling the left and roughing up Jews. When Hess, Göring, Goebbels, and the rest of their 107 delegates marched into the Reichstag to take their seats, they defiantly wore their brown outfits, though uniforms were expressly banned in the chamber.

The question Jews and worried democrats were asking was no longer who the Nazis were, but who the millions were who voted for them. Their surge at the polls was stunning. It struck Berlin's Chief Mayor Lange as positively "grotesque" that unemployed academics and students should cast their votes for them in droves.[65] A postelection analysis showed that the largest support had come not so much from the traditionally leftist workers as from the "little people"—barbers, chauffeurs, the lower salaried classes, small tradesmen, and shopkeepers. These were the class-conscious groups who had lost everything in the inflation and were again most at risk. The extreme left was no option for them, they hungered for change and were disgusted with the system, and they were also the most susceptible to anti-Semitism and fear of Jewish competition.[66]

Meanwhile the economy was going from bad to worse. By mid-1931, unemployment reached five and one-half million. A few months later almost 600,000 were without work in Berlin alone. There were seven suicides in the city every day, and 300,000 families were entirely dependent on welfare.[67] To add to the public nervousness and distress, large and small banks were failing all over Germany. The most spectacular crash was that of the Danat Bank, the country's second largest, which closed its doors and temporarily left depositors out in the cold. Thousands rushed to withdraw their savings from other banks, and many of these were pushed into default.

A world financial and banking crisis was under way, and it had spread from America to Europe, beginning with the spectacular failure of the Creditanstalt, Austria's largest. At year-end, Germany's large Bank for Commerce and Real Estate followed suit. Smaller country banks had been in trouble for some time and among the first to crumble.

In Oranienburg, the disaster struck early and with full force. With its narrow capital base and liberal lending during the exuberant good times, the small Blumenthal bank had become fatally vulnerable to defaults by farmers and the drying up of other sources of credit. Urgent appeals to Berlin's big banks had been in vain, and now the bank at Luisenplatz was permanently shut. For Martin and Ewald the embarrassment and personal tragedy could not have been greater. Their equity and wealth was gone, but the public disgrace was even worse, and there were allegations of serious mismanagement. The bank had existed for three generations, and Blumenthals had lived in or near Oranienburg for at least two hundred years and had worked themselves up to positions of honor and respect. Now all that was gone, and there was nothing left but humiliation and disgrace.

It was happening all over Germany, of course, but for Jews in a small town the experience was especially painful. The local atmosphere was tense, home-grown Nazis had made their first real gains, and the hostility against Jews was very personal. Even among themselves there was finger-pointing and fear of general reprisals.

Martin, with nowhere else to go, stayed in Oranienburg. Ewald and Valerie, however, took their two children and fled to Berlin. But no jobs were there, and it was the worst time for finding money to start something new. Everyone was stretched to the limit, and Jewish self-help organizations were mounting major drives to meet the emergency welfare needs. One in three Berlin Jews was now unemployed, and as always in times of trouble, the Jews were banding together and closing ranks. If the Jewish papers were not reporting on the latest anti-Semitic attacks, they were filled with urgent pleas for donations to retrain and support the unemployed, or even to support such worthwhile purposes as the financing of a home for "endangered young Jewish women."[68]

Many Jews, like Ewald and Valerie, were bewildered and helpless as they confronted both economic ruin and political threats. Except for the war years, Ewald had never faced such dangers to his security or material well-being, yet now there was open questioning of his rights as a German and no money. Pogroms had always been faraway events. Ignoring or downplaying Judeophobia had been his lifetime habit, yet now it was difficult to ignore such problems.

On the Kurfürstendamm, in the expensive part of Berlin, Nazi toughs openly attacked Jewish-looking pedestrians and smashed Jewish stores on Jewish New Year. In theatres and cafés Jews were being insulted and worse. All over Germany Nazi pogroms were on the rise. In several Silesian towns, Jewish businesses were being bombed, and in East Prussian Ortelsburg, where Ewald's Eloesser ancestors had once lived, two Jewish department stores had been torched. In the central district of Berlin, storm troopers marched into Jewish streets, assaulted the inhabitants, and burned their homes. On a single day sixty SA men were arrested and hauled into court but, as frequently happened, had just as quickly been released.[69]

For many Jews it was simply impossible to believe that Hitler and his toughs would really come to power or that solid law-abiding citizens would be at risk if they did. Ewald regularly wore his Iron Cross now—just in case. He was, after all, a *Frontkämpfer,* a veteran from the front lines of the war, his brother had been heavily wounded, and he had his family tree to prove that Blumenthals had lived in Prussia for hundreds of years. He told himself that Hitler's storm troopers might be shouting *Jude Verrecke* (Death to Jewry) in the streets, but that it was surely only an intemperate slogan. When all was said and done, the Nazis—though they were the country's largest party in 1932—remained in the minority, and well over half the electorate continued to oppose them. Ewald thought that was a good sign, a reason not to overreact and instead to focus on earning a living.

The Jewish leadership continued its feverish campaign against the Nazi threat, but many Jews tended to share Ewald's views and preferred to stay passive and unengaged. Though it was hard to ignore the ominous turn of events, they were determined to trust in their fellow Germans, discount the worst scenarios, and live their lives as they always had. The mayor, visiting his Jewish friends, was quite surprised that they seemed so unconcerned.[70]

Jewish leaders were urging "simplicity and modesty," but Berlin's cultural life continued even in the midst of the depression, and for those Christians and Jews who still had the means, the urge was strong to forget the talk of impending doom and to have a good time. "National failure is being conducted in *Gemütlichkeit," The New Yorker'*s correspondent reported from Berlin at the end of 1931. "Banks may close down for weeks, but cabarets rarely do before dawn. The Jockey Club on Lutherstrasse remains Europe's most pleasant nightclub and its only competition is . . . the Eden Bar's atmosphere of diehard ease and Semitic chic . . . [where] the wine is yellow and old, the ladies blonde and young, the goose livers gargantuan, the scene civilized."[71] Not all Jews, in other words, were listening to the advice to keep a low profile.

Arthur, at sixty-two, would not have been found in Berlin's bars and cabarets, but like his nephew he too stayed worried but unengaged and tried to lead a normal life. His mammoth survey of German literature was about to appear,[72] and in his weekly columns he preferred to discuss the life of a dramaturge rather than to comment on the threatening political scene.[73]

On the screen, Marlene Dietrich in *The Blue Angel* was packing them in, Fritz Lang's *M,* with Peter Lorre was a big hit, and the showing of Brecht's *Three Penny Opera* film had been disrupted by Nazi rowdies but remained one of the season's "must sees." On the stage they were doing Hemingway's *A Farewell to Arms* and at the State Opera Meyerbeer's *L'Africaine* was being revived. Max Reinhardt was dazzling audiences with his staging of smash operettas, and *The New Yorker*'s correspondent noted that even with so much poverty and joblessness outside, the theatres remained surprisingly full.

Amid the tumult and turbulence of Weimar's final months it was hard for anyone to understand the unfolding political events. Parliamentary democracy, on which the Jews counted as their principal guarantee, had effectively been dead since 1930 when Heinrich Brüning had begun to rule by emergency decree as a minority Chancellor. The secret plan of Hindenburg and the army was that at the first opportunity, he would work to restore an authoritarian monarchist form of government and eliminate the old constitution and the SPD's power once and for all.

But Brüning had hesitated and been overtaken by events. General von Schleicher, the military's éminence grise, had lost patience and in mid-1932 Brüning was forced to resign. The next choice to get the job done was Franz von Papen, a reactionary representative of the Wilhelmine old school, but even for him it was already too late. The depression was at its worst, and Hitler had struck an alliance with the barons of industry and nationalists of the far right. By summer of 1932, the Nazis were Germany's largest party, and while Papen and Schleicher maneuvered to frustrate them, Hitler's momentum was already too great. At the last minute, Papen himself was forced out, one more election had taken place, and though the Nazis had actually lost two million votes, the illusion that Hitler could still be contained with more byzantine maneuvering did not last for long. On January 30, 1933, Hindenburg appointed him German Chancellor of the Third Reich and charged him with forming a government.

Several times over the previous twelve months, the Reichstag had been dissolved and new elections held, and each time the Jewish leadership had issued its call to action and battled on. For each election they had mobilized new energies and sent out new appeals. Now the worst had happened, and the only remaining hope was that Hindenburg would protect their rights, and that Hitler in power would prove a more responsible and less ferocious foe than feared.

The moment had come to reassure the faithful and to put up a good front. "We are convinced," the CV announced once Hitler's appointment was a fact, "of the inviolability of our constitutional rights, which no one will dare touch." Germany's Jews must present a posture of dignity and calm. The phrase of the day was *Ruhig abwarten*—a quiet awaiting for events to unfold.

CHAPTER IX

DESCENDANTS

Michael

. . . a flatigious [sic] *attack upon a helpless minority that very probably has no counterpart in the course of the civilized world.*

David Buffum, U.S. Consul in Leipzig,
reporting on the *Kristallnacht* pogroms
November 1938

I would not wish to be a Jew in Germany.

Hermann Göring, after *Kristallnacht*
November 1938

1

I have virtually no recollection of Oranienburg, where I was born in 1926. We moved to Berlin in 1929, and four years later Adolf Hitler took power— I had just celebrated my seventh birthday. More than half a century has passed, and my memory of life under the Nazis has grown selective and vague.

Ewald, my father, did not easily reveal his feelings and rarely talked about the past. Given the circumstances of his ignoble departure, that was especially true when it came to the Oranienburg years. Yet the town remained for him the symbol of "die guten alten Zeiten"—the good old days—in the town where three generations of Blumenthals lie buried and where his grandfather and father were respected citizens and community leaders. In this he was no different from many Jews of his generation who looked back with nostalgia on the years before the First World War as a happy time when anti-Semitism was moderate, life was orderly, and the future was full of promise.

Much later I got to know Oranienburg quite well. With its close to thirty thousand inhabitants, sitting on the edge of Brandenburg's sandy flat-lands, the town is today mostly memorable for its ordinariness. After Na-zism, wartime destruction, and four decades of Communist mismanage-ment and neglect, it is a rather poor and drab place. Unemployment is high, and with Berlin's expanding urban sprawl Oranienburg has become just another unremarkable suburb of the capital. Yet the name has achieved a questionable fame far beyond Germany's borders. Since Hitler, the town has acquired the dubious distinction of having been, in early 1933, the site of the first Nazi concentration camp. If today tourists stop there at all, it is to visit what remains of Oranienburg-Sachsenhausen and the museum on its grounds where Jews and other Hitler opponents were tortured, mis-treated, and killed during twelve long years.

As far as I know, not a single Jew lives in Oranienburg today. Most left in the early '30s, when life in small towns became unbearable for them well before it happened in the larger cities. By the mid-1930s the synagogue was closed and the community dissolved. The handful of Jews who remained till the end were arrested, shipped east, and never heard from again. The small Jewish cemetery that Louis helped to build and where he is buried has survived and is surprisingly well preserved. The Nazis never got around to destroying it. As someone once explained this historical anomaly: "dead Jews were of no great concern to them. . . . It was only the living ones they were after."

The synagogue where Louis and Martin presided was pillaged and burned to the ground. A memorial stone now marks the spot. Virtually none of today's Oranienburgers remember Jews living in their midst and the little cemetery with its dozens of headstones is the only other evidence that Jewish life once flourished here.

On my several visits, I have always been received with courtesy and re-spect. The local paper reports my appearances as an interesting curiosity— an American ex-Oranienburger who "made good" and whom the town fa-thers gladly claim as a native son. "We remember our Jews with pleasure," several people assured me, though without much conviction. "And by the way," the mayor told me, "we've never had a Finance Minister from here, even if he is from another country!"

From the beginning, the Nazi years were a terrible time for Germany's Jews. Few had believed that Hitler would truly come to power, and when he did—suddenly and abruptly—most were utterly bewildered. In the ensuing years, as the Nazis tightened the noose, the Jews found themselves progressively deprived of their economic security and the psychological underpinnings to their self-image as members of German society. At first, there were those who hoped that the worst fears would yet prove false and that some basis for a coexistence with German "Aryans" might evolve. The CV urged quiet dignity and an emphasis on "inwardness, spirituality, attachment to the native soil, religious belief, and *Bildung*.[1] For some who had lost the connection to their Jewishness, there was a reawakened consciousness of their roots and history. Interest in Zionism increased, especially among the young. An initial wave of emigration rose and abated quickly, and thereafter those who stayed tried as best they could to wait out the anxious times and to live normal lives.

But that became steadily more difficult. The Nazi leadership's pathological anti-Jewish hatred was unrelenting. Pressures continued to build, and the slow but steady suffocation of German Jewry took its course. By the mid-'30s, most Jews found that after two thousand years on German soil, life there was increasingly intolerable and hopeless for them. The *Kristallnacht* pogroms of 1938 were the final devastating event that left few Jews not desperately pressing to leave and to save themselves. It was now clear that the worst horrors of the Middle Ages had returned. Another great wave of emigration began, until the doors closed forever on those unable to flee.

It was during these years of progressive anti-Jewish persecution that I was growing up in Berlin. Though children do not have much capacity for political sensitivity, I vaguely sensed the mood of helplessness, fear, and desperation of the adults. Yet—to be honest—I did not have an unhappy childhood. I was still a German boy, though a second-class one for reasons I could not understand. My memories of Berlin are of a city in motion, full of excitement, mass rallies, uniformed marchers, and lots of flags, songs, and oratory that sounded strong and convincing. German boys had much to be proud of, we were constantly told. Our racing cars, the Mercedes and Auto Union supermodels, were the world's best; our Autobahn would be the world's finest; Max Schmeling, our heavyweight, was a world champion (until Joe Louis knocked him out in the first round); and our athletes were a certainty for gold at the Berlin Olympics (though it was the Black American sprinter Jesse Owens who would steal the show).

My parents were perennially nervous and anxious, and I became used to their worried whispers behind closed doors. I was young and unconcerned, however, and none of that interfered with my carefree life. For a while I went to a normal German school, where there was the usual bullying but few anti-Semitic incidents I can recall. In 1936—I was ten years old—Jews were no longer welcome among "Aryans," and so I was enrolled in a quite marvelous special school for Jews, set on pleasant grounds in a calm part of West Berlin. The environment was comforting and protective, and the teachers were dedicated and sympathetic and did their best to shield us from outside pressures. In 1939 the Nazis ordered the school closed, and those students who managed to escape scattered to the far corners of the earth. Those who did not get away died in Auschwitz, Bergen-Belsen, Birkenau, Lodz, and other places of Nazi horror.[2]

Like most of my classmates from assimilated homes, it was here, at the Kaliski School, that I had my first exposure to Jewish religion and the traditions that were totally absent in our family. For my parents such emphasis on "Jewishness" had always been evidence of a flawed assimilation—a not sufficiently complete Germanness. On Friday nights, I now learned to light candles, sing Hebrew songs, and celebrate the Sabbath. Two or three times a week there were Hebrew lessons. Once I proudly reported at home that I had been selected to give a solo performance in the singing of the blessing—probably for no other reason than that I could sing louder than the other children. I distinctly recall the mixture of embarrassment and bemusement with which the news of my triumph was received at home. My parents simply did not know what to make of it. They had long since forgotten, if they had ever known it, how to be comfortable with the rituals and symbols of their Jewishness.

There is much that I have forgotten about my Berlin years, but some events remain indelibly etched in my mind. I vividly remember the torchlight parade on the night the Nazis took power and the boycott of Jewish businesses on April 1, 1933, when the takeover had become unconditional and complete. It is the image of the two jackbooted storm troopers in front of our store for women's clothes, which my parents had opened a year before Hitler took power—stern faces, the straps of their caps firmly fixed under their chins—that I can never forget. "Jew-shop," one of their signs read. "Germans don't buy from Jews," exhorted the other.

In the summer of 1935, the Nazis promulgated the Nuremberg Laws. For Germany's Jews, it was a watershed event incorporating Nazi racist theories into the formal legal framework, abrogating their equal citizenship rights granted many decades ago, and formalizing in one giant first step the process of Jewish exclusion from German life. One of the statutes was the "Law for the Protection of German Blood and German Honor." Among other things, it prohibited the employment of "Aryan" women in Jewish homes where, it was alleged, they were at risk to the predatory sexual designs of Jewish men.

We had a *Kinderfräulein* living with us, a solid member of the family who had arrived to be our nanny shortly after my older sister was born. It is because of her that I remember the time the race laws took effect. She was like my second mother, and life without her seemed inconceivable to a nine-year-old child. I feared desperately that she might have to leave and still recall my subsequent relief when it turned out that she could stay. At age forty-six, she was just above the limit specified in the Nazi law as safe from lustful Jewish designs. The far wider and serious implications of the Nuremberg Laws were lost on me.

Of course, I remember *Kristallnacht* most clearly of all—the nearby synagogue in flames, the smashed and looted family store, the shattered glass of Jewish shop windows, and my father's arrest and later return from Buchenwald concentration camp a shriveled, broken, hardly recognizable man.

I was twelve years old by then and more aware of the outside world—our isolation, the destruction of our livelihood, the fear, the urgent need to leave, and my parents' frantic search for a place that would let us in. I remember the savagery in the streets and the sense of helplessness of my parents. I remember the stolid, yet triumphant faces of the brownshirts guarding our broken store, its expropriation by the authorities, and the silent crowds watching the Fasanenstrasse synagogue burn—the very one that had once proudly welcomed the visit of the Kaiser. Nor have I forgotten my mother's tears as our possessions were sold to bargain hunters streaming through our rooms—a ritual then being repeated in Jewish homes all over Berlin. Finally, I remember the silent farewells from family and friends as we boarded the train that would take us away for good. We did not know then that most of those seeing us off would be lost and that we would never see them again.

Perhaps it is not surprising that it is the seminal events in the decline and destruction of German-Jewish life that have remained with me. Each one is a milestone in the Nazi campaign first to dehumanize and isolate, and then to strangle and destroy German Jewry. It took time for the victims to realize the extent of their predicament. No one fully grasped the depth of the Nazis' unrelenting, implacable hatred of Jews or could foresee the savagery with which they were prepared to eliminate them.

Though in an opportunistic and chaotic way, each step they took became a building block on the way to the "Final Solution." I saw them through the eyes of a child, but Germany's adult Jewish population—which included Ewald, Valerie, and Arthur—experienced them directly and with increasing desperation. It was they who bore the brunt of the burden in sustaining the blows.

2

Until the final moment, no one believed that it would happen. All weekend long, the negotiations for a new government went on behind closed doors. Berlin was rife with rumors, and the world waited and watched. "If the negotiations fail, von Papen will probably head a Presidential regime," the *New York Times* speculated on January 29, referring to the reactionary Franz von Papen, who had served as Chancellor once before.

To the French ambassador, a keen observer of German politics, Papen was "superficial, blundering, untrue, ambitious, vain, crafty, and an intriguer," not a first-rate figure, who "enjoyed the peculiarity of being taken seriously by neither his friends nor his enemies."[3] In the Weimar Republic's last days, there were far too many shortsighted and selfish men like him playing the power game. But Papen had the ear of Hindenburg, and the old Field Marshall counted on him to complete the evisceration of Weimar democracy and the restoration of a more autocratic regime. This taming of the Reichstag they called the policy of "national concentration," and in the byzantine intrigue surrounding it, Papen proved himself too clever for his own good. He expected to use Hitler as a tool for his aims while denying him the full powers he demanded, though Hindenburg was reluctant, disliking the uncouth Nazi leader, a mere corporal in the war.

Once before, the big prize had eluded Hitler, and this time he was negotiating furiously. If made Chancellor, he was ready to swear his oath on the constitution, and the *New York Times* reported him to be "in a more docile mood." The betting was that he would be restrained not only by the constitution but also by a majority of the non-Nazi cabinet members with whom Papen planned to surround him. Some people were saying that perhaps it was a good experiment to try Hitler as Chancellor, provided he were "dependent on the toleration of democratic forces."[4]

The mere possibility of a Hitler-led government sent shivers through the Jewish community. The stakes for them were extraordinarily high, yet the *Times* made no mention of that in its reports from Berlin. Throughout the fateful weekend, German Jewry watched anxiously, still hoping for a miracle and still incredulous that their most implacable enemy might emerge on top.

On January 30, there was final confirmation. For years, Hitler had been dismissed as an erstwhile Viennese derelict, police spy, and beer hall orator. Even when his party had made dramatic gains at the polls, this violent anti-Semite and muddle-headed fanatic at the outer edge of the political right, had been considered much too extreme to be a serious threat. Yet now he was to be Chancellor of Germany, and for his jubilant idolatrous Berlin *Gauleiter* Joseph Goebbels, this sudden stroke of good fortune was "like a dream."[5] For the Jews it was the worst possible news, but the world took it in stride. Wall Street hardly stirred, and the *New York Times* editorialized that given Hitler's coalition government with only three Nazis in the cabinet, "there is no warrant for immediate concern. It may be that we shall see the tamed Hitler."[6] That night, while the Nazi leadership celebrated and the frightened Jews trembled, a giant torchlight parade of uniformed storm troopers snaked its way through Berlin. Massed columns of brownshirts marched in perfect discipline to the sound of martial music and muffled drums, their flaming torches held high while singing the bloody Nazi songs the Jews dreaded.

The Jewish leadership thought it best to counsel caution and to reassure the anxious. "We confront the new government with great suspicion," the CV told its readers on February 1, pointing, however, to Hitler's promise to uphold the constitution and reprinting his solemn oath in full. "We now put our trust in *Reichspräsident* Hindenburg," the article continued, noting that Jews were loyal Germans and that hard-won civil rights would be vigorously defended.[7] While the assimilationist CV once again chose to emphasize the Jewish commitment as Germans, the Zionists took a different view. "National Socialism is an antagonistic movement," they stated flatly, and there was no denying that it had become Germany's determining force. They too counseled quiet dignity, yet their conclusion differed sharply. In their view, the developments showed more than ever the need for a Jewish consciousness and a separate identity and a Jewish state.[8] For Goebbels, nothing that the Jews or non-Nazi press was writing mattered any longer. "The Jew-Press is backpedaling furiously," he gloated in his diary. "We do nothing. We want to lull them into a sense of security . . . the better to seize them later."[9]

Papen and his right-wing friends had expected to use Hitler to install an autocratic regime under their control. To their intense surprise, however, he quickly turned the tables on them, elbowed them aside, and established a one-man, one-party dictatorship instead. From the moment he was sworn in, he unloosed a torrent of feverish activity to put himself into total control and to obliterate his opposition. Within a few short months, in a series of lightning moves combining audacity, deception, outright lies, and brutal force, he seized total power, destroyed Germany's federal structure, crushed all democratic institutions, outlawed every rival party, and achieved the total Nazification of Germany.

Neither the constitution nor the limitations of cabinet government restrained him. Two days after becoming Chancellor, Hitler maneuvered the opposition into a deadlock. Then, claiming a decision-making paralysis, he persuaded Hindenburg to dissolve the Reichstag and to allow him to govern by decree, pending new elections. Next, Hitler convinced him of the imminence of a Communist revolt and induced him to sign yet another decree "for the protection of people and state." Communist and Socialist meetings were outlawed, their headquarters raided, their newspapers banned, and the separate powers of the provincial governments restricted. Henceforth only Nazis were permitted to demonstrate in the upcoming election campaign. "Where is equality?" the *Berliner Tageblatt* asked plaintively on February 2. It would be the last time such a question could be publicly raised.

There were only two other Nazis in the government, but for Hitler that was quite enough. Wilhelm Frick was Minister of Interior, while Hermann Göring, without portfolio, had assumed the same job in Prussia. Both were longtime party stalwarts and behind a jolly, corpulent exterior Göring was an especially ruthless and cynical brute. His job gave him control of the police and he at once used it to swear in fifty thousand SA and SS "auxiliaries" for the security forces. While Hitler maneuvered politically, ignoring cabinet government but retaining a thin veil of pseudolegality for his moves, Göring's forces took to the streets. Communists and Socialists were hunted down, attacked, and arrested, and the regular police forbidden to interfere. With the opposition on the run and their media banned, Goebbels had the field all to himself and used it to inundate the public with a barrage of Nazi propaganda.

Nazi street terror exploded. For weeks the party had hoped for a sign of open protest or revolt from the Communists. If they could claim an uprising, it would be the perfect pretext for seizing absolute power for good, but to their frustration nothing happened to give them the excuse to move— until, that is, the evening of February 27. Hitler was spending a quiet few hours at the home of his Berlin *Gauleiter*, "relaxing, playing music on the gramophone and telling stories,"[10] when news was received that the Reichstag was on fire. Even today there is no complete certainty of its cause, but as Hitler and Goebbels raced to the scene, Göring, in a high state of agitation, was already there directing the police. "This is the beginning of the Communist revolution," the excited Göring shouted. "There will be no mercy . . . every Communist official must be shot. . . . Every Communist deputy must this very night be strung up! No mercy will be shown to the Socialists as well."[11]

His threats were no mere hyperbole. Within days, assured by Hitler that an emergency was at hand, the docile and tired old Hindenburg signed yet another decree—one of a total of thirty-three promulgated during the month. This time the order suspended all civil liberties, free expression, and rights to privacy, authorized extralegal searches and arrests, and empowered the Reich to take over full decision-making control from the federal states. Thus the stage was set for the next phase of the Nazi takeover— the *Gleichschaltung*—bringing under Hitler's control all governmental authority in Germany and enabling him to act at will and do as he wished.

March 5 was the last time Germans would have anything resembling a free election, and in spite of the arrest of Communist and Socialist leaders and massive intimidation of the opposition, Hitler's party still won only 43 percent of the popular vote. But none of that mattered any more. Later that month the Reichstag, stripped of its Communist and Socialist members, dutifully passed an enabling act that formally authorized Hitler to rule by decree for four years, making him the country's undisputed dictator. Subsequently it would be claimed that it had all been done by perfectly legal means, but that is at best a gross distortion of the truth. He had used a combination of deception and violence to bring a rump Reichstag to heel and to force it into surrendering him total power. The result was a reign of terror unlike anything Germany had ever seen. Freed from all constraints, Nazi gangs ran wild in the streets. Communists, Socialists, and members of opposition parties were rounded up wholesale, murdered outright, or taken to impromptu "wild" concentration camps where they were tortured and old scores were settled. Books were burned and intellectuals and opposition journalists were harassed and driven out. The hated Jews were not forgotten: they now became the principal targets.

"On March 18 our beloved son and brother, baker's apprentice Siegbert Kindermann, aged eighteen, suffered a tragic fate," an obituary announced in the *Tageblatt*. The truth of Kindermann's "tragic fate" was that he was a Jew beaten to death by Nazis because he had once complained about them to the police. Elsewhere in Berlin, a Jewish lawyer named Günther Joachim was tortured and died in hospital on March 22. Two Jewish Berliners, Leibel Vollschläger and a dentist named Phillipstal, were tortured on the streets in broad daylight and suffered a similar fate. A Jewish notary named Kurt Lange was killed and thrown into a lake.[12] No one knows how many such attacks occurred in Berlin, but throughout the length and breadth of Germany the toll rose into the hundreds.

In Kiel, a Jewish Socialist lawyer was openly murdered; in Magdeburg it was a prominent town councillor.[13] The *New York Times* reported that in Munich a rabbi "was dragged out of his bed . . . taken to a firing range . . . shown a machine gun all set for business, blindfolded and informed that his last hour had come. After he failed to show the proper respect, he was beaten and let go."[14] In Breslau, the SA engaged in one of their favorite sports by dragging Jewish judges and lawyers out of their chambers and forcing them to strip naked in the streets.

All over Germany, the brownshirts went on an unprecedented anti-Jewish rampage, and as the terror intensified the foreign press took notice and world opinion reacted with revulsion. Twenty-thousand outraged New Yorkers attended a mass protest in Madison Square Garden and thirty-five thousand more jammed the streets outside. Labor pledged its support and Jewish leaders petitioned President Roosevelt for help. In Warsaw, Polish Jews closed their businesses in protest, in London's Jewish Whitechapel district there were anti-German demonstrations, in Paris intellectuals assailed the Nazi violence, and everywhere threats of boycotting German products were being heard.

Within Germany, a complete breakdown of law and order threatened. Local SA gangs were taking matters into their own hands, murdering, looting, blackmailing, and stealing from Jews without even the pretense of any legality and with no central direction or control. Occasionally there were clashes with police, and even the SS had to be called out to protect the public against SA assaults. To be sure, Hitler had no sympathy for Jews, and at first the storm troopers were useful to him as an instrument of terror and intimidation. Göring, hearing early complaints, had been equally unconcerned and jovially expressed the view that "when planks are being planed, chips must fall somewhere."[15] Yet now even Hitler's own authority was dangerously in question, and business feared damage in export markets and a harming of the weak economy. Something had to be done to bring the SA under control.

For a while, Hitler hesitated, but on March 26, he summoned Goebbels and announced his decision: there would be a nationwide boycott against Jewish business and professionals.[16] In one bold stroke, an economic blow was to be delivered against the Jews, while SA aggression would be channeled and brought under control. The Jews themselves had to be pressured and threatened to help stop the foreign boycott of German goods. Everything would be done systematically and in an orderly way. To the outside world the boycott would be justified as a legitimate response to world Jewry's lies about German violence.

Dutiful as ever, Goebbels at once unleashed a giant propaganda campaign, announcing the boycott as "retaliation for the horror stories and atrocity tales of international Jewry against Germany." The party was instructed to begin the boycott promptly at 10 A.M. on Saturday, April 1, with SA troopers posted in front of all Jewish stores warning Aryans not to enter the premises. The action would continue until the foreign "lies" against Germany ceased. To pressure the Jews into action, Göring ordered their leaders into his presence, berated them at length, and demanded that they ask the foreign press and their coreligionists abroad to stop their accusations. Unless you put a stop to it immediately, he threatened them, "I shall no longer be able to vouch for the safety of German Jews."[17] The *New York Times* quoted Hitler as saying that "Jews must be made to realize they will feel the full effect of protest abroad," and the Nazi threats and blackmail produced the desired result. The frightened Jewish leadership urgently petitioned their confreres abroad to cease and desist, lest their situation grow even worse. The CV's newspaper, *Centralverein Zeitung,* headlined its front-page story, "565,000 GERMAN JEWS SOLEMNLY PROTEST,"[18] dutifully echoing the patently false claim that stories of Nazi atrocities were nothing but propaganda and lies.

On the day of the boycott, April 1, the public generally complied, while many Jews simply closed their shops and offices and stayed at home as storm troopers patrolled the stores with signs warning the people to stay out. It was an ominous and threatening sight, but Hitler's orders were obeyed, and the violence was over. The boycott was called off after a day, and in the following weeks business returned to normal.

Within a few short months, Weimar's weak political structure had collapsed under the Nazi pressure. Germany's only experiment with democracy had lasted a mere fourteen years, and the position of the Jews had been fundamentally changed. Their worst enemies were in control of the government and more than a century of struggle for equality had been undone.

3

After the boycott, indiscriminate street attacks ended. A measure of uneasy quiet returned. The initial phase of the Nazis' seizure of power was over, and Hitler needed a period of calm to consolidate his position.

To bring the country's institutional framework firmly under his control required dealing with unresolved problems. The churches resisted Nazification and were repelled by the lawlessness of the early weeks. Relations with the military and the *Stahlhelm,* their nationalist wing, were unstable, and the question of whether they or the SA would be the dominant factor among the armed forces required his attention. Finally, there was the strong foreign criticism and distrust of his regime from abroad. The League of Nations officially censured Germany for anti-Jewish violence in Upper Silesia, and the business community was worried about the repercussions on trade and investment. The German economy was still weak and precarious, unemployment remained very high, and delivering on his promise to alleviate it would solidify his domestic standing.

For Hitler, it was a matter not of abandoning basic aims but of adjusting their implementation to the realities of the moment. Even the boycott had taught him a valuable lesson. For the Jews, the public's passivity had been a major shock. For Hitler, their apathy and lack of enthusiasm for going after Jews, in spite of Goebbels's violent propaganda, was no less disappointing. It showed that more time was needed to rally the public to more active support of anti-Semitic measures. The risk of a helter-skelter, indiscriminate removal of Jews from the economy was also becoming clear. A case in point was the matter of the Tietz department store chain that was in trouble and needed government help to survive. Jewish-owned department stores and retail chains had long been a central target of Nazi propaganda. The zealots were eager to destroy them at once, and a government loan to Jews was anathema. Yet with thousands of employees threatened with job losses, simply letting Tietz go bankrupt was no answer. For the moment, reality had to triumph over ideology; distasteful or not, the loan to the Jews had to go forward.[19]

But though the street violence had ended, the Jews' troubles were not over. Anti-Semitism was now firmly established as official government policy, and the people, though relatively passive, seemed willing to accept Nazi propaganda's artificial abstraction of "the Jew" as at least partly responsible for their troubles. If a small number of fanatics couldn't wait to continue the anti-Jewish attacks, even fewer Germans were prepared to oppose them. The greatest number of Germans simply accepted the situation and silently acquiesced.

In the weeks and months that followed, a stream of edicts advanced the step-by-step process of Jewish exclusion from German life, with professionals, civil servants, and those active in arts and the media as the first targets. In April, there were new laws dismissing most Jewish judges and civil servants. Others restricted the access of Jewish doctors to the national health service and limited Jewish faculty and students at universities. A law to ban Jews in agriculture did not have a major impact but the exclusion of doctors, lawyers, and notaries—fields in which Jews were important—robbed many of their established livelihoods. Eventually, Jews were also removed from the stock exchanges and excluded from military service.

Once Goebbels had taken over control of the media and cultural institutions, the total exclusion of all Jews from these fields was another major blow. The large Jewish-owned Mosse and Ullstein media empires were forcibly "Aryanized" by 1934. The *Vossische* simply ceased publication, the flagship liberal *Berliner Tageblatt* began to sing the Nazi tune, and the Ullstein family was forced to surrender their properties for one-tenth the market value.[20]

At the end of the first year of Nazi rule, the flood of anti-Jewish laws finally appeared to abate. Many Jews had been financially ruined, close to 40,000 had left Germany, and another 23,000 followed the next year. Within the first three years more than 100,000 had abandoned the country. Hindenburg, their last hope, had died, and Hitler was Germany's undisputed dictator. Still, close to 400,000 German Jews were still in place. After generations of life in Germany only the specially endangered, younger Zionists, or the particularly adventurous and farsighted had left. Most others simply could not yet come to terms with the full implications of their predicament, and many still retained their poignant loyalty to Germany.

Many in fact mistook the lull in anti-Jewish measures after 1933 as a sign of hope. Quoting the fanatic and duplicitous Goebbels that "what needs to be solved concerning the Jewish question has been solved," the *Jüdische Rundschau* late in the year still found it possible to advise its readers that in spite of the hardships, "the future of our economic existence, though circumscribed, appears guaranteed."[21] It was probably what the majority wanted to hear.

Arthur Eloesser had found it necessary to make major adjustments. "Dear Meister Thomas Mann," he wrote in 1934 to his famous friend who had fled Germany. "I had withdrawn to the study of the Bible, but your Joseph trilogy has made me a reader again. . . . I hope I shall have a chance to review it in the Jewish or foreign press. The German papers are no longer open to me. I have been excluded from them. One must not be at war with one's destiny but seek in it a personal rejuvenation. . . . This summer I was in Palestine, where our son now lives. . . . It left a deeply emotional imprint on me, like a return after two thousand years. Last year I began the study of Hebrew, but at my age it is not easy."[22]

Arthur's letter to Thomas Mann reflected both new emotions and old attachments, and his struggle to come to terms with them. He had been among the first to be silenced, the *Vossische* was gone, and no German paper would employ him. His books were on the Nazi list for burning, and in a painfully emotional move he had been forced to raise money by auctioning off his treasured vast personal library. His son Max, a Zionist, had gone off to Palestine, and his daughter was planning to emigrate to Latin America.

Throughout his life he had been a patriot who treasured German culture and was deeply committed to his country. If anyone was the prototype of a thoughtful assimilated German Jew, it was Arthur. Yet now he was silenced, in increasingly precarious health with ailing lungs, and forced to question the past and confront a vastly changed present and future. In his midsixties, what was left for him, an old friend would say in a moving eulogy after his death, was "Geist, Haltung und Hoffnung" (spirit, dignity, and hope).[23]

He had to face the reality of having been rejected as a German—even the Association of the War Blind had seen fit to exclude its Jewish ex-soldier members as unworthy and unfit.[24] The further reality was that assimilation and progressive integration of the Jewish community had failed and that Jews were once again pariahs in their own land. "A few days ago," he wrote sadly, "I met several actor [friends] in the street. They turned away as if they hadn't seen me. I understand—they feared that their acquaintance with old 'Elo' might harm them."[25]

But there was also another reality, equally unfamiliar and unexpected—the discovery of a Jewishness he had long since dismissed or forgotten. Yet he could not easily finish with what had once been, and he continued to cling to it in the poignant series of essays he called *Recollections of a Berlin Jew.* The nostalgic, somewhat idealized view of the past in these articles he wrote for his Jewish readers must have appealed especially to the older ones eager to be reminded of their happier days.

Reaching back to a Jewishness he had long ignored, he turned to the Bible, struggled to master Hebrew, and discovered an admiration for Zionism after visiting his son in Palestine. When he reported on his trip in the *Jüdische Rundschau,* he described the young pioneers, children of middle-class German Jews, with a joyous awe and a touch of envy. They had "finished with Europe," he observed, adding wistfully that if he were thirty or forty years younger he would have liked to be one of them rather than merely an admirer from afar. It was as if he had found a new world, one that before the advent of Hitler he had hardly known was there: "I saw our people for the first time, with its diverse [European] cultural strains combined into something entirely new. There the young can laugh and sing proudly, and in this new land having children carries no risks. Who," he asked sadly, "can still claim that for us?"[26]

Arthur had left Nazi Germany, breathed the air of Palestine, discovered a new reality, and admired what he had seen. Yet he had returned. Why did he not simply pack up his remaining belongings, take his wife, and leave for good? The reason, one suspects, is that in those early Hitler years, Arthur's state of mind was like that of many Jews with deep German roots. He was torn and deeply conflicted, too advanced in years to make a fresh start, and his bonds to Germany were still too strong and old memories too deep to forget. All his life he had lived at a far distance from his Jewishness. Rediscovering his roots was one thing, but abandoning all he had lived for and accepting the end of the dream of Jewish assimilation into German culture as a fact and not merely as a passing nightmare—that was still too hard. He knew it would never again be quite the same, yet he was not ready to abandon all hope. Did the lull in new laws and open assaults not raise the possibility that the future in Germany might yet be stabilized? Had not Goebbels said that it was "guaranteed"?

Some Jews, in fact, had again grown complacent. At Bad Saarow, a resort near Berlin, the American journalist William Shirer noted with surprise that the hotel was filled with them—"still prospering and apparently unafraid."[27] In fact, of course, the respite was brief and Goebbels's soothing words had only been temporizing lies.

In 1934 Hitler massacred the leadership of the party and killed his old enemies on the right. Yet what to do with the Jews remained a subject for nettlesome intraparty discord and debate. For fifteen years he had preached the doctrine of racial purity and railed against the pollution of "Aryan" blood. Why, the party purists asked, were the Jews then still allowed any scope at all? Why could they still meet Aryans in public places and at work, perhaps even marry or intermingle with them?

The zealots were impatient for next steps, and occasionally there were signs that they were again willing to take matters into their own hands. The vicious Julius Streicher called Jewish contacts with Germans *Rassenschande* (racial treason). In Berlin there were new outbreaks of violence on streets and in cafés, and the wildcat banning of Jews from public facilities and parks was on the rise. In Magdeburg the locals prohibited Jews from riding on the city's trams, and in Franconia, where Streicher held sway, lurid tales of Jewish racial treason were the order of the day. Yet who was an Aryan, and who was not? Was a half or quarter Aryan still a Jew? These were matters that had to be settled, the legalists were raising all sorts of questions and objections, and old-line bureaucrats at the Interior Ministry were digging in their heels and resisting new rules.

By 1935 the party's mood threatened to turn ugly once again, and Hitler decided that it was time to act. In September, a giant party rally was scheduled for Nuremberg, and it was there that the next blow would be struck with new laws to deprive Jews formally of their citizenship rights and to define who was an "Aryan" and who was not. Henceforth Jews would be "subjects" of Germany only. Full citizenship and the right to vote would be denied them. Marriages or even sexual relations with "Aryans" were forbidden, and harsh punishments would be meted out to transgressors. No Jew could employ a female "Aryan" servant below the age of forty-five, and even a half-Jew was deemed a non-Aryan, subject to special rules. For a Jew henceforth to display the national flag would be a serious punishable offense. "National Socialism," the Nazi legal experts explained, "opposes the theories of the equality of all men" and is based "on the harsh but necessary recognition of . . . the differences between them based on the laws of nature."[28]

The Nuremberg Laws were the next step in the systematic degradation and isolation of the Jews. For some Jews, though still not for all, they were final confirmation that there was no hope left. But, incredibly, many others were still not willing to give up. Now that matters were "clarified," the CV said, perhaps it was the beginning of a "tolerable arrangement."[29]

4

There wasn't much talk in my family about leaving Germany until about 1937, when the idea began to be pursued with reluctance and no great urgency. Each phase of heightened anti-Jewish activity had been followed by a period of relative calm—a false signal to those who, like my parents, were eager for accommodation and still hoping to wait out the storm. In Hitler's first year only about 7 percent of Germany's 520,000 Jews abandoned the country for good. Then the annual exodus once again trailed off.

In my parents' circle almost no one emigrated in the early years. The one exception was my father's youngest brother, Theodor, who left with his bride to try his luck in Brazil. Their adventures in the strange and exotic South American backcountry fascinated me, but my parents showed only modest interest. "They are young and have nothing to lose," was the way they dismissed Uncle Theo as a special case. The problem was also that most countries made it hard to let a Jewish refugee in. The largest number of early departures were young Zionists bound for Palestine to work on the land, or older idealists committed to a Jewish state. For my parents, however, living in Palestine was out of the question. "We're not Zionists," they would say dismissively, "we're Europeans and don't belong in the Orient." Sometimes my father would add—only half in jest—that he couldn't imagine living with "nothing but Jews."

A handful of early emigrants fled to neighboring European countries, which, in principle, seemed a more palatable alternative, but gaining admission anywhere was difficult without money or special connections. Further away, America was everyone's first choice but it was common knowledge that getting a visa was extraordinarily hard. The Statue of Liberty might be the symbol of America as traditional haven for the downtrodden and oppressed, but letting in new immigrants had become a hot political issue, unemployment was high, and the State Department had its share of anti-Semites hiding behind a wall of bureaucratic footdragging and delays.

Nor were stories of new arrivals washing dishes and sweeping floors in New York City particularly encouraging for those who, like my parents, were still making an adequate living in Berlin. In the beginning the going had been tough, but Hitler had stimulated the economy with public works, unemployment declined steadily, people again had money to spend, and their store was doing surprisingly well. The disenfranchised Jewish professional class was in trouble, but for small businesses the economic prospects were not bad.

When Hitler took power, pessimists lamented that a thousand years of German-Jewish life had come to an end, and Zionists said they had predicted it all along. But for committed assimilationists like my parents, there was still the sense of oneness with Germany, a clinging to the values of the past, and a stubborn reluctance to throw in the towel and give up on Germany for good.

The grownups were increasingly isolated from regular German life, and so were we children. I no longer had any non-Jewish friends and my parents discouraged even casual contact with "Aryan" children as too dangerous. I was under strict orders to avoid them and to shun the ubiquitous brown uniforms in the streets. In elementary school I had once been vaguely jealous of my classmates in their snappy Hitler Youth regalia, but now I knew better. "Cross to the other side when you see them," my mother warned me, "never provoke them and if attacked run away, and above all never fight back!"

At home, adults avoided political subjects in front of the children. Sensitive matters were discussed in whispers behind closed doors. "Walls have ears," the adults preached to us. Thus, the outside environment was tense and never without risk even for a child, but I got used to it and didn't much mind. The school became my haven where I felt free. There we were among ourselves, secure from a hostile world, with dedicated teachers who did their best to protect and prepare us for the uncertainties ahead.

Gradually, however, things got worse, and by early 1938 my parents could no longer avoid the truth. Their isolation from normal German life was nearly total, the degradations and the economic squeeze increased, and there was no longer any mistaking the ominous trend. A triumphant Hitler was at the height of his power. In March he annexed Austria, where the ensuing anti-Semitic riots in Vienna surpassed the worst of the outbreaks in Germany. In the fall he seized the German parts of Czechoslovakia, and at home his secret preparations for war were moving into high gear and all those in key posts who had previously counseled caution were gone.

For years party radicals had chafed at the lack of a clear-cut policy for the total elimination of the hated Jew and fumed at Hitler's intermittent heeding of those who warned of the economic risks of indiscriminate frontal attacks. Now, however, the worst and most intemperate of the Jew-haters were in charge, and there was no longer any holding them back. The cynical, greedy Hermann Göring was the economic czar. Robbing and expropriating Jewish possessions constituted one of the ways he intended to finance Germany's armament drive. Personal enrichment appealed to him as well. Heinrich Himmler, cunning and evil, was in undisputed control of the instruments of terror of the SS, and Hitler's most fanatical vassal and Jew-hater, Joseph Goebbels, was driving the Nazi propaganda machine.

There was no love lost between these men in their ruthless internecine struggles for influence and favor at Hitler's court. But in their eagerness to rob and punish the Jew they were as one. Only the degree of vindictiveness and the inventiveness of their imaginations distinguished one from the other in the unrestrained pursuit of a common goal: to rob "the Jew," humiliate and degrade him in the public eye and—having dispossessed him—to get rid of him.

By 1938, what they called "Aryanization"—taking Jewish property and expelling Jews from economic life—had moved into high gear. First it had been the poultry trade, pharmacies, and bookshops from which Jews were banned. Real estate agents were next, then working as sales agents was forbidden. Finally even Jewish newspaper vendors and rag merchants were no longer allowed.

Large enterprises had long since been forcibly sold at nominal values and their Jewish owners thrown out. The smaller businesses and shops were next. All personal assets above five thousand marks had to be registered; special taxes, for Jews only, were steadily ratcheted up; and Jewish shops had to be publicly identified as such. At the beginning of the year, forty thousand businesses were still in Jewish hands, but over the next twelve months almost 80 percent were liquidated or forcibly sold.

By midyear, my parents were also under the gun and engaged in quiet, despairing negotiations with the one "Aryan" saleswoman my mother had trained and employed for years. The deal would involve turning over the store to her for a fraction of its true worth. She was terribly sorry, the young lady said: her boyfriend was a party member and had the money, but he simply wasn't allowed to pay more. My mother, who had worked especially hard to build the business, was sad and bitter. But at least there would be enough money to outfit us for leaving and to live on until we could find a place that would let us in.

Some Christians might sympathize with the Jewish plight, but no one really complained. When all was said and done, taking over a Jew's business for a song was an opportunity many did not want to miss.

If "Aryanization" was the main economic focus of the stepped-up attack on the Jews, dehumanizing and harassing them was an equally painful parallel thrust. Streicher's pornographic and lurid Jew-hating newspaper was now on view at street corners in every German city and town. In the parks, Jews had to sit on special yellow benches, restaurants and cafés put up "Jews not wanted here" signs, and every day a new chicanery was being announced. In June, Munich's main synagogue had been torched; a few weeks later Nuremberg had followed suit. Goebbels decreed that every male Jew add "Israel" and every female "Sara" to their names, and in October our passports were stamped with a special red *J*—which made gaining entry in another country even more difficult. For the cowed and anxious Jews, the pressure to leave was dramatically up, but though the world professed sympathy, most countries' doors remained firmly shut or, at best, open only a crack. An international conference at Evian on Lake Geneva produced much talk but no concrete results. "If you love our Jews so much, why don't you take them all," Goebbels taunted the critics from abroad. It was a challenge no country was willing to accept.

Where to go and who might admit him had become the dominant preoccupation of every German Jew, but at this late hour the options were desperately few. For America, there were quotas, waiting lists, and that most precious piece of paper—the affidavit of support from a relative or kind stranger willing to vouch that one would not become a public charge. But quota numbers were sparse, waiting lists years oversubscribed, and the magical affidavits for most of us quite impossible to get. There were stories of people imploring namesakes gleaned from American telephone directories, but the ploy rarely worked. Elsewhere one needed a "Certificate" in one place, a "Permit" in another, and in Latin America, a "Llamada"— "Schamada" we kids called them. In time my head was filled with a whole hierarchy of documents and more—or less—desirable countries to go to. America, Canada, and Australia were hardly attainable, but clearly the big prize. Brazil was OK, but there they no longer wanted Jews; Argentina and Chile were not bad, but they had practically closed their borders as well. Bolivia and Paraguay were said to be bad, though there were whispers that their consuls were bribable. Occasionally, there was talk of a few hardy souls having fled to Shanghai, a wild city in China reputed to be by far the worst place of all. I remember hearing lurid tales about horrid diseases and unfortunate sick arrivals living in misery without enough to eat. Shanghai, everyone agreed, was clearly at the bottom of the list.

Life was precarious and tense, and some thought it couldn't get any worse, yet no German Jew who lived through the climactic events of November 1938 will ever forget them as one of the most traumatic experiences of his life. History remembers it as *Kristallnacht,* or the night of the broken glass, but that sounds deceptively benign. It conveys none of the sheer fury, violence, and terror of the officially sanctioned assaults on Jews over several days. *New York Times* correspondent Tollschuss described it as "a wave of destruction, looting and incendiarism unparalled in German history since the Thirty Years War."[30] The attacks began in the early morning hours of the tenth, and by nightfall, Tollschuss reported, "there was scarcely a Jewish shop, café, office or synagogue in the country not either wrecked, burned severely or damaged," with wholesale arrests of Jewish men shipped "for their own protection" to the Buchenwald, Dachau, and Oranienburg concentration camps, where they were so brutally maltreated that many would not survive.

To David Buffum, the outraged U.S. Consul in Leipzig, it was "a flatigious [sic] attack upon a helpless minority that very probably has no counterpart in the course of the civilized world."[31] His colleague in Stuttgart described

Jews suffering "vicissitudes . . . that would sound unreal to one living in an enlightened country during the twentieth century."[32] London's *Daily Telegraph's* Hugh Carleton Greene reported that for a time mob law ruled Berlin, adding, "I have seen several anti-Jewish outbreaks in Germany during the last five years, but never anything as nauseating as this."[33] In England the archbishop of Canterbury issued a letter in the name of all English Christians, "to give immediate expression to the feeling of indignation . . . at the deeds of cruelty and destruction."[34] The United States recalled its ambassador, and the *Washington Post* observed that only the St. Bartholomew's massacre in 1572 had equaled *Kristallnacht* in ferocity and blood.[35]

The violence and brutality of the attacks deeply demoralized Germany's Jews and left scars from which many would never recover. The events were a turning point for every Jew. It was the start of a new chapter in their persecution, the final phase of their total social and economic exclusion from German life. Henceforth no one could still hope to wait out the bad times. Now everyone wanted to leave.

For Hitler, who personally ordered the attacks, it was a turning point as well—the move to an unrestrained pursuit of the three anti-Jewish objectives he had long had in mind: to take from the Jews everything they owned, to humiliate and brand them as *Untermenschen* unworthy of human consideration or pity, and to drive as many as possible across the borders of the Reich, while isolating the rest.

With his secret preparations for war in high gear, he had waited for the right moment to make the big push. The harassments had been steadily stepped up, and two weeks earlier, some seventeen thousand ex-Polish stateless Jews had been summarily seized and transported by train and cattle car to the German-Polish frontier. Poland resisted their return and barred the way, and the desperate refugees were left in a no-man's-land, without food or drink and suffering greatly.

On Monday, November 7, the weather in Paris was unseasonably mild but Herschel Grynszpan, a seventeen-year-old Jew, had other things on his mind. He was born in Hanover, where his parents, who were among the unfortunate expelled Jews languishing at the Polish border in an open field, had lived for many years. Herschel was greatly distraught, and that morning he decided that he must act. A slight young man, only five feet two inches in height, wearing a tan raincoat, he boarded the métro en route to the German Embassy at 78 rue de Lille. The German ambassador was unavailable, he was told, but Ernst vom Rath, a third secretary, received him politely in his office on the third floor. "Sale boche" (dirty Kraut) Grynszpan screamed at him in his anger and grief, drew a pistol from his pocket, and shot the hapless diplomat five times at point-blank range.

Two years earlier, a Swiss Nazi leader had been assassinated by a Jew, but the Olympics had been on, and Hitler held back. Now he was riding high and had no compunction against using the Paris shooting as pretext for an all-out assault on the Jews. "Make it look spontaneous," he instructed the eager Goebbels, who was itching to take charge. No one must wear a uniform, the Führer ordered, but "let the SA have their fling."[36] And so they did, while the SS, police, and firemen stood by. Over the next two days, at least seventy-five hundred Jewish businesses were smashed, thousands of homes wrecked, most synagogues desecrated, burned, or destroyed, and dozens of Jews killed. Hundreds were wounded, and thirty thousand men were arrested and carried off.[37]

For a day or two, vom Rath had hovered between life and death, and I remember the adults' dark forebodings of what new chicaneries might be in store for us if he should die. When he did, on the ninth, the pogroms started at once. Our store was smashed during the night, and my distraught mother rushed off in the morning to save what she could. I was left alone and under strict orders to stay indoors, but the excitement was too great. I simply had to see what was going on.

Not yet thirteen, in short pants and kneesocks, with tousled blond hair and blue eyes, I was the perfect picture of the "Aryan" boy. So much so, in fact, that a local photographer had once used my smiling face, a tooth missing, as a model for a new beverage advertisement plastered all over Berlin, with the hilarious caption—"The German boy drinks only Katreiner Kaffee." That was before 1935; thereafter the photographer wouldn't have dared using a Jew, regardless of his Germanic looks. As I raced along the Kurfürstendamm toward the Fasanenstrasse synagogue a few blocks away, I was a Jewish impostor who blended perfectly into the scene. But no one could tell, and not wearing a uniform wasn't a giveaway that day. Curious crowds were gazing at the horrendous destruction all around, yet not a single Nazi uniform was in sight. Every Jewish store had been wrecked, glass littered the sidewalks, some shops had been looted, a few were burned out, and from the direction of the synagogue rising clouds of smoke could be seen.

I have never forgotten the sight that awaited me at the scene. What had once been Berlin's finest temple was a smoldering ruin. Debris littered the ground, firemen merely protected the buildings nearby, and a large crowd of onlookers stood behind police barricades and watched in silence. Even for a child my age it was an eerie and upsetting sight, and for the first time I recall being so frightened that I quickly turned back and ran for home. Some of the Jewish shop owners were in the street attempting to sweep up the glass and the debris. No one helped, people just stared and walked on, evidently no less stunned and disturbed by what they saw than I.

On the Kurfürstendamm that morning, the crowds were subdued, but elsewhere in Germany the pogroms were violent and grim. Torah rolls were publicly burned; some Jews were forced to walk over their prayer shawls, others made to read Hitler's *Mein Kampf* aloud or sing Nazi songs. Many absorbed cruel beatings or were humiliated in especially sadistic ways. "In one Jewish section," the shocked Buffum reported from Leipzig, "an eighteen-year-old boy was hurled from a third-story window," others were thrown into a small stream, and horrified spectators were commanded to "spit at them, defile them with mud, and jeer at their plight. . . . Victims with bloody, badly bruised faces fled to this office."[38]

When it was over, the Nazi chiefs held a lengthy session to take stock. The papers said it was a "leadership summit to discuss the urgent need to solve the Jewish question" and reported that total agreement had been achieved.[39] Göring was in the chair, and Goebbels, Himmler, Frick, and virtually all other Nazi leaders were present. They decreed that Jewish stores, agencies, and trading activities had to be closed, and Jews were ordered to repair the damage at once.

In fact, there was more gloating at the predicament of the Jews than serious discussion at their meeting. The insurance companies were complaining, but that was easily fixed: Jews were ordered to clean up their own mess and pay for the damage themselves. The insurance money would go directly to the state. A billion marks fine was levied on the Jews as "punishment" for Grynszpan's deed, and a long list of additional measures were announced. Jews can no longer sit next to Germans in theatres and cinemas, Goebbels declared, and Göring dreamed of barring Jews from parks or restricting them to small parts of forests stocked with animals "which look damned similar to the Jews—the elk has a hooked nose for instance." "At the moment [the Jew] is small and ugly and stays at home," Dr. Goebbels announced to the gathering with evident satisfaction. In an ominous preview of what was to come, Göring expressed the view that for those Jews who hadn't fled, "there would be a final reckoning of our account," in the event of war. Their sadistic pleasure at the Jewish plight seemingly had no bounds: "I would not wish to be a Jew in Germany," Göring cheerfully opined. Goebbels, Himmler, Frick, and the others did not disagree.[40]

5

Ettersberg Mountain lies five miles north of Weimar in a large forest of beech trees. Once the princely domain of *Turn und Taxis* and the site of a stately manor house, the place was a favorite destination for Cranach the Elder, and for Goethe, Schiller, Wieland, Liszt, and all the great poets, painters, and composers who left their imprint on the little Thuringian city of Weimar and made its name synonomous with German culture.

Schiller brought his friend Goethe to Schloss Ettersberg to show him the corner room in the west wing where he finished writing his drama *Maria Stuart*. Goethe later recalled how they had strolled through its many rooms to admire the fine tapestries and paintings. Promenading with friends in Ettersberg Forest was one of his special pleasures, and a large oak tree where he sat to meditate and admire the view has been preserved as a national monument: "I often came here," Goethe wrote, "to look out at the world's richness and splendor. . . . It is a place where one can feel great and free."[41]

For the 238,000 prisoners who suffered here between 1937 and 1945, the German poet's celebration of Ettersberg's charms will forever ring hollow. Tortured and abused under murderous conditions, their hell in Goethe's favorite forest defies the imagination. Many did not survive. Thirty-three thousand, four-hundred and sixty-two hospital deaths were officially recorded but that does not include those who were beaten to death, executed, shot "while escaping," or killed as they were transported here. No one will ever know the true number but the best estimate puts it at sixty thousand murders or more. Ewald was one of the "lucky" ones. He spent only six weeks here and got out alive.

In 1936, SS Leader Heinrich Himmler—ever the efficient administrator—had done some forward planning and ordered the construction of a new "spacious concentration camp for up to 6,000 inmates . . . to serve the Reich not only in peace but also in war." *Gauleiter* Fritz Sauckel, another of the early Nazis, eagerly sought the honor for his province of Thuringia, and a year later he counted the opening of this place of horrors as one of his shining accomplishments.[42] The local citizenry was not in a position to object, though naming the camp after their famous Ettersberg, as had originally been intended, offended their sensibilities. The proliferation of beech trees provided Himmler's bureaucracy with a suitable alternative designation, which is why the world will forever remember it as *Konzentrationslager (KZ) Buchenwald*.[43]

They came for Ewald shortly before 6 A.M. on the morning after *Kristallnacht*. It was my mother, Valerie, who answered the door and by the time I was awake I could hear her loud, insistently repeated questions: "Why are you taking him? Where is he going? What has he done? What, for God's sake is this about?"

My mother had great reservoirs of energy, courage, and determination, and in the weeks and months ahead, she would need every ounce of these inner strengths to rescue her husband and to see us through our final ordeal in Germany. She was just forty years old then, and still a strikingly attractive woman who over the past ten years had demonstrated the toughness and unflappable smarts that would be the key to our survival as refugees from Hitler.

As a very young woman she had married a wealthy man with a seemingly solid future, but in the last several years all of that had changed. First came the disgrace of the bank's collapse and the sudden impoverishment of the family. It was she who had taken charge, moved us to Berlin, and with sheer guts, willpower, and persistence put things together again. She found the capital to open the store and built it into a thriving business. More recently, it was she who had carried on the painful "Aryanization" negotiations, while keeping her children out of harm's way in Nazi Berlin and making the rounds of consulates in search of visas for us to go somewhere—anywhere.

Now she was about to face infinitely greater challenges. Though she could not have realized it, she was one of thousands of Jewish women suddenly called upon to do things most would never have imagined possible. Some would find the task overwhelming but others—and Valerie was one of them—would rise to the occasion and accomplish the near impossible to save their husbands and sons, keep their families together, and assume critical burdens in the emigration years.

The two men who came to arrest my father were detectives from the local police station. They looked every bit like cops in their dark leather coats, and for the fifteen minutes it took him to get dressed, they stood just inside the front door, polite but visibly uncomfortable and uncommunicative. "Pack a small bag, in case it takes a few days," one of them advised helpfully. Their only answer to my mother's repeated questions was that they were just following orders and knew nothing. The last thing I remember was the look of fear on my father's face as he turned one last time to look at us, and my mother's stony gaze as he disappeared down the stairs. I think she knew.

Ewald was held most of the day at the precinct police station. One of the first to arrive, he had captured a seat in the hallway, and there he sat, silent and anxious, while the room filled with frightened neighborhood Jews clutching suitcases and squeezed on benches or squatting on the floor. None knew why they had been arrested or what lay ahead. Apart from an occasional brusque order for silence, they were being left alone, but there was little talk. A local constable recognized Ewald and with an embarrassed smile and a mumbled "Here, eat this" slipped him a bar of chocolate. It was the only food he would eat for twenty-four hours and the last act of kindness he would experience in a long time.

In the evening, two of Berlin's famous dark green enclosed police vans pulled into the courtyard, and now it was the Gestapo political police who took charge of transporting them to a central gathering place at the huge Alexanderplatz main police facility. What came next was an anxious night in a much more hostile environment, while several thousand Jews were being brought in from all over Berlin. Some were battered and bruised after rough arrests, a few sobbed and moaned, and many were in panic and badly distraught.

It was obvious now that they were victims of a major "*Aktion*." Only later would they learn that thirty thousand Jewish men, some as young as sixteen and others older than sixty, had been rounded up throughout Germany in a deliberate *Kristallnacht* move to rob them of their remaining possessions, give the men a taste of concentration camp life, and shock them into quickly leaving the country. Ewald was one of ten thousand destined for KZ Buchenwald, probably the most brutal of the camps.

The prisoners were fed at 6 A.M., pressed into trucks, and then stuffed into hopelessly overcrowded train compartments to the accompaniment of kicks and curses from a large number of SS guards. The Gestapo had been much nastier than the precinct police, and the SS now in control were worse yet. Several older men had stumbled and fallen in the scramble to get aboard the train and had been brutally beaten for it. Now they lay bleeding on the floor, and when one of the prisoners, a doctor, tried to help he was mercilessly kicked and pummelled for it by two of the guards. "Damned Jew-boys," one of them screamed, "you're KZ birds now, not sanitarium patients. We'll teach you to obey orders and do some real work."

Under heavy guard and sealed into their train, they had passed Leipzig and were headed southeast. The guard's curse confirmed their worst fears: the destination was Buchenwald.

It was when they arrived in Weimar that the real hell began. Members of the SS Death-Head Corps, Himmler's specially chosen thugs in charge of concentration camps, had formed two lines on the station platform between which the Jews had to pass. Some guards had dogs straining on their leashes while their handlers kicked, beat, clubbed, and lashed the prisoners with belts, shoulder straps, whips, and sticks, forcing them to run the gauntlet to waiting trucks accompanied by screamed curses and insults. For the prisoners, it was an indescribable moment of mayhem, pandemonium, and terror. Almost no one escaped the blows, some fell and were seriously injured by those pressing forward from the back, and it was here that the first fatalities occurred. One of the prisoners lay injured on the ground, and when he could not get up a young guard coolly drew his revolver and shot him at point-blank range. A second Jew appeared to go mad. When he began to run he was shot in the back and killed, after which the two corpses had to be dragged aboard the trucks.

Entering the camp was worse yet. The "arrival ceremony" awaiting them had long since been perfected by the guards as a deliberately murderous ritual to break down the morale of new inmates, give them a foretaste of what awaited them, and shock and dehumanize them as quickly as possible into cowed and submissive slave workers. Driven from the trucks, the prisoners were forced, one by one, to run at breakneck speed through a narrow door by the main entrance bearing the inscription "My country right or wrong" above it. Below, a gate read "To each his own" in iron letters. Inside they were greeted by guards who beat and flailed them with iron bars and whips, stoned them with rocks, and mutilated and murdered those trampled in the rush. Suitcases spilled open, and in the orgy of blows and assaults, the guards shamelessly stole whatever items of value they could find. Some prisoners were made to crawl in the dirt, or ordered to beat each other while the SS men stood by and enjoyed the show or doused them with ice-cold water. It was a macabre, nightmarish scene, and when the Jews had been reassembled on the large central assembly square, hours of more torture and abuse followed.

Dozens died that first day. Sixty-eight new arrivals went insane and were taken to the camp prison where they lay on the floor in chains. SS Sergeant Martin Sommer, long remembered as the "Hangman of Buchenwald," ran the prison and was one of the camp's most sadistic beasts. But the sixty-eight Jews brought to him did not stay long under his charge. Over the next days, Sommer took them away—four at a time—and murdered them.

Once Ewald had been a proud German, a soldier in the Kaiser's guards wearing an Iron Cross personally handed him by the Emperor. Now he was inmate No. 5349, a Jewish outcast. His head was shaved, every bone in his body ached, his hands were bloody and raw, and an ugly welt ran down the side of his face where a guard had beaten him with a whip. After four weeks as a Buchenwald prisoner, Ewald's striped ill-fitting inmate clothes with the triangular yellow patch for Jews on his left chest and right pant leg hung loosely on his shrunken frame. With the inhuman twelve to fourteen hours of hard labor in a stone quarry and the poor food, he had lost more than forty pounds.

Not long ago his father and grandfather were pillars of the community, and Oranienburgers respectfully lifted their hats when they passed them in the street. Now he was considered worse than scum and treated as such. In the perverted hierarchy of the KZ, Ewald had become the lowest of the low, and fair game for inmates and guards. Jehovah's Witnesses, homosexuals, and political inmates were considered far better than he, and even professional criminals, the "Greens," were superior beings compared to a Jew.

He had believed that German anti-Semitism was a spent force, that his equality as a citizen was anchored in the law, and that German Christians and Jews had a shared love for culture and learning quite unlike the more primitive societies in the East. He had thought that German culture and the respect for law and order were the best guarantee for gradual further progress. Yet in this place he had to live by the law of the whip, and instead of order there was caprice, despotism, and rampant corruption. With a hundred marks the guards were bribable for small favors, and several times the loudspeaker had announced that "rich Jews" who signed over their motorcycles, cars, or houses to the SS would be favorably received. The rumor was that it was the way to be released early.

He had survived the awful first days of horror and chaos in the overcrowded KZ that had been totally unprepared for the sudden influx of ten thousand *Aktionsjuden*. Since then he had been assigned to a barracks in Block 34, and now he slept in one of the shelflike bunks, each stacked four-high and so shallow that he had to enter his primitive resting place sideways and could hardly raise his head. Just outside Block 34's window he could see Goethe's Oak, a monument to German culture, which the authorities had carefully preserved, right in the middle of the camp. But the whipping block where inmates were beaten to a pulp stood not far away in roll-call square, and the perennially busy crematorium where the dead were incinerated was nearby.

At the moment, the inmates were standing at roll call—one of the four often endless ones before, during, and after work each day. SS Master Sergeant Hackmann, the one they called "Jonny," was in charge—a much feared, dangerously brutal, and cynical sadist.[44] A half hour earlier he had ordered the inmates to give the "Saxon Salute," one of his specialties. It involved standing ramrod straight with arms folded behind the back of the head. The longer it lasted the more painful it became until the agony was almost unbearable. Those who faltered were brutally beaten and risked their lives.

Ewald's arms were numb with pain, and he wondered how much longer he could last. His mind was a virtual blank and as numb as his arms. Paralyzed with fear and confusion, he hardly knew any longer who he was and what to think. Silently he cursed his misfortune, cursed his birth as a Jew, cursed his tormentors for degrading and punishing him. Most of all he cursed his own stupidity for having trusted his fellow Germans and for waiting too long to get out.

6

Two weeks passed before Valerie could confirm that her husband was alive and a Buchenwald prisoner. Thousands of Jewish wives and mothers were frantic to learn the fate of their men, but the local police professed to know nothing, and the Gestapo rudely showed them the door.

For a Jew to walk voluntarily through the dreaded portals of Hitler's Secret Police headquarters required courage and strong nerves. Valerie had risked it twice, and each time she had been summarily dismissed. But she was not one to give in easily and on her third try a Gestapo officer had been impressed with her persistence—as well as her looks—and, after a long conversation, promised to help. In a phone call late that night he confirmed Ewald's whereabouts: "He has to leave the country," he told her. "Find him a visa to somewhere, and I'll make sure they release him." Definite news came with Ewald's first letter two days later. "Protective Custody Prisoner No. 5349, Block 34, KZ Buchenwald" read the return address on the forbidding gray-green envelope, with a rigid warning in bold print:

> Each prisoner may receive and send two letters and postcards each month. Mail must be simple and legibly written . . . or it will not be handled. Packages are forbidden, though money can be transmitted. . . . National socialist newspapers may also be sent.
>
> —*The Camp Commandant*

At least it was certain now that Ewald was alive though his letter was frighteningly terse and to the point: "Dear Wally," it read. "I am well and feel good. My greetings to the children. We must emigrate at once. *Ich mache Alles.* [I'll go anyplace.] Your, Ewald."

There was no need to read between the lines. Valerie knew at once that he was desperate and that the time left for him was short. The question was what to do and who would admit them.

Every embassy and foreign consulate in Germany, even those of the smallest and least likely countries, was overrun by wretched Jews clamoring for visas. The harder they fought and the more urgently they pleaded, the stronger the resistance they encountered. Moreover, even when a visa was actually in the works, only a small part of the problem had been solved. To be allowed to leave, a nightmarish obstacle course through a thicket of bureaucratic barriers and regulations had to be negotiated to accumulate all the necessary documents. The process could take many weeks and months. A visa required a passport, the one with the special red *J*. A passport, in turn, presupposed proof that all taxes had been paid, a certified personal net worth statement (to ensure that there was nothing of value left), health certificates, good conduct reports from the local police, and much more. The list of required papers was endless and often one document depended on another whose issuance was predicated on yet a third, fourth, and fifth in the time-honored catch-22 manner of bureaucrats everywhere. The Gestapo might want them out, but each government agency insisted on strict observance of its own rules, no one was willing to bend, and everywhere there were long lines, obstacles, problems, and maddening delays.

Lack of money was another big headache. That they would leave Germany as paupers stripped of all their valuables and with only ten marks in their pocket for each person was understood. The gnawing fear of how to survive beyond Germany's border loomed large, but everything connected with getting out required money as well, and even their blocked marks for local expenses were desperately short. By virtue of Göring's Kristallnacht decree, Valerie's negotiations for the sale of the store had automatically been voided. "No more Jewish business," the *Tageblatt* headlined one of its lead stories on November 15, detailing Nazi plans for an economy without Jews, and ordering Nazi officials to step in to set the price for "Aryanized" properties.[45] Even for small businesses, arms-length sales deals were no longer permitted. An official government assessor had shown up at the store, torn up the painfully negotiated draft contract, and approved an amount only fractionally more than what was needed to cover paying off outstanding bills.

Valerie would walk away with nothing. A supplemental private under-the-table payment was strictly forbidden, the Nazi official warned. Her "Aryan" employee taking the business had expressed regret but shed hardly a tear. There was nothing she could do, she said, and so the business was hers practically as a gift. The only way to pay for emigration expenses was to sell old heirlooms, furnishings, and household goods. It wasn't at all clear that it would suffice to cover all the costs.

Who would admit them remained the critical question. By the summer of 1938, there were still 350,000 Jews left in Germany, not counting the additional 200,000 under Hitler's control since the annexation of Austria in the spring. Most now were impoverished, their men were imprisoned, and the Gestapo would release them only with proof that their departure was imminent. The Jews' desperation was at a peak; the world was outraged at their cruel treatment and professed great sympathy at their plight. But there was no softening of attitudes about taking them in, or even a temporary loosening of rigid immigration rules.

The universal refusal of help for Jewish refugees remains one of the great tragedies and scandals of the time.[46] The United States is no exception. Congress had authorized 27,370 visas annually for immigrants of German birth, yet except for the single year of 1939, that quota was never filled. In 1933, the first Nazi year, the authorities saw fit to admit only 1,450 German-Jewish immigrants, or about 5 percent of the permissible total. In 1935, as the disastrous Nuremberg race laws were announced, only 20 percent of authorized quota numbers were issued, and even in the *Kristallnacht* year of 1938 a full third of allowable slots remained unfilled. Worse yet, in the years 1933–35 more immigrants left the country than arrived, so that net U.S. immigration was actually negative. Even strong pressure from Jewish groups for allowing a few special children's transports at the height of the 1938–39 pogroms fell on deaf ears.

The U.S. record is miserable, but most other countries did even less. Canada rigidly held to highly restrictive ethnic and economic criteria that shut out most German Jews, and Australia was no more liberal. Brazil issued secret instructions to its consulates that all Jews were to be denied visas. Over a ten-year period only about twelve to fifteen thousand immigrants managed to gain admission there, and in neighboring Argentina not many more were allowed in. In Mexico and virtually every Latin American country the only means to an entry permit was through illegalities and bribes, often with the tragic and disastrous consequence that visas thus "bought" were not honored at the border, and shiploads of arriving Jewish emigrants were turned back.[47] The more time elapsed, the more desperate the Jews became, and their suicide rate escalated to two and three times the national norm. Everywhere they turned there were closed doors and regrets, long waiting lists, interminable delays, rumors that proved false, and leads that turned out to be dead ends.

A precious visa to anywhere was the key to Ewald's release, and every morning Valerie set out to make the rounds. Each night she returned home with empty hands. One day there would be a rumor that the Bolivians had opened the door a crack, and everyone would rush there to try their luck. On the next it was said that in Hamburg the vice consul of a certain small country was amenable to issue the precious stamp for a modest bribe, and she would take the train to follow up even the most tenuous lead. Some even whispered about underworld contacts who smuggled people into the Netherlands and Belgium without any papers at all, though the cost and the risks were great, and few dared to chance such a hazardous course. Switzerland in particular was known to be totally unrelenting in turning illegal immigrants back.

Only one place in the world remained where no visa was required at all—and where no one wanted to go. Transport was the big problem, but if one could get there the door was wide open and even a Jewish refugee could just walk ashore. Not all had the courage to make the move.

Shanghai was an international city where no one was effectively in charge. Its reputation was so lurid that it was everyone's last choice. To be "Shanghaied" was a prospect even the desperate refugees wanted to avoid. An island in the midst of the ongoing Sino-Japanese war, there were few rules there, fewer jobs, an unhealthy disease-ridden climate, much lawlessness and crime, indescribable poverty, and no prospects for a normal life. Shanghai was the exile of last resort, but now it was a question of staying alive, and even Shanghai was better than the Buchenwald KZ. Weeks of frustrating and fruitless efforts for a visa to anywhere else had passed. Now there was no more time left to do anything else. Valerie decided that Shanghai was the only hope, and she set out on a relentless quest to tackle shipping company waiting lists for four beds on a China-bound ship.

The first ticket, for Ewald, was bought after much intrigue and a substantial bribe, but it opened the way to petition the Gestapo for his release. In time she found a second, and the last two for the children took several nerve-wrecking weeks, more adventurous twists and turns, and negotiations till late into the night. Yet finally the die was cast: she had succeeded in keeping the family together and all would be fleeing to Shanghai. Perhaps the wait there would be mercifully short until some more normal country would allow us in.

I remember the last weeks in Berlin well. My father returned after six weeks in Buchenwald, a shrunken and broken man. One day he was back, a small, pitiful figure sitting in his old living room chair, a gaunt sixty pounds lighter, embracing me silently and hardly able to talk. I remember the two Sundays when eager buyers trooped through our apartment on the Kurfürstendamm to look for bargains among the household effects being sold at whatever price: "First-class dining room, bedroom pure mahogany, rugs, many single pieces, coffee service, lamps, dishes, bed linens, complete furnishings—any price OK," the long columns of Sunday advertisements read.

The Jews were selling out and everyone understood what it meant: their belongings were available for a very attractive price. Sometimes my mother cried, but everything had to go, and nothing could be saved. The money was needed to pay for the ship.

Thursday, April 6, 1939, was an unusually mild Berlin day. At the state opera, Wagner's *Lohengrin* was playing to a full house, though Jews were no longer allowed to attend. At Berlin's Scala Variety Theater, the famous clown Grock and a new Mexican highwire act were starring in a new show. *Broadway Melody,* an American hit, was being shown in the biggest movie house on the Kurfürstendamm.

For us these were all things of the past. At 9:15 P.M. our train was scheduled to leave, and a half hour earlier we stood quietly in a corner of Berlin's Anhalter Bahnhof to say our good-byes. The train station was full of soldiers bound for Easter leaves and others joining their regiments in Czechoslovakia, which Hitler had just taken over in violation of every commitment he had made. I was happy to be embarking on an exciting adventure, but my parents were sad and subdued.

We were leaving as our ancestors had once arrived. Poor Jews, paupers, without a country of our own.

CHAPTER X

EPILOGUE

1

We crossed the German border at the Brenner Pass on the morning of April 7, 1939. It was a final moment designed to humiliate us one last time, one more reminder that we were being driven from Germany, materially and emotionally "picked clean."

SS border guards barked at the handful of Jewish emigrants to get off the train, and tore apart even the smallest piece of their luggage with sadistic delight. Men and women were strip-searched to ensure that absolutely nothing of value was being taken out. For one more fearful hour the Jews trembled under Nazi control. Then it was over. The train crossed into Italy, and we were on our way south to the ship that would transport us to Shanghai.

I remember a brief period of elation and relief to have escaped alive and to be free. But it didn't last long. Even before we reached Naples, my parents again fell silent and looked nervous and tense.

For me, it was the beginning of a great adventure, of new experiences and unfamiliar, exotic sights and sounds—and no brown uniforms and swastikas. I sensed the adults' fears but, at thirteen, I still had childish faith in my parents' ability to cope. They had always found a way and no doubt they would again.

I did not understand how difficult it was for them. Theirs was the sinking feeling of realizing the finality of leaving and the dread of uncertainties ahead. Now there was no turning back. They were cast loose, poor, without a country and with a one-way ticket to an unpredictable, frightening place on the other side of the world. That was what was going through their minds. What would become of them? They were no longer Germans, but what were they now?

It was a deep, existential crisis and it would last a long time. They were uncomfortable to be Jews and confused about having been Germans. They abhorred the German government but remained wedded to German culture. They knew their identity as Germans was shattered but could not yet grasp what that meant. It would take time to break the bonds to the past. For the moment they were empty and drained and incapable of seeing how it could be done.

The past is not easily forgotten. It lives on and holds us in its grip. Fond memories play tricks with our emotions. To disengage is painful for anyone who has to emigrate to a new place. Even for those who go to a country where they can put down new roots, a period of adjustment is needed. Another language must be learned and a new and different culture absorbed. For a while, there is commonly a feeling of loss and nostalgia for the familiar and comfortable ways left behind.

For the eighteen thousand traumatized German and Austrian Jews who found themselves in Shanghai, the process of psychological disengagement was infinitely slower and more difficult. Some never really succeeded in making the break. Shanghai was not a normal place, but an eight-year waiting room where they lingered uncertainly while dreaming and scheming for a permanent new home elsewhere. In their inhospitable temporary shelter under difficult conditions, including two and one-half years of ghetto life under Japanese occupation during the war, the search for a new identity was extraordinarily complex. Abandoned as refugees, officially "stateless" and without passports after 1941, they were reminded every day of what they had lost. There was confusion instead of stability, nothing solid to take the place of the old, no hope for a new sense of belonging, and little that was positive to absorb their energies and ease the transition. For the older generation, having done with the past was a process that proceeded in slow motion and would not be complete until years later when they finally left China after the war. My principal memory of how the generation of my parents lived in Shanghai is their suspension in limbo between an engrained Germanness and the slow, reluctant discarding of it long after old habits had lost their relevance.

We docked in Shanghai at six o'clock in the evening on May 10. It was the beginning of the hot season and by nine in the morning, the temperature had reached eighty degrees and the humidity was 75 percent. The evening felt hot and sticky. *The North China Daily News,* Shanghai's premier foreign daily, reported the next day that the McLeans, Van Burens, and the Reverend Boynton had disembarked after returning from their home leaves. They were expatriates, and as such automatically in the top strata of the city's European elite. The arrival of close to a hundred destitute Jewish refugees was duly noted elsewhere, but our names were of no importance and not worthy of mention in the published passenger list. In Shanghai there were few rules, but who was on top, and who was not, was nevertheless clearly understood.

Shanghai was a treaty port and an anachronistic leftover of the colonial age. Situated on low-lying flatlands near the point where the Yangtze River flows into the China Sea, the city had been forcibly seized as a privileged European trading post during the Opium Wars a hundred years before. In the late 1930s it was a teeming metropolis of more than four million Chinese, cut off from its hinterland by the Sino-Japanese war. Overcrowded with untold numbers of countryside refugees who had fled the Japanese invaders, the city was run by a handful of British, French, American, and Japanese colonials administering their home countries' "extraterritorial" rights. The main beneficiaries were their businessmen, traders, and agents, who lived like potentates with legions of servants in spacious homes behind high walls.

These were the foreign tycoons who were Shanghai's ruling elite. They ran the customs, municipal affairs, and police, governed by their own rules, and settled their legal problems in their own courts. There was a French "Concession" where the street names were French, which was every bit like a colony of France. A municipal council under Anglo-American control ran a so-called International Settlement in an adjacent part of the town, and there was a Chinese area where the Japanese occupiers held sway.

The bottom of the non-Chinese pecking order was occupied by some fifteen thousand "White Russians," washed ashore in Shanghai in the 1920s after fighting on the losing side of their civil war. Many had done rather poorly and eked out a meager living in what were deemed the lowest jobs for a European. More than a few were addicted to drugs and the bottle and could be seen staggering around in disheveled rags. The ruling elite worried that they caused all "white men" to suffer a loss of "face." The arrival of the Jews from Europe only heightened their concerns.

Between the bottom and the top, there was everyone else: Russian Jews from Harbin, Sephardim from India and Iraq, Swiss, Portuguese, Italians, Koreans, and assorted missionaries, romantics, adventurers, fortune hunters, and bunco artists with murky pedigrees and questionable pasts from every conceivable part of the world. There was even a sizable colony of Germans flying the swastika flag.

Shanghai was an indigenous city, first and foremost, but the millions of Chinese who lived there had little to say. Their government presided over a polyglot place with virtually no taxes and a minimum of rules, amid a welter of conflicting jurisdictions where everything was possible and few questions were asked. Fortunes were made—and lost—overnight. All was possible, everyone was fair game, and life was cheap.

It was a city of staggering contrasts. The unhealthy subtropical climate is hot and steamy in summer and can be cold and clammy in winter; it can be miserable, especially without air conditioning, appropriate clothing, and adequate heat. Sanitation was poor. Sewers functioned imperfectly at best. When a typhoon struck, the streets were under two feet of water, the drains no longer worked at all, and the mixture became deadly.

At the waterfront, the famous Bund's imposing buildings impressed visitors, but behind the facades people lived on top of each other in rabbit-warren-like lanes and alleys where night soil was collected in buckets each day. Thousands starved and dozens of abandoned dead were daily collected in the streets. Nuns and missionaries selflessly ran schools, orphanages, and hospitals and proselytized among the poor, but nearby, little girl and boy prostitutes, eight to ten years old, were being openly offered for sale.

Cholera epidemics, and typhoid, smallpox, dysentery, and parasitic intestinal illnesses were common. The foreigners ran the police with the help of imported Sikhs from Punjab and Indo-Chinese Annamites—but they were corrupt and cruel. Gambling, drugs, prostitution, kidnapping for ransom, gang warfare, and political assassinations were common.

In Shanghai, an expatriate with foreign currency could live like a king. But there were not many jobs to be had, and if you didn't know how to live by your wits and had no money, it was one of the most miserable places in the world.

2

For all arriving refugees, to be thrust into this mad cauldron was invariably a jarring blow. For the majority, however, who had no money at all, it was an especially traumatic experience after leaving the protective cocoon of civilized shipboard life. Loaded on open trucks, they were transported by relief organizations to the *Heime*—primitive mass shelters in Hongkew, one of the worst sections in the Japanese-occupied part of town, badly damaged during the 1937 war. There they were shown to a dormitory bed, issued blankets, bedsheets, and a tin dish, cup, and spoon, fed from communal kitchens, and given some useful good advice, such as, inter alia:

> Don't drink the water
> Don't ever drink milk or eat raw vegetables and fruit
> Stay away from the Japanese military
> Don't carry valuables
> Don't trust the police
> Don't walk in the sun without a pith helmet[1]

We, however, were among the lucky ones, at first. Brazilian relatives had scraped together a little money for us—a hundred English pounds, I believe. So we took off in a convoy of rickshas and were pulled by sweaty, panting, and noisy coolies to a fleabag hotel in the better part of town. My parents were in a permanent state of shock, and that first night we made our initial acquaintance with Shanghai's ubiquitous mosquitoes, bed bugs, cockroaches, and the occasional oversized rat who would be our tormentors on and off for the next eight years.

Five days later, we moved into two tiny rooms in the modest house of a White Russian family on route Grouchy, in the "Concession Française." The paterfamilias, an elegant man with monocle who claimed to have been a colonel with the Whites fighting Bolsheviks in Siberia, drank tea during the day and vodka at night but otherwise did little else. The family's financial mainstay was his wife, who visited expatriate ladies to give them their daily massage. Each morning I would observe her, long-stemmed cigarette dangling from her lips, cursing in Russian and street Chinese while noisily bargaining with ricksha pullers over the fare to her first appointment. There were also two interesting daughters. One had a seemingly endless string of rather public lovers and worked as a hairdresser on the rue Cardinal Mercier. The other, a prostitute, rose late in the afternoon and plied her trade at night in a small Russian bar.

I was enrolled in school, learned English and fractured Chinese, and practiced my school French. My eighteen-year-old sister was packed off as a nanny to a little English girl, thus saving us an extra mouth to feed. My parents began to look around for something to do.

We had left Germany just in time. In September, Hitler invaded Poland. Europe was at war. Now, more than ever, borders were closing all over the world, and no country was willing to let us in. Even Shanghai placed restrictions against the admission of more refugees. We lived poorly from hand to mouth, and from day to day and resigned ourselves to a prolonged wait. Slowly, the news from relatives left behind in Germany grew sparser and began to dry up.

In Hongkew, five *Heime* were filled to capacity. Around them the refugees had created their own little world. Conditions were basic and primitive, no one had money, but the collective will to make life bearable was surprisingly vibrant and strong. Debris was cleared and houses made livable. Little stores and restaurants sprang up. There were synagogues, schools, a hospital, theatres, concerts, and sports for the young. Everyone spoke German and the atmosphere resembled a Jewish quarter, part Vienna and part Berlin.

Hongkew, however, was still the shabbiest and most depressing part of town, and we deemed ourselves fortunate not to be stuck there until, on December 8, 1941, the roof fell in. Early that morning, Japanese soldiers crossed out of their sector and swiftly occupied the entire town. Pearl Harbor had been bombed. The Pacific war had begun.

Shanghai had come under military occupation, extraterritoriality was a thing of the past and would never return. Its English and American guardians were repatriated or interned under the watchful eye of the International Red Cross and the neutral Swedes and Swiss. We, however, had slipped through the cracks. We were nothing—stateless "nonpersons," the flotsam and jetsam of the war. Cut off and left behind, our lives took a decided turn for the worse. Businesses closed, jobs disappeared, and without imports shortages multiplied.

For a while our new masters left us alone, but then, without much warning, the most trying phase of our enforced China exile began. On February 18, 1943, all refugees were ordered to move to a "Designated Area" in Hongkew within ninety days. To leave the area during the day would require special passes for those with a proven need. The Japanese proclamation was lengthy and its wording cloudy and indirect. The reason was "military necessity," it said, and the word *Jew* was never mentioned in the opaque text. The intent, however, was crystal clear. Alone among the remaining foreigners in Shanghai, the Jewish refugees were being singled out for confinement in nothing less than an old-fashioned ghetto. It was like the Middle Ages all over again and the refugees were in a near panic. What was the meaning of this?

At the time there were plenty of theories and wild rumors, all of them false. It would only be after the war that we would learn the truth. It was, in fact, the long arm of the Gestapo that had reached out for us one more time. We were dangerous enemies, they had told their Axis partners—and they had offered helpful suggestions and technical assistance on how to do us in. An expert on the subject had been specially dispatched to Shanghai by Himmler—via submarine, no less.[2]

The Japanese had given the Germans a polite hearing, a spirited internal debate had ensued, but in the end a less radical course was chosen. Killing us seemed unwise to them, but to placate the Germans they had decided to place us in a ghetto instead. The area they selected was less than one square mile, and besides the Hongkew Jews, one hundred thousand Chinese would continue to live there. Herding the rest of us into such limited space presented a major problem, but the Japanese made it clear that it was ours to solve.

Orders were orders, and the disciplined ex-German and ex-Austrian Jews were used to respecting authority. So we packed up our meager possessions and, in one way or another, squeezed ourselves into the narrow space. Now we lived in a single small room—more like a wooden box akin to a chicken coop, stuck onto the outside wall of a ramshackle house and reached by a set of narrow external stairs. Several families shared a single kitchen and toilet, and we washed in the open at a cold-water tap. Passes to leave the ghetto were easy to get at first, but later the rules were tightened until most gave up the effort to try.

There was no money and food was monotonous and sparse. More and more refugees were being fed from the central *Heim* kitchens. People sold their valuables and even their clothes, and stalls selling old clothing proliferated. Turning shirt collars and pants inside out and mending holes in threadbare dresses and coats kept the tailors busy. In the winter, I stuffed newspapers into my shoes to keep out the water and cover the holes in frayed soles.

It was a bizarre setting, and for people like my parents an ironic one as well. For years, they were among those who insisted they couldn't imagine living with "nothing but Jews." Yet here they were in just that situation, surrounded by a wide cross section of their coreligionists from all over Europe and getting to know them at very close quarters, for the first time in their lives. There were assimilated Germans and Austrians, journalists and intellectuals, doctors, lawyers, and businesspeople, from the better sections of Berlin, Vienna, and other larger towns. But there were also the less "Germanized" "little people" they had never really known—workers, waiters, tailors, and community retainers from the wrong side of the track, with whom they had previously had virtually no contact at all. Mixed in were the uncomfortable *Ostjuden,* and even a group of ultra-Orthodox Yiddish-speaking yeshiva students from Poland, with beards, sidelocks, wide-brimmed black hats, and long coats. My father had encountered them just once before in his life, as a German soldier in the war—and had been put off by their ancient, strange, and un-German ways.

The identity crisis was more acute than ever. Everyone was in the same boat as a "stateless Jew," yet many still clung to the past, were reluctant to abandon it, and attempted instead to recreate it in the improbable setting of our Chinese ghetto. People retained their devotion to things German— the books, music, and culture, and all the old mannerisms, habits, and prejudices. Many remained stubbornly attached to their old titles and insisted on calling each other *Herr Doktor* or *Herr Professor.* The Austrians were especially fond of *Herr Ingenieur* (Engineer). Ex-Germans criticized ex-Austrians for their sloppy ways, and the Austrians laughed at them for their Prussian affectations. The Orthodox felt superior to both, and disapproved of the assimilated Jews' un-Jewish habits.

Community life was astonishingly active and rich, tinged with a heightened awareness of Jewishness. Some rediscovered the synagogues, and there was substantial interest in Zionism and Palestine. Yet, most remained strongly wedded to the culture of the past. The Austrians put on Lehar operettas, lending libraries did a brisk business in the German classics, and in the little cafés comedians told jokes with Berlinese and Viennese themes. At one, which called itself the White Horse Inn, there was a traditional four o'clock tea and Elsa's Naturgarten advertised a restful atmosphere "just like a cure in Bad Nauheim."

The nostalgia for the past and the reluctance to shed it was understandable enough, yet somewhat quaint, if not ludicrous, in the midst of wartime Shanghai. There was still the reminiscing and the secret hankering for the old life in Berlin or Vienna, and a shrinking number still harbored the dim hope that it might be retrievable once the Nazis had lost the war. But more and more, reality intruded: the dream was over, and the history of German Jewry was finished for good; it had all been for nothing, and even if they were invited back, it was over—they couldn't, and wouldn't, return.

3

Finally the war was ending. We had seen it coming and knew that it was only a question of time. The Soviet Union was not at war with Japan until the very end, and so each night we gathered around the radio, listened eagerly to the Russian news, and followed the Red Army's advance into Germany and the progress of Allied invasion forces from the west. Even reading between the lines of optimistic Japanese war reports was no longer very hard.

Some of us had been in Shanghai close to seven years now and the last ones had been the hardest. The meager relief funds from abroad, sent through neutral channels, no longer arrived. Almost everyone was on the dole, and average daily consumption of 1,200–1,300 calories was sapping our strength.

At last, Germany surrendered. Hitler, Himmler, and Goebbels were dead and Göring was in Allied hands. Germany was in ruins and the war in Europe was over. Clearly, Japan would soon be finished as well and day by day our spirits improved. Then—just as suddenly as it had begun—Japan threw in the towel, and our Japanese jailers disappeared. The Pacific war was finished—and so was our ghetto. It was an incredible feeling of relief and joy. Now we could have hope for the future and begin to live again.

Within days, the U.S. Navy steamed into port, transport planes landed and disgorged troops, and soon these magical, healthy, boisterous American soldiers and sailors were swarming all over the town and treating us to their incredibly luxurious rations and PX treasures. Everyone was feasting on candy bars, smoking Lucky Strikes, and chewing gum.

Military bases sprang up and people were being hired—and paid in dollars, no less. I found a job as a warehouseman on a U.S. air base for sixty dollars a month. I was rich! Surely now everything would be all right. Soon we would finally be allowed to leave.

Those who had lost contact with relatives in Germany were desperate to hear from them and be reunited again. Even before the war was over we had heard Soviet reports of the mass murder of Jews, but they were so extreme and gruesome that few believed them. At first, people reassured each other that Soviet propaganda was known to exaggerate. Atrocity stories about many thousands of bodies of Jews dug up in a place called Treblinka and reports of the mass extermination of millions just did not seem real.

It took many more anxious weeks for the scope of the holocaust story to emerge. Day after day, anxious refugees crowded around the pitifully short lists of survivors posted on walls in Hongkew, and gradually the realization sank in that the worst was true, after all. Parents, brothers, and sisters, the old and the young—all were gone. As if by a miracle, Ewald's brother Hellmuth had been found alive, but Valerie's sister was lost.

Arthur had died in Berlin in early 1938, but his widow was also a victim. On June 25, 1942, Margarethe Eloesser, once the author of cheerful children's stories, had become the number A359526, one of 1,051 Berlin Jews transported to Riga on that day. Till the end, the Gestapo's bureaucracy of death administered her last moments in Berlin in meticulous detail. Her remaining property was carefully inventoried, the total value being estimated at a modest 707 marks. That was all she had left when they took her away. The list included a wastepaper basket, a small sewing table, two dresses, two small mirrors, a hairbrush, a box with ladies gloves, two of Arthur's old walking sticks, and a bird. Because of the Jewish-owned bird, fumigation of her rooms would be advisable, the Nazi officials noted in their report.

In Hongkew, no one wanted to be German anymore. Now even the language was hateful. My parents and their friends were deeply ashamed of the country to which they had once been committed with heart and soul.

Now everyone just wanted to get away to another place. It took two more years until we could leave, and eventually it was the United States and Palestine that absorbed most of the Shanghai survivors. We boarded the *Marine Adder* for America on September 8, 1947. My mother lived there for another twenty-three years; my father for thirty-two. Both were American citizens when they died. They never again looked back or gave even a moment's consideration to returning to Germany to live.

The dream had come to an end. For three hundred years, the invisible wall had never been breached. In the end, it had become a wall of death.

4

More than half a century after the event, the genocidal slaughter of Europe's Jews by Nazi Germany continues to defy human comprehension. It was not the first holocaust in history, nor the only one in modern times. Yet what Adolf Hitler and his fanatical followers did is different from Stalin's bloodbaths, Pol Pot's Cambodian killing fields, or the "ethnic cleansing" of Kurds, Armenians, and most recently, Bosnian Muslims.

The annihilation of six million or more Jews occurred in broad daylight in the heart of Europe and over the course of several years. It was the most deliberate, systematic, and highly organized killing program of any, and its perpetrators came from a country that prided itself on its culture and was considered one of the most advanced in the world.

In Germany there was no history of Cossack massacres and no tradition of government-sanctioned pogroms. There the Jews had advanced further and faster than virtually anywhere else. Germany was the cradle of modern Judaism, and its Jews considered it the best country in Europe. Yet, as Daniel Goldhagen has well documented, when Hitler and his fanatical Jew-hating followers unleashed their program of Jewish annihilation, many "ordinary" Germans obeyed his orders and participated in his crimes.[3]

The millions of Eastern European Jews who perished had little or no premonition of what awaited them. Their murderers descended on them suddenly, and few were able to escape. German Jewry, however, was more fortunate—though that assuredly is a relative term. For them, there had been ample warnings. Over six years, they were systematically excluded from German life, publicly humiliated, robbed of their possessions, progressively marginalized, and returned to the pariah status of the Middle Ages. About two-thirds managed to flee. The rest—some 150,000 in all, and mostly the older, sick, and poor—fell victim to the Nazi machinery of death.

In Shanghai, I witnessed the stunned disbelief of the survivors when the full extent of the holocaust was revealed after the war. Few of them had seen the disaster coming, and when the signs became unmistakable, not many had quickly recognized them or been willing to admit that the Nazi onslaught could long endure. Many waited until the last moment before leaving Germany for good. How could this have happened in Germany, they asked?

Are there clues in the Jewish experience over the course of the ten to twelve generations since the poor peddler Jost Liebmann first set out to walk from Hildesheim to Hamburg until my father, the Kaiser's loyal ex-guards soldier, narrowly escaped death in Buchenwald? What was it in Germany's character and history over the intervening years that could have led to this? The German soil, as we saw, had been peculiarly hospitable to Jewish talents, yet also stubbornly resistant to the minority's complete acceptance and integration. The Jewish position always remained anomalous, uncertain, and full of paradox. Still, most assimilated German Jews had never wavered in their attachment to the fatherland, nor in their hope for a better future. Should historical experience have taught them greater caution?

The history of Germany's Jews can only be understood in the larger context of German history. From the beginning, the German-Jewish relationship was a marriage of convenience. Germany needed its Jews for economic reasons, and the Jews needed Germany as a safe haven with scope for their unique talents. Germans and Jews had much in common—and in good measure this accounts for the Jews' spectacular and rapid rise. Both sides respected learning and intellectual achievement, and both believed in the ethic of hard work. Both valued an environment of law, order, and respect for authority. The Jews had traditionally looked to their rabbis; gentiles had learned to obey the Kaiser and his officials. The fortuitous circumstance of Germany's late industrialization and its coincidence with Jewish emancipation provided special opportunities for Jewish talents at just the right moment, with beneficial results for all.

To be sure, in Germany—as everywhere in Europe's Christian world—Jews encountered widespread prejudice and antipathy toward them at all levels of society. That was the heritage of a thousand years of bigotry and discrimination. German Jewry suffered greatly from these prejudices, yet it is difficult to see that the dislike of Jews was, on balance, worse in pre-Hitler Germany than anywhere else. German Jews actually believed that German anti-Semitism was, if anything, less pervasive and severe. Anti-Jewish sentiment at upper levels of society, though deep, was not demonstrably greater than in England and France. Among the rest of the population, the virulent anti-Semitism Jews traditionally encountered in Eastern Europe was largely absent, especially in Prussia.

Yet there was another side to this coin. Just as there were special conditions in Germany favoring Jewish advancement and assimilation, so there were peculiar historical factors that inhibited their true integration. Jewish successes were deceptive and obscured stubborn underlying forces arrayed against them.

In most Western countries the "Jewish Question" became part of a popular demand for democracy and social justice. In Germany the democratic ideal could not take hold; there was no concept of *liberté, égalité, et fraternité* as in France, no genuine parliamentary rule as in England, no Bill of Rights as in America. In Germany, an exclusionary political system was in place until Weimar, and its people remained obedient to a small, militaristic, authoritarian ruling elite. Jewish emancipation was not the consequence of

the democratization of society from below. It was imposed from above, reluctantly at best, on a subservient and obedient public.

As a result, there were no countervailing forces in Germany against the
use of anti-Semitism as a political weapon in times of stress, and no influential factions who understood that egregious attacks on Jews put into
question generally accepted ideals of equality and fundamental rights. Jews
remained frozen out of the key political power centers, isolated and exposed, and without powerful voices to come to their aid, as had happened
when Émile Zola led protests against the blatantly anti-Semitic Dreyfus
conspiracy in France.

There was also an element of historical chance. Germany experienced a
particularly egregious mix of economic and political reverses. Rapid industrialization caused more stress and disruption there than elsewhere, and
the very importance and prominence of their financial and industrial contributions exposed Jews to envy, resentment, and blame for the inevitable
dislocations that came with so much rapid change. Defeat in a devastating
war, the worst inflation in history, and abysmally poor leadership after Bismarck were also important factors.

If Frederick III had ruled longer than ninety days, or if the awful William
II had died at birth—as he almost did—would the Jewish experience in
Germany have been different? And how would the Jewish minority have
fared had the rise of the criminal Nazi movement not been nurtured by
Allied mistakes, economic disasters, and weak political leadership?

I do not believe that the failure of the German-Jewish relationship, and
the disaster that followed, was preordained. Basic forces in German society,
the confluence of a number of accidental factors, and the paradox of unintended consequences arising from the remarkable Jewish advance in Germany all played a role. The very impediments meant to restrict them
spurred the Jews on. Being forced into certain sectors of the economy and
the free professions, without commensurate political power, led to a dangerous exposure. Their eminence in a period of dislocation, rapid change,
and national reverses made them ready targets as scapegoats. Finally, it was
perhaps precisely the special German respect for learning in which the Jews
flourished, and the peculiar German predilection for abstract theories and
real and pseudo intellectualism, that fed the popularity of racial theories
of Jewish inferiority. The claim that Jews were different and that the differ-

ence was in their blood had originated elsewhere, but it was in Germany that it came to be most widely accepted and proved so deadly a mix in Hitler's hands.

It is all this, I believe, that shaped the special nature of gentile-Jewish relations in Germany. It is this also that put its unique stamp on Germany's assimilated Jews. It explains their character and attitudes, their dreams and fears, their striving and accomplishments—but also their frequent blindness to reality, and their defeats.

The lives and times of our principal protagonists tell their story. Jost and his contemporaries faced formidable odds in their uncertain status as society's outsiders and pariahs. The walls against them were legally sanctioned, plainly visible, and well-nigh insurmountable. Yet they had something of importance to offer. Already they were needed—even as they were disliked—and those with unusual talents could take advantage of German opportunity and lift themselves to the top. That there were a few like Jost who managed to do so in the face of so many obstacles is testimony to their relentless energy, perseverance, and drive honed over centuries of adversity and struggle. They established the foundations on which later generations could build and wrote the first chapter of the modern history of Germany's Jews.

Rahel and her contemporaries—the pioneers on the road to emancipation—wrote the next chapter. Precisely because the German world beyond the Jewish quarter was so alive with intellectual ferment and opportunity and was—to a degree—open to them, they wanted desperately to be a part of it, to be assimilated Germans at almost any cost. In the process, some moved far away from their Jewish roots but, as we saw, they were also the first to encounter invisible barriers to their complete integration, even as the formal ones were coming down. Their frustration shaped their character and outlook. It took Rahel's sensitive intelligence to realize that her Jewishness—and the limits it imposed on true acceptance as a German—was not merely a burden but also the wellspring for the creative energies that gave her life vitality and meaning.

In Giacomo's day, the special circumstances of the German-Jewish relationship had clearly emerged. For the Jews, the environment was immensely exciting and seductive. Their striving for achievement and recognition was intense. Germany was full of opportunity, and many thought

that equality and acceptance was only a matter of time. Yet their very at-
tainments and growing prominence kept alive old prejudices and generated new resentments. Gentiles valued Jewish contributions and admired
their talents, but the dislike and distance remained, and Jewish frustrations grew.

Neither side could escape the burdens of their history. In Giacomo, we
saw it deeply etched into his psyche—his incessant work and longing for
recognition in the country of his birth, but also his thin-skinned fear of
discrimination, nervous and fatalistic acceptance of gentile slights, and his
mixed sense of inferiority and defiant pride. If later observers noted the
peculiar love-hate relationship of German and Jew, it is the honors heaped
on Giacomo in his lifetime—and the German flag draped over his coffin at
Aix-la-Chapelle in death—that symbolizes one side of it. Richard Wagner's
vicious anti-Semitism and envy, and the scorn Meyerbeer's critics heaped
on the expatriate "cosmopolitan" Jew, reflects the other.

Louis and Arthur belong to the generations of those assimilated Jews
who became Germany's *Musterschüler*—its star pupils, eager to please.
When Oranienburg mayor Kahlbaum noted his Jewish councillor's passionate patriotism, or when the middle-aged Arthur volunteered for war
and later proudly idealized the experience, it reflected not only their deep
attachment to Germany but also their intense desire to belong. Arthur's
exquisite love of German culture and his monarchist nostalgia for the Kaiser's police constable as a reassuring authority figure from a better day had
their unconscious origins in similar feelings.

Louis and Arthur knew that they were Jews—society would not let them
forget it—and both experienced anti-Semitic discrimination. Yet, with the
rise of many Jews into important positions in German life, they can be
excused for their hope becoming father to the thought that the periodic
flaring up of anti-Jewish agitation in times of trouble was merely a fading
vestige of the past. They had thoroughly absorbed German *Kultur* but they
had deluded themselves that it was synonymous with liberal thinking. As
one insightful observer later noted, assimilated Jews loved an "ideal" German. The reality was that most Germans still held fast to their own distorted image of the alien Jew.[5]

Even in the best of times the relationship of German gentile and Jew
remained, as we saw, an uncomfortable marriage of convenience and a vol-

atile mixture of respect and aversion. The sociopolitical landscape stayed frozen, and the culture of militarism, obedience, and authoritarian rule by an exclusionary and reactionary elite kept the Jews in place as a special and suspect minority. Nothing the Jews did could bring the invisible wall down. Their emotional suffering continued, their insecurities remained, and their personalities reflected it. Extraordinary achievements were one consequence; the quest for titles and honors was another. Sometimes the Jewish outcast became a revolutionary and rebel; sometimes, as in the cases of Heine and Harden, merely society's acid-tongued critic and enfant terrible. And sometimes, as in the case of Walther Rathenau's complex personality, its self-hating patriot and martyr.

My father's generation would feel the full consequences of German Jewry's unresolved problems and anomalous position. Conditioned to see Jews as different and apart, envious of their successes and resentful of them as agents of unsettling modernity and change, Hitler's fanatical haters took advantage of the exposed position of Jews as they rode to power. In times of severe stress, too many Germans—though never a majority—were willing to accept the constantly repeated Nazi battle cry that it had been "the Jew" who was to blame for their troubles. Aided by luck and inept politicians, Hitler could seize control of the government, and when he subverted the constitution and installed a dictatorship, it was too late to reverse the course. Political underdevelopment and the tradition of blind obedience to authority helped lead the Jews—and many Germans—into disaster.

5

More than a hundred years ago, the German philosopher Friedrich Nietzsche observed, "I have never met a German who was favorably inclined to the Jews."[6] Hyperbole aside, Nietzsche was essentially correct. In his day, the dislike of Jews was widespread at all levels of society and, as we have seen, even in early twentieth-century Germany that was still largely the case.

Daniel Goldhagen has theorized that German anti-Semitism was not only widespread but also different from that of other countries and "annihilationist" in nature. It is this, he argues, that explains the German disaster, why "ordinary" Germans participated as perpetrators in Hitler's machinery of death while others stood by and tolerated his crimes. He is, I believe, correct that German anti-Semitism was different, and that many Germans were predisposed to dislike Jews and could more easily be aroused against them than elsewhere. Goldhagen's accumulation of the voluminous evidence shows that a surprising number—a hundred thousand or more—played an active part in the holocaust, and this is a vital, if chilling, contribution to our understanding of what actually occurred.

Yet to say that it was the German people's acceptance of a special brand of annihilationist anti-Semitism that facilitated Hitler's crimes and that because of this many were predisposed to tolerate or approve of the killing of Jews is to oversimplify and overstate the case.

The lives and times of our protagonists reflect a more nuanced and complex reality. There is no evidence to support the argument that most Germans knew of the killing, and there is nothing in German history to show that they would have approved of it if they had. Annihilating Jewish influence was one thing; annihilating them physically was quite another. As we have seen, until war broke out, the Nazis concentrated on humiliating, robbing, and disenfranchising the Jews, and on driving them out. Even the brutal *Kristallnacht* arrests had as their official goal to accelerate the Jews' departure. Whatever plan Hitler had already hatched for outright murder he kept to himself, and neither Christian nor Jew knew it.

Many Germans disliked Jews and failed to protest when the Nazis marginalized them or even when they attacked them in the street. Yet there is no clear evidence that most Germans approved of the physical violence against their Jewish neighbors. The American diplomatic reports from Leipzig and Stuttgart of shocked public reaction to the *Kristallnacht* violence made this point. The silent, stunned onlookers I observed near the burning synagogue in Berlin substantiates it. The small gestures to Jews, even as they were being arrested, show that gentile attitudes were in reality ambivalent and mixed—approval of mayhem and murder was rarely a part of it. None of this, of course, explains why "a hundred thousand or more" did become active perpetrators in the killing. Yet, awful and incomprehensible as it is, in this the Germans were not unique. Many brutalized Jew-hating non-Germans were willing helpers as well. Lamentably, in history's other holocausts willing helpers were also never lacking.

In sum, as we have seen, what was different in Germany was not so much the nature of anti-Semitism but the sociopolitical environment in which it was kept alive and could flourish, including the exposed and powerless position of the Jewish minority. Given their unusual history, too many Germans lacked civil courage and did not think for themselves. Elsewhere, democratization had placed limits on anti-Semitic excesses and changed the context of Christian-Jewish relations. In Germany that had not happened. Authoritarianism, the absence of Jews from critical power centers, the historical lack of deep social contacts between Christians and Jews, pervasive social anti-Semitism, and the postwar suffering and disillusionment of the masses—as well as Hitler's fanaticism and all of the accidents of history—each played a role. To be sure, the drumbeat of the deadly, virulent propaganda built on theories of race was also a factor, but it was only one factor of many.

6

The unrequited love affair of Germany's Jews with their native country ended in disaster. The three hundred years of their modern history had shaped their character and transformed them into a special people. There had been remarkable accomplishments and many triumphs. German Christians and Jews had deeply influenced each other. Neither side had remained the same.

For the Jews, Germany had once been the land of great opportunity and hope. They had given much—to Germany and the world—and received much in return. They had failed to see, however, that Germany was a sick society and that, when it counted most, the deck was stacked against them. Until the end, German Christian and Jew retained a distorted view of the other. It kept them apart and ultimately it contributed to the Jews' doom.

They had desperately wanted to be Germans but it hadn't worked. Was there any consolation at all for the survivors? Shortly before his death, Arthur Eloesser thought that there was: "We Jews," he wrote, "especially we who were justified to consider ourselves quite assimilated have, in the face of so many strokes of misfortune, the one compensation—the happy insight that it has enabled us to rediscover ourselves as Jews . . . to renew the long buried roots of our history."[7]

NOTES

CHAPTER I: PROLOGUE

1. The value of a taler (or thaler) in modern terms is hard to assess. It varied over time at between seven to ten times the purchasing power of a current dollar. After the nineteenth century, one taler was the equivalent of three marks.

2. Glückel von Hameln, p. xx.

3. Stern, *Dreams and Delusions: The Drama of German History,* p. 105.

4. See Cocks, p. 195; Jarausch, pp. 173–74.

5. Goldhagen, *Hitler's Willing Executioners.* The book caused a considerable stir and became an immediate bestseller, particularly in Germany where his theses were furiously debated, pro and con. German historians attacked him, often viciously and unfairly. The general public was fascinated and generally applauded him. For a good critical analysis of the Goldhagen book, see Omar Bartov, "Ordinary Monsters," *The New Republic,* April 29, 1996. Also, Clive James, "Blaming the Germans," *The New Yorker,* April 22, 1996. See also Goldhagen's reply, *The New Republic,* December 23, 1996.

    For reports on Goldhagen's reception in Germany, see Josef Joffe, "Goldhagen in Germany," *The New York Review of Books,* November 28, 1996, and Amos Alon, "The Antagonist as Liberator," *New York Times Magazine,* January 26, 1997.

6. The literature on the history of German Jewry is extensive. Gay, *The Jews of Germany,* provides an excellent survey from earliest beginnings to the present. Richarz, pp. 1–38, gives a fine short summary. Lowenthal, *The Jews of Germany,*

is an older standard. See also Ellenbogen and Sterling. There are many other good books on the subject, both in English and in German.

CHAPTER II: ORIGINS

1.   See, for example, Agus, pp. 1–20.
2.   Strabo in his *Geography,* quoted in Lowenthal, *The Jews of Germany,* p. 2. See also Gilbert, (*Jewish History Atlas*), especially pages 12 and 16–17 depicting the presence of Jews in the Roman Empire and around the Mediterranean.
3.   See Ellenbogen and Sterling, pp. 11–15; Lowenthal, pp. 1–3; Gay, *The Jews of Germany,* ch. 1.
4.   Lowenthal, p. 3; Ellenbogen and Sterling, p. 13.
5.   Abrahams, p. 265, provides a detailed list of Jewish occupations in Rome until about the fourth century C.E.
6.   This section draws, inter alia, on Gwatkin; Roth, *The Jews in the Middle Ages;* Fast, pp. 153–55; and Lowenthal, pp. 1–10.
7.   Quoted in Finucane, p. 176.
8.   Finucane, p. 187.
9.   Dahms, pp. 228–30.
10. Edom, p. 11.
11. Ibid, p. 17.
12. Ibid, p. 24.
13. Lowenthal, p. 53.
14. See *The Cambridge Medieval History,* vol. 7, 1936, p. 643.
15. Lowenthal, *The Jews of Germany,* p. 89.
16. Durant and Durant, *The Reformation,* p. 65. For additional descriptions see, for example: Castiglioni, pp. 353–60; Coulton; *Encyclopedia Judaica,* vol. 4, pp. 1063–68.
17. Ibid, p. 64
18   Roth, *A Short History of the Jewish People,* pp. 232–33.
19. Durant and Durant, *The Reformation,* p. 731.
20. For a detailed account of this episode, see Springer, pp. 17–18.
21. For descriptions of the ghetto and ghetto life see inter alia: Abrahams, pp. 78–98; Lowenthal, pp. 99–117; Ruth Gay, pp. 23–26, 62–72; Roth, *A Short History of the Jewish People,* pp. 297–311.
22. For a detailed description of Court Jews in Central Europe, see Selma Stern, *The Court Jew.*
23. See Schnee, pp. 38–47, for more on this subject.
24. Durant and Durant, *The Reformation,* p. 737.

CHAPTER III: ANCESTORS: JOST

1.   Glückel von Hameln, p. 44.
2.   For details on Jewish dress customs, see Pollack, pp. 85–95.

3. Ibid, pp. 96–98, provides details on Jewish food and drink.

4. Glückel von Hameln, p. 44.

5. Grunwald, p. 95.

6. Selma Stern, *Der Preussische Staat und die Juden,* vol. 1.2, pp. 28–31.

7. Schnee, p. 56.

8. *The New Cambridge Modern History,* vol. 5, p. 552.

9. Menga, p. 120.

10. Selma Stern, *Der Preussische Staat und die Juden,* vol. 1.2, pp. 526–37.

11. Ibid, p. 528.

12. Biereigel.

13. Holmsten, *Berlin in alten und neuen Reisebeschreibungen,* pp. 29–30.

14. *The New Cambridge Modern History,* vol. 5, p. 557.

15. For a list of Jews in Berlin at the time, see Stern, *Der Preussische Staat und die Juden,* vol. 1.2, pp. 526, 529–30.

16. See Schnee, pp. 59–65 for further details; also Stern, *Der Preussische Staat und die Juden,* vol. 1.1, pp. 149–50; Geiger, *Geschichte der Juden in Berlin,* pp. 1–27.

17. *The New Cambridge Modern History,* vol. 5, p. 398.

18. Durant and Durant, *The Age of Voltaire,* p. 437; Stern, *Der Preussische Staat und die Juden,* vol 2.1, p. 38.

19. *The New Cambridge Modern History,* vol. 5, p. 439.

20. Geiger, *Geschichte der Juden in Berlin,* pp. 32–35.

21. Wolff, pp. 162–64.

22. Schnitter, vol. 1, p. 33.

23. For details of daily life see Consentius, p. 173.

24. See Stern, *Der Preussische Staat und die Juden,* vol. 2.1, pp. 54–105, for a detailed discussion of the Jewish economic elite.

CHAPTER IV: PIONEERS: RAHEL

1. See Gaxotte, p. 174; also Mitford, p. 83.

2. See Diwald, p. 86.

3. Stade, p. 400.

4. Stern, *Der Preussische Staat und die Juden,* vol. 3.2.

5. Ibid, p. 202.

6. Geiger, *Geschichte der Juden in Berlin,* pp. 66–67.

7. The Hallesche and the Prenzlauer town gates. These are the two mentioned in the *Generalprivileg* of 1750. Earlier records also mentioned the Rosenthaler Gate. We do not know through which of these he actually passed, nor is there any evidence for the veracity of the many anecdotes later told concerning his difficulties in gaining entry.

8. The story is told that the municipal guardian recorded the event by tersely noting in the official journal that "six oxen, seven pigs and a Jew passed

through the gate this day. . ." While certainly plausible, there is no proof for this oft-repeated legend either.

9. Jewish leaders such as Jacob Emden and Isaiah Horowitz made such typical arguments. See Pollack, pp. 78–81.

10. This, for example, is the fate suffered by Gerson Jacob Bleichröder, grandfather of Bismarck's banker and adviser. Caught with a German book near Berlin's *Judenmarkt* around 1750, he was forthwith expelled from the city by the rabbis. It required Moses Mendelssohn's intercession to find him refuge in a Talmudic School in Halberstadt. See Hammer and Schoeps, pp. 31–32.

11. Scurla, p. 55.

12. Heyde, p. 91.

13. It was a last wish destined not to be honored for more than two centuries. The grave at Sans Souci where his dogs lay was considered undignified for so great a king, and his successor ordered his mortal remains placed instead into a crypt in Potsdam's more imposing Garnison Church. There they stayed until Adolf Hitler had them removed in great secrecy to the safety of southern Germany during the Second World War. Only on the 205th anniversary of Frederick's death in 1991 did the present German government finally choose to fulfill his request and returned his remains with much pomp and ceremony to the place he had designated, on the upper terrace of his beloved *Schloss* in Potsdam.

14. Arendt, *Rahel Varnhagen*, p. 5.

15. This point is made in Reich-Ranicki, p. 10.

16. Friedrich Nicolai describes the physical Berlin of the period in great detail.

17. One taler had 30 groschen, each of which was worth 12 pfennig.

18. Rachel and Wallich, p. 332.

19. See Chapter III, p. 94 above.

20. Geiger, *Berlin 1688–1840*, vol. I, pp. 585–93.

21. Friedrich Nicolai, pp. 973–74.

22. Maimon, vol. I, pp. 268–72.

23. Tewarson, *Rahel Varnhagen*, p. 54.

24. Holmsten, *Berlin in alten und neuen Reisebeschreibungen*, p. 67.

25. Schultz, p. 265.

26. von Bissing, p. 29.

27. Holmsten, *Berlin in alten und neuen Reisebeschreibungen*, pp. 53–54.

28. Ibid, pp. 67–68.

29. See Hahn.

30. See Gerhardt, p. 22.

31. See Vehse, pp. 145–47, for a description of his death.

32. Knigge, pp. 502–7.

33. See Reports of Magistrat Oranienburg, January 14 and May 15, 1792.

34. Taken from Oranienburg town records.

35. Wessling, pp. 1-70, provides an excellent summary of Meyerbeer's childhood years.

36. Arendt, *Rahel Varnhagen*, particularly ch. 7-10, has a detailed analysis of Rahel's relationship with Marwitz and the early Varnhagen. My synopsis has drawn on this material.

37. See Burg, pp. 9-58 for a biographical account of Burg's wartime service. He later became famous as that rare case—a Jew who stayed in the army and rose to the rank of major.

38. Tewarson, *German-Jewish Identity*, p. 17.

39. Becker and Becker, p. 29.

40. See Ismar Freund, vol. 1, p. 231.

41. Ibid, pp. 231-35.

42. Graetz, vol. 2, p. 338.

43. Tewarson, *Rahel Varnhagen*, p. 129.

44. Drewitz, p.67.

45. Tewarson, *Rahel Varnhagen*, p. 131.

46. Antonia Valentin, p. 87; Tewarson, *Rahel Varnhagen*, p. 12.

47. Antonia Valentin, p. 86.

CHAPTER V: ACHIEVERS: GIACOMO

1. Becker and Becker, p. 25.

2. Letter to Michael Beer, September 1, 1818, in Becker, *Giacomo Meyerbeer: Briefwechsel und Tagebücher,* vol. 1, p. 29.

3. Amalie Beer earned universal admiration for her tireless war relief work among the wounded, 1813-15. Frederick William III was so impressed that he ordered the *Luisenorder,* named in memory of his deceased wife, to be presented to her not with the standard Christian cross, but with a specially designed ribbon that, he assumed, would be more pleasing to a Jew. He also gave her a marble statue of Luise's likeness and instructed his sister-in-law to extend annual birthday greetings to Amalie in his name.

    Her reputation for grace, hospitality, and charity established her for decades as one of the grandes dames of Berlin—a most unusual role for a Jew. Heine once said of her that it seemed that Amalie would not go to bed at night without having done at least one noble deed each day.

4. Letter to Jacob Herz Beer, November 1814, in Becker, *Giacomo Meyerbeer: Briefwechsel und Tagebücher,* vol. 1, p. 32.

5. Letter to Carl Maria v. Weber, January 8, 1812, ibid, pp. 24-25.

6. Ibid, p. 27.

7. Quoted in Zimmermann, *Giacomo Meyerbeer,* p. 133.

8. Published in 1960, the somewhat reduced edited collection of Meyerbeer's correspondence entailed four substantial volumes. Family letters account for

a significant part of it. See Becker, *Giacomo Meyerbeer: Briefwechsel und Tage-bücher.*

9.   Ibid, vol. 1, p. 333.

10. See Zimmermann, *Giacomo Meyerbeer,* p. 111.

11. Ibid, p. 108.

12. Becker, *Giacomo Meyerbeer: Briefwechsel und Tagebücher,* vol. 1, p. 413.

13. Ibid, p. 74.

14. Ibid, vol. 1, p. 407.

15. Ibid, p. 371.

16. Zimmermann, *Giacomo Meyerbeer,* p. 122.

17. See Body.

18. Becker and Becker, p. 73.

19. Dettke, p. 185.

20. Herre, p. 98.

21. Ibid, p. 96.

22. Beck, pp. 478–538, gives a detailed description of Berlin conditions 1815–47.

23. See Rohrbacher, pp. 157–80, for further details.

24. See Crosten; Van Dieren; and Becker, *Giacomo Meyerbeer: Briefwechsel und Tagebücher,* for details on Meyerbeer's relations with his collaborators.

25. Zimmermann, *Giacomo Meyerbeer,* p. 180.

26. Ibid, p. 174.

27. For the literature on this phase of Giacomo's Paris years and the Paris Opéra, see inter alia Crosten; Zimmermann, ch. 5, pp. 135–86; Wessling, pp. 99–135; Kapp, pp. 65–101, 169–76; Becker, *Giacomo Meyerbeer: Briefwechsel und Tage-bücher,* pp. 17–158; Becker, *Meyerbeer,* pp. 43–54.

28. Becker, *Giacomo Meyerbeer: Briefwechsel und Tagebücher,* p. 178.

29. Becker and Becker, p. 44.

30. Becker, *Giacomo Meyerbeer: Briefwechsel und Tagebücher,* vol. 2, p. 153.

31. Body.

32. At Spa, Giacomo followed a rigorous regime, taking the waters and limiting his intake of food and drink to soothe his digestive tract. But consistency appears not to have been one of his strengths in matters of eating. Though Heine later complained that invitations for lunch in Paris involved nothing better than dried cod (*Stockfische*), Giacomo was somewhat of a gourmand and German and French cookbooks were enriched with some of his favorites: Veal Meyerbeer, lamb kidneys in madeira sauce, and rump steak with fried eggs, à la Meyerbeer.

33. Becker, *Giacomo Meyerbeer: Briefwechsel und Tagebücher,* vol. 2, for a full measure of Meyerbeer-Heine letters in this vein.

34. Ibid, p. 276.

35. Gregor-Dellin, p. 122.

36. Ibid, p. 148.

37. Becker and Becker, p. 89.
38. Ibid, p. 81.
39. Becker, *Giacomo Meyerbeer: Briefwechsel und Tagebücher,* vol. 2, p. 178.
40. Ibid, p. 305.
41. Zimmermann, *Giacomo Meyerbeer,* p. 176.
42. Keats, p. 49.
43. Zimmermann, *Giacomo Meyerbeer,* p. 231.
44. Uhlig, Nos. 7, 33 & 35.
45. Herre, p. 181.
46. For detailed statistics for this period, see Toury, and Fischer, et al.
47. See Sterling, pp. 103–12.
48. See Brandenburgisches Landeshauptarchiv Potsdam: Rep. 2A Reg. Potsdam I Pol 1910.
49. See Mendel, pp. 96 ff., for a full account of the ceremonies in Paris and Berlin.
50. Zimmermann, *Giacomo Meyerbeer,* pp. 412–13.

CHAPTER VI: PATRIOTS: LOUIS

1. For detailed accounts of the Kaiser's return to Berlin, see Savage, pp. 64–69, and Falkenau, pp. 287–88.
2. Bildarchiv Jüdischer Kulturbesitz, p. 166.
3. Hyndman, p. 102.
4. Wirth, p. 161.
5. Hyndman, p. 104.
6. See Wirth, pp. 966–71; also Kindleberger, "The Panic of 1873."
7. Mosse, *Jews in the German Economy,* pp. 116–17.
8. There is a vast literature on Bismarck and also on Bleichröder. The best account of their relationship is in Fritz Stern's classic study, *Gold and Iron.* This section, in part, draws on it.
9. Stern, *Gold and Iron,* p. 173.
10. Ibid, p. 478.
11. See Reitböck, pp. 73–74, for a detailed description of Strousberg's Castle Zbiow, near Pilsen.
12. *Der Tagesspiegel,* Berlin, March 24, 1996, p. W2.
13. Redlich is a good biographical essay on Strousberg that elaborates on this point. For more detailed accounts of Strousberg's activities see Reitböck, pp. 290–92.
14. While imprisoned in Russia in 1875–76, he wrote his autobiography: *Dr. Strousberg und sein Wirken von ihm selbst geschildert,* Berlin 1876.
15. Brandenburgisches Landeshauptarchiv Potsdam: Rep. 8 OR762, Blatt 138.
16. Ibid, Blatt 155.
17. Ibid, Blatt 205.

18. Kindleberger, "The Panic of 1873," pp. 69–73, provides a good discussion of the background to the crash.

19. Dahrendorf, pp. 49–64.

20. Massing, p. 41.

21. Ibid, p. 88.

22. Pulzer, p. 10.

23. For a detailed description of Dühring's life and career as an anti-Semitic agitator, see Mogge. No one would later be cited more favorably and often by Hitler's Nazis than he.

24. See Treitschke, p. 378.

25. See Heinrich von Treitschke, "Unsere Aussichten," in *Deutsche Kämpfe,* Leipzig 1896, p. 364.

26. Ibid, p. 381.

27. Iggers, p. 73.

28. See Treitschke.

29. Iggers, p. 73.

30. Reinharz, p. 16. See also Ellenbogen and Sterling, pp. 261–81.

CHAPTER VII: DREAMERS: ARTHUR

1. Holborn, *A History of Modern Germany 1840–1945,* p. 299.

2. Quoted in Annemarie Lange, p. 158: In translation it reads:
   "Even if Fritz is hoarse,
   The Reich will scarcely wobble;
   The German Kaiser's force
   A soft voice cannot hobble."

3. Kracke, p. 84.

4. Ibid, p. 87.

5. Pakula, p. 394.

6. Röhl, p. 198.

7. Eloesser, *Die Strasse meiner Jugend,* p. 11. Eloesser published this nostalgic little book of reminiscence about his Berlin youth in 1919. Full of warmth and affection for the city of his birth, it presents a picture of an uncomplicated childhood and cordial gentile-Jewish relations prior to the poisonous wave of virulent anti-Semitism of later years. In 1987, it was republished by Arsenal Press, though a chapter describing his experiences as a soldier in the war was omitted for unknown reasons. Perhaps it was because generally favorable reviews of the original version had criticized its, for him, uncharacteristic sentiments of military enthusiasm. See *Die Weltbühne,* January 15, 1920, pp. 93–94.

8. Eloesser, *Erinnerungen eines Berliner Juden.* This series of articles appeared in Berlin's Jewish paper *Jüdische Rundschau* between September 21 and November 16, 1934, when Eloesser was forbidden to publish anywhere else. By then, his views on the position of German Jews had been greatly altered by the shock of Hitler's rise to power. Yet his deeply engrained affinity for Germany

and German culture still shows through. Sections 2 and 3 of this chapter draw in part on the 1920 and 1934 publications.

9. Ibid, October 26, 1934, p. 6.

10. Ibid, October 10, 1934, p. 10.

11. Hamburger, *Jews in Public Service under the German Monarchy,* p. 222.

12. Cecil, *The German Diplomatic Service,* pp. 97–103.

13. Westphal, p. 25.

14. *Ignaz Jastrow* (1856-1937), the son of Posen Jews. Jastrow had already made a name for himself as an economic historian. Because of his religion, he had been rejected for a regular professorship, but was allowed to lecture intermittently as a *Privatdozent,* a kind of adjunct professor. He later became the dean of Berlin's foremost school of commerce, an important position, though not comparable in status and prestige to a tenured professorship at the university.

15. Eloesser, *Erinnerungen eines Berliner Juden,* November 11, 1934, p. 12.

16. Pulzer, p. 10.

17. Festbuch, Studentisches Breslau, p. 42.

18. Eloesser, *Erinnerungen eines Berliner Juden,* October 26, 1934, p. 6.

19. Ibid, p. 7.

20. Ibid, p. 31.

21. Reinharz and Schatzberg, pp. 164–69.

22. Ibid, p. 167.

23. He was Ernst von Wildenbruch (1845-1909), a grandson of Prince Louis Frederick Christian of Prussia.

24. Quoted in Marschall, p. 397.

25. Masur, p. 175.

26. Albret and Aldo, p. 4.

27. Mommsen, pp. 119–140.

28. Eloesser, "Die ältesten Übersetzungen Molièrischer Lustspiele."

29. Eloesser, *Das Bürgerliche Drama.*

30. Eloesser, *Erinnerungen eines Berliner Juden,* November 10, 1934, p. 10.

31. *Paul Ehrlich* (1854-1915), Germany's greatest bacteriologist and the discoverer of "606" (Neo-Salversan), a remedy against syphillis, continued to be refused even after he had won the Nobel Prize. It took six years of heated debate until the University of Frankfurt finally relented and appointed him to a regular chair, just one year before his death.

32. Eloesser, *Aus der Werkstatt eines Kritikers,* p. 4.

33. Monty Jacobs, at Eloesser's funeral: *Abschied von Arthur Eloesser,* Febuary 17, 1938.

34. Holmsten, *Die Berlin-Chronik,* p. 292.

35. See Holborn, *A History of Modern Germny 1840-1945,* pp. 367-91; Henderson, pp. 173-207; Berghahn, pp. 1-11.

36. Grunow, p. 26; Masur, p. 88.

37. Balfour, p. 140.

38. *Die Chronik Berlin's,* p. 295.

39. Ibid.

40. Ibid, p. 294.

41. The proliferation of the media continued unabated for years. In the feverish days of the Weimar Republic, the capital eventually was home to a bewildering assortment of some two hundred dailies, weeklies, and monthlies of every conceivable political type and stripe.

42. Mosse, *Jews in the German Economy,* p. 208.

43. The *Militärwochenblatt* and the *Fürstenkorrespondenz.*

44. Grunow, p. 62.

45. Masur, p. 72.

46. Cecil, *Kaiser Wilhelm und die Juden,* pp. 334, 336.

47. *Allgemeine Zeitung des Judentums,* Berlin, January 24, 1896.

48. Stern, *Dreams and Delusions,* pp. 97–114.

49. *Berliner Illustrierte,* October 16, 1906.

50. *Allgemeine Zeitung des Judentums,* Berlin, August 31, 1894.

51. Jarausch, pp. 171–90.

52. Ibid, pp. 191–205. The roster of German-Jewish pioneers is long. At least seven were awarded the Nobel Prize. See Osborne, pp. 22–29.

53. For a detailed account of Jews in the textile industry, also see Westphal.

54. *Berliner Illustrierte Zeitung,* July 7, 1895.

55. Berghahn, p. 104. Also Mosse, *Jews in the German Economy,* ch. 5, pp. 172–217, an excellent compilation of financial data on the prewar Jewish "wealth elite."

56. Reinharz, p. 43.

57. Ibid, pp. 31–32.

58. *Allgemeine Zeitung des Judentums,* February 25, 1898.

59. *Allgemeine Zeitung des Judentums,* February 6, 1900.

60. *Allgemeine Zeitung des Judentums,* August 18, 1911.

61. Eloesser, *Erinnerungen eines Berliner Juden,* September 28, 1934, p. 6.

62. Huret, pp. 311–12.

63. Ibid, pp. 342–43.

64. Ibid, p. 315.

65. In contrast, it was often joked, in rhyme, that old William I had been the *Greise* (venerable), Frederick III, the *Weise* (wise) Kaiser.

66. *Chronik der Deutschen,* p. 702.

67. For details on the League, see Massing, pp. 141–46, and Pulzer, pp. 191, 222–24.

68. For a description of The Army League, see Coetzee.

69. Cecil, *Albert Ballin,* p. 131.

70. See the column "From the Camp of the Antisemites" *in Mitteilungen aus dem Verein zur Abwehr des Antisemitismus,* Berlin, 1895–1914.

71. Quoted in Massie, p. 683.

72.   Chamberlain, pp. 388–89.

73.   Hitler, p. 64.

74.   Ibid, p. 65.

75.   Ibid, p. 161.

CHAPTER VIII: SURVIVORS: EWALD

1.   *Berliner Tageblatt,* June 29, 1914, p. 1.

2.   *Berliner Tageblatt,* July 3, 1914, Insert p. 1.

3.   Ibid.

4.   See Mai, pp. 9–30, for a good description of these events.

5.   Ibid, p. 14.

6.   Zweig, *The World of Yesterday,* pp. 223–29.

7.   *Die Zukunft,* vol. 22, no. 44, August 1, 1914, pp. 137–8.

8.   *Allgemeine Zeitung des Judentums,* August 6, 1914.

9.   *Jüdische Rundschau,* Berlin, No. 32, August 7, 1914, pp. 343–44.

10.   Centralverein der deutschen Juden, *Im deutschen Reich,* vol. 20, Berlin, 1914, p. 342.

11.   See von Rieben for a detailed account of the Second Guard Regiment's wartime battles.

12.   Ibid, p. 23.

13.   Bundesministerium der Verteidigung, p. 13.

14.   Reichsbund Jüdischer Frontsoldaten, p. 21.

15.   *Oranienburger Generalanzeiger,* August 4, September 9, 1914.

16.   *Auf Vorposten,* quoted in *Allgemeine Zeitung des Judentums,* No. 32, August 11, 1916.

17.   *Jüdische Rundschau,* "Kriegsantisemitismus," December 1914–1916.

18.   *Allgemeine Zeitung des Judentums,* January/February 1916.

19.   Gilbert, *The First World War,* p. 275. Pages 258–300 relate the events of the battle of the Somme in detail.

20.   Angress, *The German Army's "Judenzählung,"* p. 117.

21.   Rieben, p. 248.

22.   Cowles, p. 405. The events surrounding the Kaiser's abdication have been described in detail many times. See, for example, Kürenberg, pp. 367–72; Cowles, pp. 400–3; Ludwig, pp. 337–47.

23.   Diwald, p. 297.

24.   See *Oranienburger Generalanzeiger,* No. 133, June 9, 1918.

25.   Gilbert, *The First World War,* pp. 437, 477.

26.   *Vossische Zeitung,* October 15–22, 1918.

27.   Grosz, p. 134. George Grosz was a keen observer and reporter not only with his brush but equally so with the written word. Chapters 8–10, pp. 115–152, give a fascinating picture of Berlin life in the immediate postwar years.

28.   *Im Deutschen Reich,* No. 24, 1918, p. 455.

29. Zechlin, p. 559.

30. See Lohalm, pp. 15–19, 77–134; Dunker, p. 32.

31. Mosse, *Deutsches Judentum in Krieg und Revolution,* p. 463.

32. Hitler, pp. 202–3.

33. *Jüdische Rundschau,* November 2, 1919.

34. Arrias.

35. Dunker, p. 32.

36. Cecil, *Albert Ballin,* pp. 345–46. There is no agreement whether he intended to kill himself or merely sought to quiet his nerves. Most of his friends apparently concluded that it was suicide.

37. Nelson, p. 107.

38. Friedrich, pp. 124–25.

39. Blaich, p. 10.

40. See Reichsbund Jüdischer Frontsoldaten's *Der Schild,* no. 9, August 22, 1923.

41. *Jüdische Rundschau,* November 1923, no. 11, p. 11; no. 95, p. 1.

42. Friedrich, pp. 215–16.

43. Rathenau, *An Deutschland's Jugend,* p. 9.

44. Rathenau, "Höre Israel."

45. *Frankfurter Zeitung,* October 2, and 9, 1922.

46. Benoist-Méchin, vol. 2, p. 321.

47. Friedrich, pp. 171–73.

48. Friedrich Lange, p. 171.

49. Eloesser, *Thomas Mann: Sein Leben und Sein Werk* and *Elisabeth Bergner.*

50. Eloesser, *Die Deutsche Literatur von der Romantik bis zur Gegenwart.*

51. See *Weltbühne,* March 6, 1928, quoted in Carl von Ossietsky, *Lesebuch, Rowohlt,* Hamburg 1989.

52. Friedrich, p. 22.

53. See *Der Schild,* February 1, 1925.

54. Mosse, *Entscheidungsjahr 1932,* pp. 87–131.

55. Bab, p. 98.

56. Hitler, p. 327.

57. Ibid, p. 326.

58. Ibid, p. 325.

59. Goebbels, *Kampf um Berlin, 1926–7,* p. 21.

60. Ibid, p. 18.

61. Ibid, p. 86.

62. Ibid, p. 138.

63. Paucker, p. 437.

64. *Deutsche Allgemeine Zeitung,* June 26, 1930.

65. Friedrich Lange, p. 161.

66. *Chronik der Deutschen,* p. 844.

67. *Die Chronik Berlin's,* p. 379.

68. See *Centralverein Zeitung* no. 10, January 9, 1931, p. 1. Also *Jüdische Rundschau*, no. 37, October 7, 1932, p. 1.

69. *Die Chronik Berlin's*, p. 376.

70. Friedrich Lange, p. 167.

71. *The New Yorker*, January 9, 1932.

72. See *Vossische Zeitung*, October 30, 1930.

73. *Centralverein Zeitung*, Berlin, February 2, 1933, p. 1.

CHAPTER IX: DESCENDANTS: MICHAEL

1. Cited in Boas, p. 242.

2. Busemann, et al., pp. 311–30.

3. François-Ponçet, pp. 23–24.

4. *New York Times*, January 29, 1933, pp. 1, 5.

5. Goebbels, *Vom Kaiserhof zur Reichskanzlei*, p. 251.

6. *New York Times*, January 31, 1933, p. 16.

7. *Centralverein Zeitung*, Berlin, February 1, 1933, pp. 1, 4.

8. *Jüdische Rundschau*, February 1933, p. 2.

9. Goebbels, *Vom Kaiserhof zur Reichskanzlei*, p. 255.

10. Shirer, *The Rise and Fall of the Third Reich*, p. 191.

11. Diels, p. 143.

12. Burkert, et al., p. 113.

13. François-Ponçet, p. 59.

14. *New York Times*, March 27, 1933, p. 5.

15. François-Ponçet, p. 59.

16. See Schleunes, pp. 71–91, for a detailed summary account of the history and organization of the anti-Jewish boycott of April 1, 1933.

17. Ibid, p. 77.

18. *Centralverein Zeitung*, Berlin, March 30, 1933, p. 1.

19. Schleunes, p. 93.

20. Even that, however, proved illusory compensation. Like many others, Hermann Ullstein waited too long to flee, and when he finally left at the end of 1938, it would be like all others—with no more than 10 marks in his pocket.

21. *Jüdische Rundschau*, November 17, 1933.

22. Arthur Eloesser letter to Thomas Mann, August 26, 1934.

23. Monty Jacobs, at Eloesser funeral, February 17, 1938.

24. Bab, p. 105.

25. Renée Christian-Hildebrandt on Arthur Eloesser, *Neue Zeitung*, Berlin, September 7, 1949.

26. Arthur Eloesser, "*Palästina Reise*," in *Jüdische Rundschau*, June 12, June 15, 1934.

27. Shirer, *The Nightmare Years*, p. 161.

28. Noakes and Pridham, *Nazism 1919–45: A History in Documents*, p. 537.

29. *Centralverein Zeitung*, Berlin, September 26, 1935.

30. *New York Times,* November 11, 1938, p. 1.

31. Buffum, Confidential Report, *Anti-Semitic Onslaught in Germany as seen from Leipzig,* November 21, 1938. National Archives, Washington, D.C.

32. Morse, p. 223.

33. Reed and Fisher, p. 68.

34. *New York Times,* November 12, 1938, p. 1.

35. Ibid, p. 4.

36. See Lowenberg, pp. 309–23.

37. Ibid, p. 313.

38. Buffum, pp. 3, 7.

39. *Berliner Tageblatt,* November 13, p. 1.

40. Lowenberg, pp. 315–19.

41. International Buchenwald Committee, pp. 17–18; Hackett, p. 32.

42. For his crimes as Commissioner of Manpower in the Occupied Territories during the war, Sauckel was hanged at Nuremberg as a war criminal.

43. The description of KZ Buchenwald and the experiences there of Ewald and the more than 10,000 other Jews is based, inter alia, on accounts from International Buchenwald Committee; Hackett, Kogon; Angress, *Generation Zwischen Furcht und Hoffnung,* pp. 69–78; and Broszat, et al., pp. 78–97.

44. Heinrich Hackmann was sentenced to death by hanging in 1947, a verdict that was later commuted to life imprisonment.

45. *Berliner Tageblatt,* November 15, p. 3.

46. See Strauss, *Jewish Emigration from Germany,* pp. 343–409, for a detailed account of immigration legislation and statistics for major countries during the period.

47. The most famous case is that of the German ship *St. Louis,* with 930 refugees, which was forced to return them to Europe in 1939 when their visas to enter Cuba were not honored. A substantial number of these refugees did not survive.

CHAPTER X: EPILOGUE

1. This comes from an ex-refugee's recollection cited in Heppner, p. 41.

2. He was SS Colonel Josef Meisinger, otherwise known as the "Butcher of Warsaw." In 1946, he was hanged in Poland. The German role in the action against us was officially confirmed after the war by the then German consul in Tientsin, Fritz Wiedemann.

3. See page 17 above.

4. Report of the *Geheime Staatspolizei* (Gestapo), Berlin, February 9, 1942.

5. Leschnitzer, p. 143.

6. Nietzsche, p. 563.

7. Eloesser, *Erinnerungen eines Berliner Juden,* p. 2.

SELECTED BIBLIOGRAPHY

Abrahams, Israel. *Jewish Life in the Middle Ages.* London: Edward Goldstein, 1932.

Achenholtz, J. W. von. *Geschichte des 7-jährigen Krieges.* Leipzig: E. F. Attelangs Verlag, 1911.

Adler-Rudel, S. *Ostjuden in Deutschland.* Tübingen: JCB Mohr (Paul Siebeck), 1958.

Ages, Arnold. *The Diaspora Dimension.* The Hague: Martinus Nijhoff, 1973.

Agus, Irving R. *The Heroic Age of Franco-German Jewry.* New York: Yeshiva University Press, 1969.

Ahlwardt, Hermann. *Der Verzweiflungskampf der arischen Völker mit dem Judentum.* Berlin: Th. Fritsch, 1890.

Albret, Helga, and Karl Aldo. *Die Majestätsbeleidigungsaffaire des Simplicissimus-Verlegers Albert Langen.* Frankfurt/Main: Verlag Peter Lang, 1985.

Altmann, Alexander. *Moses Mendelssohn.* University: University of Alabama Press, 1973.

Altmann, Wilhelm, ed. *Letters of Richard Wagner.* New York: E. P. Dutton & Co., 1927.

Angress, Werner T. *The German Army's "Judenzählung" of 1916.* Leo Baeck Institute Yearbook, vol. 23, 1978.

———. *Generation Zwischen Furcht und Hoffnung.* Hamburg: Hans Christians Verlag, 1985.

Arendt, Hannah. *Rahel Varnhagen: The Life of a Jewish Woman.* New York and London: Harcourt Brace Jovanovich, 1974.

Aretin, Karl Otmar von. *Vom Deutschen Reich zum Deutschen Bund.* Göttingen: V&R, 1993.

Arrias, Otto. *Die Juden im Heere,* Berlin: 1919.

Awerbuch, Marianne, and Stefi Jersch-Wenzel. *Bild und Selbstbild der Juden Berlin's Zwischen Romantik und Aufklärung.* Berlin: Historische Kommission zu Berlin, Band 75, Colloquium Verlag, 1992.

Bab, Julius. *Leben und Tod des Deutschen Judentums.* Berlin: Argon Verlag, 1988.

Bähtz, Dieter, ed. *Rahel Varnhagen: Briefe und Aufzeichnungen.* Frankfurt/Main: Insel Verlag, 1986.

Balfour, Michael. *The Kaiser and His Times.* New York: W. W. Norton & Co., 1962, 1974.

Barkley, Richard. *The Empress Frederick.* London: MacMillan & Co., 1956.

Beck, C. H. *Geschichte Berlin's,* vol. 1. Munich: C. H. Beck Verlag, 1987.

Becker, Heinz. *Der Fall Heine-Meyerbeer.* Berlin: Walter de Gruyter & Co., 1958.

———. *Meyerbeer.* Hamburg: Rowohlt, 1980.

Becker, Heinz, ed. *Giacomo Meyerbeer: Briefwechsel und Tagebücher.* Berlin: Walter de Gruyter & Co., 1960.

Becker, Heinz, and Gudrun Becker. *Giacomo Meyerbeer: A Life in Letters.* London: Christopher Helm, 1983.

Benoist-Méchin, J. *Jahre der Zwietracht, 1919–25.* Oldenburg and Hamburg: Gerhard Stalling Verlag, 1965.

Benz, Wolfgang. *Das Exil der Kleinen Leute.* Munich: C. H. Beck Verlag, 1991.

———. *Die Juden in Deutschland.* Munich: C. H. Beck Verlag, 1989.

Berghahn, Volker R. *Imperial Germany 1871–1914.* Providence and Oxford: Berghahn Books, 1994.

Bering, Dietz. *Der Name als Stigma.* Stuttgart: Klett-Otta Verlag, 1987.

Biereigel, Hans. *Oranienburg—kurz vorgestellt.* Unpublished manuscript.

Bildarchiv Jüdischer Kulturbesitz. *Juden in Preussen.* Harenberg: 1981.

Bissing, W. M. Fohr von. *Friedrich Wilhelm II: König von Preussen.* Berlin: 1967.

Blaich, Fritz. *Der Schwarze Freitag.* Munich: dtv Verlag, 1985.

Blasius, Dirk and Dan Diner, eds. *Zerbrochene Geschichte.* Frankfurt/Main: Fischer Taschenbuch Verlag, 1991.

Boas, Jacob. *The Shrinking World of German Jewry.* New York: Leo Baeck Institute Yearbook, vol. 31, 1986.

Body, Albin. *Meyerbeer aux Eaux de Spa.* Brussels: V. J. Rodez, 1885.

Boeckel, Otto. *Die Juden—Die Könige unserer Zeit.* Berlin: G. A. Dewald, 8th ed., 1887.

Born, Karl Erich. *Von der Reichsgründung bis zum I. Weltkrieg.* Munich: dtv Verlag, 1975.

Börner, Karl Heinz. *Kaiser Wilhelm I.* Cologne: Pahl-Rugenstein Verlag, 1984.

Bracher, Karl Dietrich. *The German Dictatorship.* New York: Praeger, 1970.

Bräker, Ulrich. *The Life Story and Real Adventures of the Poor Man of Toggenburg.* Reprint, Edinburgh University Press, 1970.

Brod, Max. *Some Comments on the Relationship between Wagner and Meyerbeer.* New York: Leo Baeck Institute, vol. 9, 1964.

Broszat, Martin, et al. *Anatomie des SS-Staates,* vol. 2. Olten and Freiburg: Walter Verlag, 1965.

Bruer, Alfred. *Geschichte der Juden in Preussen, 1750–1820.* Frankfurt and New York: Campus Verlag, 1991.

Buch, Willi. *50 Jahre Antisemitische Bewegung.* Munich: Deutscher Volksverlag, 1937.

Bundesministerium der Verteidigung. *Deutsche Jüdische Soldaten, 1914–45.* Freiburg: 1982.

Burg, Meno. *Geschichte meines Dienstlebens.* Leipzig: M. W. Kaufmann, 1916.

Burkert, Hans-Norbert, et al. *Machtergreifung, Berlin 1933.* Berlin: Edition Albert Hentrich im Rembrandt Verlag, 1982.

Büsch, Otto. *Militärsystem und Sozialleben im Alten Preussen.* Berlin: Berliner Historische Kommission, Band 7, 1962.

Busemann, Hertha-Louise, et al. *Insel der Geborgenheit: Die Private Waldschule Kaliski, Berlin 1932–9.* Stuttgart, Weimar: Verlag J. B. Metzler, 1992.

Butler, E. M. *Heinrich Heine.* London: The Hogarth Press, 1956.

Caro, Georg. *Sozial und Wirtschaftsgeschichte der Juden.* Hildesheim: Georg Olms Verlagsbuchhandlung, 1964.

Carsten, F. L. *The Rise of Brandenburg.* In *The New Cambridge Modern History,* vol. 5. Cambridge: Cambridge University Press, 1961.

Castiglioni, Arturo. *History of Medicine.* New York: Alfred A. Knopf, 1941.

Cecil, Lamar. *Albert Ballin.* Princeton: Princeton University Press, 1967.

———. *Jew & Junker in Imperial Berlin.* New York: Leo Baeck Institute Yearbook, vol. 20, 1975.

———. *The German Diplomatic Service.* Princeton: Princeton University Press, 1976.

Chamberlain, Houston Stewart. *Foundations of the Nineteenth Century,* vol. 1. London: John Lane, 1910.

Christiansen, Rupert. *Paris-Babylon.* New York: Penguin Books, 1994.

Chronik Verlag. *Chronik der Deutschen.* Gütersloh, Munich: Bertelsmann, 1995.

———. *Die Chronik Berlin's.* Dortmund, 1986.

Cocks, Geoffrey. *Partners and Pariahs: Jews and Medicine in Modern German Society.* Leo Baeck Institute Yearbook, vol. 36, 1991.

Coetzee, Marilyn Shevin. *The German Army League.* New York and Oxford: Oxford University Press, 1990.

Cohen, Carl. *The Road to Conversion.* Leo Baeck Institute Yearbook, vol. 6, 1961.

Consentius, Ernst. *Alt Berlin, Anno 1740.* Berlin: C. A. Schwetschke und Sohn, 1907.

Conti, Egon C. C. *The English Empress.* London: Cassell & Co., 1957.

Coulton, G. G. *The Black Death.* London: Ernest Bems, 1929.

Cowie, Leonard W. *Eighteenth Century Europe.* London: G. Bell & Sons, 1963.

Cowles, Virginia. *The Kaiser.* New York: Harper & Row, 1963.

Cowley, Malcolm. *Exile's Return.* New York: W. W. Norton & Co., 1934.

Craig, Gordon A. *The Politics of the Prussian Army 1640–1945.* Oxford: Clarendon Press, 1955.

———. *Germany 1866–1945.* New York and Oxford: Oxford University Press, 1978.

———. *The Germans.* New York: Meridien, 1983.

Crankshaw, Edward. *Bismarck.* New York: The Viking Press, 1981.

Crosten, William M. *French Grand Opera: An Art and a Business.* New York: Kings Crown Press, 1948.

Dahms, Joseph. *Dictionary of Medieval Civilization.* New York: Macmillan Publishing Co., 1984.

Dahrendorf, Ralf. *Society and Democracy in Germany.* New York: Doubleday & Co., 1967.

Dettke, Barbara. *Die Asiatische Hydra.* Berlin and New York: Historische Kommission zu Berlin, Band 89, Walter de Gruyter & Co., 1995.

Diels, Rudolf. *Lucifer Ante Portas.* Zürich: Intertag, 1950.

Dinter, Artur. *Die Sünde Wider das Blut.* Leipzig: Matthes und Thost, 1920.

Diwald, Hellmut. *Heros wider Willen.* In *Preussen's Könige,* Friedrich Wilhelm Prinz von Preussen, ed. Gütersloh, Munich: Bertelsmann, 1971.

Drewitz, Ingeborg. *Berliner Salons.* Berlin: Haude & Spener, 1979.

Dubnow, S. *Weltgeschichte des Jüdischen Volkes.* Berlin: Jüdischer Verlag, 1925–29.

Dühring, E. *Die Parteien in der Judenfrage.* Leipzig: Verlag Theodor Fritsch, 1885.

Dunker, Ulrich. *Der Reichsbund Jüdischer Frontsoldaten.* Düsseldorf: Droste Verlag, 1977.

Durant, Will and Ariel Durant. "The Jews." In *The Reformation, The Story of Civilization,* part 6, New York: Simon & Schuster, 1967.

———. *The Age of Voltaire.* In *The Story of Civilization,* part 9, New York: Simon & Schuster, 1967.

———. *Rousseau and Revolution.* In *The Story of Civilization,* part 10, New York: Simon & Schuster, 1967.

Edom. *Berichte Jüdischer Zeugen und Zeitgenossen über die Judenverfolgungen während der Kreuzzüge.* Berlin: Jüdischer Verlag, 1919.

Ellenbogen, Ismar, and Eleonore Sterling. *Die Geschichte der Juden in Deutschland.* Frankfurt/Main: Athenäum Verlag, 1988.

Eloesser, Arthur. *Das Bürgerliche Drama.* Berlin: 1890. Reprint, University of Geneva, 1970.

———. *Die Strasse meiner Jugend.* Berlin: Das Arsenal, 1987 (first published 1919).

———. *Aus der Werkstatt eines Kritikers.* In *Blaue Hefte,* Freie Deutsche Bühne, vol. 1. Halbjahr, 1921.

———. *Thomas Mann: Sein Leben und Sein Werk.* Berlin: S. Fischer, 1925.

———. *Elisabeth Bergner.* Berlin: Williams, 1928.

———. *Die Deutsche Literatur von der Romantik bis zur Gegenwart.* Berlin: Bruno Cassirer, 1931.

———. *Modern German Literature.* New York: Alfred A. Knopf, 1933.

————. *Erinnerungen eines Berliner Juden.* In *Jüdische Rundschau,* nos. 76–92, September 21–November 11, 1934.

————. *Vom Ghetto nach Europa.* Berlin: Verlag Erwin Löwe, 1936.

————. "Literatur" in Kaznelson, Sigmund, *Juden in Deutschen Kulturbereich.* Berlin: Jüdischer Verlag, 1959.

Embden, Baron Ludwig von. *Heinrich Heine: Ein Familienleben.* Hamburg: Hoffman und Campe Verlag, 1892.

Encyclopedia Judaica. Jerusalem: Keter, Corrected Edition, n.d.

Engels, Bernhard. *Oranienburg.* Berlin: Verlag Wilhelm Bänsch, 1902.

Eyck, Erich. *Das Persönliche Regiment Wilhelm's II.* Erlenbach and Zürich: Eugen Rentsch Verlag, 1948.

Falkenau, Walter Schimmel. *Unter den Linden.* Berlin: Rembrandt Verlag, 1963.

Fast, Howard. *The Jews: Story of a People.* New York: Dell, 1968.

Fay, Sidney. *The Rise of Brandenburg-Prussia to 1786.* New York: Henry Holt & Co., 1937.

Feingold, Henry L. *The Politics of Rescue.* New Brunswick: Rutgers University Press, 1970.

Fervers, Kurt. *Berliner Salons: Die Geschichte einer grossen Verschwörung.* Munich: Deutscher Volksverlag, 1940.

Fest, Joachim C. *Hitler.* New York: Harcourt Brace Jovanovich, 1973.

Finkelstein, Louis, ed. *The Jews: Their History.* New York: Schocken Books, 1977.

Finucane, Ronald C. *Soldiers of the Faith.* New York: St. Martin's Press, 1983.

Fischer, Wolfram, et al., eds. *Sozialgeschichtliches Arbeitsbuch 1815–1870.* Munich: Verlag C. H. Beck, 1982.

Fischer-Fabian, S. *Herrliche Zeiten.* Munich: Droemer-Knaur, 1983.

Fontane, Theodor. *Wanderungen durch die Mark Brandenburg.* Stuttgart: Cotta, 1910–14.

François-Ponçet, André. *The Fateful Years.* New York: Harcourt, Brace & Co., 1949.

Frank, Walter. *Hofprediger Adolf Stoecker und die Christliche Bewegung.* Hamburg: Hanseatische Verlagsanstalt, 1935.

Freitag, Gustav. *Bilder aus der Deutschen Vergangenheit.* Leipzig: S. Hirzel Verlag, 1873.

Freund, Ismar. *Die Emanzipation der Juden in Preussen,* vols. 1, 2. Berlin: M. Poppelauer, 1912.

Freund, Michael. *Das Drama der 99 Tage.* Cologne and Berlin: Kiepenheuer und Witsch, 1966.

Friedman, Saul S. *No Haven for the Oppressed.* Detroit: Wayne State University Press, 1973.

Friedrich, Otto. *Before the Deluge.* New York: Harper Perennial, 1972, 1995.

Fritsch, Theodor. *Handbuch der Judenfrage.* Hamburg: Steipner Verlag, 1919.

Gall, Lothar, et al. *Die Deutsche Bank.* Munich: Verlag C. H. Beck, 1995.

Gaxotte, Pierre. *Frederick the Great.* New Haven: Yale University Press, 1942.

Gay, Peter. *Weimar Culture: The Outsider as Insider.* New York: Harper & Row, 1970.

———. *Freud, Jews and Other Germans*. New York and Oxford: Oxford University Press, 1978.

Gay, Ruth. *The Jews of Germany: A Historical Portrait*. New Haven: Yale University Press, 1992.

Geiger, Ludwig. *Berlin 1688–1840*. Orig. pub., Berlin: Gebrüder Paetel, 1893. Reprint, Aalen: Scientia Verlag, 1987.

———. *Die Deutschen Juden und der Krieg*. Berlin: C. U. Schwetschke & Sohn, 1916.

———. *Geschichte der Juden in Berlin*. Reprint, Leipzig: Arani-Verlag, 1988.

Gerhardt, Marlis. *Rahel Varnhagen: Jeder Wunsch wird Frivolität genannt*. Frankfurt/Main: Luchterhand Literaturverlag, 1983.

Gidal, Nachum T. *Die Juden in Deutschland*. Gütersloh, Munich: Bertelsmann, 1988.

Gilbert, Felix. *Bänker, Künstler und Gelehrte*. Tübingen: JCB Mohr (3 Paul Siebeck), 1975.

———. *Bismarckian Society's Image of the Jew*. New York: Leo Baeck Memorial Lecture, vol. 22, 1978.

Gilbert, Martin. *Jewish History Atlas*. New York: George Weidenfeld & Nicolson, 1969.

———. *The First World War*. New York: Henry Holt & Co., 1994.

Gilman, Sander L. *Jewish Self-Hatred*. Baltimore: The Johns Hopkins University Press, 1986.

Glagau, Otto. *Der Börsen und Gründungsschwindel in Berlin*, vol. 1. Leipzig: Frohberg, 1876.

Glatzer, Ruth, ed. *Berlin wird Kaiserstadt*. Berlin: Siedler Verlag, 1993.

Glückel von Hameln. *The Memoirs*. M. Lowenthal, trans. New York: Harper & Bros., 1932.

Goebbels, Joseph Paul. *Kampf um Berlin, 1926–7*. Munich: Verlag Franz Eher Nachf., 1932.

———. *Vom Kaiserhof zur Reichskanzlei*. Munich: Verlag Franz Eher Nachf., 1940.

Goldhagen, Daniel J. *Hitler's Willing Executioners*. New York: Alfred A. Knopf, 1996.

Gordon, Harold J. *Hitler and the Beer Hall Putsch*. Princeton: Princeton University Press, 1972.

Grab, Walter. *Der Deutsche Weg der Judenemanzipation, 1789–1938*. Munich and Zurich: Piper Verlag, 1991.

Graetz, Heinrich. *Geschichte der Juden*. Leipzig: Oskar Leiner Verlag, 1900.

Graml, Hermann. *Reichskristallnacht*. Munich: dtv Verlag, 1988.

Grattenauer, Karl W. F. *Wider die Juden*. Berlin: John Wilh. Schmidt, 1803.

Grayzel, Solomon. *The Church and the Jews in the Thirteenth Century*. Philadelphia: Dropsie Coll., 1933.

Gregor-Dellin, Martin. *Richard Wagner: Sein Leben, Sein Werk, Sein Jahrhundert*. Munich: Piper-Schoft, 1980.

Gribetz, Judah, et al. *The Timetables of Jewish History*. New York: Simon & Schuster, 1993.

Gronberger, Richard. *The Twelve-Year Reich.* New York: DaCapo Press, 1971.

Grosz, George. *Ein Kleines Ja und ein Grosses Nein.* Hamburg: Rowohlt Verlag, 1974.

Grube, Frank, and Gerhard Richter. *Die Weimarer Republik.* Hamburg: Hoffmann und Campe, 1983.

Grunow, Alfred. *Der Kaiser und die Kaiserstadt.* Berlin: Haude & Spenersche Verlagsbuchhandlung, 1970.

Grunwald, Max. *Vienna.* Philadelphia: The Jewish Publication Society of America, 1936.

Gwatkin, H. M. *Constantine and His City.* Cambridge Medieval History, vol. 1. Cambridge: Cambridge University Press, 1936.

Hackett, David. *The Buchenwald Report.* Boulder: Westview Press, 1995.

Haffner, Sebastian. *Von Bismarck zu Hitler.* Munich: Kindler Verlag, 1987.

Hahn, Barbara. "Die Salons der Rahel Levin Varnhagen." In: Hannelore Gärtner/ Annette Purfürst (ed.), *Berliner Romantik. Orte, Spuren, Begegnungen.* Berlin: Trescher Verlag, 1992.

Hamburger, Ernst. *Jews in Public Service under the German Monarchy.* New York: Leo Baeck Institute Yearbook, vol. 9, 1964.

―――. *Jews, Democracy and Weimar Republic.* New York: Leo Baeck Memorial Lecture vol. 16, 1972.

Hamburger, Ernest, and Peter Pulzer. *Jews as Voters in the Weimar Republic.* New York: Leo Baeck Institute Yearbook, vol. 30, 1985.

Hamerow, Theodore S. *The Age of Bismarck.* New York: Harper & Row, 1973.

Hammer, Manfried, and Julius Schoeps, eds. *Juden in Berlin, 1671-1945.* Berlin: Nicolai, 1988.

Harden, Maximilian. *Kaiserpanorama.* Berlin: Buchverlag der Morgen, 1983.

Harttung, Arnold, et al. *Walther Rathenau: Schriften.* Berlin: Berlin Verlag, 1965.

Heiber, Helmut. *Die Republik von Weimar.* 2nd ed. Munich: dtv Verlag, 1993.

Heid, Ludger, and Julius Schoeps, eds. *Juden in Deutschland.* Munich and Zurich: Piper, 1994.

Henderson, W. O. *The Rise of German Industrial Power 1834-1914.* London: Temple-Smith, 1975.

Heppner, Ernest G. *Shanghai Refuge.* Lincoln and London: University of Nebraska Press, 1993.

Herre, Franz. *Kaiser Wilhelm I.* Cologne: Kiepenheuer & Witsch, 1980.

Hertz, Deborah. *Jewish High Society in the Old Regime.* New Haven: Yale University Press, 1988.

―――. *"Why Did the Christian Gentleman Assault the Jüdischer Elegant?": Four Conversion Stories from Berlin, 1816-25.* New York: Leo Baeck Institute Yearbook, vol. 40, 1995.

Heyde, Johann Friedrich. *Der Roggenpreis und die Kriege des Grossen Königs, 1740-86.* Berlin: Akademie Verlag, 1988.

Hitler, Adolf. *Mein Kampf.* Ralph Manheim, trans., Boston: Houghton Mifflin Co., 1971.

Holborn, Hajo. *A History of Modern Germany 1648–1840.* Princeton: Princeton University Press, 1964.

———. *A History of Modern Germany 1840–1945.* Princeton: Princeton University Press, 1969, 1982.

Holmsten, Georg. *Die Berlin-Chronik.* Düsseldorf: Droste Verlag, 1984.

———. *Berlin in alten und neuen Reisebeschreibungen.* Düsseldorf: Droste Verlag, 1989.

Huret, Jules. *En Allemagne.* Paris: Bibliothèque-Charpentier, 1909.

Hyndman, H. M. *Commercial Crises of the Nineteenth Century.* New York: Charles Scribner & Sons, 1892.

Iggers, Georg. *Heinrich von Treitschke.* In Hans-Ulrich Wehler, ed., *Deutsche Historiker II.* Göttingen: Vandenhoeck & Ruprecht, 1971.

International Buchenwald Committee. *Buchenwald: Mahnung und Verpflichtung.* Berlin: Kongress Verlag, 1961.

Isherwood, Christopher. *The Berlin Stories.* New York: New Directions, 1945.

Jacobs, Monty. Abschied von Arthur Eloesser. February 17, 1938, unpublished.

Jacobson, Jacob. *Die Judenbücher der Stadt Berlin 1809–1851.* Berlin: Walter de Gruyter & Co., 1962.

Jarausch, Konrad. *Jewish Lawyers in Germany 1848–1938.* New York: Leo Baeck Institute Yearbook, vol. 36, 1991.

Jersch-Wenzel, Stefi. *Juden und Franzosen in der Wirtschaft des Raumes Berlin/Brandenburg.* Historische Kommission zu Berlin, Band 23. Berlin: Colloquium Verlag, 1978.

Jessen, Hans, ed. *Friedrich der Grosse und Maria Theresa.* Düsseldorf: Karl Rauch Verlag, 1965.

Jöhlinger, Otto. *Bismarck und die Juden.* Berlin: Dietrich Reiner, 1921.

Johnson, Herbert C. *Frederick the Great and His Officials.* New Haven: Yale University Press, 1975.

Johnson, Paul. *A History of the Jews.* New York: Harper & Row, 1987.

Kaes, Jay, and Dimenberg Kaes, eds. *The Weimar Sourcebook.* Berkeley: University of California Press, 1994.

Kahn, Lothar. *Biography of Ludwig Robert.* New York: Leo Baeck Institute Yearbook, vol. 19.

Kamnitzer, Heinz. *Die Wirtschafliche Struktur Deutschlands zur Zeit der Revolution 1848.* Berlin: Volk und Wissen Verlag, 1952.

Kampmann, Wanda. *Deutsche und Juden.* Heidelberg: Verlag Lambert Schneider, 1963.

Kapp, Julius. *Giacomo Meyerbeer.* Berlin: Max Hesses Verlag, 1932.

Karpeles, Gustav. *Heinrich Heine's Autobiographie.* Berlin: Verlag Robert Oppenheim, 1988.

Katz, Jacob. *Out of the Ghetto.* Cambridge: Harvard University Press, 1973.

Kaufmann, David. *Wann ist Heinrich Heine Geboren?* In *Gesammelte Schriften,* Frankfurt/Main: Kommissions Verlag J. Kaufmann, 1908.

Keats, Jonathan. *Stendhal.* London: Sinclair-Stevens, 1991.

Keller, Werner. *Diaspora: The Post-biblical History of the Jews.* New York: Harcourt Brace & World Inc., 1966.

Kennan, George F. *The Decline of Bismarck's European Order 1875–90.* Princeton: Princeton University Press, 1974.

Kerbs, Diethart, and Henrick Stahr. *Berlin 1932.* Berlin: Edition Hentrich, 1992.

Kerr, Alfred. *Walther Rathenau.* Amsterdam: Querido Verlag, 1935.

Kessler, Count Harry. *Walther Rathenau: His Life and His Work.* London: Gerald Howe, 1929.

Kindleberger, C. P. *Manias, Panics and Crashes.* New York: Basic Books, 1978.

———. "The Panic of 1873." In Eugene N. White, ed., *Crashes and Panics.* New York: Dow Jones-Irwin, 1990.

Knigge, Baron Adolf von. *Über den Umgang mit Menschen.* Hanover: Schmidtsche Buchhandlung, 1788.

Kobler, Franz, ed. *Juden und Judentum in Deutschen Briefen aus 3 Jahrhunderten.* Vienna: Saturn Verlag, 1935.

Kogon, Eugen. *Der SS-Staat.* Stockholm: Bermann-Fischer Verlag, 1947.

König, Anton Balthasar. *Annalen der Juden in den Preussischen Staaten.* Berlin: Kammergericht RG 3618, 1790.

Korfi, Ernst. *Biografische Karakteristik.* Berlin: Eichler, 1870.

Kracke, Friedrich. *Prinz und Kaiser.* Munich: Günter Olzog Verlag, 1960.

Kraemer, Mario. *Berlin im Wandel der Jahrhunderte.* Berlin: Rembrandt Verlag, 1956.

Krüger, Peter. *Versailles.* Munich: dtv Verlag, 1986.

Kulka, Otto Dov. *Die Nürnberger Rassengesetze und die Deutsche Bevölkerung.* In *Vierteljahreshefte für Zeitgeschichte,* December, 1984.

Kürenberg, Joachim von. *The Kaiser.* New York: Simon & Schuster, 1955.

Kurtz, Harold. *The Second Reich, Kaiser Wilhelm and His Germany.* New York: American Heritage Press, 1970.

Küster, Bernd. *Max Liebermann.* Hamburg: Ellert & Richter Verlag, 1988.

Kuznets, Simon. *Economic Structure and Life of the Jews.* In Louis Finkelstein, ed., *The Jews: Their History, Culture & Religion.* New York: Harper, 1949.

Lamberti, Marjorie. *Jewish Activism in Imperial Germany.* New Haven: Yale University Press, 1978.

Landsberg, Hans. *Rahel: Ein Buch des Andenkens.* Berlin: Verlag Leonhard Simon, 1904.

Lange, Annemarie. *Das Wilhelminische Berlin.* Berlin: Dietz Verlag, 1967.

Lange, Friedrich C. A. *Gross-Berliner Tagebuch, 1920–33.* Berlin and Bonn: Westkreuz Verlag, 1982.

Leschnitzer, Adolf. *Saul and David.* Heidelberg: Lambert Schneider, 1954.

Levy, Richard S. *The Downfall of the Anti-Semitic Political Parties in Imperial Germany.* New Haven and London: Yale University Press, 1975.

Linday, J. O., ed. *The Old Regime: 1713–63.* In *The New Cambridge Modern History,* vol. 7. Cambridge: Cambridge University Press, 1957.

Liptzin, Solomon. *Germany's Stepchildren.* Philadelphia: The Jewish Publication Society of America, 1944.

Lohalm, Uwe. *Völkischer Radikalismus.* Hamburg: Leibniz-Verlag, 1970.

Löschburg, Winfried. *Unter den Linden.* Berlin: Buchverlag der Morgen, 1971.

Low, Alfred D. *Jews in the Eyes of the Germans.* Philadelphia: Institute for the Study of Human Issues, 1976.

Lowenberg, Peter. *The Kristallnacht as a Public Degradation Ritual.* New York: Leo Baeck Institute Yearbook, vol. 32, 1987.

Lowenthal, Marvin. *The Jews of Germany: A Story of Sixteen Centuries.* New York and Toronto: Longmans, Green & Co., 1936.

———. *A World Passed By.* New York: Behrman's Jewish Book House, 1938.

Ludwig, Emil. *Kaiser Wilhelm II.* London and New York: G. P. Putnam & Sons, 1926.

Magee, Bryan. *Aspects of Wagner.* New York: Stein and Day, 1969.

Mai, Gunther. *Das Ende des Kaiserreiches.* 2nd ed. Munich: dtv Verlag, 1993.

Maimon, Salomon. *Gesammelte Werke,* vol. 1, Hildesheim: Georg Olms Verlagsbuchhandlung, 1965.

Marcus, Jacob. *The Jew in the Medieval World.* Cincinnati: The Sinai Press, 1938.

Marcuse, Ludwig. *Heine: A Life Between Love and Hate.* New York: Farrar & Rinehart, 1933.

Marr, Wilhelm. *Der Sieg des Judentums über das Germanentum.* Bern: Rud. Costenoble, 1879.

Marriott, J.A.R., and C. G. Robertson. *The Evolution of Prussia.* Oxford: Clarendon Press, 1937.

Marschall, Birgit. *Reisen und Regieren.* Heidelberg: Winter, 1991.

Maser, Werner. *Zwischen Kaiserreich und NS-Regime.* Bonn and Berlin: Bouvier Verlag, 1992.

Massie, Robert K. *Dreadnought: Britain, Germany and the Coming of the Great War.* New York: Random House, 1991.

Massing, Paul W. *Rehearsal for Destruction.* New York: Harper & Bros., 1949.

Masur, Gerhard. *Imperial Berlin.* New York and London: Basic Books, 1970.

Mayer, Hans. *Anmerkungen zu Richard Wagner.* Frankfurt/Main: Suhrkamp Verlag, 1966.

———. *Der Widerruf: Über Deutsche und Juden.* Frankfurt/Main: Suhrkamp Verlag, 1994.

Mendel, Herman. *Giacomo Meyerbeer.* Berlin: Verlag L. Heiman, 1869.

Menga, Wolfgang. *So Lebten Sie Alle Tage. . . .* Cologne: Quadriga Verlag, J. Severin, 1984.

Meyer, Michael. *Origin of the Modern Jew.* Detroit: Wayne University Press, 1967.

Meyer, Michael E. *Von Moses Mendelssohn zu Leopold Zunz: Jüdische Identität in Deutschland 1749–1824.* Munich: Verlag C. H. Beck, 1992.

Meyer, Rudolph. *Politische Gründer und die Corruption in Deutschland.* Leipzig: E. Bidder Verlag, 1877.

Mitchem, Jr., Samuel W. *Why Hitler?* Westport and London: Praeger, 1996.

Mitford, Nancy. *Frederick the Great.* London: Hamish Hamilton, 1970.

Mogge, Brigitta. *Rhetorik des Hasses.* Neuss: Verlag Gesellschaft für Buchdruckerei, 1977.

Möller, Horst. *Die Unvollendete Demokratie.* Munich: dtv Verlag, 5th ed., 1994.

Mommsen, Wolfgang J. *Imperial Germany 1867–1918.* London: Arnold, 1995.

Morse, Arthur D. *Why Six Million Died.* New York: Random House, 1967.

Morton, Frederic. *A Nervous Splendor.* New York: Little Brown, Penguin Books, 1979.

Mosse, George L. *The Crisis of German Ideology: The Intellectual Origins of the Third Reich.* New York: Grosset & Dunlop, 1964.

Mosse, Werner E. *Entscheidungsjahr 1932.* Munich: JCB Mohr (Paul Siebeck), 1965.

———. *Germans & Jews.* New York: Howard Fertig, 1970.

———. *Deutsches Judentum in Krieg und Revolution.* Tübingen: JCB Mohr (Paul Siebeck), 1971.

———. *Juden Im Wilhelminischen Deutschland 1890–1914.* Munich: JCB Mohr (Paul Siebeck), 1976.

———. *Jews in the German Economy.* Oxford: Clarendon Press, 1987.

———. *The German-Jewish Economic Elite.* Oxford: Clarendon Press, 1989.

Mühr, Alfred. *Rund um den Gendarmenmarkt: Von Iffland bis Gründgens.* Oldenburg and Hamburg: Gerhard Stalling Verlag, 1965.

Mun, Richard. *Die Juden in Berlin.* Leipzig: Hammer Verlag, 1924.

Nachana, Andreas. *Der Grosse Kurfürst.* Berlin: Stapp Verlag, 1989.

Nelson, Walter Henry. *The Berliners.* New York: David McKay & Co., 1969.

The New Cambridge Modern History, vols. 5, 7. Cambridge: Cambridge University Press, 1960.

Nicolai, Friedrich. *Beschreibung der Königlichen Residenzstädte Berlin und Potsdam.* Berlin: 1786; reprint, Berlin: Haude und Spenersche Verlagsbuchhandlung, 1986.

Nicolaiische Buchhandlung. *Wegweiser für Fremde und Einheimische durch Berlin und Potsdam.* Berlin: Nicolai, 1833.

Nietzsche, Friedrich. *Beyond Good and Evil: The Philosophy of Nietzsche.* New York: Random House, 1937.

Niewyk, Donald L. *The Jews in Weimar Germany.* Baton Rouge and London: Louisiana State University Press, 1980.

Nipperdey, Thomas. *Deutsche Geschichte, 1800–66.* Munich: Verlag C. H. Beck, 1983.

Noakes, J., and G. Pridham, eds. *Nazism 1919–45: A History in Documents.* New York: Schocken Books, 1983.

———. *Nazism 1919–45,* vol. 1, *The Nazi Party, State and Society.* New York: Schocken Books, 1983.

Oertzen, Dietrich V. *Adolf Stoecker: Lebensbild.* Schwerin: Volksausgabe, 1912.

Osborne, Sidney. *Germany and Her Jews.* London: The Soncino Press, 1939.

Osten-Sacken, Peter V., ed. *Juden in Deutschland.* Berlin: Inst. Kirche und Judentum, 1980.

Pakula, Hannah. *An Uncommon Woman: The Empress Frederick.* New York: Simon & Schuster, 1995.

Pangels, Charlotte. *Friedrich der Grosse.* Munich: Eugen Diederichs Verlag, 1995.

Paret, Peter. *"The Enemy Within": Max Lieberman as President of the Prussian Academy of Art.* New York: Leo Baeck Institute Memorial Lecture no. 28, 1984.

Paucker, Arnold. *Der Jüdische Abwehrkampf.* Hamburg: Leibniz Verlag, 1968.

Peukert, Detlev J. K. *The Weimar Republic.* New York: Hill & Wang, 1987.

Pierson, Ruth. *Embattled Veterans: The Reichsbund Jüdischer Frontsoldaten.* New York: Leo Baeck Institute Yearbook, vol. 19, 1974.

Pois, Robert A. *Walther Rathenau's Jewish Quandary.* New York: Leo Baeck Institute Yearbook, vol. 13, 1968.

Pollack, Herman. *Jewish Folkways in Germanic Lands (1648–1806).* Cambridge: MIT Press, 1971.

Pörtner, Rudolf, ed. *Alltag in der Weimarer Republik.* Munich: dtv Verlag, revised ed., 1993.

Prawer, S. S. *Heine's Jewish Comedy.* Oxford: Clarendon Press, 1983.

Press, Volker. *Kriege und Krisen, Deutschland 1600–1750.* Munich: Verlag C. H. Beck, 1991.

Prinz, Arthur. *New Perspectives on Marx as a Jew.* New York: Leo Baeck Institute Yearbook, vol. 15, 1970.

Pulzer, Peter. *The Rise of Political Antisemitism in Germany and Austria.* Boston: John Wiley & Sons, 1964; revised edition, Cambridge: Harvard University Press, 1988.

Rachel, Hugo, and Paul Wallich. *Berliner Grosskaufleute und Kapitalisten, vol. 2, 1648–1806.* Berlin: Walter de Gruyter & Co., 1967.

———. *Berliner Grosskaufleute und Kapitalisten, vol. 3, 1806–56.* Berlin: Walter de Gruyter & Co., 1967.

Rathenau, Walther. "Höre Israel." In *Impressionen.* Leipzig: S. Hirzel Verlag, 1908.

———. *An Deutschland's Jugend.* Berlin: S. Fischer Verlag, 1918.

Read, Anthony, and David Fisher. *Kristallnacht.* New York: Peter Bedrick Books, 1989.

Redlich, Fritz. "Two Nineteenth Century Financiers and Autobiographies." In *Economy and History* vol. 10. Sweden: Institute of Economic History, University of Lund, 1967.

Reich-Ranicki, Marcel. "Die Verkehrte Krone." *Aufbau,* August 18, 1995.

Reichsbund Jüdischer Frontsoldaten. *Kriegsbriefe Gefallener Deutscher Juden.* Berlin: Vortrupp Verlag, 1935.

Reinharz, Jehuda. *Fatherland or Promised Land.* Ann Arbor: University of Michigan Press, 1975.

Reinharz, Jehuda, and Walter Schatzberg. *The Jewish Response to German Culture.* Hanover: University Press of New England, 1985.

Reitböck, Gottfried. *Der Eisenbahnkönig Strousberg und seine Bedeutung für das Europäische Wirtschaftsleben.* In Conrad Matschoss, ed. *Jahrbuch des Vereins Deutscher Ingenieure,* Band 14, Berlin: 1924.

Reuth, Ralf Georg. *Goebbels.* Munich: Piper, 1990.

Ribbe, Wolfgang, ed. *Geschichte Berlins.* Munich: C. H. Beck Verlag, 1987.

Richarz, Monika, ed. *Jewish Life in Germany.* Bloomington and Indianapolis: Indiana University Press, 1991.

Richter, Werner. *Bismarck.* Brian Battershaw, trans. New York: G. P. Putnam & Sons, 1965.

Rieben, Lt. Col. von. *Das 2. Garderegiment zu Fuss.* Zeulendroda: Verlag Bernhard Sporn, 1934.

Rodenberg, Julius. *Bilder aus dem Berliner Leben.* vols. 1–3, Berlin: Gebr. Paetel, 1891.

Röhl, John C. G. *The Kaiser and His Court.* Terence F. Cole, trans. Cambridge: Cambridge University Press, 1994.

Rohrbacher, Stefan. *Gewalt im Biedermeier.* Schriftenreihe des Zentrums für Antisemitismus-Forschung, Band 1, Frankfurt and New York: Campus Verlag, 1993.

Roper, Katherine. *German Encounters with Modernity: Novels of Imperial Berlin.* New Jersey and London: Humanities Press International, 1991.

Rose, Paul Lawrence. *Revolutionary Antisemitism in Germany from Kant to Wagner.* Princeton: Princeton University Press, 1990.

Rosenberg, Alfred. *Der Mythus des 20. Jahrhundert.* Munich: Hoheneichen Verlag, 1934.

———. *Kampf um die Macht.* Munich: Franz Eher, 1938.

Rosenberg, Hans. *Grosse Depression und Bismarckzeit.* Berlin: Walter de Gruyter & Co., 1967.

———. *Probleme der Deutschen Sozialgeschichte.* Frankfurt/Main: Suhrkamp Verlag, 1969.

Rosenthal, Ludwig. *Heinrich Heine als Jude.* Frankfurt: Verlag Ullstein, 1973.

Roth, Cecil. *A Short History of the Jewish People.* London: E&W Library, 1953.

———. *The Jews in the Middle Ages.* In *Cambridge Medieval History,* vol. 8. Cambridge: Cambridge University Press, 1937.

Rottenberg, Dan. *Finding Our Fathers.* New York: Random House, 1977.

Runciman, Steven. *The First Crusade.* Cambridge: Cambridge University Press, 1951.

Ruppin, Arthur. *Soziologie der Juden.* Berlin: Jüdischer Verlag, 1930.

Rürup, Reinhard. *The Tortuous and Thorny Path to Legal Equality.* Leo Baeck Institute Yearbook, vol. 31, 1986.

———. *Deutschland im 19.Jahrhundert, 1815–71.* Göttingen: Vandenhoeck & Ruprecht Verlag, 1992.

———, ed. *Jüdische Geschichte in Berlin.* Berlin: Edition Hentrich, 1995.

Salamander, Rachel, ed. *Die Jüdische Welt von Gestern.* Vienna: Verlag Christian Brandstätter, 1995.

Savage, Pierre-Paul. *1871: Berlin/Paris.* Berlin: Propyläen Verlag (Ullstein), 1971.

Schaaf, Doris. *Der Theaterkritiker Arthur Eloesser.* Berlin-Dahlem: Colloquium Verlag, 1962.

Scheiger, Brigitte. *Juden in Berlin.* In Stefi Jersch-Wenzel and Barbara John, eds., *Von Zuwanderern zu Einheimischen,* Berlin: Nicolai Verlag, 1990.

Schimmel-Falkenau, Walter. *Kommen und Gehen unter den Linden.* Berlin: Rembrandt Verlag, 1963.

Schleunes, Karl A. *The Twisted Road to Auschwitz.* Urbana: University of Illinois Press, 1970.

Schnee, Heinrich. *Die Hoffinanz und der Moderne Staat.* Berlin: Duncker, 1953–67.

Schnitter, Helmut, ed. *Gestalten um den Soldatenkönig.* Berlin: Preussischer Militärverlag, 1994.

Schoeps, Hans-Joachim. *Preussen: Geschichte eines Staates.* Berlin: Propyläen Verlag, 1967.

Schoeps, Julius H. *Bismarck und Seine Attentäter.* Frankfurt/Main, Berlin, Vienna: Ullstein Verlag, 1984.

Schuder, Rosemarie, and Rudolph Hirsch. *Der Gelbe Fleck.* Cologne: Rugenstein Verlag, 1988.

Schultz, Helga. *Berlin 1650–1800.* Berlin: Akademie Verlag, 1992.

Schulz, Gerhard. *Deutschland Seit dem Ersten Weltkrieg 1918–45.* Göttingen: Vandenhoeck & Ruprecht, 1982.

———. *Revolutionen und Friedensschlüss 1917–20.* Munich: dtv Verlag, 6th ed. 1985.

Schütz, Hans. *Juden in der Deutschen Literatur.* Munich: Piper Verlag, 1992.

Scurla, Herbert. *Rahel Varnhagen.* Düsseldorf: Claasen Verlag, 1962.

Shirer, William. *The Rise and Fall of the Third Reich.* New York: Simon & Schuster, 1960.

———. *The Nightmare Years.* Boston: Little, Brown & Co., 1984.

Simon, Hermann. *Majestäten in Berliner Synagogen.* In Ludgerheid and Joachim H. Knoll (eds.), *Deutsch-Jüdische Geschichte im 19. und 20. Jahrhndert.* Sachsenheim: Burg Verlag, 1992.

Snyder, Louis L. *The Blood and Iron Chancellor.* Princeton: D. Van Nostrand & Co., 1967.

Sombart, Werner. *Juden und Wirtschaftsleben.* Leipzig: Duncker & Humblot, 1911.

Sorkin, David. *The Transformation of German Jewry, 1780–1840.* New York and Oxford: Oxford University Press, 1987.

Spencer, Stewart, and Barry Millington. *Selected Letters of Richard Wagner.* London: J. M. Dent & Sons, 1987.

Springer, Robert. *Berlin: Die Deutsche Kaiserstadt.* Berlin: Verlag Friedrich Lange, 1876.

Stade, Martin. *Der König und sein Narr.* Berlin: Buchverlag der Morgen, 1975.

Sterling, Eleonore. *Jewish Reaction to Jew-Hatred in the First Half of the Nineteenth Century.* New York: Leo Baeck Institute Yearbook, vol. 3, 1958.

Stern, Fritz. *The Politics of Cultural Despair.* Berkeley and Los Angeles: University of California Press, 1961.

———. *The Failure of Illiberalism.* New York: Alfred A. Knopf, 1972.

———. *Gold and Iron: Bismarck, Bleichröder and the Building of the German Empire.* New York: Vintage Books, 1977.

———. *Dreams and Delusions: The Drama of German History.* New York: Vintage Books, 1989.

Stern, Selma. *Jud Süss.* Berlin: Akademie Verlag, 1929.

———. *The Court Jew.* Philadelphia: Jewish Publication Society of America, 1950.

———. *Der Preussische Staat: Akten.* Tübingen: JCB Mohr (Paul Siebeck), 1962.

———. *Der Preussische Staat und die Juden, vols. 1–6.* Tübingen: JCB Mohr (Paul Siebeck), 1962–75.

Stern-Taeubler, Selma. *The First Generation of Emancipated Jews.* New York: Leo Baeck Institute Yearbook, vol. 15, 1970.

Stevenson, William B. *The First Crusade.* In *Cambridge Medieval History,* vol. 5. Cambridge: Cambridge University Press, 1936.

Stolper, Gustav. *The German Economy: 1870 to Present.* New York: Harcourt, Brace & World, 1967.

Strauss, Bruno. *Moses Mendelssohn in Potsdam.* Berlin: Edition Hentrich, 1994.

Strauss, Herbert A. *Jewish Emigration from Germany.* Leo Baeck Institute Yearbook, vol. 26, 1981.

———. *Hostages to Modernization: Studies of Modern Antisemitism 1870–1933/9.* Berlin and New York: Walter de Gruyter & Co., 1993.

Streckfuss, Adolph. *Berlin im 19.Jahrhundert.* Berlin: Wilhelm Seidel Verlag, 1860.

Strube, Rolf, ed. *Sie Sassen und Tranken am Teetisch.* Munich: R. Piper, 1991.

Sucher, C. Bernd. *Luther's Stellung zur Judenfrage.* Nieukoop: De Graaf, 1977.

Suchy, Barbara. *The Verein zur Abwehr des Antisemitismus.* Leo Baeck Institute Yearbook, vol. 28, 1983.

Susman, Margarete. *Frauen in der Romantik.* Frankfurt/Main: Insel Verlag, 1996.

Tal, Uriel. *Christians and Jews in Germany.* Ithaca: Cornell University Press, 1975.

Taylor, James, and Warren Shaw. *The Third Reich Almanac.* New York: World Almanac, 1987.

Teske, Hermann. *Berlin und Seine Soldaten.* Berlin: Haude and Spenersche Verlagsbuchhandlung, 1968.

Tewarson, Heidi Thomann. *Rahel Varnhagen.* Reinbek and Hamburg: Rowohlt, 1988.

———. *German-Jewish Identity in the Correspondence Between Rahel Levin Varnhagen and her Brother, Ludwig Robert.* New York: Leo Baeck Institute Yearbook, vol. 39, 1994.

Toury, Jacob. *Die Politische Orientierung der Juden in Deutschland.* Tübingen: Mohr, 1966.

————. *Soziale und Politische Geschichte der Juden in Deutschland 1847-71*. Düsseldorf: Droste Verlag, 1977.

Traverso, Enzo. *The Jews and Germany*. Lincoln: University of Nebraska Press, 1995.

Treitschke, Heinrich von. *Deutsche Geschichte im 19. Jahrhundert*. 5 vols., Leipzig: 1879-84.

Treue, Wilhelm. *Gesellschaft, Wirtschaft und Technik im 19. Jahrhundert*. Munich: dtv Verlag, 1975.

Tuchman, Barbara. *The Guns of August*. New York: The MacMillan Co., 1962.

Uhlig, Theodor. *Zeitgemässe Betrachtungen*. In *Neue Zeitschrift für Musik,* nos. 33-37, Leipzig: 1850.

Ullstein, Herman. *The Rise and Fall of the House of Ullstein*. New York: Simon & Schuster, 1943.

Valentin, Antonia. *Poet in Exile*. New York: The Viking Press, 1934.

Valentin, Veit. *The German People*. New York: Alfred A. Knopf, 1946.

Van Dieren, Bernard. *Down Among the Dead Men*. London: Oxford University Press, 1935.

Vehse, Carl Eduard. *Die Höfe zu Preussen*. Leipzig: Gustav Kiepenheuer Verlag, 1993.

Verdrow, Otto. *Rahel Varnhagen: Ein Lebensbild*. Stuttgart: Greiner & Pfeiffer, 1900.

Vogel, Rolf. *Ein Stück von Uns: Deutsche Juden Deutschen Armeen, 1813-1976*. Mainz: Von Hase & Köhler Verlag, 1977.

Vogel, Werner. *Führer durch die Geschichte Berlins*. Berlin: Arani Verlag, 1993.

Vogelstein, Hermann. *Rome*. Philadelphia: The Jewish Publication Society of America, 1940.

Volkov, Shulamit. *Antisemitism as a Cultural Code: Reflections on the History and Historiography of Antisemitism in Imperial Germany*. New York: Leo Baeck Institute Yearbook, vol. 23, 1978.

Wagner, Cosima. *Die Tagebücher, vols. 1, 2*. Munich: Serie Piper, 1976.

Walter, H. *Moses Mendelssohn*. New York: Block Publishing Co., 1930.

Wassermann, Henry. *The Fliegende Blätter as a Source for the Social History of German Jewry*. New York: Leo Baeck Institute Yearbook, vol. 28, 1983.

————. *Jews in Jugendstiel: The Simplicissimus 1896-1914*. New York: Leo Baeck Institute Yearbook, vol. 31, 1986.

Wehler, Hans-Ulrich. *Deutsche Gesellschaftsgeschichte, vol. 2, 1815-49*. Munich: Verlag C. H. Beck, 1987.

Weiner, Marc A. *Richard Wagner and the Antisemitic Imagination*. Lincoln and London: University of Nebraska Press, 1995.

Weiss, John. *Ideology of Death: Why the Holocaust Happened in Germany*. Chicago: Ivan R. Dee, 1996.

Wertheimer, Jack. *Unwelcome Strangers: East European Jews in Imperial Germany*. New York and London: Oxford University Press, 1987.

Wessling, Berndt W. *Meyerbeer*. Düsseldorf: Droste Verlag, 1984.

Westphal, Uwe. *Berliner Konfektion und Mode*. Berlin: Edition Hentrich, 1986.

Wile, Frederic William. *Men Around the Kaiser*. Philadelphia: J. B. Lippincott & Co., 1913.

Willett, John. *Art and Politics in the Weimar Period*. New York: Pantheon Books, 1978.

Winteroll, Michael. *König der Eisenbahn—König der Pleiten*. In *Tagesspiegel* (Berlin) May 24, 1996.

Wirth, Max. *Geschichte der Handelskrisen*. Frankfurt/Main: J. D. Sauerländer Verlag, 1858.

Wolbe, Eugen. *Geschichte der Juden in Berlin und in der Mark Brandenburg*. Berlin: Verlag Keden, 1937.

Wolff, Richard, ed. *Berichte des Braunschweiger Gesandten*. Berlin: Mittler, 1914.

Woloch, Isser. *Eighteenth Century Europe: Tradition and Progress 1715–89*. New York and London: W. W. Norton & Co., 1982.

Wyman, David S. *Paper Walls: America and the Refugee Crisis 1938–1941*. New York: Pantheon Books, 1968.

Zechlin, Egmont. *Die Deutsche Politik und die Juden im I. Weltkrieg*. Göttingen: Vandenhoeck und Ruprecht, 1969.

Zedlitz-Trütschler, Robert. *Zwölf Jahre am Deutschen Kaiserhof*. Stuttgart: Deutsche Verlagsanstalt, 1924.

Ziegler, Dieter. *Eisenbahnen und Staat im Zeitalter der Industrialisierung*. Stuttgart: Franz Steiner Verlag, 1995.

Zielenziger, Kurt. *Juden in der Deutschen Wirtschaft*. Berlin: Der Heine Bund, 1930.

Zimmermann, Reiner. *Giacomo Meyerbeer: Eine Biographie nach Dokumenten*. Berlin: Henschel Verlag, 1991.

——. *Die Opern Giacomo Meyerbeer auf den Dresdner Bühnen*. In *Schriftenreihe der Hochschule für Musik*, Heft 24, Dresden: 1991.

Zivier, Georg. *Das Romanische Café*. Berlin: Haude und Spenersche Verlag, 1965.

Zweig, Stefan. *The World of Yesterday*. New York: The Viking Press, 1943.

——. *Bilanz der Deutschen Judenheit*. Leipzig: Reclam, 1991.

NEWSPAPERS AND PERIODICALS

Allgemeine Musikalische Zeitung, Leipzig
Allgemeine Zeitung des Judentums, Berlin
Berliner Illustrierte Zeitung, Berlin
Berliner Tageblatt, Berlin
Centralverein Zeitung, Berlin
Deutsche Allgemeine Zeitung, Berlin
Frankfurter Zeitung, Frankfurt/Main
Jüdische Rundschau, Berlin
Neue Zeitschrift für Musik, Leipzig
The New Yorker Magazine
The New York Times

The North China Daily News, Shanghai
Oranienburger Generalanzeiger, Oranienburg
The Shanghai Jewish Chronicle
Der Tagespiegel, Berlin
Vossische Zeitung, Berlin

INDEX